Norman W. Paton
Editor

Active Rules in Database Systems

With 55 Illustrations

Norman W. Paton
Department of Computer Science
University of Manchester
Oxford Road
Manchester M13 9PL
UK

Series Editors:
David Gries
Department of Computer Science
Cornell University
Upson Hall
Ithaca, NY 14853-7501
USA

Fred B. Schneider
Department of Computer Science
Cornell University
Upson Hall
Ithaca, NY 14853-7501
USA

Library of Congress Cataloging-in-Publication Data
Paton, Norman W.
      Active rules in database systems / Norman W Paton.
          p.   cm. — (Monogrpahs in computer science)
      Includes bibliographical references and index.
      ISBN 978-1-4612-6448-4   ISBN 978-1-4419-8656-6 (eBook)
      DOI 10.1007/978-1-4419-8656-6
      1. Database Management.   I. Paton, Norman W.   II. Title.
      III. Series.
      QA76.9.D3P3487   1998
      005.74—dc21   98-17537
Printed on acid-free paper.

Production managed by Anthony K. Guardiola; manufacturing supervised by Jacqui Ashri.
Camera-ready copy prepared from the author's TeX files.

9 8 7 6 5 4 3 2 1

ISBN 978-1-4612-6448-4   SPIN 10678033

Monographs in Computer Science

Editors

David Gries
Fred B. Schneider

Springer
Science+Business Media, LLC

Monographs in Computer Science

Preface

Active database systems extend their passive predecessors with rules that describe how the database should respond to events as they take place. Active rules can be used either to extend the range of applications that can be supported effectively by a database system, or to change the way in which existing applications are developed.

Active rules have been recognized as important for databases both in the research community and in commercial settings. In the database research community, active databases have received widespread attention for at least ten years, with many languages, architectures and systems developed and evaluated. In commercial settings, the relational vendors have been quick to incorporate active rule (trigger) facilities into their products, and the SQL-3 standard supports active rules (see Chapter 10). Many new and existing application areas are considered likely to benefit from the judicious use of active facilities.

This book aims to provide a comprehensive introduction to the field of active database systems. The book introduces the fundamental facilities of active databases for readers new to the area, provides chapters on many of the important areas of relevance to active rule support, compares a range of proposals for active database systems within a common framework, and describes how active facilities can be used in different categories of application.

The book should be useful to anyone with a background in database systems who is interested in finding out more about active databases. Such people will include researchers and graduate students who need a comprehensive overview of the field, university teachers who want to include material on active databases in courses, developers of database systems who want to have a clear understanding of the state of the art in active databases, and potential users who need to know if current systems are suitable for their applications.

The book is structured as follows:

Part I – Fundamentals: An introduction is given to the basics of active databases, and a framework is provided that summarizes key active facilities. The consequences of design decisions for implementation architectures is considered in Chapter 2.

Part II – Advanced Topics: Chapters are provided on different issues that are important to the development of active systems or applications. These chapters are largely independent of each other.

Part III – Systems: Many proposals have been made for active database systems over different data models. This part has chapters on a cross-section of recent proposals, which can be compared using the framework presented in Part I.

Part IV – Applications: Exploitation of any new technology presents challenges to application developers. This part provides insight into experience using active rules in different settings, and pointers as to how they can be more fully exploited in the future.

Part V – Summary: This part provides a brief summary of the areas covered in parts I to IV.

The book is intended to provide the most thorough and wide-ranging coverage of active databases in a single text. Anyone who reads the whole book should have a good grasp of the area. However, there are many possible routes through the material contained in the book, and rather few chapter dependencies. Chapter 1 provides the bulk of the background material and terminology that is required by other chapters, which can then be selected according to the interests of the reader.

Norman W. Paton
Manchester

Contents

II Advanced Topics   49

V Summary   427

22 Summary   429
Norman W. Paton

Contributors

Elena Baralis: Dipartimento di Automatica e Informatica, Politecnico di Torino, Corso Duca degli Abruzzi 24, I10129 TORINO ITALY. e-mail: BARALIS@polito.it.

Mikael Berndtsson: University of Skovde, Department of Computer Science, Box 408, 541 28 SKOVDE, SWEDEN. e-mail: mikael.berndtsson@ida.his.se.

Alejandro P. Buchmann: Technische Universitat Darmstadt, Fachbereich Informatik, Wilhilminenstr. 7, 64283 Darmstadt, Germany. e-mail: buchmann@dvs1.informatik.th-darmstadt.de.

Roberta Cochrane: IBM Almaden Research Center, San Jose, CA, USA. e-mail: bobbiec@almaden.ibm.com.

Christine Collet: LSR - IMAG, B.P. 72, F-38402 Saint Martin d'Heres Cedex, France. e-mail: Christine.Collet@imag.fr.

Oscar Díaz: Departamento de Lenguajes y Sistemas Informaticos, University of the Basque Country, San Sebastián, Spain. e-mail: jipdigao@si.ehu.es.

Andrew Dinn: Department of Computing and Electrical Engineering, Heriot-Watt University, Riccarton, Edinburgh EH14 4AS, Scotland. e-mail: andrew@cee.hw.ac.uk.

Klaus R. Dittrich: Department of Computer Science, University of Zurich, Winterthurerstr. 190, CH-8057 Zurich, Switzerland. e-mail: dittrich@ifi.unizh.ch.

Suzanne M. Embury: Department of Computer Science, University of Wales, Cardiff, P.O. Box 916, Cardiff CF2 3XF, UK. e-mail: S.M.Embury@cs.cf.ac.uk.

Alvaro A.A. Fernandes: Department of Computer Science, University of Manchester, Oxford Road, Manchester M13 9PL. e-mail: alvaro@cs.man.ac.uk.

Piero Fraternali: Politecnico di Milano, Dipartimento di Elettronica e Informazione, via Ponzio 34/5, 20133 Milan, Italy. email: fraterna@elet.polimi.it.

Stella Gatziu: Department of Computer Science, University of Zurich, Winterthurerstr. 190, CH-8057 Zurich, Switzerland. email: gatziu@ifi.unizh.ch.

Andreas Geppert: Department of Computer Science, University of Zurich, Winterthurerstr. 190, CH-8057 Zurich, Switzerland. email: geppert@ifi.unizh.ch.

Peter M.D. Gray: Department of Computing Science, University of Aberdeen, King's College, Aberdeen, UK. email: pgray@csd.abdn.ac.uk

Eric N. Hanson: 301 CSE, P.O. Box 116120, University of Florida, Gainesville, FL 32611-6120, USA. email: hanson@cis.ufl.edu.

Jörgen Hansson: University of Skovde, Department of Computer Science, Box 408, 541 28 SKOVDE, SWEDEN. email: jorgen.hansson@ida.his.se.

Arne Koschel: Forschungszentrum Informatik (FZI), Haid-und-Neu-Str. 10-14, D-76131 Karlsruhe, Germany. email: koschel@fzi.de.

Angelika Kotz-Dittrich: UBS, Bahnhofstrasse 45, CH-8021 Zurich, Switzerland. email: kotz-dittrich@ubs.ch

Krishna Kulkarni: IBM Corporation, 555 Bailey Avenue, Room C320, San Jose, CA 95141, USA. email: krishnak@us.ibm.com

Peter C. Lockemann: Fakultät für Informatik, Universität Karlsruhe, D–76128 Karlsruhe, Germany. email: lockeman@ira.uka.de.

Nelson Mattos: IBM Almaden Research Center, San Jose, CA, USA. email: mattos@vnet.ibm.com.

Stefano Paraboschi: Politecnico di Milano, Dipartimento di Elettronica e Informazione, via Ponzio 34/5, 20133 Milan, Italy. email: parabosc@elet.polimi.it

Norman W. Paton: Department of Computer Science, University of Manchester, Oxford Road, Manchester M13 9PL. email: norm@cs.man.ac.uk.

Alexandra Poulovassilis: Department of Computer Science, King's College London, Strand, London WC2R 2LS. e-mail: alex@dcs.kcl.ac.uk.

Swarup Reddi: 45 Marchmont Street, London WC1N 1AP. e-mail: swarup @desktopsoft.com.

Tore Risch: Department of Computer and Information Science, Linkoping University, S-581 83 Linkoping, Sweden. e-mail: torri@ida.liu.se.

Eric Simon: INRIA, 78153 Le Chesnay, France. e-mail: simon@laure.inria.fr.

Martin Sköld: Department of Computer and Information Science, Linkoping University, S-581 83 Linkoping, Sweden. e-mail: marsk@ida.liu.se.

Carol Small: Prebon Yamane (UK) Limited, 155 Bishopsgate, London, EC2N 3DA, UK. e-mail: carols@prebon.co.uk.

Guenter von Bültzingsloewen: Schweizerischer Bankverein, IT Architectures & Standards, Hochstr. 16, CH-4002 Basel, Swiss. e-mail: von-bueltzingsloewen.guenter@ch.swissbank.com.

Hans-Dirk Walter: Schweizerischer Bankverein, IT Architectures & Standards, Hochstr. 16, CH-4002 Basel, Swiss. e-mail: Walter.Hans-Dirk@ch.swissbank.com.

M. Howard Williams: Department of Computing and Electrical Engineering, Heriot-Watt University, Riccarton, Edinburgh EH14 4AS, Scotland. e-mail: howard@cee.hw.ac.uk.

Jürgen Zimmermann: Object Design Software GmbH, Kreuzberger Ring 64, D-65205 Wiesbaden, Germany. e-mail: zim@odi.com.

Part I

Fundamentals

1

Introduction

Norman W. Paton
Oscar Díaz

ABSTRACT

This chapter introduces the main features of active database systems, outlines how these features can be exploited in a range of application domains, and presents a framework that is used later in the book to characterize the functionality of different active systems. The framework is the major contribution of the chapter, but an important side-effect of its presentation for the book is that much of the terminology associated with active database systems is introduced and defined.

1.1 Introduction

Database management systems are at the heart of current information system technology. They provide reliable, efficient, and effective mechanisms for storing and managing large volumes of information in a multi user environment. In recent years, there has been a trend in database research and practice towards increasing the proportion of the semantics of an application that is supported within the database system itself. Temporal databases, spatial databases, multimedia databases, and database programming languages are examples of this trend. *Active databases* can be considered as part of this trend, where the semantics that are supported reflect the *event-based behavior* of the domain.

According to the dictionary, an event is a thing that happens, especially when it has some *relevance*. Relevance can be measured by whether some sort of action has to be taken as a result of the event. Consequently, an *event* can be seen as a specific situation to which one or more reactions may be necessary. For instance, a user may be interested in undertaking an action linked to a certain event or set of events, such as showing a new window when the mouse is moved over a certain rectangle of the display, or updating the value of x when y is changed and both are related by $x + y = 1$. In a database system, events can be any operation relating to the data. For instance, adding a new tuple to the *child* table can lead to the automatic insertion of a new tuple in the *bus_stops* table to indicate that the school bus now has to stop at the new child's address.

Event Detection	Reaction Execution	Classification
Application	Application	Call-driven
Application	Development System	Event-driven
Development System	Application	Event-source
Development System	Development System	Active

TABLE 1.1. System classification based on reactive behavior support.

This behavior, whereby actions are carried out in response to happenings, can be described as *reactive behavior*, which involves: (1) *defining* the happening of interest (i.e., the *event*) and the associated reaction (2) *detecting* when the relevant circumstance has taken place, and (3) *reacting* to the event.

Table 1.1 classifies systems according to where responsibility is vested for event detection and action execution [FD95].

Call-driven systems don't provide system support for reactive behavior. Applications have to detect relevant circumstances and execute the associated reactions. Reactive behavior can be *programmed* in any system supporting a conditional branch primitive construct (e.g., if – then – else). In a database context, an application program accessing the database using an embedded query language could take responsibility for detecting any violations of an integrity constraint and reacting to them.

Event-driven systems include event detection within the application, which then notifies events to the system that must respond to the event by executing the reaction. In a database context, a forms interface could support automatic detection of user interaction events, which are then notified to the database as a call to a stored procedure, so that the database manages the reaction to an externally detected occurrence.

Event-source systems do support event detection. The application can then explicitly enquire about events detected by the system and carry out the reaction. This is usually achieved by continuously polling the development system or by *call-back* mechanisms: in the first case, the names *event bus* or *event queue* are used for the polled system; in the second case, the application is wakened at certain points when the interesting event takes place, much like interrupts are used to signal external events. In a database context, a management information system application might have the role of reporting certain occurrences in the database to members of staff. The database system might then log the information of interest in specific tables, which are periodically polled by the management information system software.

Active systems support both event detection and action execution. The response is achieved through the run time support part of the system, in accordance with the reaction definitions given by the application. Section 1.2 outlines a range of applications that can benefit from active behavior. In the meantime, the constraints example used above to illustrate call-driven systems can be revisited to show how active facilities can be of use. Rather than implementing the constraint within a range of application programs, it can be supported using rules within the database, so that whenever an event takes place that can violate the constraint, the condition checks to see if the constraint really has been violated, and the action performs the response (e.g., by blocking the update or recording the error).

Active database management systems (ADBMS's), as examples of active systems, are able to monitor and react to specific circumstances of relevance to an application. Traditional (DBMS's) are *passive* in the sense that commands are executed by the database (e.g., query, update, delete) as and when requested by the user or application program. However, some situations cannot be modeled effectively by passive systems. As an example, consider a railway database where data is stored about trains, timetables, seats, fares, and so on, which is accessed by different terminals. In some circumstances (e.g., shortage of seats, public holidays, cultural events) it may be beneficial to add additional coaches to specific trains if the number of spare seats a month in advance is below a threshold value. To address this situation, two options are available to the administrator of a passive database system. One is to add this additional monitoring functionality to all booking programs so that each time a seat is sold, the above situation is checked for. However, this approach leads to the semantics of the monitoring task being distributed, replicated, and hidden among different application programs. The second approach relies on a polling mechanism that periodically checks the number of seats available. Unlike the first approach, here the semantics of the application is represented in a single place, but the difficulty stems from ascertaining the most appropriate polling frequency. If too high, there is a cost penalty. If too low, the reaction may be too late (e.g., the coach is added, but only after several customers have been turned away).

Active databases support the above application by moving the reactive behavior from the application (or polling mechanism) into the DBMS. This implies that the active DBMS has to provide some mechanism for users to describe the reactive behavior (generally referred to as the *knowledge model*), as well as support for monitoring and reacting to relevant circumstances (generally referred to as the *execution model*), and for maintaining, browsing, and debugging reactive behavior (i.e., *management tasks*). In addition, application design methods have to be extended to capture and express reactive functionality. This book addresses these issues describing both current practice and research topics.

A common approach for the knowledge model uses rules that have up to three components: an event, a condition, and an action. The *event* part of a rule describes a happening to which the rule may be able to respond. The *condition* part of the rule examines the context in which the event has taken place. The *action* describes the task to be carried out by the rule if the relevant event has taken place and the condition has evaluated to true. In the train booking application described above, the following rule could be used to monitor new bookings and to add extra coaches if necessary:

```
on insert to booking
if (days_between(new.train.date,today) > 30 and
    new.train.percentbooked() > 60)
do set new.train.carriages = new.train.carriages + 1;
```

This and other event-condition-action rules in this chapter use on to specify the event, if to specify the condition, and do to specify the action. Conditions or actions access event parameters using old to refer to the value that a data item held before an event updated it, new to refer to a newly inserted value, old to refer to a recently deleted value, and new to refer to attributes of a data item that were unaffected by an update event.

In the example above, the *event* to be monitored is the insertion of a new *booking* (on insert to booking). The *condition* performs two tests: that the date when the train departs is more than 30 days ahead of the current date, and that more than 60% of the seats have been booked. The *action*, if the condition is true, then extends the train with extra carriages. The reserved word new allows access from the condition and the action of the rule to the newly inserted tuple.

Most active database systems support rules with all three of the components described above; such a rule is known as an event-condition-action or *ECA rule*. In some proposals the event or the condition may be either missing or implicit. If no event is given, then the resulting rule is a condition-action rule, or *production rule*. If no condition is given, then the resulting rule is an event-action rule.

A range of proposals have been made for execution models that determine how a set of rules is processed at runtime to respond to events that are taking place. Figure 1.1 describes the principal information stores (in ovals) and processes (in rectangles) that are required within all but the most rudimentary of active rule systems.

The following are the steps taken during rule execution:

1. The *DBMS* notifies the *Event Detector* of occurrences within the database in which the event detector has registered an interest. The event detector may then read or update the *History*, which is a log of information of relevance to the event detector about what has happened in the database.

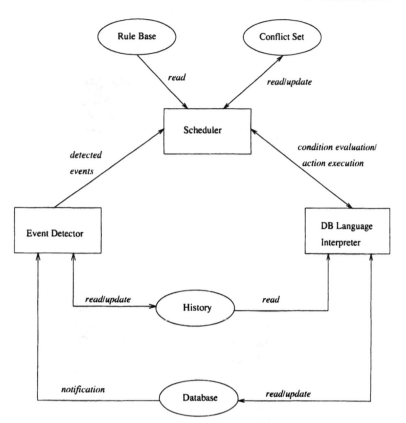

FIGURE 1.1. Abstract active rule system architecture.

2. The *Scheduler* requests information about detected events from the event detector, and reads from the *Rule Base* descriptions of rules that are associated with the events that have taken place. Information about rules that have been triggered (i.e., for which the relevant event has taken place) but which the scheduler may wish to process later, is stored in the *Conflict Set*.

3. The *DB Language Interpreter* is called by the scheduler whenever a rule condition is to be evaluated or action executed. This process may require information to be read from or written to the database, and it may be possible for the language interpreter to service certain requests about what has happened, using information in the history. These accesses to and updates of the database may in turn lead to the detection of further events, thereby causing the rule execution process to be repeated.

The above description of execution model behavior is not very detailed. This is because different rule systems support very different execution models, and the description is intended to be general enough to account for most existing proposals, if in a rather abstract way. Further details of rule execution model features are given in section 1.4.

In addition to support for a knowledge model and execution model, an active rule system must provide facilities for managing the rule base. For example, mechanisms are required for selectively activating or deactivating rules, for browsing large rule sets, and to support rule programming.

Before continuing the presentation of these three aspects of rule systems (i.e., the knowledge model, the execution model, and rule management), the next section provides further motivation for the use of rules by describing some applications that can benefit from the facilities provided by active database systems.

1.2   Applications

As mentioned above, database research often aims to extend the range of facilities within the database system for representing application concepts. Hence, additional capabilities are largely dependent on the applications that are being targeted. In the case of active rules, different categories of applications can be distinguished, and are described in the following subsections.

1.2.1   Database System Extensions

Active rules can be used as a primitive mechanism for supporting the implementation of other parts of a database system. For example, ECA rules have been used to support integrity constraints, materialized views, derived data, coordination of distributed computation, transaction models, advanced data modeling constructs, and automatic screen updating in the context of database change. In [WC96], these extensions are further classified into *internal* or *conventional*, where rules are used as a substitute for a special-purpose mechanism that could be available in the database system (e.g., integrity constraint maintenance or view support), and *extended* or *novel*, where rules are used to support nonstandard database tasks (e.g., version management).

Such extensions to core database functionality are usually supported by defining a high-level syntax for the extended functionality, plus a mapping onto sets of active rules. For example, the following syntax could be used to express the constraint that all employees earn less than their bosses:

```
employee.salary < employee.boss.salary
```

This constraint can be violated by a range of different update operations (e.g., a new `employee` is inserted with a salary higher than that of his/her boss, the `salary` of an employee or a boss is changed, etc.), that can then be monitored by a set of system-generated active rules. For example, to check for violation of the constraint on insertion of a new **employee**, the following active rule could be used:

```
on insert to employee
if new.salary > new.boss.salary
do <action>
```

In this example, the action could be defined in different ways–the update operation could be blocked by aborting the transaction, the constraint could be repaired by increasing the salary of the boss, etc.

1.2.2   Closed Database Applications

This category of application involves the use of active functionality to describe some of the behavior to be manifested by a software system without reference to external devices or systems. Such applications can generally be classified according to whether they support monitoring or control of aspects of an application. For example, rules might be used to describe repair actions in a protein modeling database, to monitor sales in a stock control database, to propagate load calculations in an architectural design database, or to anticipate market activity in a portfolio management database. In these applications there may not be any mapping from a higher-level description onto the active rule language–ECA rules are used directly to support the semantics of the application. For example, in a student exam results database, a rule can be written that records all increases to the **grade** of a student, along with the date when the change is made and the user making the change:

```
on update to grade of student
if new.grade > old.grade
do insert into grade_log
   values (new.reg#, old.grade, new.grade, TODAY(), USER())
end
```

A point to note is that both the condition and the action of this rule require access to information on the update event that triggered the rule. The value of the **grade** attribute after the update is accessed using **new**, and the value before the update using **old**.

1.2.3   Open Database Applications

In this category of application, a database is used in conjunction with monitoring devices to record and respond to situations outside the database. For example, rules could be used in command and control applications to respond to evolving battlefield scenarios, in medical applications to warn physicians of changes in a patient's condition, in transport applications to anticipate traffic holdups, and in air-traffic control to detect potentially dangerous aircraft movements [NI94]. For example, in an aircraft monitoring database, the following rule adapted from [NI94] could inform a controller when two aircraft are approaching each other:

```
on update to pos of aircraft
if exists (select *
           from aircraft Other
           where distance(Other.pos,new.pos) < 5000 and
                 distance(Other.pos,old.pos) > 5000)
do <send message to controller>
```

In this example, the situation being monitored is the position of an aircraft notified to the database from an external device, and the action taken is a change to a display that the air traffic controller is monitoring. Both the new value and the old value for the pos affected by the event are accessed from within the condition.

The situation is more complicated if the environment to be controlled by the DBMS is loosely integrated. If triggered actions cannot be executed under the control of the local transaction manager, these actions are no longer within the scope of the recovery mechanism, and thus special-purpose contingency actions should be provided to reestablish a valid situation in the event of a failure. As an example, consider a federated database where autonomous database systems are integrated to provide a global view, the federated schema, that describes data stored in the component database systems. While site autonomy is preserved, the correctness of the federated schema implies that relevant changes made at each site have to be propagated to the federated schema. A solution based on rules is proposed in [BIPG92]. As an example, consider the case where tuple changes (i.e., extensional modifications) are significant to the federated schema. Here propagation cannot occur in a per-tuple basis, as this will incur a large communication cost. Hence, propagation is delayed until a significant number of tuples are affected (i.e., inserted or deleted). Meanwhile, extensional changes can be stored in a file using a rule such as:

```
on insert or delete of student
if true
do <write inserted or deleted tuples to file F>
```

In this example, the insertion or deletion of tuples in *student*, a relation of relevance to the federated schema, causes a set of records to be written to the file *F*. However, if an error occurs subsequent to the firing of this rule whereby the transaction is invalidated, the recovery mechanism of the database will not undo the updates to the file *F* as this file is outside the control of the local transaction manager. In this context, an active DBMS should provide the user with contingency mechanisms that can be used to undo the updates to *F*. Greater problems arise with certain kinds of external action. For example, it is not possible to undo the effect of an instruction to an industrial robot to drill a hole at a particular position. In this case, the contingency action could be to scrap the part and start again. The use of rules in open systems is discussed more fully in [BBKZ94].

1.2.4   Example Application

This section introduces a straightforward stock control database for a chain of stores that is used throughout the chapter to exemplify the functionality of active database systems. The relations used are:

```
Stock(item#,desc,cost)
Holds(store#,item#,level,sales)
Store(store#,name,address,area)
```

The Stock table stores information on the lines that stores in the chain may hold. The Holds table indicates which stores hold which lines of Stock. The Store table provides some basic information on individual stores.

Specific examples of active behavior that can be used in this application are introduced when they are used to illustrate concepts. Where rules are presented in this chapter, the syntax used is not that of any specific active rule system, but rather a notation based on SQL that should require minimal explanation.

1.2.5   Conclusions

In general, active DBMS's allow reactive behavior to be managed in a centralized way, rather than being distributed, replicated, and embedded in application programs. This leads to what has been called *knowledge independence*, from which the following advantages can be drawn: (1) easy evolution: active semantics can be modified by changing a few rules rather than ascertaining the set of applications in which the reactive behavior is implemented; and (2) guaranteed policy enforcement: any application accessing the database must obey the policies described by the rules–responsibility for policy enforcement lies with the DBMS rather than with the application. The application of active databases is discussed further in Part IV.

1.3   Knowledge Model

The knowledge model of an active database system indicates *what* can be said about active rules in that system. This is in contrast with the execution model, which determines *how* a set of rules behaves at runtime, as presented in section 1.4. As the knowledge model essentially supports the description of active functionality, the features dealt with in this section will often have a direct representation within the syntax of the rule language. Rather than using any particular rule language to illustrate features of the knowledge model, this section is based around a number of dimensions of active behavior [PDW+94, PD98]. These dimensions itemize the principal characteristics of an active database system, and can be used both for comparing different proposals for systems and for describing the requirements of applications.

The concepts supported as dimensions are not new–the aim is to provide a framework for characterizing well-understood active database functionality. The dimensions of rule functionality considered in this chapter are presented in a tabular form. In the tables, the symbol $\subset$ is used to indicate that the particular dimension can take on more than one of the values given, whereas $\in$ indicates a list of alternatives.

Knowledge Model	
Event	**Type** $\subset$ {Primitive, Composite} **Source** $\subset$ {Structure Operation, Behavior Invocation, Transaction, Abstract, Exception, Clock, External} **Granularity** $\subset$ {Member, Subset, Set} **Role** $\in$ {Mandatory, Optional, None}
Condition	**Role** $\in$ {Mandatory, Optional, None} **Context** $\subset$ {DB$_T$, Bind$_E$, DB$_E$, DB$_C$}
Action	**Options** $\subset$ {Structure Operation, Behavior Invocation, Update-Rules, Abort, Inform, External, Do Instead} **Context** $\subset$ {DB$_T$, Bind$_E$, Bind$_C$, DB$_E$, DB$_C$, DB$_A$}

TABLE 1.2. Dimensions for the knowledge model.

The knowledge model of an active rule is considered to have (up to) three principal components; an *event*, a *condition*, and an *action*. The dimensions associated with these structural components of an active rule are presented in Table 1.2 and discussed in the following subsections.

1.3.1 Event

The event part of a rule describes occurrences that are of interest to the
rule. The *Type* of an event can be:

- *primitive*, in which case the event is raised by a single, low-level occurrence that belongs to one of the categories described in *Source* in
  Table 1.2. For example, the event on insert to Store monitors the
  insertion of new tuples into the Store relation.

- *composite*, in which case the event is raised by some combination of
  primitive or composite events using a range of operators that constitute the *event algebra*. For example, the event on insert to Holds
  or update to sales of Holds is a composite event using the operator or that is signaled if either of the operand events take place.
  The design of languages and systems for describing and detecting
  composite events has been a major focus of work on active database
  systems, and is discussed below.

Primitive Events

An event is something that happens at a point in time. Specifying an
event therefore involves providing a description of the happening that is
to be monitored. The nature of the description and the way in which the
event can be detected largely depends on the *Source* or *generator* of the
event. Possible alternatives are:

- *structure operation*, in which case the event is raised by an operation
  on some piece of structure (e.g., *insert* a tuple, *update* an attribute,
  access a tuple).

- *behavior invocation*, in which case the event is raised by the execution
  of some user-defined operation (e.g., the message *display* is sent to an
  object of type *widget*). It is common for event languages to allow
  events to be raised *before* or *after* an operation has been executed.

- *transaction*, in which case the event is raised by transaction commands (e.g., abort, commit, begin-transaction).

- *abstract* or *user-defined*, in which case the programming language of
  the database explicitly signals the occurrence of the event (e.g., in
  response to some information entered by a user).

- *exception*, in which case the event is raised as a result of some exception being produced (e.g., an attempt is made to access some data
  without appropriate authorization).

- *clock*, in which case the event is raised at some point in time. Absolute
  (e.g., the 13th of November 1998 at 15:00), relative (e.g., 10 days after

the shares are sold), and periodic (e.g., the first day of every month) time events are reported in the literature.

- *external*, in which case the event is raised by a happening outside the database (e.g., the temperature reading goes above 30 degrees [DBM88]).

The *Event Granularity* of an event indicates whether an event is defined for every object in a *set* (e.g., every instance of a class), for given *subsets* (e.g., all staff members except professors), or for specific *members* of the set (e.g., to prevent unauthorized access to specific instances).

The *Role* of an event indicates whether events must always be given for active rules, or whether the explicit naming of an event is not necessary. If the role is *optional*, then when no event is specified *condition-action* rules are supported, which have significantly different functionality and implementations from event-condition-action (ECA) rules, as described in Chapter 5. If the role is *none*, then events cannot be specified, and all rules are *condition-action* rules. If the role is *mandatory*, then only ECA rules are supported.

Composite Events

The design of languages that can specify precisely when a rule should be triggered has been important to most of the later work on active database systems. Early work on composite event detection took place in the HiPAC project [DBM88], and a range of active OODBs refined and extended the early results [GJS92, GD94, CKAK94, CFPT96].

Composite events definitions exploit event algebras that include a range of operators to indicate the combinations of events that are of interest to an application. For example, if a rule should be triggered when a new Holds tuple is created or if the store# of a Holds tuple is changed, this can be expressed using the operator or thus:

`on insert to Holds or update to store# of Holds`

The or operator is very straightforward to support, as a rule monitoring the above event can easily be rewritten as two rules, each monitoring one of the operands of the or. However, other operators require the system to record partially detected events. For example, if an event is to be triggered when the level attribute and the sales attribute of a stock item is changed, this can be expressed as:

`on update to level of Holds and update to sales of Holds`

The above definition is probably not what is required, however, as it seems to allow the composite event to be triggered whenever a level and a sales are updated, whether or not the updates are to the same tuple in the Holds relation. Thus, to make the specification more precise, the parameters of the component events can be used to restrict when composition takes place, as in the following case, which is based on the syntax for SAMOS [GD94]:

```
on update to level of Holds and
   update to sales of Holds : same Holds
```

Other common event composition operators identify sequences of event occurrences, raise an event once when another event occurs a specific number of times, or raise an event if another event has not occurred within some interval. Individual proposals differ in terms of the default or allowed intervals over which an event can be detected. Some systems only accumulate components of composite events within transactions, while others allow event detection to span transaction boundaries.

Another factor that influences when composite events are raised is the way in which the event detector consumes event instances. As an example, consider a composite event CE that is the sequence of events $EV1$ and $EV2$. If two occurrences of event $EV1$, first $ev1$ and later $ev1'$, have already been signaled, and an occurrence of event $EV2$, e.g., $ev2$, is now produced, there is a question as to what instances of CE should be raised. Possibilities include $sequence(ev1,ev2)$, or $sequence(ev1',ev2)$, or $sequence(ev1,ev2) \cup sequence(ev1', ev2)$. The alternatives are distinguished using $consumption$ $policies$. In [CKAK94], four possible consumption policies are introduced: a $recent$ context, which considers the most recent set of events that can be used to construct the composition (in the previous example, $sequence(ev1', ev2)$ is detected when $ev2$ arises, after which $ev1'$ and $ev2$ are no longer considered for the detection of CE); a $chronicle$ context, which consumes the events in chronological order ($sequence(ev1, ev2)$ is signaled when $ev2$ arises, after which $ev1$ and $ev2$ are no longer considered for the detection of CE); a $continuous$ context, which defines a sliding window and starts a new composition with each primitive event that takes place (two sequence events would begin to be constructed when $ev1$ and $ev1'$ arise, and both sequence events would be signaled as $ev2$ is detected); and a $cumulative$ context, which accumulates all the primitive events until the composite event is finally raised (a sequence event is signaled only once when $ev2$ arises, where the first parameter of the sequence includes the parameters of all the occurrences of EV1, i.e., $ev1$ and $ev1^{1}$). The rationale for each context can be found in [CKAK94].

---

[1]Unlike the continuous context, an event occurrence does not participate in more than one composite computation in the cumulative context.

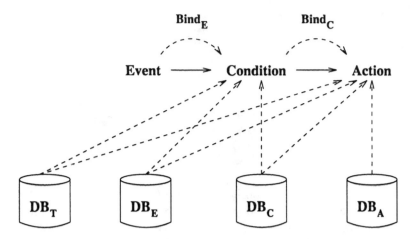

FIGURE 1.2. The context within which a rule is processed.

1.3.2 *Condition*

The *Role* of a condition indicates whether or not it must be given. In ECA rules, the condition is generally *optional*, or a dummy condition true can be given. When no condition is given for an ECA rule, or where the role is *none*, an *event-action* rule results. In systems in which both the event and the condition are optional, it is always the case that at least one is given.

The *Context* indicates the setting in which the condition is evaluated. The different components of a rule are not evaluated in isolation from the database or from each other, and furthermore they may not be evaluated in quick succession, as described in section 1.4. As a result, the processing of a single rule can potentially be associated with at least four different database states: DB_T–the database at the start of the current transaction; DB_E–the database when the event took place; DB_C–the database when the condition is evaluated; and DB_A–the database when the action is executed. Active rule systems may support facilities within the condition of a rule that allow the condition to access zero or more of the states DB_T, DB_E, and DB_C, and may also provide access to bindings associated with the event ($Bind_E$). The availability of information to the different components of a rule is illustrated in Figure 1.2. As an example of the utility of such information, the following rule is used to respond to the situation in which the level of a stock item held by a store drops to 0.

```
on update to level of Holds
if new.level = 0
do <action>
```

In this rule, information from the event (DB_E) is used to identify when the level field has been set to 0, so that an appropriate response can be made (e.g., more stock is ordered, the manager is informed).

1.3.3   Action

The range of tasks that can be performed by an action is specified as its *Options*. Actions may update the *structure* of the database or *rules*, perform some *behavior invocation* within the database or an *external* call, *inform* the user or system administrator of some situation, *abort* a transaction, or take some alternative course of action using *do-instead* [SJGP90].

The following example shows a typical rule action that performs a *structure operation*. The rule supports the behavior that when the cost of an item of stock is set to NULL, the tuples recording the stock level in the Holds relation can be removed.

```
on update to cost of Stock
if new.cost is NULL
do delete from Holds
   where Holds.item#=new.item#
```

As an example of *do-instead*, if an attempt was made to delete a tuple from the Holds relation that has sales > 1000, then rather than allow the operation to proceed, the store manager could be informed of the attempted operation:

```
on delete to Holds
if old.sales > 1000
do instead <inform store manager>
```

This is in contrast with the more standard semantics, in which the tuple is deleted *and* the store manager is informed:

```
on delete to Holds
if old.sales > 1000
do <inform store manager>
```

Whereas rules are mainly used to expand the effects of operations on the database, *do-instead* rules specify alternative behaviors that are appropriate in specific circumstances.

The *Context* of the action is similar to that of the condition, and indicates the information that is available to the action, as illustrated in Figure 1.2. It is sometimes possible for information to be passed from the event or condition of a rule to its action as DB_E or $Bind_C$.

1.4   Execution Model

The execution model specifies how a set of rules is treated at run time, and is characterized by the dimensions presented in Table 1.3. While the

---

Execution Model

Condition-Mode ⊂ {Immediate, Deferred, Detached}
Action-Mode ⊂ {Immediate, Deferred, Detached}
Transition Granularity ⊂ {Tuple, Set}
Net-effect policy ∈ {Yes, No}
Cycle policy ⊂ {Iterative, Recursive}
Priorities ∈ {Dynamic, Numerical, Relative, None }
Scheduling ∈ {All Parallel, All Sequential, Saturation, Some}
Error handling ⊂ {Abort, Ignore, Backtrack, Contingency}

TABLE 1.3. Dimensions for the execution model.

execution model of a rule system is closely related to aspects of the underlying DBMS (e.g., data model, transaction manager), there are a number of phases in rule evaluation, illustrated in Figure 1.3, that transcend considerations that relate to specific software environments:

1. The *signaling* phase refers to the appearance of an *event occurrence* caused by an event source.

2. The *triggering* phase takes the events produced so far, and triggers the corresponding rules. A rule that has been associated with its event occurrence forms a *rule instantiation*, and is also known as a *triggered rule*. The triggered rules are stored in the *conflict set*.

3. The *scheduling* phase indicates how the rule conflict set is processed, and in particular *when* the conditions of rules are evaluated and their actions executed.

4. The *evaluation* phase evaluates the condition of the triggered rules. Although this is not shown in Figure 1.3, in some systems condition evaluation can lead to event signaling (e.g., in object-oriented databases where the invocation of a method can be monitored as an event, and conditions can invoke methods).

5. The *execution* phase carries out the actions of the chosen rule instantiations. The execution of the action of a rule is also known as *firing* a rule. During action execution other events can in turn be signaled, which may produce *cascaded* rule firing.

These phases are not necessarily executed contiguously, but depend on the *event-condition* and *condition-action* coupling modes. The former determines when the condition is evaluated relative to the event that triggers the rule. The condition-action coupling mode indicates when the action is

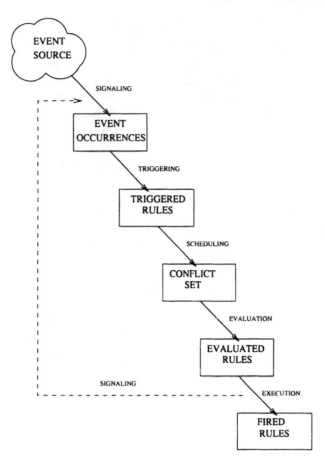

FIGURE 1.3. Principal steps that take place during rule execution.

to be executed relative to the evaluation of the condition. The options for coupling modes most frequently supported are:

- *immediate*, in which case the condition (action) is evaluated (executed) immediately after the event (condition). Immediate coupling modes can be used, for example, to enforce security constraints or to propagate updates.

- *deferred*, in which case the condition (action) is evaluated (executed) within the same transaction as the event (condition) of the rule, but not necessarily at the earliest opportunity. Normally, further processing is left until the end of the transaction, or until a program requests that rule processing take place at a *rule assertion point*. Deferred coupling modes can be used, for example, to defer constraint checking until the end of the transaction, thereby allowing temporary inconsistencies within a single transaction.

- *detached*, in which case the condition (action) is evaluated (executed) within a different transaction from the event (condition). The execution of the action can be *dependent* upon or *independent* of the committing of the transaction in which the event took place or the condition was evaluated. Detached coupling modes are normally associated with the control of activities external to the database, but can also be used, for example, to monitor access to sensitive information, as running a *detached independent* transaction will record information on the access even if the transaction in which the access took place is aborted.

The nature of the relationship between events and the rules they trigger is partially captured by the *transition granularity*. This indicates whether the relationship between event occurrences and rule instantiations is 1:1 or many:1. When the transition granularity is *tuple*, a single event occurrence triggers a single rule. When the transition granularity is *set*, a collection of event occurrences are used together to trigger a rule. For example, if a rule R with a condition-action coupling mode of *deferred* is monitoring an event E, and occurrences e_1, e_2, and e_3 of E have taken place during a transaction, then the transition granularity indicates how many instantiations of R are created by the triggering phase. If the transition granularity is *tuple*, then a separate instantiation of R is created for each of e_1, e_2, and e_3; if the transition granularity is *set*, then a single instantiation of R is created to respond to the set of events $\{e_1, e_2, e_3\}$.

An example in which a transition granularity of *tuple* is required is in an immediate rule that wishes to block access to particular items of data:

```
on access to sales of Holds
if AUTHORITY(USER()) < 5
do abort
```

In this case, it is necessary to abort the transaction as soon as the access is attempted, and thus the rule must run with *immediate* condition and action coupling modes and a transition granularity of *tuple*.

An example in which a transition granularity of *set* is required is when the overall effect of a set of updates has to be considered together. For example, a constraint might abort any transaction in which more than 50 tuples are deleted from the Holds table:

```
on delete to Holds
if count(select * from deletedHolds d) > 50
do abort
```

In this case, as a single rule is associated with a set of events, the event binding DB_E is represented as a table, named in the example as deletedHolds.

Another feature that influences the relationship between events and the rules they trigger is the *Net effect policy*, which indicates whether the net effect of the event occurrences rather than each individual event occurrence should be considered. The difference between the two strategies stems from cases in which several updates on the same data item can be considered as a single update: if an instance is updated and then deleted, the net effect is deletion of the original instance; if an instance is inserted and then updated, the net effect is the insertion of the updated instance; if an instance is inserted and then deleted, the net effect is no modification at all [Han92]. The net effect policy is not generally meaningful in the context of immediate rule processing.

The question of what happens when events are signaled by the evaluation of the condition or action of a rule is addressed by the *Cycle policy* of the execution model. In general, there are two options. If the Cycle policy is *iterative*, then events signaled during condition and action evaluation are combined with those from the original event source illustrated in Figure 1.3, and are subsequently consumed by rules from this single, global repository of signaled events. This means that condition or action evaluation is never suspended to allow responses to be made to events signaled by those conditions or actions. By contrast, if the Cycle policy is *recursive*, events signaled during condition and action evaluation cause the condition or action to be suspended, so that any immediate rules monitoring the events can be processed at the earliest opportunity. In practice, a recursive cycle policy is only likely to be considered in systems that support immediate rule processing, and some systems support a recursive cycle policy for immediate rules and an iterative cycle policy for deferred rules.

The *Scheduling* phase of rule evaluation determines what happens when multiple rules are triggered at the same time. The two principal issues are:

- *The selection of the next rule to be fired.* This topic has received much attention in the expert system community, as it is seen as fundamental to understanding and controlling the behavior of a set of rules [Win84]. Indeed, rule order can strongly influence the result and reflects the kind of *reasoning* followed by the system. Examples of well-known *Dynamic* approaches (referred to as *conflict resolution policies*) are those that prioritize rules based on either the recency of update (i.e., the time of event occurrence) or the complexity of the condition. The former makes the system focus on a line of reasoning, since the most recently modified data is that associated with the most recently fired rule (i.e., the search space is traversed depth-first). The latter reflects the assumption that condition complexity indicates the specificity of the rule (i.e., the extent to which the rule fits the current situation). However, mechanisms available in active database systems, that have to cope with large quantities of data efficiently in a context where deterministic behavior is held to be highly desirable, tend to support schemes in which rules are associated with a priority at rule definition time (staticly).

Static priorities are often determined either by the system (e.g., based on rule creation time) or by the user as an attribute of the rule. In the latter case, a rule is selected from a collection of simultaneously triggered rules for execution using a *Priority* mechanism. Rules can be placed in order using a *numerical* scheme, in which each rule is given an absolute value that is its priority, or by indicating the *relative* priorities of rules by stating explicitly that a given rule must be fired before another when both are triggered at the same time.

- *The number of rules to be fired.* Possible options include (1) To fire *all* rule instantiations *sequentially.* (2) To fire *all* rule instantiations in *parallel.* (3) To fire all instantiations of a specific rule before any other rules are considered, which is known as firing a rule to *saturation.* (4) To fire only one or *some* rule instantiation(s). Which approach is most appropriate depends on the task that is being supported by the rule. The first alternative is suitable for rules supporting integrity maintenance: an update is successful once all constraints have been validated. The second option is described in HiPAC [DBM88] in a bid to encourage more efficient rule processing. The third option is most popular among expert-system practitioners, as it yields more focused inference than the other approaches. The fourth option can be of use to support derived data–different derivation criteria may be available (each of them supported by a rule), but only one is used.

A further aspect to be considered is how *Error handling* is supported during rule firing. Most systems simply *abort* the transaction, as this is standard behavior in databases. However, other alternatives may be more convenient [HW93]: to *ignore* the rule that raised the error and to continue processing other rules; to *backtrack* to the state when rule processing started and either restart rule processing or continue with the transaction; to adopt some *contingency* plan that endevours to recover from the error state, possibly using the exception mechanism of the underlying database system.

The following example should help to illustrate how some of the execution model dimensions impact upon rule behavior at runtime. In what follows, the following simple rulebase will be used, where we assume that the rules are monitoring abstract events:

```
rule r1: on e1 if true do raise(e2)
rule r2: on e1 if true do raise(e3)
rule r3: on e2 or e3 if true do nothing
rule r4: on e2 if true do nothing
rule r5: on e3 if true do nothing
```

When rules are defined without priorities, this increases the level of non-determinism in the behavior of the system. However, in this case, we will assume a total order of rule priorities as follows:

r1 > r3 > r2 > r4 > r5

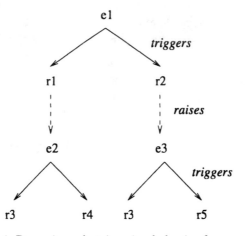

FIGURE 1.4. Recursive rule triggering behavior for example rules.

In addition, it will be assumed that all rules have a transition granularity of tuple, and that rule processing is initiated by an occurrence of the event e1. Two execution models and cycle policies will be compared:

- *Immediate condition and action coupling modes, with a recursive cycle policy.* It is common for immediate rules to operate with a recursive cycle policy. In this case, the processing that results from the occurrence of e1 is illustrated in Figure 1.4. The figure illustrates which events trigger which rules, and which rules raise which events. In immediate rule processing with a recursive cycle policy, the tree structure in Figure 1.4 is traversed depth first. The event e1 triggers rules r1 and r2. As r1 has a higher priority than r2, r1 is chosen for execution first. When its action is executed, this in turn raises the event e2, which in turn triggers r3 and r4. These rules then have their conditions and actions executed before the scheduler returns to process r2, which was triggered earlier by r1. The overall order in which the rules are fired is: r1, r3(e2), r4, r2, r3(e3), r5.

- *Deferred condition and immediate action coupling modes, with an iterative cycle policy.* It is common for deferred rules to operate with an iterative cycle policy. In this case, the way in which rules are scheduled is quite different from the previous case. The first difference is that rules are not scheduled for execution as soon as e1 takes place, but rather at a rule assertion point or at the end of the transaction. Rules are then scheduled using a global conflict set, and processing proceeds as illustrated in Figure 1.5. The occurrence of e1 triggers rules r1 and r2, which are added to the conflict set. As r1 has the highest priority in the conflict set, it is scheduled next, and in turn raises event e2, which triggers r3 and r4, which are added to the conflict set. As r3 now has highest priority of any rule in the conflict set, it is scheduled next, and so on. The overall order in which rules are scheduled for execution in this case is r1, r3(e2), r2, r3(e3), r4, r5.

It should be clear from the above that even with simple rule bases, the interleaving of rule behavior can become quite complex, and that the order in which rules are fired may not be immediately obvious from the rule base and the rule priorities. In practice, application development using rules is likely to require effective tool support for analyzing (Chapter 3) and debugging (Chapter 7) rule bases.

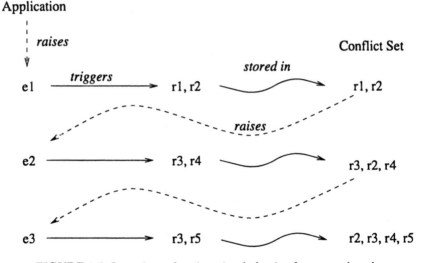

FIGURE 1.5. Iterative rule triggering behavior for example rules.

1.5 Management

Sections 1.3 and 1.4 have, respectively, described the structural characteristics of individual active rules and the run time evaluation of sets of such rules. This section considers the facilities provided by the system for managing rules–specifically what operations can be applied to rules, how rules are represented, and programming support for rules. Possible dimensions are shown in Table 1.4.

The *Description* of rules refers to how rules are normally expressed using either a database *programming language*, a *query language*, or as *objects* in an object-oriented database. These categories are not exclusive.

Management of Rules

Description $\subset$ {Programming Language, Query Language, Objects}
Operations $\subset$ {Activate, Deactivate, Signal}
Adaptability $\in$ {Compile Time, Run Time}
Data Model $\in$ {Relational, Extended Relational, Deductive, Object-Oriented}

TABLE 1.4. Dimensions for rule management.

For example, it is possible for an extended query language facility in an object-oriented database to arrange for rules to be stored as objects.

Besides creation and deletion, which are taken to be mandatory, other *Operations* commonly found are *activate, deactivate,* and *signal.* Activation (deactivation) of rules makes the system start (stop) monitoring the rule's event or condition. Since rules can persist for long periods, this mechanism helps the database administrator to temporarily switch on (off) some rules without deleting them. Among other things, such deactivation mechanisms may be convenient for improving efficiency, for debugging, or for loop prevention (e.g., by deactivating rules once they have been fired).

The operation *Signal* is required to support *abstract events*, and is invoked explicitly by the application to notify the rule system of external occurrences.

Although all active DBMS's support creation and deletion of rules, they can differ in the level of *Adaptability* supported. In some systems it is only possible to change the rules associated with an application by recompiling the application code, and thus the rules can only be modified at *compile time.* Others support more dynamic *run time* rule modification, including the ability of rule actions to modify the rule base. Clearly there is a sliding scale of degrees of *Adaptability*–in the context of the dimensions, any system that allows rules to be created without recompiling application code can be considered to support *run time* adaptability.

There is an extent to which the *Data Model* with which an active rule system is associated is independent of the other dimensions of rule system functionality. However, the data model is likely to significantly influence the designers of an active rule system, and is thus included as a dimension.

Also of importance for the developers of applications are the tools for reasoning about rule behavior (Chapter 3), designing active applications (Chapter 7), and debugging active applications (Chapter 7).

1.6   Conclusion

This chapter has explained how active database systems extend the capabilities of passive database systems with mechanisms for responding automatically to events as they take place. The utility of this sort of behavior has been motivated by describing a range of classes of application for which active behavior may be useful. It has been shown how active behavior can be expressed using event condition action rules, and a framework has been presented that summarizes important features of active database systems, and in particular the syntax (knowledge model) by which rules are described, the semantics (execution model) of how rules are executed, and the environment (management model) within which rule programs are developed. The chapter has thus provided a brief overview of the fundamentals of active database systems. One area that is central to active rule systems but that has received only limited attention is implementation architectures, which are addressed in the remainder of Part I. A complementary view of important features for active databases is provided by the Active Database System Manifesto [DGG95].

1.7   REFERENCES

[BBKZ94]   H. Branding, A. Buchmann, T. Kudrass, and J. Zimmermann. Rules in an Open System: The REACH Rule System. In N.W. Paton and M.H. Williams, editors, *Rules in Database Systems*, pages 111–126. Springer-Verlag, 1994.

[BIPG92]   J.M. Blanco, A. Illarramendi, J.M. Perez, and A. Goni. Making a Federated Database System Active. In A.M. Toja and I. Ramos, editors, *Proc. DEXA*, pages 345–350. Springer-Verlag, 1992.

[CFPT96]   S. Ceri, P. Fraternali, S. Paraboschi, and L. Tanca. Active Rule Management in Chimera. In J. Widom and S. Ceri, editors, *Active Database Systems: Triggers and Rules for Active Database Processing*, pages 151–175. Morgan Kaufmann, 1996.

[CKAK94]   S. Chakravarthy, V. Krishnaprasad, E. Anwar, and S.-K. Kim. Composite Events for Active Databases: Semantics, Contexts and Detection. In J. Bocca, M. Jarke, and C. Zaniolo, editors, *Proc. 20th Intl. Conf. on Very Large Data Bases*, pages 606–617. Morgan-Kaufmann, 1994.

[DBM88]   U. Dayal, A.P. Buchmann, and D.R. McCarthy. Rules Are Objects Too: A Knowledge Model for an Active Object Oriented Database System. In K.R. Dittrich, editor, *Proc. 2nd Intl. Workshop on OODBS*, volume 334, pages 129–143. Springer-Verlag, 1988. Lecture Notes in Computer Science.

[DGG95]   K.R. Dittrich, S. Gatziu, and A. Geppert. The Active Database Management System Manifesto: A Rulebase of ADBMS Features. In T. Sellis, editor, *Rules In Database Systems: Proc. of the 2nd Intl. Workshop*, pages 3–17. Springer-Verlag, 1995.

[FD95]   R. Fernandez and O. Diaz.   Reactive Behaviour Support: Themes and Variations. In T. Sellis, editor, *2nd Intl. Workshop on Rules In Database Systems (RIDS)*, pages 69–85. Springer-Verlag, 1995.

[GD94]   S. Gatziu and K.R. Dittrich.   Events in an Active Object-Oriented Database. In N.W. Paton and M.H. Williams, editors, *Proc. 1st Intl. Workshop on Rules in Database Systems*, pages 23–39. Springer-Verlag, 1994.

[GJS92]   N.H. Gehani, H.V. Jagadish, and O. Shmueli. Event Specification in an Active Object-Oriented Database. *ACM SIGMOD*, pages 81–90, 1992.

[Han92]   E.N. Hanson. Rule Condition Testing and Action Execution in Ariel. In *Proc. SIGMOD*, pages 49–58. ACM, 1992.

[HW93]   E.N. Hanson and J. Widom. An Overview of Production Rules in Database Systems.   *The Knowledge Engineering Review*, 8(2):121–143, 1993.

[NI94]   W. Naqvi and M.T. Ibraham. Rule and Knowledge Management in an Active Database System. In N.W. Paton and M.H. Williams, editors, *Proc. 1st Intl. Workshop on Rules In Database Systems*, pages 58–69. Springer-Verlag, 1994.

[PD98]   N.W. Paton and O. Diaz. Active Database Systems. *Computing Surveys*, 1998. To be published.

[PDW+94] N.W. Paton, O. Diaz, M.H. Williams, J. Campin, A. Dinn, and A. Jaime. Dimensions of Active Behaviour. In N.W. Paton and M.H. Williams, editors, *Proc. 1st Intl. Workshop on Rules In Database Systems*, pages 40–57. Springer-Verlag, 1994.

[SJGP90]   M. Stonebraker, A. Jhingran, J. Goh, and S. Potamianos. On Rules, Procedures, Caching and Views in Database Systems. In *Proc. ACM SIGMOD*, pages 281–290, 1990.

[WC96]   J. Widom and S. Ceri. *Active Database Systems*. Morgan Kaufmann, 1996.

[Win84]   P.H. Winston.   *Artificial Intelligence (Second Edition)*. Addison-Wesley, 1984.

2

Architecture of Active Database Systems

Alejandro P. Buchmann

ABSTRACT
The architecture of an active DBMS determines both its functionality and
the components that are required for its implementation. This chapter addresses first some issues that have an impact on the architecture of an
active database system, and presents the various architectural alternatives.
The basic functions of an ADBMS are identified and then related to the
architectural alternatives. This chapter discusses rule specification and registration, and rule execution. Special attention is devoted to the execution
of transactions and its relationship to the execution of ECA rules.

2.1 Introduction

The architecture of an active DBMS determines both its functionality and
the components that are required to realize it. Since an ADBMS by definition must provide the active capabilities in addition to full DBMS features,
it can be viewed as an extension of a passive DBMS. There are various
properties of the underlying DBMS and of the architectural strategy used
for implementing the active extensions that will have an impact on the functionality and the performance of the active DBMS. The major dimensions
that need to be considered are:

- the degree of integration between the underlying DBMS and the active capabilities,

- the system architecture of the underlying DBMS, and

- the data model of the DBMS and the programming language used
  for the active extensions.

In this chapter we will briefly discuss the various architectural alternatives. We will then identify the basic functions and components of an
ADBMS and will relate them to the various architectural alternatives and
will point out the effect of an architecture on the implementation of a given
feature. We will address first the rule specification and registration functionality and then the rule execution subsystem. A central aspect of rule

execution is the integration of the active functionality with the transaction manager of the underlying DBMS. Therefore, special attention is given to the transaction model supported by the underlying DBMS and how the execution of ECA rules is integrated with the execution of transactions. Since existing products and prototypes of active systems are mostly centralized, the discussion will concentrate on centralized active database systems.

2.2   Degree of Integration

An important dimension along which architectures can be distinguished is the degree of integration between the underlying DBMS and the active functionality. The two extremes along this line are a layered architecture in which the active components of the ADBMS are built on top of the existing DBMS in a user process, and a fully integrated architecture that tightly couples the components providing the active features with the rest of the DBMS. Depending on the degree of integration, some of the active capabilities may not be implementable or may be implemented only in a very inefficient manner.

2.2.1   Layered Architecture

Layered architectures are popular because they allow the implementation of the active functionality *on top* of an existing system with little or no modification to the underlying database management system. Event detection and rule execution is done separately from the underlying DBMS and typically on the client-side in the user's address space. Application programs are often preprocessed and modified in such a way that events can be appropriately detected. Since communication between application and DBMS is always via the client, it is relatively easy to generate the events on the client-side when a method is executed. However, the server must communicate transaction events that are required by the active component. Further, the server generally is not aware of the active component and is not prepared to signal the necessary events. Most commercial DBMS's do not allow access to or direct communication with internal components such as the transaction manager, the lock manager, and the access control module. In most cases the interfaces to these components are not laid open. Some commercial systems go as far as isolating the user processes in a proprietary programming environment curtailing the ability to make system calls. In addition, some basic functions that are already performed by the underlying DBMS, such as logging, must be reimplemented in the user space. Other extensions, such as nested transactions, may not be implementable in a layered architecture.

    The advantage of low cost extensibility and the fact that the active extensions can sometimes be used on different DBMS's is balanced by the limitation of functionality derived from the lack of open interfaces of the underlying DBMS and its internal components, and a strong performance penalty.

2.2.2 Integrated Architecture

In a fully integrated architecture, the active functionality is embedded in the basic components of the DBMS. While some of the extensions may be realized on the user side, others must be implemented by extending the basic DBMS functionality. The advantages of a fully integrated architecture are most evident when dealing with the transaction manager, the concurrency control and rollback mechanisms. Important portions of the DBMS that must be adapted when extending a DBMS with active functionality are the dispatch mechanism, the lock manager, and the commit and abort processes. To modify these components it is necessary to have access to the source code of the underlying DBMS. Unfortunately, sources of full-fledged OODBMS's are not readily available to research groups, which has slowed progress in the development of active OODBMS's. Extensions to commercial products have occurred mostly within companies or through partnerships between a research group and a company. An example of this route is the NAOS project and its cooperation with O2 [CCS94]. The use of available OODBMS research prototypes, such as Texas Instruments' OpenOODB [WBT92], is a compromise. OpenOODB is built as a client to the Exodus Storage Server [CDRS86]. While the source code for both systems is made available to research groups, some of the problems remain, since the OODBMS runs as a client to the Exodus server and modifications to the Exodus transaction manager are not trivial. Some of these problems are discussed in the next section.

The advantage of fully integrating the active capabilities with the DBMS lies both in the broader range of functionality that can be provided and in the potential performance gains. The main drawback is the high entry price when building from scratch or the lack of availability of a stable platform to research groups.

2.3 Client-Server Architecture of the Underlying DBMS

All active database systems we know of are implemented as extensions to a DBMS based on the client-server principle.

Relational systems are usually implemented as fat servers, meaning that event detection and trigger execution is essentially carried out on the server side. The old and/or new states of the database on which a trigger operates are typically handled in the form of delta-relations. Because tuple identification in the relational model is done strictly by value, passing of tuples as parameters is easy.

Object systems are typically distinguished based on their architecture as page-server or object-server systems. The impact of underlying system architecture can be seen clearly when we compare object-server and page-server architectures for object-oriented DBMS's.

In a page-server architecture, the server manages I/O, page buffering, and page locks. The data transfer unit between server and client is a page. The client is responsible for unpacking the page and accessing individual objects. This means that the server does not know how to interpret objects, nor how to execute methods, and object-level locking is not provided by the server. Therefore, most of the active functionality, such as event detection and composition, must be realized on the client-side. On the other hand, transaction control is clearly located on the server-side. Transaction commit and abort is controlled by the server and the corresponding transaction events are generated by the server.

Object servers, on the other hand, unpack pages and do understand objects and can execute their methods. Their transport unit is an object. They can provide either page or object-level locking, which simplifies the implementation of nested transactions. Because the server can execute methods, method events may be generated both at the client-side and the server-side, and event handling and rule execution could be executed on either side. In general, more degrees of freedom exist in an object-server architecture.

Most active OODBMS prototypes we are aware of have been built as extensions to a page-server architecture, either directly at the user level on a commercial OODBMS or as extensions to a prototype OODBMS, such as Texas Instruments' OpenOODB. In the latter case, OpenOODB runs as a client process of Exodus and an application must be bound to an instantiation of OpenOODB. Different applications run on different instances of OpenOODB, thus having different address spaces. This makes the passing of object references impossible and requires that parameter passing be done strictly by value across applications.

2.4   Data Model and Programming Language Issues

The main difference between the relational and an object model when dealing with active capabilities lies in the variety of the events that may have to be detected. In a relational system, the triggering events are usually limited to insert, delete, and update operations with a few systems providing also read access as an event. Therefore, event detection on these predefined operations can be hard-wired into the system. In an object model in which the user may define new classes with arbitrary methods, every method can represent an event and must be detected. The problem is compounded because of inheritance and the issues of encapsulation. Object-oriented systems and their languages have more complex scoping rules than relational systems.

A major difference with respect to rule definition exists between interpreted and compiled languages. The addition of a new rule is trivial in an interpreted environment, such as Smalltalk, but is a major problem in a statically compiled environment, such as C++. In a C++ environment, relinking is at least required, thus making fully dynamic addition of rules almost impossible. We will pick up these issues as we discuss the individual components of an ADBMS architecture.

2.5 Rule Specification and Registration

Any ADBMS needs some capability for describing rules and registering them with the system. In this section we identify the basic functions involved in the specification of rules and their registration with the system, and discuss the components needed to implement this functionality. The important issues from an architectural point of view are:

- the model and language used,

- the time and method of creation and modification of rules,

- the process of subscription to events, and

- the handling of privileges associated with the definition of rules.

We distinguish here between the functions and components that are part of the DBMS and those that are part of design tools. A function that is typically associated with aDB design tools is the testing for correctness of a rule set, specifically static tests for termination and confluence. We do not address those. However, since new rules that are added may conflict with the current database state, we analyze the implications in the context of rule creation and modification privileges. Some ADBMS's include checking capabilities that include the current state of the database as part of the rule specification and registration subsystem.

Rule definition: ECA rules are defined through a rule specification language that is an extension of the schema definition language. Depending on the data model used, the rule specification language is typically an extension of SQL in the relational case or an extension to a (persistent) OO-programming language. The corresponding precompiler must be provided.

In the case of SQL, ECA rules are specified as triggers that are defined on a specific relation. Triggers are compiled with the corresponding relation and registered in the catalogue. In an object model, the issues are more diverse. Depending on the actual object model used, it may either be possible to define rules as instances of a single class Rule, or the underlying model may in effect require the creation of a single-instance class for each new rule. The implication from an operational point of view will be that the definition of a new ECA rule in the latter case requires the recompilation of the schema. A commonly used subterfuge that has an impact on system architecture is to break up a rule into simple C-functions that are placed into libraries that only need to be relinked when new rules are added.

Rule registration: The registration of a new rule with the ADBMS also implies a series of administrative processes for which the necessary infrastructure must be provided. When a new rule is registered with the system, the event definition must be extracted and the corresponding event handler must be initialized. If the triggering event is an event already known to the system, then the new rule must subscribe to that event. If the event was not previously known to the ADBMS as a triggering event, the corresponding mechanisms for event detection/composition must be initialized. Initialization implies the creation of the necessary event detector/composer structures as well as the necessary metadata entries about coupling-modes, priorities, and activation/deactivation of rules. The initialization process may require changes to the application, for example, to include new wrappers, unless a very flexible approach for the detection of base events is provided. This is discussed in more detail in section 6.1 on primitive event detection.

Privileges: Last but not least are the architectural issues related to privileges associated with rule creation and manipulation. As much as we would like to view rules as any other object, they are metadata that can modify the behavior of other objects. This can range from the addition of new behaviors (e.g., an alarm when a threshold value is exceeded), to substitution of behaviors (e.g., by using the instead modifier provided by several ADBMS's), or (unauthorized) tracking of data usage, and activation/deactivation of consistency constraints. All these are effects that require careful consideration of how and to whom the privilege of rule creation and modification is granted and what support structures must be provided by the ADBMS to make rule definition safe. We illustrate this point by analyzing the effects of creation, activation, and deactivation of constraints modeled by ECA rules. If consistency constraints may be added dynamically or consistency-related rules may be deactivated and reactivated, the ADBMS must provide the mechanisms for validating existing data against the new rule and taking the proper action if a conflict arises between existing data and the new rule. Such action could be the time-stamping of data and rules to be able to reconstruct valid states, the elimination of instances that do not conform to the new constraint, or the flagging of these instances to request human intervention. Some of these actions have a major impact upon system architecture.

Figure 2.1 shows schematically the architecture of the rule registration portion of an ADBMS.

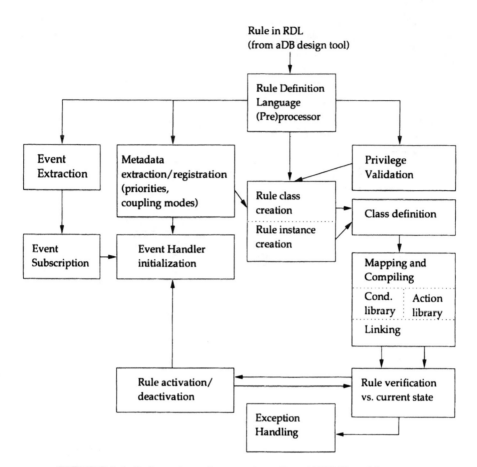

FIGURE 2.1. Rule registration portion of an ADBMS architecture.

2.6   Rule Processing

Once rules have been defined and registered, the rule execution component takes over. The rule execution component of an ADBMS is responsible for

- primitive event detection,

- composition of events,

- signaling of events,

- scheduling of rule execution,

- processing rules and synchronizing them with the execution of user transactions, and

- recovery and garbage collection of events.

Figure 2.2 shows schematically a basic architecture for the run time component of an ADBMS. We will expand this basic architecture in the sequel.

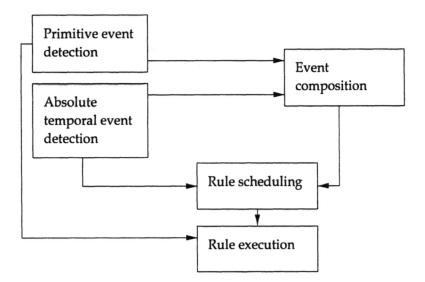

FIGURE 2.2. Schematic representation of the run time component architecture.

2.6.1   Primitive Event Detector Architecture

Detection of primitive events is a basic function in an ADBMS and must be realized in a very efficient manner. How primitive event detection is implemented will have an impact on the overall flexibility of an ADBMS and on the rule registration process. Depending on the underlying model, different primitive events are typically identified.

Relational systems generally handle the modification events *insert*, *delete*, and *update*. Object models consider method invocation as the basic primitive event. To account for the duration of a method execution, modifiers *before* and *after* have been introduced, meaning that a rule subscribing to a method event should execute either before the method is invoked or after it returns. Depending on the particular object model used, state changes may be considered. State change events are typically introduced when an object model distinguishes between attributes that are modified through methods and values that are manipulated through generic accessor functions. Temporal events may be absolute or relative. Absolute temporal events are considered primitive events that are signaled by the system clock. Another class of primitive events that deserves special attention from the architectural point of view comprises the transaction events, such as *begin of transaction*, *end of transaction*, *commit*, and *abort*. Some ADBMS's also provide explicit external events. We will discuss each class briefly for its architectural implications.

A variety of mechanisms exist to detect primitive method events (we will subsume *insert*, *delete*, and *update* events). Early implementations used an existing DBMS-component, such as the lock manager, to detect update events. The disadvantage of such an approach is that the signaling of a primitive event is tied to another property of the data, such as persistence. Monitoring of primitive events should be independent of other properties of an object. Expressed differently, we want to be able to detect a primitive event, such as a method event, independently of an object being persistent or transient, being a system-object or a user-defined object. This property is known as orthogonality of monitoring and type [BZBW95].

Among the mechanisms that have been proposed for method-event detection, the most popular is method wrapping. Method wrapping consists in bracketing a method with a begin-method and an end-method signal. Depending on whether a rule exists that subscribes to this method event (either before or after), the corresponding primitive method-event is signaled. If no rule subscribed to this event, execution just continues. Figure 2.3 illustrates the principle of method wrapping. The dashed return line indicates that control is immediately returned only if no rule will require this event. If a rule has subscribed, the event is propagated and control is returned after some additional processing.

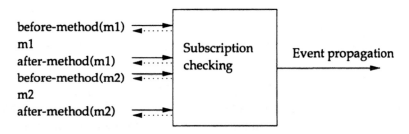

FIGURE 2.3. Method wrapping and subscription checking.

A basic difference from an architectural point of view is whether method wrapping is done manually or by the rule preprocessor, and whether all methods are wrapped or only those methods for which rules are known to exist. Wrapping every method improves flexibility since a new rule that consumes a given method event that has no previous subscription can be added without having to wrap the corresponding method and recompiling the object class definition. This approach was taken in [BZBW95, BDZH95]. However, this flexibility comes at a price. If every method is wrapped independently of whether a rule subscribes to that event or not, some overhead is paid before and after the execution of each rule to check if a subscription exists. Hand-wrapping a method that should be monitored was used in [GD93, GGD95]. A compromise solution adopted in [CKAK94, Cha97] consists in distinguishing between passive objects, reactive objects, and notifiable objects. The interface for reactive objects is modified and only methods in reactive objects are wrapped.

Detection of state change events requires modification of the generic accessor functions. The detection of transaction events requires redefinition of the transaction bracketing and the commit and abort mechanism to signal the corresponding event to the event handler.

Detection of external events is a somewhat controversial issue. While external events are a needed extension in relational systems that otherwise are restricted to insert, delete, update, and selection events, they are easily represented in an object system through methods. In an object system, anything that is known to the system is represented by an object, an attribute, or a method. Therefore, external events can be easily handled by the method-event detector. In relational systems, external events may be represented explicitly in the database and signaled through an update event. However, many systems, both relational and object-oriented, provide an additional, explicit signaling mechanism for external events that interprets messages.

Absolute temporal events are signaled by the system clock. This mechanism is straightforward if all processes run on a single machine. However, in a client-server environment, in which clients are running on different machines, the options are either to have one master providing the absolute temporal events, in which case different propagation delays are possible, or have multiple clocks which may drift apart. For practical reasons, most prototypes opt for one common clock with a coarse time granularity that is assumed to be greater than the expected propagation delays.

2.6.2   Composite Event Detector Architecture

Event composition is an essential feature of any active system that provides more than the basic active functionality. The basis of composite events is the event algebra that is supported by the ADBMS. Event algebras may vary in expressive power, but they all offer at the minimum the basic composition for sequences of events, disjunctions, and conjunctions. A popular optimization is the closure operator, which accumulates repeated occurrences of the same event and triggers the corresponding rule only once. Negation and other history operators are also common.

From an architectural point of view, the event composer consists of the data structures needed to describe event types and their instantiations, and the operations on these structures. The most popular structures are finite state automata, variations of Petri-nets, and query-graphs. When finite state automata are used, a separate automaton is constructed for each event. A problem of finite state automata is their inability to associate the state of objects. The same is true for basic Petri-nets and is corrected by colored Petri-nets, for example. In a Petri-net, a primitive event-token enters the Petri-net and progresses through the net according to the state at the decision points. In the case of query-graph-like composers, the structure of the composite event is represented as a tree with the operators of the algebra at the inner nodes. Primitive events and their parameters enter the graph through the leaf nodes and the event composition is completed when the root node is processed.

Garbage collection of semicomposed events is necessary, whenever the validity interval of a composite event expires. This could be either at the time a transaction commits or aborts, or after an interval defined by temporal or other events has lapsed. Once the validity interval has expired, we know that the missing primitive events that are required to complete a composition will never occur. To prevent the system from being swamped with semi-composed events, garbage collection is needed.

A major distinction in event composer architectures is whether the composite event graph is kept as a single monolithic structure or as specialized graphs, one for each event. There are advantages and disadvantages to each approach, particularly with respect to parameter passing, distribution, and garbage collection.

A single event graph minimizes redundancy. This is particularly the case whenever the same primitive event is used by many composite events limited to a single address space. On the negative side, it can be a bottleneck. It makes implementation in a distributed environment difficult and is very time-consuming to garbage-collect, since an extensive graph needs to be traversed and the semicomposed events need to be identified and removed.

Specialized event composers keep a separate event composition graph for each composite event. This carries an overhead in passing the appropriate parameters but makes distribution and garbage collection much easier. Particularly garbage collection is more efficient, since the whole graph can be eliminated once the validity interval has expired. Each specialized event composer corresponds to a specialized event handler. Therefore, each event handler has all the necessary information about the rules that need to be triggered or what other event handlers need to be notified. This eliminates the lookup process in a centralized rule manager.

2.6.3 Event Consumption and Logging

An important architectural issue related to event composition is the event consumption policy that is enforced by the ADBMS. First, it must be clear whether events may participate in multiple composite events or not. It is generally accepted that events may participate in multiple compositions. This requires either event replication or additional bookkeeping mechanisms to decide when an event can be discarded.

When composing events, there exist multiple event consumption strategies that are application-dependent. Events could actually be consumed in *chronological* order (typical for workflow applications), in a *most recent* manner in which the latest event of a kind supersedes previous occurrences (typical for control applications), *continuous*, in which windows are established by two events and other events of interest in that window are detected (typical for trend monitoring applications), or a *cumulative* policy, in which all instances of the participating primitive events are accumulated and consumed at once when the composition is completed [CKAK94].

To support any of these policies, events and their parameters must be logged. Event logging can be a major performance factor in an ADBMS. For every event of interest, i.e., an event that has at least one subscriber, its occurrence must be recorded with a time stamp, the transaction in which the event occurred (if it is an event that can be associated with a particular transaction), and the necessary parameters that must be passed. Since events and their parameters may be used in a non immediate mode, they must be recorded for later use. This means multiple write operations to the log and a potential bottleneck. To avoid this hotspot, some systems use distributed logging with deferred consolidation of the partial logs [BZBW95].

2.6.4   Guarded Events, Light-Weight Vs. Heavy-Weight Events

An important design decision that is still debated concerns how much information should be attached to events and how much processing should be done by the event detectors. One school of thought (represented, for example, by the HiPAC project [DBM88]) states that events should be as lightweight as possible, i.e., they should only signal that a rule is to be processed and get out of the way. Any further testing as to whether the action ought to be executed should be pushed into the condition part of a rule. This has the advantage of not blocking further event detection, and that the condition is processed as any other query. The other school of thought (represented among others by the Ode project [GJS92]) states that lightweight events cause too many rules to be triggered unnecessarily just to detect in the condition evaluation part that no action is required. Therefore, events are provided with additional conditions, so-called guards, that allow the specification of rather complex conditions on the events. In the extreme, such an approach would make the condition evaluation superfluous and revert to (complex) event-action rules. The implication is also that the event handler must contain filtering mechanisms that otherwise are provided by the query processor.

2.6.5   Rule Scheduling

Once an event is raised, the rule(s) triggered by that event must be identified and scheduled for execution. The identification of the rule(s) that are triggered by an event can be done either by a specialized event handler that knows locally what rules are to be fired once the event has been raised, or through the use of a separate registration mechanism and an additional lookup. The rules that are fired are then scheduled and the requests for their execution must be passed to the DBMS's transaction manager. Condition and action can either be processed together or separate.

Depending on the coupling mode specified and the origin and type of the triggering event, a rule may either execute within the transaction in which the triggering event was raised or outside the user transaction.

If the rule executes within the triggering transaction, it may either be immediately after the event was raised, in which case the transaction's execution is halted until the rule completes execution (immediate coupling mode), or at the end of the triggering transaction and before the triggering transaction commits (deferred coupling mode). If a rule executes outside the triggering transaction in a separate transaction, then it may either begin in parallel and finish independently of the triggering transaction (detached coupling mode), it may begin in parallel but wait for the triggering transaction to commit before being allowed to commit (parallel causally dependent coupling mode), it may have to wait until the triggering transaction commits before being allowed to execute (sequential causally dependent coupling mode), or it may not begin execution unless the triggering transaction aborts (exclusive causally dependent coupling mode).

Rules triggered by absolute temporal events always execute in separate transactions. Rules triggered by events that are composed from events originating in multiple transactions must execute as detached transactions. If they execute in causally dependent detached mode, the causal dependence exists with *all* transactions in which the component events were raised [BZBW95].

Rule scheduling and execution is highly dependent on the DBMS's transaction management and must be synchronized with the execution of user transactions. How the user transactions and rule executions are synchronized depends on the transaction model supported by the underlying DBMS, the interfaces to the transaction manager provided by the underlying DBMS, and the way the active database system takes advantage of the provided facilities. We briefly review the alternatives.

2.6.6   Transaction Models

The two main alternatives when dealing with transaction models are flat transactions and nested transactions.

Within both groups, special extensions are needed to properly execute rules.

Flat transactions are the transactions commonly supported by today's DBMS's and need little further explanation. However, when building active functionality on top of a flat transaction model, several limitations arise. Flat transaction models support only a single transactional thread of control. Therefore, whenever a rule needs to be executed, it has to be done one at a time without any parallelism. The transaction manager must provide a transaction handle to the rule system. It must further signal the end of the user transaction and transfer control to the rule manager and allow for the execution of deferred rules before committing the transaction and releasing the locks. No locks may be released prior to the execution of the deferred rules. Since rules may require new locks during their execution, two-phase locking would be violated otherwise. Flat transaction models typically do not provide for spawning additional transactions. Extensions for spawned detached transactions are straightforward, as long as no parameters are passed. If parameters that refer to objects modified within the transaction are passed to the spawned transaction, the isolation is compromised and the spawned transaction may execute with dirty data. If extended with the capability of spawning causally dependent transactions, the possibility exists that the spawned transaction competes with the spawning transaction for the same data, thus causing a deadlock. The transaction manager must be modified in such a way that the spawned transaction is always declared the victim when resolving a conflict. In [Mar95], these transactions are introduced as *weak transactions*.

Nested transactions have been proposed to increase intra-transaction parallelism. Common to all nested transaction models is the fact that new subtransactions can be spawned from within a transaction, and that the related transactions are organized in the form of a transaction tree. In the basic nested transaction model proposed in [Mos85], a nested subtransaction is started explicitly by the parent transaction, which is suspended until the nested transaction commits or aborts. Commitment of a subtransaction is conditional and occurs through the top. If the top transaction aborts, the whole transaction tree is aborted. In [HR93], a variation to the basic nested transaction model is proposed. This model allows for exploitation of intra-transaction parallelism through the introduction of downward inheritance of locks. This mechanism modifies the visibility rules for nested transactions and makes it possible for children to access the data manipulated by the parent.

For parallel execution of rules in active databases under a variety of coupling modes, a modified nested transaction model is presented in [DHL90]. The nested subtransactions of [Mos85] are used for the execution of immediate rules. In addition, three more types of nested (sub)transactions are defined. *Deferred subtransactions* are subtransactions whose execution is explicitly delayed until the end of the user's top transaction. If more than one deferred subtransaction is spawned within a user's transaction, they all execute in parallel at the end of the user's transaction. If any of these deferred subtransactions spawns itself another subtransaction, this is executed immediately if the rule is to be executed in immediate mode or it is deferred until all deferred transactions from the level above have finished. *Nested top-transactions* are top transactions started from within another transaction and are represented by their own tree. However, a nested top-transaction has no privileges with respect to the spawning transaction, i.e., it may not see any non-committed objects and is not automatically aborted when the spawning transaction aborts. *Causally-dependent-top-transactions* (CDtop) are spawned from within another transaction and are like nested top-transactions that have their own transaction tree but are commit-dependent on the parent. Aborting the spawning transaction aborts the CD-top transaction. However, aborting the CD-top transaction has no effect whatsoever on the spawning transaction. A combination of this transaction model with downward inheritance of locks is a meaningful extension.

2.6.7   Rule Execution

Rules that are executed in immediate coupling mode just cause the execution of the user transaction to pause until the rule finishes and then control is returned to the user transaction. For all rules that are executed in a non-immediate coupling mode, the corresponding scheduler elaborates a schedule that is then passed for processing. Depending on the correctness criteria supported by the ADBMS, the transaction model provided and the number of rule processing threads, a scheduler may either create an ordering of the rules or allow for their parallel execution.

The execution of sets of rules triggered by the same event or sets of rules that are to be executed in a deferred mode at the end of the transaction requires either an ordering of the rules and their sequential execution in priority order as an extension of the user transaction, or it requires a nested transaction model to execute the rules as parallel subtransactions. The nested transactions presently offered by commercial DBMS's do provide transaction hierarchies but with *sequential* execution of the subtransactions. Since none of the commercial DBMS's offers *parallel* nested transactions, they must be implemented as part of the active extensions.

Some aOODBMS prototypes [Cha97] implement nested transactions in user space on top of the flat transaction model provided by the server. For example, if the underlying page server offers only flat transactions and page locks, it is possible to implement an additional object-locking mechanism in the user address space and provide the visibility and local commit and abort dependencies of the nested subtransactions proposed in [HR93]. However, in case of failure, the whole user transaction must be rolled back by the server.

Rules that execute in a detached mode as separate transactions can be scheduled like any other user transaction. However, a major problem arising when executing transactions in any detached mode that allows for parallel execution is the passing of the parameters. Quite often the parameters to be passed include the state of the object that was just modified in the user transaction. If the user transaction has not.committed, the lock on the object has not been released. Waiting for the commit of the user transaction before the rule can execute precludes parallelism, but making dirty data visible to other transactions reduces the isolation level. Some prototypes have opted for implementing lock sharing mechanisms between the triggering and the triggered transaction. Others restrict the detached execution of rules to those rules that do not share data between the triggering and the triggered transaction.

The causally dependent coupling modes imply additional commit or abort dependencies that are typically not supported by a DBMS's transaction manager. Therefore, the causally dependent coupling modes are often not implementable in layered architectures in which the active capabilities run completely at the user level or where modifications to the commit and abort process are not possible.

Processing may be done either by a single rule processor or in parallel among multiple rule processors. Most rule processors we are aware of are implemented as user processes or threads within a user process in the user's address space. This may be acceptable for prototypes but poses risks of interference in case of rule failure. Some systems [KRSR97] offer the possibility of dynamically assigning new threads for additional rule processors or giving up rule processors when the load falls below a threshold.

2.7   Recovery

Recovery, i.e., the ability to restore the database to a consistent state in the case of transaction or system failure, is one of the distinguishing features of database management systems. Therefore, active databases must provide the same resilience to failure.

The problem of recovery in active databases is more complex mainly because of three reasons: some events may be non-recoverable, some external actions may be irreversible, and certain coupling modes may allow transactions to commit ahead of the triggering transaction.

Closed nested transactions that always commit through the top are perfectly recoverable and do not require additional precautions. In general, to guarantee recoverability, a transaction should not be allowed to commit unless *both* its database updates and the events signaled by it are logged on stable storage.

The exact meaning of recoverability of events is still an open research issue and might have to be considered in the context of specific applications.

Database events are always recoverable. Other events, such as temporal events, may or may not be recoverable. The event log should contain explicitly all the relevant events, including temporal events, that either triggered a rule or were part of an event composition. As a general rule it is stated in [DHL90] that events signaled by committed transactions and for which the action was executed before the failure occurred should always be recovered. Events that are signaled by committed transactions and whose action had not completed before failing should only be signaled on reexecution if they are recoverable.

Rules that were triggered and are scheduled for execution in a detached mode must be guaranteed execution. An interesting situation arises when a rule that is being executed in a causally dependent transaction does not terminate because of a system failure during its execution while the spawning transaction committed. The active DBMS must provide the mechanisms to guarantee the execution of these rules, since the triggering transaction already committed and the user cannot be aware of the failure of the triggered transaction.

The problem of non-recoverable actions arises when the active database system allows either detached transactions that may commit independently of the spawning transaction, or when external actions that are irreversible are carried out as actions of a rule. To deal with the latter situation, [BBKZ93] introduced the detached sequential causally dependent coupling mode, in which a triggered action may only begin execution once the triggering transaction committed. Detached transactions that have no dependencies upon the spawning transaction should be used only in those situations in which their execution can be tolerated independently of the spawning transaction or where a compensating transaction can be defined.

Figure 2.4 puts the components of the rule processing subsystem together and shows schematically their interplay.

2.8 Conclusion

In this chapter the major factors affecting the architecture of active DBMS's were outlined. These are the degree of integration between the active functionality and the underlying DBMS, the architecture of the underlying DBMS, and the data model and language of implementation used. We discussed the basic subsystems of the active component: the rule specification and registration component, and the event detection and rule execution component. For each component we analyzed its functionality and tried to view it in the perspective of integration, and in terms of the limitations imposed by the underlying DBMS and language of implementation.

As with any generic architecture, much detail had to be omitted. Details about individual components can be found in the corresponding chapters

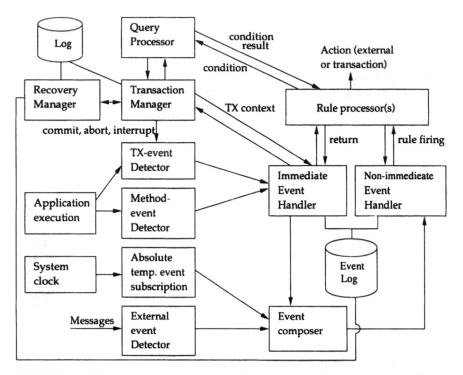

FIGURE 2.4. Schematic representation of the rule execution subsystem architecture.

that will treat each topic in depth. Details on the design decisions that were made in specific systems can be found in the chapters describing each of them. Hopefully this discussion served to set the stage for the more detailed discussions to follow.

2.9   REFERENCES

[BBKZ93]   H.Branding, A.P. Buchmann, T.Kudrass, and J.Zimmermann. Rules in an Open System: The REACH system. In N. W. Paton and M. H. Williams (Eds.), *Rules in Database Systems, Proc. 1st Intl. Workshop on Rules in Database Systems*, August 1993.

[BDZH95]   A.P. Buchmann, A.Deutsch, J.Zimmermann, and M.Higa. The REACH Active OODBMS. In *Proc. of the 1995 ACM SIG-MOD Intl. Conf. on Management of Data*, May 1995.

[BZBW95]   A.P. Buchmann, J.Zimmermann, J.Blakeley, and D.Wells. Building an Integrated Active OODBMS: Requirements, Architecture, and Design Decisions. In *Proc. 11th Intl. Conference on Data Engineering*, Taipei, Taiwan, March 1995.

[CCS94]   C.Collet, T.Coupaye, and T.Svensen. NAOS Efficient and Modular Reactive Capabilities in an Object-Oriented Database System. In *Proc. of the 20th Intl. Conf. on Very Large Data Bases,* Santiago, Chile, September 1994.

[CDRS86]   M.J. Carey, D.J. DeWitt, J.E. Richardson, and E.J. Shekita. Object and File Management in the EXODUS Extensible Database System. In *Proc. 12 Intl. Conf. on Very Large Data Bases,* Kyoto, Japan, August 1986.

[Cha97]   S.Chakravarthy. SENTINEL: An Object-Oriented DBMS with Event-Based Rules. In *Proc. of the ACM SIGMOD Intl. Conf. on Management of Data,* Tucson, AZ, May 1997.

[CKAK94]   S.Chakravarthy, V.Krishnaprasad, E.Anwar, and S.-K. Kim. Composite Events for Active Databases: Semantics, Contexts, and Detection. In *Proc. of the 20th Intl. Conf. on Very Large Data Bases,* Santiago, Chile, September 1994.

[DBM88]   U.Dayal, A.P. Buchmann, and D.McCarthy. Rules are Objects Too: a Knowledge Model for an Active, Object-Oriented Database Management System. In *Proc. 2nd Intl. Workshop on Object-Oriented Database Systems,* Bad Muenster am Stein, Germany, September 1988.

[DHL90]   U.Dayal, M.Hsu, and R.Ladin. Organizing Long-Running Activities with Triggers and Transactions. In *Proc. of the 1990 ACM SIGMOD Intl. Conf. on Management of Data,* Atlantic City, NJ, May 1990.

[GD93]   S.Gatziu and K.R. Dittrich. Events in an Active Object-Oriented Database System. In N. W. Paton and M. H. Williams (Eds.), *Rules in Database Systems, Proc. 1st Intl. Workshop on Rules in Database Systems,* Edinburgh, August 1993.

[GGD95]   S.Gatziu, A.Geppert, and K.R. Dittrich. The SAMOS Active DBMS Prototype. In *Proc. of the 1995 ACM SIGMOD Intl. Conf. on Management of Data,* San Jose, CA, May 1995.

[GJS92]   N.H. Gehani, H.V. Jagadish, and O.Shmueli. Composite event specification in active Databases: Model and Implementation. In *Proc. of the 18th Intl. Conf. on Very Large Data Bases,* Vancouver, Canada, August 1992.

[HR93]   T.Haerder and K.Rothermel. Concurrency Control Issues in Nested Transactions. *VLDB Journal,* 2(1), 1993.

[KRSR97] G.Kappel, S.Rausch-Schott, and W.Retschitzegger. A Tour of the TriGS Active Database System–Architecture and Implementation. Technical report, Department of Information Systems, Johannes Kepler University, Linz, 1997.

[Mar95]   J.Marschner. *Non-Standard Transaktionsmanagement in Einem Aktiven Objektorientierten Datenbanksystem.* Dipl. Thesis, Dept. of Computer Science, Darmstadt University of Technology, Darmstadt, 1995.

[Mos85]   E.Moss. *Nested Transactions.* MIT Press, Cambridge, MA, 1985.

[WBT92]   D.L. Wells, J.A. Blakeley, and C.W. Thompson. Architecture of an Open Object-Oriented Database Management System. *IEEE Computer,* 25(10), 1992.

Part II

Advanced Topics

3

Rule Analysis

Elena Baralis

ABSTRACT
Rules in active database systems can be very difficult to program, due to the
unstructured and unpredictable nature of rule processing. In this chapter
static analysis techniques for predicting useful properties for active rule sets
are described. In particular, we focus on methods to determine at compile-
time whether a given rule set is guaranteed to terminate, and whether rule
execution is confluent (guaranteed to have a unique final state).

3.1 Introduction

During rule processing, rules can interact in complex and sometimes unpredictable ways: they may trigger and "untrigger" each other, and the
intermediate and final states of the database can depend upon which rules
are triggered and executed in which order. For this reason, developing active rule applications may become a difficult task; methods and tools are
needed to assist the design, prototyping, implementation, and testing of
active rules.

Active rule analysis is aimed at defining compile-time techniques that allow a rule designer to predict in advance important aspects of rule behavior
such as termination of rule execution. These techniques are used to statically analyze a set of rules before installing them in the database. Thus,
static rule analysis can provide a fundamental building block for both a
design methodology and a programming environment for the development
of active rule applications.

Two important and desirable properties of active rule behavior are *termination* and *confluence*. These properties are defined for a given rule set
and arbitrary user-defined modifications and database states.

- *Termination*: A rule set is guaranteed to terminate if, for any database
  state and initial modification, rule processing cannot continue forever
  (i.e., rules cannot activate each other indefinitely).

- *Confluence*: A rule set is confluent if, for any database state and
  initial modification, the final database state after rule processing is
  unique, i.e., it is independent of the order in which activated rules
  are executed.

A considerable body of work has been devoted to the development of static techniques to detect termination and confluence of rule execution, such as [AHW95, BW94, BCP95b, KU94, vS93, WH95, ZMU96]. Rule analysis techniques have addressed active rules that follow the event condition action paradigm, where events and actions are restricted to database operations, and the considered execution modes are immediate and deferred.

Since both termination and confluence are undecidable in the general case, static analysis techniques only give sufficient conditions for guaranteeing the property searched for. For example, if appropriate conditions hold, they guarantee that a rule set always terminates execution. When these conditions do not hold, it is conservatively concluded that rule execution may not terminate (although it will not necessarily continue indefinitely). Furthermore, anomalous rule behaviors may occur only when rules are executed on particular database states. Since rule analysis is performed at compile-time, it does not take into account the actual state of the database on which the rule set may be executed. In particular, it will disregard whether a database state giving rise to anomalous behaviors is actually forbidden (e.g., by an integrity constraint) or never occurs at run time.

A different approach has been used to provide design support for triggers in commercial systems: either syntactic limitations are imposed in order to guarantee run time termination or confluence for any rule set (see, e.g., the forthcoming SQL3 standard [ISO94]), or run time counters are used to prevent infinite rule execution (see, e.g., [Ora92]). The first approach severely limits the expressiveness of the active rule language, while appropriately setting the counters, as pursued in the second approach, may be difficult. Indeed, a low threshold may cause abnormal termination of rule processing even when rule execution would have ended successfully in a few more steps, while a high threshold may reveal a loop only after expensive processing.

We finally mention *observable determinism* [AHW95] and *conflicting updates* [KU91, ZH90] as interesting properties that may provide additional insight in rule behavior. A rule action is observable when its effect is visible from the execution environment (e.g., a data retrieval or a rollback statement are observable actions). A rule set is observably deterministic if the rule execution order does not affect the order in which observable actions become visible. Although this property can be detected analogously to confluence, it is in fact orthogonal to confluence (i.e., a rule set may be observably deterministic, but not confluent, and vice versa).

Two updates are conflicting when the action performed by one rule may undo changes made by the action of a previously executed rule (e.g., the same data should not be inserted by one rule and subsequently deleted by another rule). Although not essential, this last property may be useful in detecting potential mistakes in rule applications.

3.2   Termination Analysis

An active rule is triggered, i.e., is eligible for evaluation, when any event specified in the rule's event set occurs. If the rule includes a condition, the condition must be true on the current database state for the rule's actions to be executed.

Termination for a rule set is guaranteed if rule processing always reaches a state in which no rule is triggered. Hence, informally, rule processing does not terminate if and only if rules cause each other to execute indefinitely. For a rule r_i to cause the execution of a rule r_j, it is necessary that: (1) rule r_i triggers r_j, i.e., r_i's actions generate one or more events that trigger r_j, and (2) either r_j's condition is true, or rule r_i activates r_j, i.e., it executes an action that causes r_j's condition to become true.

Several methods have been proposed in the literature to perform compile-time termination analysis. Many techniques [AHW95, CW90, KU96] are based on building a triggering graph by considering the type of triggering events and of events generated by the execution of rule actions. Non termination may occur if the graph contains cycles. Other techniques [BCW93, BW94, TC94, WH95] rely mostly on the semantic information contained in the rule condition and actions, using which a Activation Graph is built. Cycles are then searched for in this graph. A synthesis of the two techniques is proposed in [BCP95b], which allows the discarding of some "false" cycles that are detected by the former methods. Termination analysis based on triggering and activation graphs is discussed in Section 3.2.1. When a (partial) ordering is defined on the rule set, the analysis technique may be improved [BCP95b, ZMU96], as described in Section 3.2.3.

A rather different approach [KU94] to active rule analysis is based on reducing active rules to *conditional term rewrite rules*, then applying known analysis techniques for termination of term rewriting systems. This approach is powerful, since it exploits the body of work on Conditional Term Rewrite Systems (CTRS). The intuition behind the technique is that conditional rewrite steps progressively reduce the "size" of a term. If the reduction ordering is well-founded, there does not exist an infinite rewriting chain of terms with decreasing size, and therefore the rewrite process terminates. When a CTRS has a decreasing ordering, it is called a decreasing CTRS and termination is guaranteed for it. As mentioned in [KU94], finding an appropriate decreasing ordering for an arbitrary CTRS to show its termination is not a trivial task.

In [vS93], the property of termination within some fixed number of steps (and of confluence) is shown to be decidable using an approach based on "typical databases." A typical database contains all possible data instances that could affect the outcome of rule processing. The rule set is "run" over the typical database and the outcome is checked for the desired property. The sufficient condition for termination in n steps is based on the notion of a "flag," which is selected by the query that represents the condition of a rule r. The flag is progressively lowered by r's action. When the flag is lowered in less than n steps, then termination is guaranteed. This approach is clearly unfeasible in practical applications, so lower complexity algorithms are proposed, but the details and applicability of these algorithms are not completely described.

A more design-oriented perspective is taken in [BCP96, ZH90], by proposing techniques to generate rule sets that are guaranteed to terminate execution. In particular, [BCP96] proposes a technique to group homogeneous rules, typically associated with a well-defined applicative objective, into modules. Termination of rule execution within each module is assumed, and inter module termination is guaranteed when the modules present appropriate behavioral or structural properties.

Unfortunately, it is not always possible to guarantee for a given rule set that rule processing terminates at compile-time. A complementary approach [BCP95c] to termination analysis is based on monitoring rule execution at run time to detect when rule processing enters a loop causing infinite execution. This technique identifies loops, based on recognizing that a given state has already occurred in the past and therefore will occur an infinite number of times in the future. Since it requires a comparison of successive states of an active database, this technique is potentially very expensive. Several methods, which exploit compile-time analysis results, are proposed in [BCP95c] to implement this technique with limited computational effort.

Tools performing compile time analysis of active rules can provide considerable help to a rule designer in understanding the interaction among active rules. While many efforts have been devoted to the development of powerful rule debuggers, currently not many tools are available for the compile time analysis of rule behavior.

ARACHNE (Active Rules Analyzer for Chimera) [BCP95a] is a tool for the compile-time analysis of active rules, developed in the context of the IDEA project. It performs termination analysis of active rules in Chimera (see Chapter 17) and it detects rules which may exhibit a non terminating behavior. The tool proposes a graphical representation of triggering and activation graphs and allows the rule designer to separately consider each cycle, i.e., each group of rules that may cause infinite rule executions. More details on ARACHNE can be found in Chapter 17.

VITAL [BGB95] is a toolbox for active rule analysis and debugging. It includes a tool for the static analysis of an active rule set, a step by step simulator of rule execution, a graphical interface with navigation and browsing facilities, and statistical information on the evolution of the database content. In particular, its analysis tool builds the triggering graph for the analyzed rule set and detects cycles; the simulator, among other features, allows the rule designer to trace rule executions on the triggering graph.

3.2.1   Triggering and Activation Graphs

A very general compile time analysis technique is based on the distinction
between mutual triggering and mutual activation of rules. This distinction
motivates the introduction of two graphs defining rule interaction, called
Triggering Graph and Activation Graph, respectively.

Let R be an arbitrary active rule set.

- The **Triggering Graph (TG)** is a directed graph where each node
  corresponds to a rule $r_i \in R$. A directed arc $\langle r_j, r_k \rangle$ means that the
  action of rule r_j generates events that trigger rule r_k.

- The **Activation Graph (AG)** is a directed graph where each node
  corresponds to a rule $r_i \in R$. A directed arc $\langle r_j, r_k \rangle$, with $j \neq k$,
  means that the action of rule r_j may change the truth value of rule
  r_k's condition from **false** to **true**. An arc $\langle r_j, r_j \rangle$ means that rule
  r_j's condition can be **true** after the execution of r_j's action.

The Triggering Graph can be built by performing a simple syntactical
analysis of each rule pair r_j, r_k. An arc $\langle r_j, r_k \rangle$ is included in the Triggering Graph if r_j performs a modification type included in r_k's set of
triggering events. When rule processing does not terminate, rules cyclically
retrigger each other. Hence, acyclicity of the Triggering Graph provides a
sufficient condition to guarantee termination. This result, initially introduced in [CW90], was proved in [AHW95], where Triggering Graphs were
carefully analyzed.

Activation Graphs are complementary to Triggering Graphs; indeed,
acyclicity of the Activation Graph implies the absence of non terminating
behaviors, because non terminating behaviors may only occur if conditions
remain true after rule execution or if rules cyclicly change the truth values
of conditions, so that they become true before being evaluated [BW94]. The
accuracy of the analysis depends on the accuracy by which it is possible
to determine when an arc should be included in the graph, i.e., when one
rule may activate another rule. However, while Triggering Graph arcs are
syntactically derivable, it is very difficult to precisely determine the arcs of
an Activation Graph. In Section 3.2.2, we describe a technique to derive
the Activation Graph for a given active rule set.

An example of a combined representation of Triggering and Activation
Graphs is presented in Figure 3.1. Several cycles can be detected in the
graphs, e.g., one including rules r_1, r_2 in the Triggering Graph, and one
including rules r_3, r_4, r_5 in the Activation Graph. Then, if either analysis
based only on the Triggering Graph or on the Activation Graph is applied,
it would conclude that the rule set may cause infinite rule executions. These
techniques may be improved by considering the combined information provided by the two graphs.

Given the information in the Triggering and Activation Graphs, it is
possible to generate from a rule set R its *irreducible active rule set*, i.e.,

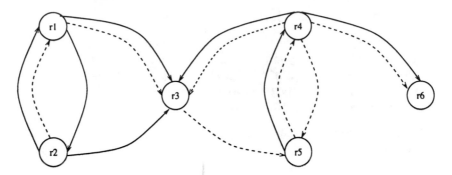

FIGURE 3.1. A Triggering (solid arcs) and Activation (dashed arcs) Graph.

the subset of R that includes all rules that may execute an infinite number of times. This subset is generated by applying to R the *rule reduction algorithm* presented in Figure 3.2. At each iteration the algorithm discards a rule that does not have an incoming arc in either the TG or the AG, and removes all its outgoing arcs. The process iterates until all the rules have been removed, or until all the remaining rules have incoming arcs both in the TG and in the AG.

Based on the irreducible active rule set, it is possible to give a sufficient condition for termination of rule execution: If the irreducible active rule set obtained by applying the rule reduction algorithm to an active rule set R is empty, then R is guaranteed to terminate for any database state and user modification. This result is proved in [BCP95b].

Consider the active rule set in Figure 3.1. The application of the rule reduction algorithm to it yields an empty irreducible active rule set. Thus, although both the TG and the AG include separate cycles, rule execution is guaranteed to terminate.

When instead the irreducible active rule set I is not empty, rule set R may exhibit a non terminating behavior. In particular, since I contains *all* the rules that can be executed an infinite number of times, any rule in I may be involved in some non terminating behavior. The irreducible active rule set produced by the rule reduction algorithm applied to the rule set in Figure 3.3 contains rules $r_1, r_2, r_3, r_4, r_5, r_6$. Then, it is possible to conclude that rule execution may not terminate for this rule set.

The irreducible active rule set can be further divided in smaller subsets which may separately cause non termination, called *non terminating rule sets*. A non terminating rule set is any subset S of rules in I such that no rule of S is eliminated by applying the rule reduction algorithm to the set S itself. All non terminating rule sets of I constitute a lattice. Consider the rule set in Figure 3.3, which may execute infinitely, since its irreducible active rule set is not empty. Its corresponding lattice of non terminating rule sets is depicted in Figure 3.4.

```
L := ∅;
For each rule rᵢ ∈ R
    If (rᵢ.T = 0) or (rᵢ.A = 0) then
        L := append(L,rᵢ);
while not Empty(L)
    {rᵢ := pop(L);
    R := R - rᵢ;
    For each rule rⱼ ∈ outₜ(rᵢ)
        {rⱼ.T := rⱼ.T - 1;
        If rⱼ.T = 0 and rⱼ ∈ R and rⱼ ∉ L then
            L := append(L,rⱼ); }
    For each rule rⱼ ∈ outₐ(rⱼ)
        {rⱼ.A := rⱼ.A - 1;
        If rⱼ.A = 0 and rⱼ ∈ R and rⱼ ∉ L then
            L := append(L,rⱼ); } }
return(R);
```

FIGURE 3.2. The Rule Reduction Algorithm applied to a rule set R. $out_T(r_i)$ and $out_A(r_i)$ are the endpoints of arcs originating from r_i in the TG and AG graphs, respectively; $r_i.T$ and $r_i.A$ are the counters of arcs incoming into r_i in either the TG or the AG; L is a list of rules. The algorithm returns the irreducible active rule set into R.

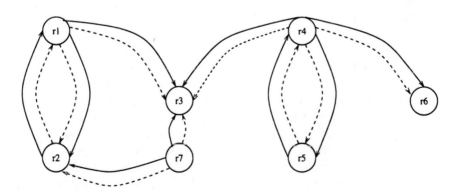

FIGURE 3.3. Active rule set with non terminating behavior.

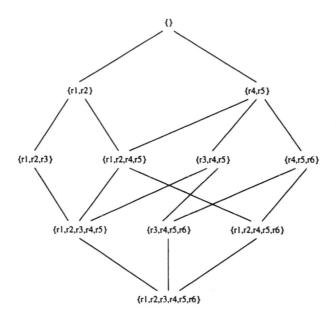

FIGURE 3.4. Lattice for the rule set in Figure 3.3.

3.2.2 Building the Activation Graph

Consider two rules r_i and r_j with $i \neq j$. Rule r_i may activate rule r_j if the execution of r_i's action may cause the truth value of r_j's condition to change from false to true. A syntactic analysis of r_i's action and r_j's condition can be used to determine if the arc $\langle r_i, r_j \rangle$ belongs in the Activation Graph. This analysis was initially performed in [CW90] by deriving all events that may cause r_j's condition to become true. If the event generated by r_i's action execution is included in this set, the arc is included in the AG.

More accurate results can be achieved by considering the algebraic structure of r_j's condition and r_i's action. An algorithm described in [BW94] evaluates the effect of the execution of an insert, delete, or update action on relations that are used by a condition. The condition is interpreted as a query and expressed in relational algebra; in this context, the truth value of the condition changes to true when new tuples are produced in the query. This algorithm, called the *Propagation Algorithm*, evaluates if inserts, deletes, or updates on relations due to the action of r_i cause inserts, deletes, or updates on the condition query of r_j. If the algorithm yields an *insert* or *update* operation, then r_i may activate r_j, and the arc $\langle r_i, r_j \rangle$ is included in the AG. If only a *delete* operation or no operation is produced by the algorithm, then r_i cannot cause r_j's condition to become true, and the arc is not included in the graph.

The Propagation Algorithm discards operations based on unsatisfiability of the relational expression characterizing them.[1] It behaves conservatively, i.e., it guarantees that potential activation arcs are always detected, at the cost of pessimistically including into the Activation Graph some arcs that at rule execution time, due to the actual values contained in the database, do not actually cause rule activation.

A different technique, based on the notion of the *self-disactivating rule*, is used to decide whether an arc $\langle r, r \rangle$ belongs in the Activation Graph. A rule r is self-disactivating when either: (1) its condition references event bindings so as to become false after it is evaluated, or (2) the execution of its action causes its condition to become false, e.g., by deleting all data that satisfied it. Detection of self-disactivating rules may be based on the Propagation Algorithm. A complete characterization of self-disactivating rules can be found in [BW], where they are called *quasi-CA* rules owing to their activation semantics, which is identical to that of condition-action (CA) rules.

When a rule r is not self-disactivating, its condition may remain true after the rule is executed. This effect is taken into account by introducing a ring $\langle r, r \rangle$ in the Activation Graph. Observe that if no rule is self-disactivating, then considering the Activation Graph does not allow any improvement with respect to the analysis performed by means of the Triggering Graph. We finally note that self-disactivating rules are quite common in practice: for example, rules written for constraint enforcement and view maintenance applications are typically self-disactivating.

3.2.3 Termination with Priorities

Some active rule systems provide the possibility of specifying a–possibly partial–ordering of rules, e.g., by means of user-specified or system-specified priorities among rules in the rule set. When rules are ordered, during the scheduling phase some rules may not be selected, due to the fact that rules higher in the ordering (i.e., with higher priority) are triggered. The knowledge of rule ordering may be exploited to strengthen the termination analysis technique described in the previous section.

The analysis improvement is based on the concept of inhibited cycle. A cycle is inhibited when it contains a rule r that, because of rule ordering, is never ready for reexecution after its first execution. This rule is called an *inhibited rule* and prevents infinite looping of rules in the cycle that contains it.

A rule r is inhibited when its activation depends on rules at lower priority than rules providing triggering. Then, when r's condition is evaluated, it is

---

[1] Although the general problem of detecting relational expressions' satisfiability is undecidable, in the cases of interest it is possible to base it on the detection of contradictory predicates.

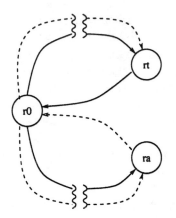

FIGURE 3.5. An inhibited rule.

false. A subsequent change of the truth value of the condition due to the execution of the activating rule has no effect, since the triggering event(s) has already been consumed. More precisely, let r_0 be a self-disactivating rule triggered by a rule r_t and activated by a rule r_a, and $p(r_0), p(r_t)$ and $p(r_a)$ denote the corresponding rule priorities, with $p(r_a) < p(r_0)$ and $p(r_a) < p(r_t)$ (i.e., r_a has lower priority than both r_0 and r_t). The execution of r_t, which precedes that of r_a due to rule ordering, will cause retriggering of r_0. Since $p(r_0) > p(r_a)$, r_0's condition is evaluated before r_a can execute and change the truth value of r_0's condition. Hence, r_0's condition will be false at reconsideration, and r_0's action will not be executed. Then, r_0 is an inhibited rule.

Observe that, without rule ordering, no assumption on the execution order of rules can be made. Therefore, a scheduling order in which activation precedes triggering (i.e., the execution of r_a precedes that of r_t) must be pessimistically assumed, because it can indeed be nondeterministically chosen by the system.

Detecting rule and cycle inhibition is quite complex and we only give an intuition here; details of the method can be found in [BCP95b]. Consider a non terminating rule set NT; let C denote the rules belonging to a cycle of the TG. Let r_0 be a self-disactivating rule in C that is triggered by rule r_t and activated by rule r_a, with $r_t \neq r_a$. This situation is depicted in Figure 3.5. To detect if r_0 is inhibited, all sets of rules that can independently cause the execution of r_t or r_a given that r_0 has executed must be considered. These sets are called *reaching sets* and are denoted as $reach(r_0, r_t)$ and $reach(r_0, r_a)$, respectively. There can be many distinct reaching sets for the same rule pair. Next, to each reaching set is associated its dominant priority, which is the priority of its lowest-priority rule. Such a rule is the bottleneck in the execution of rules belonging to the corresponding reaching set. Let p_t be the lowest dominant priority among all the reaching sets $reach(r_0, r_t)$, and p_a the highest dominant priority among all reaching sets

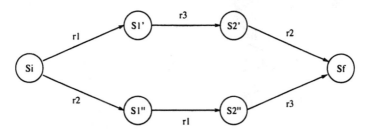

FIGURE 3.6. Representing rule execution by means of rule execution sequences.

$reach(r_0, r_a)$. If $p_a < p_t$ and $p_a < p(r_0)$, rule r_0 is inhibited and cycle C is an inhibited cycle. Then, cycle C cannot cause non terminating executions.

3.3   Confluence Analysis

At each execution of the scheduling phase of rule processing, multiple rules may be triggered, and hence be eligible for execution. A rule set is confluent if the final state of the database does not depend on which eligible rule is chosen for execution at any iteration of the rule execution cycle.

The rule execution process can be described by means of the notions of *rule execution state* and *rule execution sequence*. Consider a rule set R. A rule execution state S has two components: (1) a database state d, and (2) a set of triggered rules $R_T \subseteq R$. When R_T is empty, no rule is triggered and the rule execution state is quiescent. A rule execution sequence consists of a series of rule execution states linked by (executed) rules.[2] A rule execution sequence is *complete* if its last state is quiescent.

In Figure 3.6, two rule execution sequences for rule set $R = \{r_1, r_2, r_3\}$ are represented. The initial state S_i is characterized by database state db_i and triggered rule set $R_T = \{r_1, r_2\}$ and the (unique) final state is characterized by a database state db_f and an empty triggered rule set. Each state transition is labeled with the rule whose execution caused the transition.

Confluence can be defined in terms of execution sequences. A rule set is confluent if, for every initial rule execution state S (produced by an initial database state followed by some user modification(s)), every complete rule execution sequence beginning with S reaches the same quiescent state. Then, confluence analysis would require the exhaustive verification of all possible execution sequences for all possible initial states. This technique is clearly unfeasible even for a small rule set.

A different approach to confluence analysis is based on the *commutativity* of rule pairs. Two rules r_i and r_j commute if, starting with any rule execu-

---

[2]We assume rule execution sequences to be correct: only triggered rules with a true condition are executed, and pairs of adjacent states properly represent the effect of executing the corresponding rule.

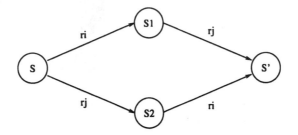

FIGURE 3.7. Commutativity of a rule pair.

tion state S, executing r_i followed by r_j produces the same rule execution state as executing r_j followed by r_i; this is depicted in Figure 3.7.

If all pairs of rules in a rule set R commute, any two execution sequences with the same initial state and executed rules have the same final state. Furthermore, again under the assumption of commutativity, two sequences with the same initial execution state must have the same executed rules. Based on these properties, proved in [BW94], it is possible to state a sufficient condition to guarantee confluence of a rule set: A rule set R is confluent if all pairs of rules in R commute.

This requirement for confluence may seem rather strong, but there is no way to weaken it without specifying some (partial) ordering on the rules in the rule set. This issue is further discussed in Section 3.3.2 where an algorithm for confluence analysis of prioritized rules is presented.

Commutativity of rule pairs forms the basis of most methods for analyzing confluence of database rules, e.g., [AHW95, BW94, vS93]. A technique to test commutativity of rule pairs that have the set transition granularity is described in section 3.3.1.

An alternative approach to confluence analysis is proposed in [KU94], where rules are reduced to conditional term rewrite rules. Confluence analysis is based on finding *contextual critical pairs* (terms that can be rewritten in two different ways, equivalent to rules triggered by the same events on the same classes) and analyzing their feasibility. Unfeasibility is determined by detecting that two rule conditions cannot be true at the same time.

3.3.1   Analyzing Commutativity

Criteria for guaranteeing commutativity of active rules adopting the set transition granularity have been proposed in [AHW95, BW94]. In particular, the following are sufficient conditions for the commutativity of two distinct active rules r_i and r_j: (1) r_i cannot trigger r_j; (2) r_i cannot "untrigger" r_j, i.e., r_i cannot undo all changes triggering r_j[3]; (3) r_i cannot

---

[3]For example, consider a rule r_j triggered by insertions in some table t. A rule r_i untriggers r_j if it deletes from t all inserted data that trigger r_j before r_j is executed.

activate r_j; (4) r_i cannot deactivate r_j, i.e., r_i's action cannot delete all data that satisfies r_j's condition; (5) conditions (1)–(4) with i and j reversed; (6) r_i's action and r_j's action commute. Note that even though conditions (1)–(6) are not necessarily satisfied when $r_i = r_j$, a rule always commutes with itself.

Condition (1) is satisfied if r_i's actions do not generate events triggering r_j; similarly, condition (2) is verified if r_i does not delete from any table t for which *insert(t)* or *update(t)* are included in r_j's triggering event set. For checking condition (3), we determine that r_i cannot activate r_j as described in section 3.2.2. To verify condition (4), which requires that r_i cannot deactivate r_j, we must show that r_i's action(s) cannot "take away" data from r_j's condition. This happens only if the Propagation Algorithm (see section 3.2.2) applied to r_i's actions and r_j's condition produces a *delete* operation. Hence, one application of the Propagation Algorithm is sufficient for verifying (3) and (4). For (5), we reverse the roles of r_i and r_j in the analysis of (1)–(4).

Two database modification operations commute if, for all database states, executing them in either order always yields the same final database state. Then, for (6) we must determine if any of r_i's actions can change the effect of any of r_j's actions, and vice versa. Again, this can be detected by applying the Propagation Algorithm. Consider two actions A_i and A_j. First, A_j is transformed into a query Q_{A_j},[4] such that if the result of query Q_{A_j} cannot be affected by the execution of A_i, then A_i cannot change the effect of action A_j. Then the Propagation Algorithm is applied to A_i and Q_{A_j}: if it produces an empty result, then A_i cannot change the effect of A_j. Then, the roles of A_i and A_j are reversed. If again the algorithm produces an empty result, then A_i and A_j commute.

We finally observe that if a rule is self-disactivating, we can improve the commutativity check. In particular, if rule r_j is self-disactivating, conditions (1) and (2) can be dropped for r_i. Analogously, if r_i is self-disactivating as well, the same conditions can be dropped also with i and j reversed.

3.3.2 Confluence with Priorities

Consider a prioritized rule set R. If a total ordering is defined on the rules in R, when multiple rules are triggered only one rule at a time is eligible for evaluation. Then, rule processing is always characterized by a single rule execution sequence, which yields a unique final state, and confluence is guaranteed. When instead the rule set is partially ordered, there may exist some execution state S in which several unordered rules are eligible for execution (see Figure 3.8). In this case, a rule is selected randomly

---

This phenomenon is disallowed in some active systems and rather rare in practice.

[4]Details of how the query is derived can be found in [BW94].

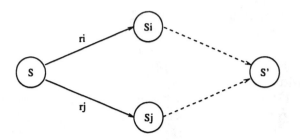

FIGURE 3.8. A commutative rule pair.

$R_1 \leftarrow \{r_i\}$
$R_2 \leftarrow \{r_j\}$
repeat until unchanged:
$\qquad R_1 \leftarrow R_1 \cup \{r \in R | r \in Trig(r_1) \text{ and } r_1 \in R_1$
$\qquad\qquad$ and $p(r) > p(r_2)$ for some $r_2 \in R_2$
$\qquad\qquad$ and $r \neq r_j$
$\qquad R_2 \leftarrow R_2 \cup \{r \in R | r \in Trig(r_2) \text{ and } r_2 \in R_2$
$\qquad\qquad$ and $p(r) > p(r_1)$ for some $r_1 \in R_1$
$\qquad\qquad$ and $r \neq r_i$

FIGURE 3.9. Algorithm to build sets R_1, R_2 for testing confluence of active rules. $Trig(r_1)$ is the set of rules triggered by r_1's actions.

among all eligible rules. If n rules are eligible for execution in state S, then n different rule execution sequences originate from S, one per eligible rule. These sequences may yield different final states, hence a nondeterministic execution.

Intuitively, to guarantee confluence, it may be tempting to restrict the commutativity test to all pairs of unordered rules. Unfortunately, since rules interact in quite an intricate way, this technique may yield incorrect results. Consider the execution sequences originating from state S in Figure 3.8. Although it may seem that commutativity of r_i and r_j should guarantee the existence of a common state S', this is actually not a sufficient condition. This is due to the fact that, e.g., r_i may trigger a rule r with precedence over r_j, thus preventing r_j from being executed from state S_i. Furthermore, the execution of r may cause additional rules with precedence over r_j to become triggered.

The algorithm presented in Figure 3.9 has been proposed in [AHW95] in the context of the Starburst active rule system. It applies to all pairs of unordered rules in a rule set R. For each pair r_i, r_j, it recursively builds two rule sets R_1 and R_2 that contain all rules whose commutativity must be checked to guarantee confluence. In particular, rule set R_1 (respectively R_2) includes all rules that may be triggered by r_i and by any r triggered by r_i (respectively by r_j and by any r triggered by r_j) that have precedence over any rule in rule set R_2 (respectively R_1). If, for each unordered pair

r_i, r_j, each pair of $r_1 \in R_1$ and $r_2 \in R_2$ commutes, then rule set R is confluent. Correctness of the algorithm is proved in [AHW95].

3.4 Conclusion

Compile-time analysis of active rules allows the rule designer to predict relevant aspects of rule behavior before the rule set is installed in the database. Hence, tools implementing the algorithms described in this chapter can simplify the rule design task by providing a deeper understanding of the interaction among active rules.

Unfortunately, only a few tools that perform compile-time analysis of active rules are currently available. In particular, the VITAL toolbox [BGB95] performs termination analysis by building the Triggering Graph. A more sophisticated termination analysis is performed by the ARACHNE tool [BCP95a], which builds both the Triggering and Activation Graphs to perform termination analysis of Chimera active rules (see Section 3.2 for more details on both systems). These prototypes may be enhanced by adding more advanced features, such as the exploitation of priority information.

To our knowledge, no tool is available to analyze the confluence property of an active rule set. Although confluence may be guaranteed by imposing a total ordering on the active rule set, weakening this requirement may provide more flexibility to the design of complex rule applications. In this case, tools detecting confluence would provide to the designer a means to accurately verify the correctness of all the different execution sequences allowed in the system.

3.5 REFERENCES

[AHW95] Alexander Aiken, Joseph M. Hellerstein, and Jennifer Widom. Static Analysis Techniques for Predicting the Behavior of Active Database Rules. *ACM Transactions on Database Systems*, 20(1):3 41, March 1995.

[BCP95a] Elena Baralis, Stefano Ceri, and Stefano Paraboschi. ARACHNE: A Tool for the Analysis of Active Rules. In *Proc. of the Second Int. Conf. on Applications of Databases–ADB'95*, Santa Clara, California, December 1995.

[BCP95b] Elena Baralis, Stefano Ceri, and Stefano Paraboschi. Improved Rule Analysis by Means of Triggering and Activation Graphs. In Timos Sellis, editor, *Proc. of the Second Workshop on Rules in Database Systems*, LNCS 985, pages 165–181, Athens, Greece, September 1995.

[BCP95c] Elena Baralis, Stefano Ceri, and Stefano Paraboschi. Run-Time Detection of Non-Terminating Active Rule Systems. In *Proc. of the Conf. on Deductive and Object-Oriented Databases, DOOD '95*, LNCS 1013, pages 38–54, Singapore, December 1995.

[BCP96] Elena Baralis, Stefano Ceri, and Stefano Paraboschi. Modularization Techniques for Active Rules Design. *ACM Transactions on Database Systems*, 21(1):1–29, March 1996.

[BCW93] Elena Baralis, Stefano Ceri, and Jennifer Widom. Better Termination Analysis for Active Databases. In N.W. Paton and M.H. Williams, editors, *Proc. of First Workshop on Rules in Database Systems*, WICS, pages 163–179, Edinburgh, Scotland, August 1993. Springer-Verlag, Berlin.

[BGB95] Emmanuel Benazet, Hervé Guehl, and Mokrane Bouzeghoub. VITAL: a Visual Tool for Analysis of Rules Behavior in Active Databases. In Timos Sellis, editor, *Proc. of the Second Workshop on Rules in Databases Systems*, LNCS 985, pages 182–196, Athens, Greece, September 1995.

[BW] Elena Baralis and Jennifer Widom. Better Static Analysis for Active Database Systems. Submitted for publication.

[BW94] Elena Baralis and Jennifer Widom. An Algebraic Approach to Rule Analysis in Expert Database Systems. In *Proc. Twentieth Intl. Conf. on Very Large Data Bases*, pages 475–486, Santiago, Chile, September 1994.

[CW90] Stefano Ceri and Jennifer Widom. Deriving Production Rules for Constraint Maintenance. In Dennis McLeod, Ron Sacks-Davis, and Hans Schek, editors, *Proc. Sixteenth Int'l Conf. on Very Large Data Bases*, pages 566–577, Brisbane, Australia, August 1990.

[ISO94] ISO-ANSI Working Draft: Database Language/SQL Foundation, August 1994. Document DBL:RIO-004 and X3H2-94-329.

[KU91] A.P. Karadimce and Susan D. Urban. Diagnosing Anomalous Rule Behavior in Databases with Integrity Maintenance Production Rules. In *Proc. Third Int. Workshop on Foundations of Models and Languages for Data and Objects*, pages 77–102, Aigen, Austria, September 1991. Technische Universitaat Clausthal.

[KU94] A.P. Karadimce and Susan D. Urban. Conditional Term Rewriting as a Formal Basis for Analysis of Active Database Rules. In *Proc. Fourth International Workshop on Research Issues in Data Engineering RIDE-ADS '94*, pages 156–162, Houston, Texas, February 1994.

[KU96] A.P. Karadimce and Susan D. Urban.   Refined Triggering Graphs: A Logic-Based Approach to Termination Analysis in an Object-Oriented Database. In *Proc. Twelfth Intl. Conference on Data Engineering*, pages 384–391, New Orleans, Louisiana, February 1996.

[Ora92] Oracle Corporation, 500 Oracle Parkway, Redwood City CA 94065. *Oracle 7 Server SQL Language Reference Manual*, December 1992. Part Number 778-70.

[TC94] H.Tsai and A.M.K. Cheng. Termination Analysis of OPS5 Expert Systems. In *Proc. of the AAAI National Conference on Artificial Intelligence*, Seattle, Washington, 1994.

[vS93] L.van der Voort and A.Siebes. Termination and Confluence of Rule Execution. In *Proc. of the Second International Conference on Information and Knowledge Management*, Washington DC, November 1993.

[WH95] T.Weik and A.Heuer. An Algorithm for the Analysis of Termination of Large Trigger Sets in an OODBMS. In *Proceedings of the International Workshop on Active and Real-Time Databases Systems*, Skövde, Sweden, June 1995.

[ZH90] Y.Zhou and M.Hsu. A Theory for Rule Triggering Systems. In Francois Bancilhon, Costantino Thanos, and Dennis Tsichritzis, editors, *Proc. Second Intl. Conf. on Extending Database Technology*, volume 416, pages 407–421, Venice, Italy, March 1990. Lecture Notes in Computer Science.

[ZMU96] Detlef Zimmer, Axel Meckenstock, and Rainer Unland. Using Petri Nets for Rule Termination Analysis. In *Proc. of Workshop on Databases: Active and Real-Time*, Rockville, Maryland, November 1996.

4

Optimization

Norman W. Paton
Andrew Dinn
M. Howard Williams

ABSTRACT
This chapter describes how system supported optimization techniques can be applied to ECA rules to improve their runtime performance. In so doing, it is indicated how existing optimization techniques for passive databases can be adapted and extended for use with active rules, and in particular, how the results of rule analysis can be combined with multiple query optimization techniques to support effective optimization of rule bases.

4.1 Introduction

Active databases are sometimes said to provide a declarative framework for describing certain aspects of the behavior of an application, in that they indicate what events are to be monitored, what conditions must hold and what reactions are to take place without being prescriptive about the details of how this behavior is to be enacted. This means that the system may have some latitude in determining exactly what is done, when, and how, in order to support the active behavior. In extreme cases, for example, this may involve compiling away ECA rules, which instead of being supported directly at runtime, are incorporated into application code by the compiler [SJGP90]. Such an approach, however, is only possible when a restricted rule language is used, and will not be considered further in this chapter. However, it does indicate that the system has some freedom when it comes to transforming active database rules. Indeed, if active databases are to be successful, it is important that they are seen to provide good value, by performing useful tasks at minimal cost in terms of execution overhead. The declarative framework provided by active rules can therefore be seen as something of a challenge to the developers of active database systems, who must ensure that tasks are carried out as efficiently as possible and with minimal duplicated effort.

As with optimization in passive databases, the scope that exists for developing practical optimizers depends very largely on the nature of the languages used. In general, declarative languages are more amenable to optimization, as are languages that avoid side effects. Active database systems have been developed that exploit a wide range of programming paradigms for expressing conditions and actions, some of which are more amenable to optimization than others, but it is not the aim of this chapter to provide a comparison or analysis of alternative approaches. Instead, it will be assumed in what follows that the condition language used by the active rule system is amenable to optimization, without addressing details of how transformations might be performed for any specific language. Event specifications will be assumed to exploit operators along the lines of those presented in Chapter 1, and features assumed of action languages should be clear from the context. A further assumption made in the text is that rules with an event-condition coupling mode of immediate are processed by a recursive rule processor, and that rules with an event-condition coupling mode of deferred are processed by an iterative rule processor (for definitions of these terms, see Chapter 1).

In active databases, considerable effort has been directed at methods for efficient evaluation of condition-action rules. As this has become a significant research topic in itself, it is not covered here; for more details, see Chapter 5.

4.2   Optimizing Single Rules

This section considers opportunities for optimizing individual rules without regard to what other rules exist in the database. The optimization of multiple rules is considered in section 4.3. These sections do not discuss standard optimizations on declarative rule conditions (it is assumed that such optimizations are necessary when declarative condition languages are exploited), as the focus is on extensions to standard optimizations in the context of ECA rules.

4.2.1   Exploiting Parameters

Rule conditions are evaluated in the context of the events that triggered the rule, and the parameters of the events that have triggered the rule are often passed onto the condition of the rule. These parameters can often be used as a starting point for evaluating the truth or otherwise of the condition. For example, the following rule monitors the insertion of new composite_part objects with components that are of lower quality than that of the composite_part. It is assumed that this rule is triggered in response to a set of insertions, that inserted collects together the composite_part objects inserted since the rule was last considered for firing, and that composite_part is a subclass of part.

```
DEFINE RULE R1 AS
ON insert OF composite_part
IF EXISTS (SELECT *
           FROM p in part, new in inserted
           WHERE p in new.components and
                    p.quality < new.quality)
DO ...
```

In evaluating the condition, the optimizer has the option of iterating over the extension of **part**, and then testing to see if the parts retrieved are components of the **inserted** composite parts, or, alternatively, of iterating over the **inserted** composite parts and then retrieving the associated component objects. In general, the most efficient evaluation is likely to result from starting the search from the event parameters, as they are likely to be small in number and resident in main memory. Any optimizer for use with an active database system is likely to need the modest extensions required to optimize queries parameterized by main memory collections that represent the event parameters.

In condition-action rules, where events are not explicit, optimizations have been proposed that essentially involve identifying events and their parameters when evaluating rule conditions [BW95].

4.2.2   Moving Constraints

Together, the event and the condition describe the situation that a rule is monitoring. As such, given a situation, an event language and a condition language, an important question is how the description of the situation should be partitioned between the event and the condition of a rule. In most systems, the event language is exclusively concerned with questions about what has happened and cannot perform tests on values associated with the event (e.g., that the *update id* event that has taken place is assigning the value *0*), but some event languages provide filtering mechanisms that can perform tests on event parameters [GJS92, RPS95, DPWF96, CFPT96]. (See also the chapters on Chimera, PFL, and ROCK & ROLL). In general, optimization involves trying to exploit constraints on the values of interest as early as possible in the evaluation process, with a view to minimizing the amount of redundant effort expended. This, in turn, implies that if constraints from the condition can be enforced by the event detector, this may improve efficiency.

As an example, consider the following rule, which monitors the setting to 0 of **part** identifiers. It is assumed that this rule is triggered once in response to a single update, and that **new** is used to refer to the value assigned to id by the update.

```
DEFINE RULE R2 AS
ON update TO id OF part
IF new.id = 0
DO ...
```

An optimizer might then elect to rewrite rule R2 as R3, so that the restriction on the id of the updated part is checked by the event detector, thereby removing the need to invoke the condition evaluator.

```
DEFINE RULE R3 AS
ON update TO id OF part WITH 0
DO ...
```

In a case such as this, a rule optimizer could do one of two things: it could exploit the filtering facilities of the event language to rewrite rule R2 as R3, or, if the event language does not support user-defined matching facilities, it could push into the event detector the constraint that only events updating the id to 0 are of interest, thereby enforcing the constraint at event detection time, even though the event language does not allow the user to specify that the constraint should be enforced by the event detector.

The validity of the above transformation, however, depends upon various conditions being satisfied regarding the semantics of the rule language and the context within which R2 exists. For example, if the expression new.id is interpreted as meaning the value assigned to the id attribute by the update operation, then the transformation is likely to be valid (subject to some consistent semantics on deletion of the modified object). However, if new.id is interpreted as meaning the value of the updated object's id attribute at condition evaluation time (i.e., the new keyword serves to identify the updated object in its current state), then R2 and R3 will only be equivalent if the value of the id of new cannot be changed between the occurrence of the event and the evaluation of the condition of R2.

The challenge for an optimizer working with an active rule system is to identify meaning preserving transformations, a challenge that is made significant in active databases by the close integration of updates in actions with conditions in queries. If we assume the second interpretation given above for event parameters, namely that new in R2 is the object identifier of the updated object, then pushing the constraint from the condition into the event detector is only valid if:

1. The condition coupling mode of the rule is *immediate*. If the condition coupling mode is deferred, then there is clearly a possibility that the id of the object new might be modified by the application or by another rule before the condition of the rule is evaluated at a rule assertion point.

2. There is no other (immediate) rule that may be triggered by the same event that may update the id attribute of new before the condition

of R2 is evaluated. Any other immediate rule that is monitoring the update of the id attribute of part objects, and that has a priority higher than or equal to that of R2, may interfere with the evaluation of the condition of R2.

The general situation is depicted in Figure 4.1. The condition of each rule reads from a portion of the database, which is referred to as the *read set* of the rule. The action of a rule updates a portion of the database, known as the *write set* of the rule. It is only valid to push a constraint from the condition of a rule, say *R1*, to its event if there is no other rule, say *R2*, such that:

1. *R2* can be triggered by the same event as *R1* and has a priority at least as high as that of *R1*, and the write set of *R2* intersects with the read set of *R1*.

2. *R2* triggers (directly or indirectly) immediate rules that have write sets that intersect with the read set of *R1*.

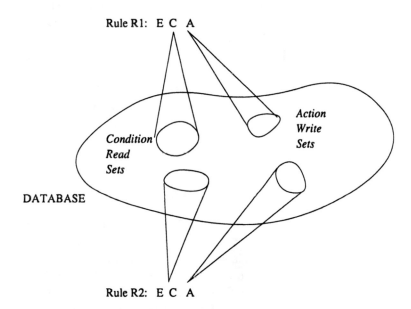

FIGURE 4.1. Rule condition/action read/write sets.

The analyses that are required to characterize the read and write sets of rules for optimization purposes are essentially the same as those that are required in rule analyses to determine how rules interact, as discussed in Chapter 3. The more conservative the rule analysis supported, the more opportunities will be identified in which rule optimization is possible. In what follows, rules that have nonintersecting read and write sets will be said to be *ca-independent*.

In the same way as events and conditions may perform related tasks in describing the situation that is being monitored, it is possible for the condition and action to be seen as having shared responsibility for identifying objects to which some operation should be applied. For example, rule R4 below sets the cost of each newly inserted part to the minimum cost of existing parts with the same type:

```
DEFINE RULE R4 AS
ON insert OF part
IF EXISTS (SELECT *
           FROM p IN part, new IN inserted
           WHERE new.type = p.type AND p.cost < new.cost)
DO SET new.cost = (SELECT MIN(q.cost)
                   FROM q IN part
                   WHERE q.type=new.type)
   FROM p IN part, new IN inserted
   WHERE new.type = p.type AND p.cost < new.cost;
```

In this example, the query that forms the condition is essentially repeated in the action. This repetition of work would normally be avoided by rule programmers using language mechanisms to transfer information directly from the condition to the action, but it is potentially possible, where the action is run immediately after the condition and where there is no interference from other rules, for the optimizer to identify common subqueries in the condition and the action that are repeating work. The extent to which this is practical depends to a significant degree on the choice of action language.

4.3   Optimizing Multiple Rules

The previous section was concerned with local optimization of active behavior, and essentially involved the exploitation of existing optimization techniques in active systems. This section considers how more global optimization can be performed, with a view to minimizing the overall cost of evaluating rule conditions, rather than focusing on individual rules in isolation. This more global examination of rule behavior exploits earlier results on rule analysis [AHW95] and on multiple query optimization [RC88]. As an example, consider the two rules R4 and R5, which respond to changes to the type of composite_part objects in different ways:

```
DEFINE RULE R4 AS
ON update TO type OF composite_part
IF new.type = 'Widget' AND
   MAX(SELECT weight FROM new.components) > 100
DO SET new.description = 'Large widget';
```

```
DEFINE RULE R5 AS
ON update TO type OF composite_part
IF new.type = 'Widget' AND
   MAX(SELECT weight FROM new.components) <= 100
DO SET new.description = 'Small widget';
```

These two rules, if triggered in the absence of facilities for optimizing multiple rule conditions at the same time, will duplicate the work required to identify the maximum weight of the components of the updated composite_part.

In general, it is only feasible to apply multiple query optimization to the conditions of several rules if:

1. The rules are triggered at the same time. If the rules cannot be triggered at the same time, then there is no point in considering effort that may be duplicated by their conditions. In fact, where deferred rules are supported, it is very common for rules with different triggering events to be triggered at the same time. In the case of rules with immediate event-condition coupling modes, simultaneous triggering is reserved for rules monitoring common events.

2. The rules are *ca-independent*, i.e., the order in which the rules are chosen for processing has no impact on the truth of their conditions. This is important because, if the action of one rule can change the result of the condition of another, then the fact that they have overlapping conditions can be rendered irrelevant by the fact that the conditions are evaluated over different database states. It happens that *ca-independence* is a weaker version of the confluence property discussed in Chapter 3 (i.e., all confluent rules are also *ca-independent*), and it is shown in [DPW96] that a variant of the confluence analysis presented in [AHW95] can be used to identify whether a pair of rules chosen from a given rule set are *ca-independent*. Alternatively, analysis can be based on confluence, although this stronger condition will give rise to fewer cases being found in which multiple query optimization is valid.

A general definition for the *ca-independence* follows, in which *condition-read-set* and *action-write-set* must take account of whatever cascaded active behavior may be interleaved with the evaluation of r_i and r_j.

ca-independent(r_1,r_j) → Boolean
      return (condition-read-set(r_i) ∩ action-write-set(r_j) = {} and
          condition-read-set(r_j) ∩ action-write-set(r_i) = {})

To return to rules R4 and R5 above, assuming that they have an event-condition coupling mode of immediate, and are the only rules monitoring updates to the types of composite_parts, it is clear that these rules do satisfy the above conditions: they are sure to be triggered simultaneously as they monitor the same event, and they are *ca-independent* because the updates performed by their actions have no effect on their conditions.

The challenge, then, for an optimizer is to identify collections of rules where it is both *valid* and *beneficial* to exploit multiple query optimization. Given an event definition E and a rule base R, the following simple algorithm returns a set of rules that can be considered together by a multiple query optimizer immediately after an occurrence of E:

optimizable(E:Event $\times$ R:{Rule}) $\rightarrow$ {Rule}
      precondition: confluent(R)
      return {r:Rule |
          $r \in R$,
          event_condition_coupling_mode(r) = *immediate*,
          triggering_event(r) = E}

This algorithm essentially states that, when the whole rule set is confluent, all immediate rules that are triggered by an individual event can be considered together by the multiple query optimizer. The basic algorithm for determining the confluence of a set of rules is assumed to be that of [AHW95], adapted to reflect the execution model and rule language being used.

In fact, the above algorithm is unnecessarily conservative, and multiple query optimization can be exploited whenever all rules monitoring the triggering event E are *ca-independent*:

optimizable(E:Event $\times$ R:{Rule}) $\rightarrow$ {Rule}
      let *candidates* = {r:Rule |
          $r \in R$,
          event_condition_coupling_mode(r) = *immediate*,
          triggering_event(r) = E}
      in if ca-independent(*candidates*)
          then return *candidates*
          else return $\emptyset$

For immediate rule processing, detailed examination of rule priorities and of the interactions between smaller sets of rules can be used to identify opportunities for multiple query optimization that are missed by the above algorithm. For details, see [DPW96].

For rules with an event-condition coupling mode of deferred, it may be possible to exploit multiple query optimization across rules that are monitoring different events. This is because when rules are scheduled for condition evaluation at the end of a transaction or at a rule assertion point, these rules will have been triggered by a range of events that have taken place over a period of time, either as a result of operations performed by user programs or as a result of rule processing. This provides a larger search space for opportunities in which to perform multiple query optimization, but also requires that groups of less directly related rules are *ca-independent*.

If the whole rule base is confluent, then the following variant on the first definition of *optimizable* can be used, where R is the rule base:

optimizable(R:{Rule}) $\rightarrow$ {Rule}
 precondition: confluent(R)
 return R

In this case, the event is not given as a parameter to *optimizable*, as many different events may have occurred, depending on the application. In essence, where the whole rule base is confluent and rules are deferred, the problem reduces to a search for cases where it is beneficial to apply multiple query optimization across collections of rules.

As with immediate rules, however, there are cases in which multiple query optimization can be exploited in rule bases that are not necessarily confluent. For example, the following algorithm identifies sets of rules that can be considered together for multiple query optimization:

optimizable(R:{Rule}) $\rightarrow$ {{Rule}}
 let *candidates* = {S:{Rule} |
   $S \subseteq$ {DR:Rule |
     DR $\in R$,
     event_condition_coupling_mode(DR) = deferred },
   ca-independent(S),
   ($\nexists\, r \in R$ - S |
     priority(r) $\geq$ min {$s.priority$:Int | $s \in S$},
     priority(r) $\leq$ max {$s.priority$:Int | $s \in S$})
   ($\forall\, r \in$ (triggered_by(S) $\cap$ deferred(R)),
     priority(r) $<$ min {$s.priority$ | $s \in S$})}
 in return (candidates)

Given a rule base, this algorithm identifies sets of deferred rules that are guaranteed not to be interleaved at runtime with any other rules. The algorithm has the following components:

1. The set variable S is bound in turn to all sets of deferred rules in the rulebase R.

2. The sets bound to S are then filtered, so that it is known that:

 (a) The rules in S are *ca-independent*.

 (b) No deferred rules triggered at a rule assertion point with the rules in S can be interleaved with the rules in S.

 (c) No deferred rules that can be triggered by the execution of rules in S can be interleaved with the rules in S.

This algorithm exploits the fact that *ca-independent* must take account of immediate rules in determining the independence of rule conditions and actions, and thus is valid for rule bases with both immediate and deferred rules.

The extent to which the above algorithms can be applied in real systems is directly dependent upon the effectiveness of the rule analyzer, in that a conservative rule analyzer will fail to identify some rule sets that are amenable to multiple query optimization. However, the ability to obtain performance gains by reusing the rule analyzer in support of optimization should encourage the developers of active rule systems to develop effective analyzers. Although early work on confluence analysis tended to be performed with simple rule systems, it is shown in [DPW96] that analyses can also be carried out in the context of more powerful rule languages.

Given the above algorithms for identifying when it is valid to perform multiple query optimization in active databases, two additional issues remain, namely when to exploit this facility, and how to tell whether or not it is beneficial in a particular context. It is probably most appropriate to identify opportunities for rule optimization at rule compilation time, as query optimization, especially involving multiple conditions, is not cost-free. However, it would be worthwhile to investigate the trade offs associated with compile time and run time optimization for deferred rule processing, when it is difficult to anticipate in advance which rules will be triggered at the same time. As for the benefits that derive from multiple query optimization, these have to be assessed by examining the results of cost analyses on alternative plans. Some aspects of multiple query optimization involve trade offs, in which units of work can only be shared by enforcing some constraints later than would be possible in a query-specific execution plan. Detailed results on when to apply multiple query optimization await further experimentation with implemented systems.

Related results to those presented above are described by [CM95], in the context of the NAOS active database system (see Chapter 15). In that work, rules defined using an execution model that assumes sequential rule processing are analyzed to identify when they can be executed in parallel without changing their meaning. It is shown that rules can be executed in parallel when they are *ca-independent*. Thus, the work on NAOS shares with that presented here the use of analysis to influence evaluation, but does not consider the use of multiple query optimization.

4.4   Conclusion

This chapter has described how query optimization techniques can be applied in ECA rule systems. The optimization of individual rules involves the use of techniques originally developed for use with passive databases, slightly adapted to take into account the facilities supported by and the information provided by the event detector. The optimization of multiple rules, however, involves the application of earlier results on active rule analysis and on multiple query optimization. It has been shown how, when all or part of a rule set can be shown to be *ca-independent*, multiple query optimization techniques can be applied to prevent work being duplicated in different rules. This has the effect of performing global optimization of active behavior, taking into account all the active behavior carried out by the system and the execution model used to support that behavior.

4.5 Acknowledgments

This work has been supported by the UK Engineering and Physical Sciences Research Council (Grant GR/H43847), and the EU Human Capital and Mobility Network ACT-NET.

4.6 References

[AHW95] A. Aiken, J.M. Hellerstein, and J. Widom. Static Analysis Techniqies for Predicting the Behaviour of Active Database Rules. *ACM TODS*, 20(1):3–41, 1995.

[BW95] E. Baralis and J. Widom. Using Delta Relations to Optimize Condition Evaluation in Active Databases. In T. Sellis, editor, *Proc. 2nd Intl. Workshop on Rules In Database Systems (RIDS)*, pages 292–308. Springer-Verlag, 1995.

[CFPT96] S. Ceri, P. Fraternali, S. Paraboschi, and L. Tanca. Active Rule Management in Chimera. In J. Widom and S. Ceri, editors, *Active Database Systems: Triggers and Rules for Active Database Processing*, pages 151–175. Morgan Kaufmann, 1996.

[CM95] C. Collet and J. Manchado. Optimization of Active Rules With Parallelism. In M. Berndtsson and J. Hansson, editors, *Proc. Active and Real Time Database Systems (ARTDB)*, pages 82–103. Springer-Verlag, 1995.

[DPW96] A. Dinn, N.W. Paton, and M.H. Williams. Active Rule Analysis and Optimisation in Object-Oriented Databases. 1996. Submitted for publication.

[DPWF96] A. Dinn, N.W. Paton, M.H. Williams, and A.A.A. Fernandes. An Active Rule Language for ROCK & ROLL. In R. Morrison and J. Kennedy, editors, *Proc. 14th British National Conference on Databases*, pages 36–55. Springer-Verlag, 1996.

[GJS92]   N.H. Gehami, H.V. Jagadish, and O. Shmueli. Composite Event Specification in Active Databases: Model & Implementation. In *18th Intl. Conf. on Very Large Data Bases, Barcelona*, pages 327–338. Morgan Kaufmann, 1992.

[RC88]   A. Rosenthal and U.S. Chakravarthy. Anatomy of a Multiple Query Optimiser. In *Proc. 14th VLDB.*, pages 230–239, 1988.

[RPS95]   S. Reddi, A. Poulovassilis, and C. Small. Extending a Functional DBPL With ECA-Rules. In T. Sellis, editor, *Proc. 2nd Intl. Workshop on Rules in Database Systems*, pages 101–115. Springer-Verlag, 1995.

[SJGP90]   M. Stonebraker, A. Jhingran, J. Goh, and S. Potamianos. On Rules, Procedures, Caching and Views in Database Systems. In *Proc. ACM SIGMOD*, pages 281–290, 1990.

5

Monitoring Complex Rule Conditions

Tore Risch and Martin Sköld

ABSTRACT

This chapter describes and discusses the problem of efficient checking of complex rule conditions expressed as database queries. For this, several methods have been proposed that are based on the technique of *incremental evaluation*. With incremental evaluation, the state of a rule condition is materialized and, after an update, the new state of the condition is defined incrementally in terms of differences to the materialized state generated by the update. First an overview of the traditional methods for incremental evaluation is given. Then a *partial differencing calculus* is defined for set algebra and is then mapped to the relational operators. Examples are given on how the calculus has been used to define an algorithm that allows trade offs between space and time efficiency when checking complex rule conditions.

5.1 Introduction

The discussion in this chapter concerns the efficient evaluation of complex rule conditions. The discussion is applicable both to CA and ECA rules with complex rule conditions. Systems based on CA rules (e.g., AI production rule systems) have traditionally used more complex rules than ECA rules of active databases. However, as more advanced active database systems are being developed, the need for efficient handling of complex rule conditions will increase for ECA rules as well.

The condition part of a rule is allowed to be more or less complex in different active database systems. If it is expressed as a general database query, it can span very large parts of the database. A *naive* method of checking such a rule condition is to execute the complete rule condition whenever an event that triggers the rule has occurred. This, however, can be very costly. For example, a rule attached to update events of the salaries of employees might have a rule condition that specifies that the rule action is executed only when the sum of the incomes of all employees is larger than the salary budget. The execution cost for a query that adds together all employee salaries is proportional to the number of employees in the database.

It would be very inefficient if the ADBMS would check the complete query representing the condition every time the salary of an employee is updated.

The example illustrates that for optimization of rule conditions it is not always sufficient to rely solely on conventional query optimization techniques. Special optimization techniques are needed to execute complex rule conditions with reasonable efficiency. Such optimizations can make use of special knowledge about rules. In our example, it is favorable to store the sum of all employee salaries in the database and then incrementally update the sum whenever the salary of some employee is changed. The condition checking only has to check whether the materialized sum is larger than the budget.

The example illustrates the need for an important class of optimization techniques for rule conditions based on *incremental evaluation* of rule conditions. Incremental evaluation avoids recomputing the rule condition completely for every event by incrementally computing the influence of an update event on a materialized part of a condition. In the example, when an income of an employee or manager is updated, we use the incremental difference between the old and the new income to calculate the influence on the sum on the update.

This chapter first makes an overview of some well-known incremental evaluation techniques and how they have been used in databases. In particular, we discuss how well-suited the various techniques are for monitoring rule conditions in active databases.

To illustrate and formalize the technique, a *partial difference calculus* is presented that formally defines incremental changes to rule conditions in an active DBMS. The calculus is based on a form of incremental evaluation named *partial differencing* of rule conditions. The calculus gives us a formalism to optimize rule condition checking with respect to both space and time. Space optimization is achieved since the calculus does not presuppose materialization of all intermediate results of monitored conditions to find its previous state. As an alternative to complete materialization of the rule condition, the calculus provides a method to do a *logical rollback* from the new database state to the old one. Thus by using the calculus, a rule optimizer has the choice of not materializing when favorable.

The calculus has been applied in the implementation of an incremental algorithm that efficiently monitors complex rule conditions [SR96]. To optimize space usage, the algorithm uses a *breadth-first, bottom-up* propagation based on the calculus combined with the possibility to do logical rollbacks. Time optimization is achieved by materializing some (but not all) intermediate results and then incrementally computing as little as possible at each update. The algorithm is particularly favorable for database transactions with few updates and where the rule conditions are complex and the rule checking is deferred until the end of transactions (deferred coupling mode). However, the technique can also be used for immediate coupling mode. The algorithm and the calculus are applicable both to CA (production) rules and to ECA rules.

5.2   Incremental Evaluation Techniques

Finite differencing [PK92] is an incremental evaluation method to calculate changes to functions in terms of changes to its arguments. As a simple example, if we have a function

```
netpay = income - taxes - fees
```

and increase the income with Δincome while taxes and fees stay fixed, we get the same change in `netpay`, i.e.:

Δnetpay = Δincome

If the old state of `netpay` is materialized, the new state can be computed by just incrementing `netpay` with Δincome. It is favorable to use such incremental evaluation if it is cheaper to look up the materialization than to compute the subtraction.[1] The example illustrates that it is often (but not always) cheaper to incrementally compute the incremental difference to the value of a function than to fully recompute it.

The example illustrates the *chain rule* [PK92] for the minus function: If $F = X - Y$ then $\frac{\Delta F}{\Delta X} = \Delta X$ and $\frac{\Delta F}{\Delta Y} = -\Delta Y$, where $\frac{\Delta F}{\Delta X}$ denotes the change to F, given the change ΔX to X and $\frac{\Delta F}{\Delta Y}$ denotes the change to F given the change ΔY to Y. Thus, we get the *partial difference* expressions $\Delta F = \frac{\Delta F}{\Delta X} = \Delta X$ if ΔY is empty and $\Delta F = \frac{\Delta F}{\Delta Y} = -\Delta Y$ if ΔX is empty.

Early work on finite differencing was done by Paige and Koenig [PK92], who used the technique for improving the efficiency of programs in the set-oriented programming language SETL by program transformations. In that work, differentiation operators were defined for the basic set functions in the SETL language. The transformed programs were faster since results of functions could then be materialized to avoid recomputations of large sets.

Paige and Koenig also discovered that finite differencing could be applied on materialization of derived data in databases [KP81]. In [KP81], finite differencing is used for materializing derived data in a functional data model. Finite differencing for maintaining materialized views in the relational model was first developed in [BLT86], where it was shown how to incrementally maintain materialized relational Select-Project-Join (SPJ) views. Work on incremental maintenance of materialized views in Datalog can be found in [GM95, KM92, DS93]. In [QW91], the relational algebra is extended with some incremental operators that can be used for differencing relational algebra expressions.

---

[1] This is actually not the case here, but would be so if the operator had been more expensive, e.g., a set or an aggregation operator.

[RCBB89] proposed incremental evaluation of relational Select-Project-Join (SPJ) queries in ECA rule conditions. The motivation for this was that ECA rules with complex rule conditions need incremental evaluation techniques for efficient evaluation of the condition part. The work was based on defining an algebra for computations over database changes, Δ-relations. Each relation had an associated Δ-relation where the tuples that got added and deleted during an update operation were stored. Each SPJ-view also had Δ-relations that were computed though a *chain-rule* for SPJ queries. An incremental evaluation algorithm for rule condition monitoring was also proposed by [HD91].

In [CW91], it is shown how active rules can be used for maintaining materialized views. The rules are semi-automatically generated from the user-defined views to be materialized. The generated ECA rules are parameterized to allow for a simple form of incremental evaluation.

A classical algorithm for incremental evaluation of rule conditions in AI is the RETE algorithm [For82]. It is used to incrementally evaluate rule conditions (called patterns) in the OPS5 [BFKM85] expert system shell. OPS5 is a forward-chaining production rule system where all patterns are checked using RETE. Thus, in difference to active database systems, all the instantiations of all patterns (i.e., all queries) in the current OPS5 program are incrementally maintained, and regular demand-driven database queries are not supported. In RETE the system records each incremental change (insertions or deletions, called tokens) to the stored data. For patterns that reference other patterns (i.e., derived patterns), a *propagation network* is built that incrementally maintains the instances of the derived patterns. The propagation network may contain both selections (represented as *alpha nodes*) and joins (represented as *beta nodes*). The alpha nodes (selections) are always propagated before the beta nodes (joins).

The main problem with using RETE for rule matching in large databases is that RETE is very space-inefficient for large databases since RETE saves all intermediate results for all rule conditions. RETE furthermore does not do join optimizations which may result in a combinatorical explosion of the size of the working memory [Mir87]. Its memory usage therefore often becomes substantially larger than the database itself. To improve the performance of RETE, the TREAT [Mir87] and A-TREAT [Han92] algorithms were developed. These algorithms are shown to be more efficient for large databases [WH92]. TREAT avoids the combinatorical space explosion by using relational database optimization techniques [Mir87]. A-TREAT further reduces the memory usage by avoiding to materialize some intermediate results by defining some selection nodes in the propagation network as simple relational expressions [Han92] (named *virtual alpha nodes*). A related approach is proposed in [FRS93a], where an algorithm is presented that can take a set of rules and return the set of relational expressions that is most profitable to materialize to support efficient execution of the rules. These are examples of how to trade query execution time for space in rule condition checking.

By contrast, relational differencing techniques [RCBB89] transform relational expressions into one or several incremental expressions. The nodes in the propagation network do not reflect hard-coded primitive operations as in alpha and beta nodes, but represent temporary storage of data propagated from the nodes below. The arcs represent variables in these expressions.

In the partial differencing technique described below, the propagation network will contain separate relational expressions associated with each *arc* of the network representing the specific changes coming from each input node. These partial changes are accumulated in the nodes through a special operator, called *delta-union* ($\cup_\Delta$). This has the advantage that the partial incremental expressions are simpler and more efficient to optimize and evaluate, in particular for deferred rules where few changes are made in the transaction [SR96, Sko97].

In Heraclitus [GHJ96], a database programming language is proposed that supports incremental evaluation by having deltas, i.e., incremental changes, as first class data types. This allows for different rule semantics to be implemented, but leaves it to the programmer to define how to incrementally evaluate database expressions. Since incremental expressions can be rather complicated, it is preferable if the system could automatically generate them, rather than letting the programmer explicitly define them. The Heraclitus approach is very similar to ECA rules, which also can be used to manually maintain materialized views [SJGP90].

5.3 Differencing Relational Expressions

Let P be a relation whose values depend on the values of the relations Q and R which we call the *influents* of the *affected* relation P. Thus, the definition of P is defined as some function $P = op(Q, R)$, where $op(x, y)$ is some set (or relational algebra) operator.

In *full differencing*, the changes to P are defined in terms of some combination of changes to Q and R that depend on the operator op. Thus, $\Delta P = op'(\Delta Q, \Delta R)$, where $op'(x, y)$ is an incremental version of $op(x, y)$. Full differencing of relational algebra was done by [RCBB89, BLT86] and of Datalog by [GM95, KM92, DS93]. The problem with full differencing of relational algebra or Datalog expressions is that the differential operator, $op'(x, y)$, is complex for many expressions such as SPJ joins and aggregation operators. It is therefore difficult to use conventional query optimization techniques to optimize the differentiated expressions. Also, we notice that transactions are often small with few updates, and therefore it is common that ΔP and ΔQ are not both updated in the same transaction.

Instead of full differencing, we define *partial differencing* rules where changes to P are defined in terms of separate changes for each of its influents. Let $\frac{\Delta P}{\Delta Q}$ and $\frac{\Delta P}{\Delta R}$ denote changes to P, given changes in Q and R, respectively. ΔP can be expressed as a function of the *partial differential* functions $\frac{\Delta P}{\Delta Q}$ and $\frac{\Delta P}{\Delta R}$. We will define how to automatically derive the partial differentials $\frac{\Delta P}{\Delta Q}$ and $\frac{\Delta P}{\Delta R}$ from the definition of P, and how to calculate the total change ΔP from the partial differentials. If there is an update of R, but not of Q, we can use the partial differential $\frac{\Delta P}{\Delta R}$ to compute $\Delta P = \frac{\Delta P}{\Delta R}(\Delta R)$. Analogous for changes to Q, but not to R, we define ΔP as $\Delta P = \frac{\Delta P}{\Delta Q}(\Delta Q)$. The partial differential operators $\frac{\Delta P}{\Delta Q}$ and $\frac{\Delta P}{\Delta R}$ give much less complicated expressions than the full differential operator op'.

Also notice that the partial differencing calculus itself does not say anything about what intermediate relational expressions (views) are materialized or not; it just tells how to calculate a change of an expression given a change to one of its influents. It is up to the rule compiler to use the calculus and to materialize intermediate results in the best possible way. In some cases, the incremental expressions need to refer back to the old value of some intermediate result. If the intermediate result is materialized, this a straightforward data access. If it is not materialized, the old value can still be computed by a so-called *logical rollback* defined in the calculus below.

Partial differencing has the following properties compared to other approaches for incremental evaluation:

- Often the number of updates in a transaction is small, and often one or very few tables are updated. Therefore, only one or very few partial differentials are affected and need to be checked in each transaction. Compared to using conventional finite differencing [BLT86, RCBB89], each partial differential becomes a relatively simple database query that can be optimized using traditional cost-based query optimization techniques [SAC+79]. The partial differentials can be automatically generated by a rule compiler. The regular query optimizer is then applied on the partially differenced expression, assuming few changes to a single influent. The cost model of the query optimizer should be adapted to support this assumption.

- Insertions are more common than deletions, and the calculus for deletions is much more complicated and costly than the calculus for insertions. The partial differentials for handling insertions and deletions do not have the same structure, since conditions that depend on deletions are actually historical queries that must be executed in the old database state when the deleted data were present. This makes negative differentials different, more complicated, and not easily mixable with positive ones. We therefore separately define *positive* and *negative* partial differentials, denoted $\frac{\Delta P}{\Delta_{+} Q}$ and $\frac{\Delta P}{\Delta_{-} Q}$, respectively.

Based on the calculus, an algorithm has been developed [SR96] for efficient rule condition monitoring. The algorithm propagates incremental changes through a *propagation network* that describes how each monitored condition is defined in terms of its subconditions. For correct and efficient handling of both insertions and deletions in the absence of materializations, the algorithm requires a *breadth-first, bottom-up* propagation through the propagation network. The propagation of deletions is performed only when records are deleted since the more complicated calculus for deletions make their partial differencing slower than insertions.

In order to significantly reduce permanent memory utilization, the algorithm immediately releases intermediate change materializations as the propagation proceeds upwards in the propagation network. One can regard this as if a wavefront of change materializations is propagated breadth-first up through the network.

A rule system has been implemented that uses the algorithm for monitoring complex rule conditions [SR96]. The default semantics of our active rules [RS92] uses the CA model where each rule is a pair, <Condition,Action>, where the condition is a declarative database query, and the action is a database procedural expression. ECA rules have also been implemented [Mac96] and the techniques presented here are applicable for evaluating complex rule conditions of ECA rules as well; the event part just further restricts when the condition is tested. Set-oriented action execution [WF90] is supported since data instances can be passed from the condition to the action of each rule by using shared query variables. Deferred condition evaluation is supported by delaying the condition checking until a *check* phase usually at commit time. In the check phase, change propagation is performed only when changes affecting activated rules have occurred, i.e., no overhead is placed on database operations (queries or updates) that do not affect any rules. After the change propagation, one triggered rule is chosen through a *conflict resolution method*. Then the action of the rule is executed for each instance where the rule condition is true based on the net changes of the rule condition.

Next we proceed by presenting an example incremental condition monitoring of active rules. The example will illustrate incremental evaluation by showing how our calculus is used to efficiently implement active rules in the AMOS DBMS [SR96].

5.4   Monitoring Active Rule Conditions in AMOS

Active rules have been introduced into AMOS [RS92, FRS93b] (Active Mediators Object System), an object relational DBMS. The data model of AMOS is based on the functional data model of Daplex [Shi81] and Iris [FAC⁺89]. AMOSQL, the query language of AMOS, is a derivative of OSQL [Lyn91]. The data model of Iris is based on *objects, types,* and *functions.* In AMOS, the data model is extended with *rules.* Everything in the data model is an object, including types, functions, and rules. All objects are classified as belonging to one or several types, which are equivalent to classes. Functions can be stored, derived, or foreign. Stored functions equal object attributes or base relational tables, derived functions equal methods or relational views, and foreign functions are functions written in some procedural language.[2] Stored procedures can be defined as functions that have side-effects. AMOSQL extends OSQL with active rules, a richer type system, and multidatabase functionality.

5.4.1   Rules in AMOSQL

The condition in an AMOSQL rule is a query, and the action is a procedural expression.

The syntax for the CA rules is as follows:

create rule *rule-name parameter-specification* **as**
    [**for each** *variable-declaration-commalist*]
      when *predicate-expression*
      do *procedure-expression*

The *predicate-expression* can contain any boolean expression, including conjunction, disjunction, and negation. Rules are activated and deactivated separately for different parameters.

The semantics of a rule is as follows: If an event of the database changes the truth value for some instance of the condition to *true*, the rule is marked as *triggered* for that instance. If something happens later in the transaction that causes the condition to become false again, the rule is no longer triggered. This ensures that we only react to net changes, i.e., *logical* events. A non empty result of the query that represents the condition is regarded as *true*, and an empty result is regarded as *false*.

Let us define an example database for a factory inventory:

```
create type item;
create type supplier;
create function quantity(item) -> integer;
create function max_stock(item) -> integer;
create function min_stock(item) -> integer;
create function consume_freq(item) -> integer;
create function supplies(supplier) -> item;
create function delivery_time(item,supplier) -> integer;
create function threshold(item i) -> integer as
        select consume_freq(i) * delivery_time(i, s)
                + min_stock(i)
```

---

[2]Foreign functions allow for extending the DBMS with new operations for specific database applications.

```
      for each supplier s where supplies(s) = i;
create rule monitor_items() as
      for each item i
      when quantity(i) < threshold(i)
      do order(i,max_stock(i) - quantity(i));
```

The monitor_items rule monitors the quantity of all items in stock and
orders new items when the quantity of some item drops below the threshold,
considering the time to get new items delivered. The procedure order does
the actual ordering. The consume-frequency defines how many instances of
a specific item are consumed on average per day.

Next we populate the database and activate the rule monitor_items:

```
create item instances :item1, :item2;
set max_stock(:item1) = 5000;
set max_stock(:item2) = 7500;
set min_stock(:item1) = 100;
set min_stock(:item2) = 200;
set consume_freq(:item1) = 20;
set consume_freq(:item2) = 30;
create supplier instances :sup1, :sup2;
set supplies(:sup1) = :item1;
set supplies(:sup2) = :item2;
set delivery_time(:item1, :sup1) = 2;
set delivery_time(:item2, :sup2) = 3;
activate monitor_items();
```

The activated rule will now monitor the items and trigger if the quantity falls below the threshold (i.e., below 140 of :item1 and below 290 of
:item2).

5.4.2   Rule Compilation

The rule compiler generates the condition function cnd_monitor_items
from the condition of the rule monitor_items. This function returns all
the items with quantities below the threshold. Condition monitoring is
then regarded as monitoring changes to the condition function [Ris89].

```
create function cnd_monitor_items() -> item as
      select i for each item i
      where quantity(i) < threshold(i);
```

The action part of the rule generates a stored procedure that takes an
item as argument and orders new items to fill the inventory.

```
create function act_monitor_items(item i) -> boolean as
      order(i, max_stock(i) - quantity(i));
```

At run time the `act_monitor_items` procedure will be applied to *the set of changes* calculated from the differential denoted Δcnd_monitor_items:
```
for each item i in Δcnd_monitor_items()
do act_monitor_items(i);
```
We distinguish between *strict* and *nervous* rule execution semantics [SR96]. With strict semantics, the action procedure is executed *only* when the truth value of the monitored condition changes from false to true in some transaction (i.e., we consider exactly the changes to the condition function since the last time it was checked). With nervous semantics, the rule sometimes also triggers when there has been an update that causes the rule condition to become true without having been false previously. Nervous semantics is often sufficient; however, in our example strict semantics is preferable since we only want to order an item once when it becomes low in stock.

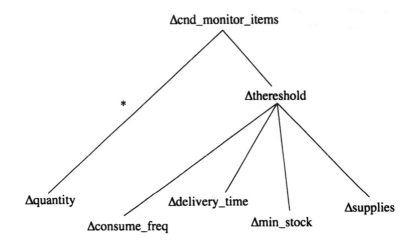

FIGURE 5.1. Dependency network of the rule condition.

By looking at the definition of `cnd_monitor_items`, we can define a *dependency network* (Figure 5.1) that specifies what changes can affect the differential Δcnd_monitor_items. Each edge in the dependency network defines the influence from one function to another. With each edge, we will later associate the partial differentials that calculate the actual influence from a particular node. For instance, Δquantity is an influent of Δcnd_monitor_items with a partial differential:

$$\frac{\Delta cnd\_monitor\_items}{\Delta quantity}$$

(the edge marked * in Figure 5.1). The dependency network is constructed from the definition of the condition function and its sub functions.

In our system, AMOSQL functions are compiled into a domain calculus language called ObjectLog [LR92], which is a variant of Datalog [Ull89], where facts and Horn Clauses are augmented with type signatures. In AMOS, stored functions are compiled into facts (base relations) and derived functions are compiled into Horn Clauses (derived relations). In our example, the system can deduce the dependency network by examining the definitions of the functions cnd_monitor_items and threshold:

$$\text{cnd\_monitor\_items}_{item}(\text{I}) \leftarrow$$
$$\quad \text{quantity}_{item,integer}(\text{I},\text{G1}) \ \wedge$$
$$\quad \text{threshold}_{item,integer}(\text{I},\text{G2}) \ \wedge$$
$$\quad \text{G1} < \text{G2}$$

$$\text{threshold}_{item,integer}(\text{I},\text{T}) \leftarrow$$
$$\quad \text{consume\_freq}_{item,integer}(\text{I},\text{G1}) \ \wedge$$
$$\quad \text{delivery\_time}_{item,supplier,integer}(\text{I},\text{G2},\text{G3}) \ \wedge$$
$$\quad \text{supplies}_{item,supplier}(\text{I},\text{G2}) \ \wedge$$
$$\quad \text{G4} = \text{G1} * \text{G3} \ \wedge$$
$$\quad \text{min\_stock}_{item,integer}(\text{I},\text{G5}) \ \wedge$$
$$\quad \text{T} = \text{G4} + \text{G5}$$

5.5   Partial Differencing

We first define a *difference calculus* as the theory for incremental computation of changes in set expressions using an extension of set algebra. The calculus is then mapped to relational algebra by defining partial differentials for the basic relational operators. The calculus is our basis for incremental evaluation of rule conditions. It formalizes update event detection and incremental change monitoring. The calculus is based on the usual set operators *union* ($\cup$), *intersection* ($\cap$), *difference* ($-$), and *complement* ($\sim$). Three new operators are introduced, *delta-plus* (Δ_+), *delta-minus* (Δ_-), and *delta-union* ($\cup_\Delta$). Δ_+ returns all tuples added to a set over a specified period of time, and Δ_- all tuples removed from the set. A *delta-set* (Δ-set) is defined as a disjoint pair $< \Delta_+S, \Delta_-S >$ for some set S, and $\cup_\Delta$ is defined as the union of two Δ-sets. The calculus is general and the section ends with partial differencing formulae of the relational algebra operators.

Separate *partial differentials* are generated for monitoring insertions and deletions for each influent of a derived relation. Positive partial differentials (insertions) are calculated in the new state of the database, while the negative partial differentials (deletions) are calculated in the old state where the deleted tuples were present in the database. The database updates are made in place, i.e., the current database state always reflects the new state.

5.5.1 Breadth-First Propagation

In some cases the old state, S_{old}, of some Δ-set is needed. This is particularly important when dealing with deletions (see [SR96, Sko97] for details).

The old state of a relation can be calculated from the new state by performing a *logical rollback* that inverts all the updates. Given the value of S_{new}, we can calculate S_{old} by inverting all operations done to S, i.e., by using

$$S_{old} = (S_{new} \cup \Delta_-S) - \Delta_+S$$

The calculus is based on accumulating all the relevant updates to base relations during a transaction. These accumulated changes are then used to calculate the partial differentials of derived relations. To make the logical rollback possible, the changes must be propagated in a breadth-first, bottom-up manner through a propagation network where the Δ-sets can be seen as temporary wave-front materializations (Figure 5.2). This is required for the logical rollback since calculating the old state, S_{old}, requires every instance of the propagated changes that influence S, i.e., the complete new Δ_+S and Δ_-S are needed in order to compute the complete S_{old}. Next we define how to accumulate these changes and how to generate partial differentials.

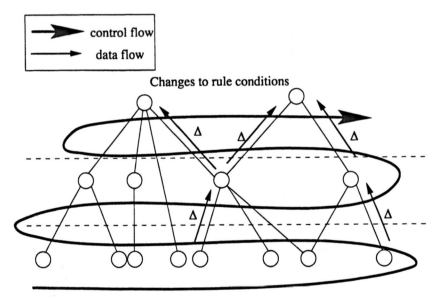

FIGURE 5.2. Breadth-first, bottom-up propagation.

In the implementation, Δ-sets are represented as temporary materializations done in the propagation algorithm and are discarded as the propagation proceeds upwards. Changes, i.e., Δ-sets, which are not referenced by any partial differentials further up in the network are discarded. This assumes that there are no loops in the network, i.e., non recursive functions. The algorithm propagates changes breadth-first by first executing all affected partial differentials of an edge (i.e., stored functions or base relations) and then by accumulating the changes in the nodes above. Here is an outline of the quite simple algorithm (see [Sko97] for more details):

```
for each level (starting with the lowest level)
      for each changed node (a non-empty Δ-set)
            for each edge to an above node
                  execute the partial differential(s)
                  and accumulate the result in the
                  Δ-set of the node above using ∪Δ
```

The Δ-sets of each node are cleared after the node has been processed, i.e., after the partial differentials that reference the Δ-sets have been executed.

5.5.2 Differencing Base Relations

All changes to base relations, i.e., stored functions, are logged as *physical events* in an undo/redo log. If there is a change to a base relation, the physical events are accumulated in a Δ-set that reflects all *logical events* of the updated relation. Only those relations that are influents of some rule condition need Δ-sets. Before the physical update events are accumulated, a simple check is made if the base relation that was updated is influencing some activated rule condition. The Δ-sets can be discarded when the changes of the affected relations have been calculated, which saves space compared to other propagation algorithms where all the change data during the complete propagation need to be retained. Since rules are only triggered by net changes, the physical events have to be added with the *delta-union* operator, $\cup_\Delta$, that cancels counteracting insertions and deletions in the Δ-set. The Δ-set for a base relation B is defined as:

$$\Delta B = \;\; <\Delta_+B, \Delta_-B>$$

where Δ_+B is the set of added tuples to B, and Δ_-B is the set of removed tuples. They are defined as:

$$\Delta_+B = \;\; B - B_{old}$$
$$\Delta_-B = \;\; B_{old} - B$$

Therefore, it holds that

$$B_{old} = (B \cup \Delta_- B) - \Delta_+ B$$

We define $\cup_\Delta$ formally as:

$$\Delta B_1 \cup_\Delta \Delta B_2 = \quad < (\Delta_+ B_1 \cup \Delta_+ B_2) - (\Delta_- B_1 \cup \Delta_- B_2),$$
$$(\Delta_- B_1 \cup \Delta_- B_2) - (\Delta_+ B_1 \cup \Delta_+ B_2) >$$

The $\cup_\Delta$ operator ensures that we only consider the net effect of updates to a function. Updates to stored functions are made by first removing the old value tuples and then adding the new ones. For example, let us update the minimum stock of some item twice, assuming that min_stock was originally 100:

```
set min_stock(:item1) = 150;
set min_stock(:item1) = 100;
```

This produces the physical update events:

```
-<min_stock,:item1,100>,
+<min_stock,:item1,150>,
-<min_stock,:item1,150>,
+<min_stock,:item1,100>.
```

The Δ-set for min_stock changes accordingly with:

```
Δ min_stock = <{},{<:item1,100>}>
Δ min_stock = <{<:item1,150>},{<:item1,100>}>
Δ min_stock = <{},{<:item1,100>}>
Δ min_stock = <{},{}>
```

i.e., there is no net effect of the updates.

5.5.3 Partial Differencing of Views

As for base relations, the Δ-set of a relational view is defined as a pair:

$$\Delta P = < \Delta_+ P, \Delta_- P >$$

We need to define how to calculate the Δ-set of an affected view in terms of the Δ-sets of its influents. To motivate our calculus, we next exemplify change monitoring of views for positive changes (adding) and negative changes (removing), respectively. We then show how to combine partial differentials into the final calculus.

Positive Partial Differentials

For a view P defined as a Horn Clause with a conjunctive body, let Ip be the set of all its influents. The positive partial differentials $\frac{\Delta P}{\Delta_+ X_i}, X_i \in I_p$ are constructed by substituting X_i in P with its positive differential $\Delta_+ X_i$.

For example, if

$$p(X, Z) \leftarrow q(X, Y) \wedge r(Y, Z)$$

then

$$\frac{\Delta p(X, Z)}{\Delta_+ q} \leftarrow \Delta_+ q(X, Y) \wedge r(Y, Z)$$

and

$$\frac{\Delta p(X, Z)}{\Delta_+ r} \leftarrow q(X, Y) \wedge \Delta_+ r(Y, Z)$$

If the old database state consists of the stored relations (facts)

```
q(1, 1)
r(1, 2)
r(2, 3)
```

then we can derive

```
p(1, 2)
```

A transaction performs the updates

```
assert q(1, 2)
assert r(1, 4)
```

The new state of the database now becomes

```
q(1, 1)
q(1, 2)
r(1, 2)
r(1, 4)
r(2, 3)
```

and we can derive

```
p(1, 2)
p(1, 3)
p(1, 4)
```

The updates give the Δ-sets,

```
Δq = <{<1,2>},{}>
Δr = <{<1,4>},{}>
```

Then

$$\frac{\Delta p(X,Z)}{\Delta_+ q} = <\{<1,3>\},\{\}>$$

and

$$\frac{\Delta p(X,Z)}{\Delta_{+}r} = <\{<\text{1,4}>\},\{\}>$$

and joining with $\cup_{\Delta}$ finally gives

$$\Delta p = <\{<\text{1,3}>,<\text{1,4}>\},\{\}>$$

The AMOSQL compiler expands as many derived relations as possible to have more degrees of freedom for optimizations. The condition function of our running example will be expanded to:

cnd_monitor_items$_{item}$(I) $\leftarrow$
        quantity$_{item,integer}$(I,G1) $\wedge$
        consume_freq$_{item,integer}$(I,G2) $\wedge$
        delivery_time$_{item,supplier,integer}$(I,G3,G4) $\wedge$
        supplies$_{item,supplier}$(I,G3) $\wedge$
        G5 = G2 * G4 $\wedge$
        min_stock$_{item,integer}$(I,G6) $\wedge$
        G7 = G5 + G6 $\wedge$
        G1 < G7

The positive partial differential based on the influent quantity is defined as:

Δcnd_monitor_items$_{item}$(I)/Δ_{+}quantity $\leftarrow$
        Δ_{+}quantity$_{item,integer}$(I,G1) $\wedge$
        consume_freq$_{item,integer}$(I,G2) $\wedge$
        delivery_time$_{item,supplier,integer}$(I,G3,G4) $\wedge$
        supplies$_{item,supplier}$(I,G3) $\wedge$
        G5 = G2 * G4 $\wedge$
        min_stock$_{item,integer}$(I,G6) $\wedge$
        G7 = G5 + G6 $\wedge$
        G1 < G7

The other differentials

Δcnd_monitor_items/Δ_{+}consume_freq
Δcnd_monitor_items/Δ_{+}supplies
Δcnd_monitor_items/Δ_{+}min_stock

are defined likewise. Using these partial differentials, we can build a *propagation network* for cnd_monitor_items by associating the partial differentials with the arcs of a flattened version of the dependency network in Figure 5.1.

The propagation network for cnd_monitor_items is flat since the AMOS query compiler expands functions as much as possible. In the case of *late binding*[3] [FR95], this is not possible and the result is a more bushy network.

---

[3]Late binding means that some types of information cannot be determined at compile

Bushy networks are sometimes preferable since they can promote node sharing between nodes shared by different rule conditions.

Negative Partial Differentials

Often the rule condition depends only on positive changes, as for the monitor_items rule. However, for negation and aggregation operators, negative changes must be propagated as well. For strict rule semantics, propagation of negative changes is also necessary for rules whose actions negatively affect other rules' conditions. See [SR96] for details.

Partial Differentials of Intersection, Union, and Set-Complement

Let $\Delta_+ P$ be the set of additions (positive changes) to a view P, and $\Delta_- P$ be the set of deletions (negative changes) from P. As before, the Δ-set of P, ΔP, is a pair of the positive and the negative changes of P:

$$\Delta P = < \Delta_+ P, \Delta_- P >$$

As for base relations, we formally define the delta-union, $\cup_\Delta$, over differentials as:

$$\Delta P_1 \cup_\Delta \Delta P_2 = \begin{aligned} &< (\Delta_+ P_1 \cup \Delta_+ P_2) - (\Delta_- P_1 \cup \Delta_- P_2), \\ &(\Delta_- P_1 \cup \Delta_- P_2) - (\Delta_+ P_1 \cup \Delta_+ P_2) > \end{aligned}$$

Next we define the partial differential, $\frac{\Delta P}{\Delta X}$, that incrementally monitors changes to P from changes of each influent X. Partial differencing of a relation is defined as generating partial differentials for all the influents of the relation. The net changes of the partial differentials are accumulated (using $\cup_\Delta$) into ΔP.

Let I_p be the set of all relations that P depends on. The Δ-set of P, ΔP, is then defined by:

$$\Delta P = \cup_\Delta \frac{\Delta P}{\Delta X} = \cup_\Delta < \frac{\Delta P}{\Delta_+ X}, \frac{\Delta P}{\Delta_- X} >, \forall X \in I_p$$

For example, if P depends on the relations Q and R, then:

$$\Delta P = \frac{\Delta P}{\Delta Q} \cup_\Delta \frac{\Delta P}{\Delta R} = < \frac{\Delta P}{\Delta_+ Q}, \frac{\Delta P}{\Delta_- Q} > \cup_\Delta < \frac{\Delta P}{\Delta_+ R}, \frac{\Delta P}{\Delta_- R} >$$

To detect changes of derived relations, we define intersection (conjunction), union (disjunction), and complement (negation) in terms of their differentials as:

---

time (early binding) and must instead be determined at run time.

$$\Delta(Q \cap R) = \quad < (\Delta_+Q \cap R) \cup (Q \cap \Delta_+R), \{\} >$$
$$\cup_\Delta$$
$$< \{\}, (\Delta_-Q \cap R_{old}) \cup (Q_{old} \cap \Delta_-R >$$

$$\Delta(Q \cup R) = \quad < (\Delta_+Q - R_{old}) \cup (\Delta_+R - Q_{old}), \{\} >$$
$$\cup_\Delta$$
$$< \{\}, (\Delta_-Q - R) \cup (\Delta_-R - Q) >$$

$$\Delta(\sim Q) = \quad\quad\quad < \Delta_-Q, \Delta_+Q >$$

Note that for unions, any overlaps between the added (removed) tuples and the old state (new state) of the other part of the union are removed. From the expressions above, we can easily generate the simpler expressions in the case of, e.g., insertions only. For example, when only considering insertions, changes to intersections are defined as:

$$\Delta_+(Q \cap R) = (\Delta_+Q \cap R) \cup (Q \cap \Delta_+R)$$

Partial Differencing of the Relational Operators

The calculus of partial differencing can easily be applied to the relational algebra to incrementally evaluate its operators. This is illustrated in table 5.1. This was generated by separating the expressions above for insertions and deletions and by using the definitions of the relational operators in terms of set operations. Note the table assumes set-oriented semantics and that $Q - R$ can be rewritten as $Q \cap (\sim R)$. See [Sko97] for more details.

P	$\dfrac{\Delta P}{\Delta_+Q}$	$\dfrac{\Delta P}{\Delta_+R}$	$\dfrac{\Delta P}{\Delta_-Q}$	$\dfrac{\Delta P}{\Delta_-R}$
$\sigma_{cond}Q$	$\sigma_{cond}\Delta_+Q$		$\sigma_{cond}\Delta_-Q$	
$\pi_{attr}Q$	$\pi_{attr}\Delta_+Q$		$\pi_{attr}\Delta_-Q$	
$Q \cup R$	$\Delta_+Q - R_{old}$	$\Delta_+R - Q_{old}$	$\Delta_-Q - R$	$\Delta_-R - Q$
$Q - R$	$\Delta_+Q - R$	$Q \cap \Delta_-R$	$\Delta_-Q - R_{old}$	$Q_{old} \cap \Delta_+R$
$Q \times R$	$\Delta_+Q \times R$	$Q \times \Delta_+R$	$\Delta_-Q \times R_{old}$	$Q_{old} \times \Delta_-R$
$Q \bowtie R$	$\Delta_+Q \bowtie R$	$Q \bowtie \Delta_+R$	$\Delta_-Q \bowtie R_{old}$	$Q_{old} \bowtie \Delta_-R$
$Q \cap R$	$\Delta_+Q \cap R$	$Q \cap \Delta_+R$	$\Delta_-Q \cap R_{old}$	$Q_{old} \cap \Delta_-R$

Table 5.1 Partial differencing of the relational operators.

5.6   Conclusion

This chapter presented incremental evaluation techniques for efficient monitoring of complex rule conditions. An overview of incremental evaluation techniques was given. A difference calculus was presented for incremental evaluation of queries, based on database updates. The calculus defines partial differentials of rule conditions as separate queries that each considers changes to a single relation that influences a monitored rule condition. The advantage of incremental evaluation in general is the efficiency that comes from the assumption that most transactions only perform small changes to rule conditions, and it is therefore cheaper to incrementally change a materialized rule condition than to recompute it in every transaction. Partial differencing has the additional advantages that only a few (or just one) partial differentials are normally executed in each transaction. The partial differentials are much simpler and more efficient than the combined full differentials, in particular when combining partial differentials for both positive (insertions) and negative (deletions) changes. The calculus also defines how to calculate the old database state without materializing. A breadth-first, bottom-up propagation algorithm is used where changes can be discarded as the propagation proceeds upwards in the propagation network. This propagation algorithm is fast, space-efficient, and supports logical rollbacks.

5.7 REFERENCES

[BFKM85] L.Brownston, R.Farrell, E.Kant, and N.Martin. *Programming Expert Systems in OPS5.* Addison-Wesley, 1985.

[BLT86] J.A. Blakely, P-Å. Larson, and F.W. Tompa. Efficiently Updating Materialized Views. In *SIGMOD Conf.*, pages 61–71, 1986.

[CW91] S.Ceri and J.Widom. Deriving Production Rules for Incremental View Maintenance. In R.Camps, G.M.Lohman, A.Sernadas, editors, *17th Intl. Conf. on Very Large Data Bases*, pages 577–589. Morgan Kaufmann, 1991.

[DS93] G.Dong and J.Su. First-Order Incremental Evaluation of Datalog Queries. In *4th Intl. Workshop on Database Programming Languages*, pages 295–308, 1993.

[FAC+89] D.Fishman, J.Annevelink, E.Chow, T.Connors, J.W. Davis, W.Hasan, C.G. Hoch, W.Kent, S.Leichner, P.Lyngbaek, B.Mahbod, M.A. Neimat, T.Risch, M.C. Chan, and W.K. Wilkinson. Overview of the Iris DBMS. In W. Kim and F.H. Lochovsky, editors, *Object-Oriented Concepts, Databases, and Applications*, pages 219–250. ACM Press, 1989.

[For82] C.L. Forgy.   Rete: A Fast Algorithm for the Many Pattern/Many Object Pattern Match Problem. *Artificial Intelligence*, 19(1):17–37, 1982.

[FR95]   S.Flodin and T.Risch. Processing Object-Oriented Queries
            with Invertible Late Bound Functions. In *21st Intl. Conf. on
            Very Large Data Bases (VLDB'95)*, pages 335–344, 1995.

[FRS93a]   F.Fabret, M.Regnier, and E.Simon. An Adaptive Algorithm
            for Incremental Evaluation of Production Rules in Databases.
            In R.Agrawal, S.Baker, and D.Bell, editors, *19th Intl. Conf.
            on Very Large Data Bases*, pages 455–466. Morgan Kaufmann,
            1993.

[FRS93b]   G.Fahl, T.Risch, and M.Sköld. AMOS–an Architecture for Ac-
            tive Mediators. In *Intl. Workshop on Next Generation Infor-
            mation Technologies and Systems (NGITS'93)*, pages 47–53,
            1993.

[GHJ96]   S.Ghandeharizadeh, R.Hull, and D.Jacobs. Heraclitus: Ele-
            vating Deltas to be First-Class Citizens in a Database Pro-
            gramming Language. *ACM Transactions on Database Systems*,
            21(3):370–426, 9 1996.

[GM95]   A.Gupta and I.S. Mumick. Maintenance of Materialized Views:
            Problems, Techniques and Applications. *IEEE Quarterly Bul-
            letin on Data Engineering*, 18(2), 1995.

[Han92]   E.N. Hanson. Rule Condition Testing and Action Execution in
            Ariel. In *Proc. SIGMOD*, pages 49–58. ACM, 1992.

[HD91]   J.D. Harrison and S.W. Dietrich. Condition Monitoring in an
            Active Deductive Database. Technical Report TR-91-022, Ari-
            zona State University, 12 1991.

[KM92]   A.G.D. Katiyar and I.S. Mumick. Maintaining Views Incre-
            mentally. Technical Report, AT&T Bell Laboratories, 1992.

[KP81]   S.Koenig and R.Paige. A Transformational Framework for the
            Automatic Control of Derived Data. In *Proc. 7th Intl. Conf.
            on Very Large Data Bases*, pages 306–318. IEEE, 1981.

[LR92]   W.Litwin and T.Risch. Main Memory Oriented Optimization
            of OO Queries Using Typed Datalog with Foreign Predicates.
            IEEE Transactions on Knowledge and Data Engineering, 4(6),
            12 1992.

[Lyn91]   P.Lyngbaek. OSQL: A Language for Object Databases. Tech-
            nical Report HPL-DTD-91-4, Hewlett-Packard Laboratories, 1
            1991.

[Mac96]   S-A. Machani.   Events in an Object Relational Database System. Technical Report LiTH-IDA-Ex-9634, University of Linköping, 1996.

[Mir87]   D.P. Miranker. TREAT: A Better Match Algorithm for AI Production Systems. In *Proc. AAAI*, pages 42–47, 1987.

[PK92]   R.Paige and S.Koenig. Finite Differencing of Computable Expressions. *ACM Transactions on Programming Languages and Systems*, 4(2):402–454, 1992.

[QW91]   X.Qian and G.Wiederhold. Incremental Recomputation of Active Relational Expressions. *IEEE Transactions on Knowledge and Data Engineering*, 3(3):337–341, 1991.

[RCBB89]   A.Rosenthal, S.Chakravarthy, B.Blaustein, and J.Blakeley. Situation Monitoring for Active Databases. In M.G. Apers and G. Wiederhold, editors, *Proc. 15th Intl. Conf. on Very Large Data Bases*, pages 455–464, 1989.

[Ris89]   T.Risch. Monitoring Database Objects. In P.M.G. Apers and G. Wiederhold, editors, *Proc. 15th Intl. Conf. on Very Large Databases*, pages 445–453, 8 1989.

[RS92]   T.Risch and M.Sköld. Active Rules Based on Object Oriented Queries. *IEEE Quarterly Bulletin on Data Engineering*, Special Issue on Active Databases, 1992.

[SAC+79]   P.Selinger, M.M. Astrahan, R.A. Chamberlin, R.A. Lorie, and T.G. Price. Access Path Selection in a Relational Database Management System. In *SIGMOD Conf.*, pages 23–54. ACM, 1979.

[Shi81]   D.W. Shipman. The Functional Data Model and the Data Language Daplex. *ACM Transactions on Database Systems*, 6(1), 3 1981.

[SJGP90]   M.Stonebraker, A.Jhingran, J.Goh, and S.Potamianos. On Rules, Procedures, Caching and Views in Database Systems. In *Proc. ACM SIGMOD*, pages 281–290, 1990.

[Sko97]   M.Skold. *Active Database Management Systems for Monitoring and Control.* Dissertation No. 494. Linköping University, 9 1997.

[SR96]   M.Sköld and T.Risch. Using Partial Differencing for Efficient Monitoring of Deferred Complex Rule Conditions. In Stanley Y.W. Su, editor, *Proc. 12th Intl. Conf. on Data Engineering*, pages 392–401. IEEE Computer Society Press, 1996.

[Ull89]   J.D Ullman. *Principles of Database and Knowledge-Base Systems*, Volume I & II. Computer Science Press, 1989.

[WF90]   J.Widom and S.J. Finkelstein. Set-Oriented Production Rules in Relational Database Systems. In *Proceedings of the ACM SIGMOD International Conference on Management of Data*, pages 259–270, 1990.

[WH92]   Y-W Wang and E.N. Hanson. A Performance Comparison of the Rete and TREAT Algorithms for Testing Database Rule Conditions. In *Proc. Data Engineering*, pages 88–97. IEEE, 1992.

6

Performance Assessment

Andreas Geppert and Klaus R. Dittrich

ABSTRACT
This chapter addresses performance evaluation of active database systems.
We first analyze potential performance gains and losses of ADBMS applications in comparison to passive solutions, and identify performance-critical
aspects of ADBMS's. We then describe the Beast benchmark which has
been proposed for measuring the performance of object-oriented ADBMS's
and present results obtained from running Beast on SAMOS. We conclude
the chapter by identifying possibilities for optimizing ADBMS's and tuning
their applications.

6.1 Introduction

Like any other kind of software system, ADBMS's have to provide their
functionality in an efficient way. Thus, tools and frameworks are needed
that allow assessment of the performance of ADBMS's in a systematic, fair,
and reproducible way. In other words, *benchmarks* [Gra93, Jai91], have to
be developed that allow evaluation and comparison of ADBMS's from a
performance point of view.

Such a benchmark should make it possible to enhance the knowledge
about ADBMS implementation in several ways:

- it allows comparison of ADBMS implementations from a performance
  point of view,

- it helps to identify trade-offs between functionality and performance,

- it contributes to better understanding of tuning techniques,

- it enables users to select an ADBMS appropriate for application domains with certain characteristics and requirements.

Current ADBMS's differ in various respects. For instance, different architectural styles have been proposed (namely, layered or integrated; see Chapter 2 in this volume), and thus the impact of style on performance needs
to be investigated. For instance, as has been stated elsewhere [BZBW95],
integrated architectures are expected to exhibit better performance. Likewise, different techniques have been proposed for some ADBMS tasks such

as composite event detection (e.g., finite state automata [GJS92, LGA96], event trees [CKAK94], Petri-Nets [GD94], and arrays [Eri93]). It is worthwhile to assess the impact of these different techniques on performance.

ADBMS's also differ with respect to functionality, for instance, according to the set of event type constructors or the consumption mode(s) they support. Thus, it is necessary to analyze whether and which trade-offs between functionality and performance exist.

Finally, the understanding of bottlenecks and performance trade-offs shows where tuning facilities are required and need to be developed. A benchmark also helps to evaluate the quality of tuning techniques. Once these issues are better understood, a benchmark helps with selection of an ADBMS for their specific application domains.

Thus, a benchmark dedicated to ADBMS's is definitely needed, and performance issues in general and benchmarks in particular are commonly seen as urgent research issues in the field [Wid94]. However, while a benchmark usually proposes a *typical application* for the kind of system under consideration, this is not straightforward for ADBMS's. (Note that potential applications range from DBMS internal tasks like integrity constraint and view maintenance to complex applications such as workflow and energy management [CW96]). Thus, before the selection of ADBMS's based on benchmark results can be addressed, potential applications must be understood to a much greater degree [Day95] than is currently the case. This paper hence focuses on the other purposes of ADBMS performance assessment (the first three issues itemized early in this section).

6.2   Performance-Critical Aspects of Active Database Systems

In this section, we analyze the factors that are likely to influence the performance of an ADBMS or ADBMS application. We first consider performance of ADBMS applications, followed by an investigation of performance-critical features of ADBMS's.

6.2.1   Performance of Active Database Applications

From a user and application-oriented point of view, the most interesting question is how efficient applications of ADBMS's are in comparison to passive applications addressing the same tasks. Since current ADBMS applications typically use a relational DBMS, we implicitly assume a relational ADBMS for the remainder of this section.

When comparing the performance of passive and active applications, it is crucial to compare *equivalent applications*, i.e., an application using ECA rules with an application that implements the semantics of the ECA rules in a purely passive way. A conclusion can then be drawn as to whether or not the usage of ECA rules is beneficial with respect to performance. Additionally, the applications considered should comprise tasks that are commonly supported by ECA rules, i.e., they should implement consistency constraints, materialized views, etc.

Currently, such systematic comparisons are not available. The obvious difficulty is that real applications are too complex to reimplement on top of an ADBMS purely for the sake of carrying out performance comparisons. Implementing a (real and large) active application a second time without using ECA rules is time-consuming and thus does not make sense either. As a result, only a few reports on experiences exist [SKD95, BZB97].

Subsequently, we analyze the factors that are likely to influence performance of ADBMS applications. The hypotheses presented tend to confirm the experiences reported in [SKD95]. The impact of most of these factors on performance should yet be validated by measurements.

Active applications are likely to be less efficient than passive ones for a number of reasons. First, in a typical application of current (relational) ADBMS products, everything that can be done with triggers can also be done in the application. A typical transaction reads input data, reads data elements out of the database, perhaps gathers more input data, performs checks, and updates the retrieved data. In this way, consistency constraints can be checked perfectly adequately in the application program, especially since for many constraints the data already resides in the buffer of the application. On the other hand, if triggers are used for constraint maintenance, modified tuples have to be identified, deltas may have to be collected, and rules have to be fired. Intuitively, the latter approach is less efficient than the former. This may be different if constraints concern other tuples (not yet in the application's buffer). In such a case, control must cross the interface between the application and the DBMS multiple times, which is unnecessary in the active solution.

Second, in current ADBMS products, triggers are executed *within* the triggering transaction, since decoupling of trigger execution from the triggering transaction is not supported. The overall transaction size is thus roughly the same, regardless of whether triggers are used or their effect is implemented in a hard-wired way. However, transaction size can be decreased by decoupling trigger execution. This has been identified as a major performance gain in simulative studies [CJL91]. Since the flexibility of using triggers also implies more overhead (within the DBMS) while transaction size is not reduced, again the overall result is worse performance.

Third, there is so far little experience and know-how in optimizing transactions that can fire triggers [SKD95], while the tuning of passive transactions is a well-understood issue.

On the other hand, there are also reasons giving rise to the expectation of better active application performance. First, the number of context switches between an application and the DBMS (i.e., how often the interface between the two must be crossed during a transaction) is a factor. Using triggers, a significant number of actions to be performed "move into the DBMS server" and thus require fewer context switches, which finally can lead to better performance.

Second, triggers can be disabled (either internally by the ADBMS or explicitly by the database administrator) if they are known not to be fired for a certain period of time, while switching off code fragments in an application program is more difficult. Disabling triggers results in fewer triggers fired, fewer conditions to be evaluated, and thus in smaller transaction size.

Third, if trigger executions can be decoupled from the triggering transaction, performance can be improved. Although this "transaction chopping" [SLSV95] leads to a higher number of (concurrent) transactions, each of these is smaller and holds locks for shorter periods of time. Thus, overall performance of sets of concurrent transactions will be better in this way.

Finally, advanced ADBMS can provide functionality that is only hard to implement in a passive way (and subject to performance overhead). This is especially the case for those rules needing composite events. For instance, consider events modeling specific evolutions of an object/tuple, e.g., dynamic consistency constraints. As an example, consider a sequence of operations on (or state changes to) an object that are required or prohibited, e.g., a maximal number of salary raises that are permitted during one year. Such situations can be modeled with powerful event constructors; they are, however, hard to monitor passively. In addition, keeping track of such developments in a passive way requires additional data to be kept in the database and additional actions in applications, and thus is likely to be less efficient in a passive application.

Note that the last two of the aforementioned concepts are supported by some prototypes, while they are not yet implemented in current products. This helps to explain why the performance of ADBMS product applications is experienced to be worse when compared to passive solutions.

6.2.2   Performance-Critical Aspects of Active Database Management Systems

In this section, we investigate the performance-relevant factors of ADBMS's. We consider ADBMS's with powerful rule definition languages and execution models. Since these are typically found in object-oriented ADBMS's, we consider such systems for the rest of the section.

Event Detection. The event detection method employed is expected to have a great impact on performance, since there are different strategies that can be pursued:

- event detection can be done locally or centrally,
- it can be implemented according to different techniques (e.g., finite state machines, syntax trees, Petri-Nets).

Local event detection means that events are detected within objects or that dedicated event detectors are used. For instance, Ode uses class-specific local event detectors [LGA96], and events/rules are specified as a part of class definitions. In this case, each object (whose class defines one or more triggers) detects events that happen at that object. Event-specific local detection uses one event detector per event type (e.g., each method event type used in one or more ECA rules has its own event detector). Programs or objects that can generate events of a certain type maintain references to the corresponding event detector, which is notified whenever the event occurs. This approach partitions the global event detector. It is thus beneficial with respect to performance, since the relevant portion of the global event detector need not be identified upon event occurrences, and because each detector can exactly maintain the information, e.g., on component events, that is needed.

The *centralized approach* uses a small set of event detectors, each one responsible for a class of event types (e.g., transaction events, composite events). Thus, all events are signaled through the same function, and relevant structures needed for composite event detection have first to be identified and retrieved before composite event detection can proceed and rules to be executed can be determined. Such a centralized detector is likely to become a bottleneck especially in multi-user mode.

In event-specific and centralized approaches, event and rule definitions are likely to be stored as database objects, while in the class-specific approach, they are part of class definitions. Since storing ECA rules as database objects means pursuing a (partially) interpretive approach, we expect performance to be worse than for a compilation-based alternative using class-specific ECA rules and event detection (see also [AMC93] for that matter).

Ultimately, different techniques have been proposed for composite event detection. It is therefore necessary to compare them from a performance point of view.

Event (History) Management and Event Consumption. Since a composite event is built using component events, the composite event detector has to check whether there are candidate components available, and, if so, it has to select appropriate ones for forming the new composition. Thus, it is performance-critical to maintain these histories in such a way that retrieval of component occurrences is fast, since the set of component candidates can be very large.

The consumption mode can also be performance-critical—especially if large sets of component occurrences exist (and therefore have to be browsed in order to determine components for composition). In particular, we expect the **recent** mode to be the most efficient consumption mode, since it is rather immune to large backlogs of component occurrences.

Rule Execution. Condition evaluation and action execution also influence ADBMS performance. In the brute-force solution, each condition evaluation or action execution interrupts application program execution and the ADBMS process; if there are multiple rules to be triggered, the ADBMS executes them sequentially. In more sophisticated implementations, the ADBMS is able to evaluate conditions and to execute actions concurrently with its "normal" processing. If there are multiple rules to be executed at one point in time, they could also be executed concurrently (unless their execution order is constrained by priorities). Such concurrent execution is likely to speed up the ADBMS.

Furthermore, a sophisticated ADBMS might apply techniques proposed for query evaluation and production rule processing to optimize condition evaluation (e.g., several similar or even identical conditions may have to be evaluated together at times. Then, the optimizer could recognize that the common parts need to be evaluated only once, decreasing overall condition evaluation time; See Chapter 4 in this volume).

Impact of Architectural Style. By architectural style, we mean how the ADBMS is structured. In an integrated architecture, the active components are integrated with the passive parts. Components such as event detectors and rule execution components can easily interface with other components and can access their information. It is also possible to modify the passive part when implementing the active behavior. In the layered architecture, the active functionality is implemented on top of a passive one, and passive components cannot be extended or modified. It has been claimed elsewhere [BZBW95] that better opportunities to integrate active and passive components in the integrated architecture leads to better performance.

Impact of (Growing) Rulebase Size. While the aforementioned aspects refer to the ADBMS itself and its components, the final performance-critical aspect is the rulebase, i.e., the set of currently defined event types and rules. A practically useful ADBMS must be able to handle large rulebases with reasonable performance, i.e., it should scale well, preferably (almost) constantly for growing rulebases. The ADBMS should thereby not only scale well for growing numbers of event types, but also for growing sets of event occurrences (i.e., large event histories).

Cross-Effects. Each of these aspects cannot be considered separately, but there will typically be dependencies between them. For instance, performance can be traded for functionality, and the efficiency of an event detection technique depends on the event consumption mode.

6.3   Performance Measurement of Active Database Management Systems

In this section we elaborate on the Beast benchmark [GGD95a], which is the first benchmark addressing the aspects mentioned above, and which has been used to assess the performance of multiple ADBMS's [GBLR96]. The following elaborations follow the description of Beast in [GBLR96].

6.3.1   Benchmark Design

Beast is a benchmark for object-oriented ADBMS's. It uses the OO7 benchmark [CDN93] schema and programs to populate the databases. One reason for reusing parts of OO7 is to obtain a schema and database easily. Moreover, for a given object-oriented ADBMS, Beast and OO7 together measure the performance of both the active and the passive parts of a system, respectively. Beast defines several tests for event detection, rule management, and rule execution. Thus, the result of running Beast is a collection of figures instead of a single figure for each ADBMS (much like OO7). Note that we cannot test the performance of each component directly, due to lack of access to internal interfaces of an ADBMS. Therefore, most Beast tests specify one or more rules that are triggered when executing the test, i.e., the test actually causes the event occurrence. To stress the performance of single phases (event detection, rule retrieval, action execution), we keep all other phases as small as possible. For instance, a rule testing event detection performance simply defines the condition to be false, so that condition evaluation is cheap and no action is executed. Additionally, only one rule is triggered by such an event to minimize the rule management overhead.

Subsequently, we present the various tests. The rules used are specified in pseudo-syntax. Unless stated otherwise, the coupling mode is **immediate** and no priorities are used.

Tests for Primitive Event Detection. Two Beast tests refer to primitive detection:

1. detection of method invocation (ED-02),

2. detection of transaction events (ED-03).

We illustrate the execution of tests with the test ED-02. First, the actual time is obtained, and then the event is forced to occur multiple times (in this case, a method is invoked). Note that in this way, we know the point in time of event occurrence. The ADBMS subsequently detects the event, determines attached rules, and executes them. It then returns control to the test program. Finally, the test program again records the time and computes the elapsed time.

The tests ED-02 and ED-03 (see Figure 6.1) measure detection of single events. The corresponding rules for all tests have a false condition and an empty action in order to restrict the measured time to event detection, as far as possible. Coupling modes for actions and conditions are immediate.

```
RULE ED-02
ON    before AtomicPart->DoNothing // method event
IF    false
DO    ...


Rule ED-03
ON    before commit(ED03_TX)        // commit event
IF    false
DO    ...
```

FIGURE 6.1. Beast tests for primitive event detection.

Composite Event Detection. Composite event detection typically starts after a (primitive or other composite) event has been detected. The event detector then checks whether the detected event participates in a composite event. This is generally done in a stepwise manner, e.g., by means of syntax trees [CKAK94], automata [LGA96], or Petri-Nets [GD94]. Composite event detection is measured through tests ED-06-11.

In order to stress the time needed for composite event detection, we use abstract events in the definitions of composite events wherever possible. Using abstract events enables more accurate measurements, since only the time for event signaling is required and primitive event detection is not necessary. In order to measure the entire event composition, the tests raise the component events directly one after the other.

Beast contains six tests for the detection of composite events (Figure 6.2):

1. detection of a sequence of primitive events (ED-06),

2. detection of the non-occurrence of an event within a transaction (negative event, ED-07),

3. detection of the repeated (ten times) occurrence of a primitive event (ED-08),

4. detection of a sequence of events that are in turn composite (ED-09),

5. detection of a conjunction of method events occurring for the same object (ED-10),

6. detection of a conjunction of events raised within the same transaction (ED-11).

```
RULE ED-06
ON    EvED-061 ; EvED-062 //composite event: sequence

RULE ED-07 //negative event within a named transaction
ON    ! EvED-07 within [begin(ED07_TX), commit(ED07_TX)]

RULE ED-08
ON    times (EvED-081, 10) //EvED-081 occurs ten times

RULE ED-09 //times event, then disjunction and abstract event
ON    times (EvED-091, 3) ; (EvED-092 | EvED-093) ; EvED-094

RULE ED-10 //method event sequence with identical receivers
ON    Module->DoNothing ; Module->setDate : same object

RULE ED-11 //conjunction of method events in same trans.
ON    AtomicPart->setX & AtomicPart->setY : same transaction
```

FIGURE 6.2. Beast tests for composite event detection.

Tests ED-06 through ED-08 measure event detection for common composite event constructors. Test ED-09 considers one specific constructor applied to events that are in turn composite. Finally, ED-10 and ED-11 measure the performance of event detection when the events of interest are restricted by event parameters.

Tests for Rule Management. Another group of tests considers rule management. It is based on the observation that an ADBMS has to store and retrieve the definition and implementation of rules, be it in the database, as external code linked to the code of the ADBMS, or as interpreted code. Clearly, the time it takes to retrieve rules influences ADBMS performance. Rule management tests measure rule retrieval time, but they do not consider rule definition and rule storage. These services are used infrequently, and thus their efficient implementation is less important.

The test RM-1 (see Figure 6.3) raises an abstract event, evaluates a condition to false, and therefore does not execute any action. The three parts are kept so simple in order to restrict the measured time to the rule retrieval time as far as possible.

```
RULE RM-01
ON    EvRM-01 // abstract event
IF    false
DO    ...
```

FIGURE 6.3. Beast test for rule management.

Tests for Rule Execution. The tests for rule execution are separated into two groups: one for the execution of single rules, and one for the execution of multiple rules. The first group of tests (RE-01 through RE-03) determines how quickly rules can be executed. The execution of a single rule consists of loading the code for conditions and actions and of processing or interpreting these code fragments. Different approaches for linking and processing condition and action parts can be compared by means of the tests in this group. Different strategies can also be applied for executing multiple rules all triggered by the same event (e.g., sequential or concurrent execution). The performance characteristics of these approaches are tested by the second subgroup.

```
RULE      RE-01
ON        EvRE-01     // abstract event
IF        true
DO        print("Executing RE-01");


RULE      RE-02
ON        EvRE-02     // condition and action as in RE-01
COUPLING (immediate. deferred)


RULE      RE-03
ON        EvRE-03     // condition and action as in RE-01
COUPLING (immediate. decoupled)


RULE RE-04a
ON    Document->DoNothing     // method event
IF    oid->searchString("I am") > 0     // oid is the receiver
DO    print("Document contains 'I am'");


RULE RE-04b ...                //event and condition as in RE-04a
DO    oid->setAuthor();


RULE RE-04c ...                //event and condition as in RE-04a
DO    oid->setDate();


RULE RE-04d ...                //event and condition as in RE-04a
DO    oid->replaceText("I am","This is");
```

FIGURE 6.4. Beast tests for primitive event detection.

For the execution of single rules, we consider three rules with different coupling modes. An abstract event is used, the condition is always true, and the action is a print command in rules RE-01, -02, and -03. The coupling mode of the condition is always **immediate**. The coupling modes of the actions are immediate (RE-01), deferred (RE-02), and decoupled (RE-03). The intention of these tests is to measure the overhead needed for storing the fact that the action still needs to be executed at the end of the transaction (RE-02), as well as the overhead necessary to start a new transaction in RE-03. In order to stress these aspects of rule execution, we use an abstract event to avoid event detection, and use a simple true condition and a simple action. Note that the performance of condition evaluation and action execution is not of interest, because it is determined by the passive part of the DBMS.

The fourth test (RE-04, see Figure 6.4) for rule execution considers four rules all triggered by the same event. Conditions and actions are more complex than in the previous tests, in order to observe the effects of optimizing the condition evaluation and of concurrency. All RE-04 rules have the same condition. Hence, an ADBMS that recognizes that the actions do not affect the truth of the condition and that the conditions are identical (e.g., if it is able to optimize sets of conditions) will perform better than a non-optimizing ADBMS. All rules have the coupling modes (immediate, immediate). No ordering is defined for the four rules. An ADBMS that is able to process conditions and actions in parallel or at least concurrently will thus perform better in this test. The test RE-05 is similar to RE-04, with the exception that priorities are specified.

6.3.2   Factors and Modes

A crucial step when designing a benchmark is the proper identification of factors [Jai91], i.e., parameters that influence performance measurements. Several parameters of a database can have an impact on the performance of an ADBMS. In addition to the database parameters relevant for benchmarking a passive DBMS (e.g., database size, buffer size, page size, etc.), these include:

- the number of defined event types,

- the number of defined rules,

- the number of partially processed (i.e., not yet consumed) event occurrences in the system.

In the ideal case, the time to detect events is constant, i.e., independent of the number of defined event types. However, especially for composite events, it may be the case that the event detection process for single events slows down as more events are added to the system. Furthermore, an ADBMS needs to store and retrieve internal information on event definitions during (or after) event detection. Clearly, a large number of event definitions can increase the time needed to retrieve event information. It is thus worth investigating how large execution times are when the number of events increases. This number is therefore included as a factor. In general, about 50 percent of the events are defined as composite events.

Furthermore, the total number of rules defined is relevant for performance. Recall that rule information has to be retrieved before rule execution. While a small number of rules can be entirely loaded into main memory without problems when the ADBMS starts execution, this is no longer possible if the rulebase is large–rules must be selectively loaded upon rule execution. Thus, determining how efficiently an ADBMS can handle large sets of rules and how the system behaves when the number of rules grows larger is important.

Ultimately, the performance of composite event detectors can depend on the previous event history. Specifically, we expect the performance of event composition to depend on the number of event occurrences that are candidate components for composite event detection. For the tests ED-06 and ED-09 through ED-11, the number of component events that are used to initialize the composite event detector is thus a parameter.

factor	rulebase size			
	empty	small	medium	large
#events	0	50	250	500
#rules	0	50	250	500
# of component event occurrences	0	25	50	100

TABLE 6.1. Parameter values for different rulebase sizes.

For the three factors, we choose four possible values for an empty, a small, a medium, and a large rulebase (see Table 6.1). Tests for larger rulebases are simple to produce, since the values of all factors can be specified as parameters of the rulebase creation program. Each rulebase will contain the event types and rules needed for the tests. Those events/rules defined for the four rulebase sizes are not used by Beast and solely serve the purpose to measure performance under increasing rulebase size. They are therefore viewed as dummies and indicate whether the ADBMS is able to handle large sets of rules with a performance comparable to small numbers of rules.

6.3.3   Results for SAMOS

Figure 6.5 shows the results we obtained from running Beast on SAMOS [GGD91] (see also Chapter 14). For detailed statistical information and results for further systems (ACOOD [Ber94], NAOS [CCS94], and Ode [GJS92, LGA96]), see [GBLR96]. SAMOS has been tested on a SUN-SparcServer 4/690 under SUNOS 4.1.3.

The test series on which we report here consisted of several dozen test iterations. Within each iteration, each test was executed once. Within each

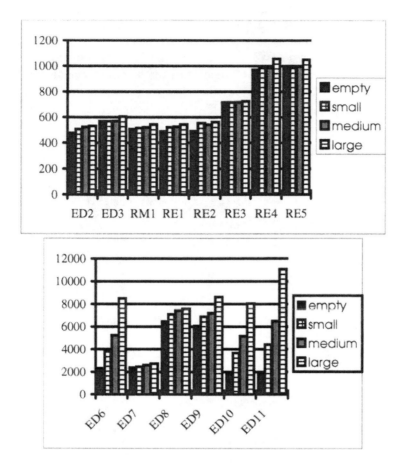

FIGURE 6.5. Beast results for SAMOS.

test, the corresponding event was generated ten times. Time was measured directly before and after the event generation (i.e., as soon as the control returned to the test program). Figure 6.5 refers to average execution times. The measure is wallclock time in milliseconds.

The major reasons for the high execution times in SAMOS are the complexity of the system, the powerful functionality it has, and the way event detection is implemented. SAMOS scales quite well for growing rulebases as far as primitive event detection and rule execution is concerned. This is due to indexing and clustering event descriptions and rule information [GGD+95b]. Measured times are rather high for composite event detection, since (1) lots of objects forming the Petri-Net used for composite event detection are stored on disk, and (2) no clustering is applied to those objects.

Furthermore, SAMOS (i.e., its composite event detector) is sensitive to the number of existing component event occurrences. In ED-11 for the large rulebase, e.g., 100 component events are raised before the tests actually start. These events are stored persistently and are considered for event composition during each test ED-11. Without these useless component events, the average execution time of ED-11 is 2515 ms for the large rulebase (Figure 6.6); thus, the execution time is almost constant for this test.

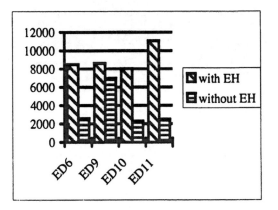

FIGURE 6.6. Beast results for SAMOS (large rulebase, with and without event history).

6.3.4   Lessons and Observation

Below, we interpret the results obtained form running Beast on SAMOS.
Event Detection. A major performance degradation stems from SAMOS's centralized approach to event detection (see above). Each event is signaled through one global function (in SAMOS called `raise_event`). This function determines the appropriate event detector (or parts thereof) and notifies it about the event occurrence. It is also necessary at this time to retrieve the event type definition from the rulebase.

Alternatively, in the *local* approach to event detection, events are detected at the objects for which they occur (as in Ode [LGA96]) or the corresponding event detector is directly notified about the event occurrence by the object or program that generates the event (as in REACH [BZBW95]). In both cases, event type information does not need to be retrieved, and thus event detection and composition are faster.
Event History Management. For some tests, the number of initially raised component events is a factor, i.e., the event history is not empty when the tests start. Especially if event parameters are required for subsequent rule execution, then the event history must be maintained, either explicitly or implicitly in the state of the event detector(s). Three observations are apparent with respect to event history management:

- The need to maintain the event history at all slows down SAMOS, since upon event detection and consumption, the event history must be updated.

- The `chronicle` consumption mode used in SAMOS seems to degrade performance, since upon event composition the entire event history might have to be scanned. In the `recent` consumption mode, however, old candidate component events are replaced by newer ones, and so the event history is much smaller than in the case of `chronicle`. (Note, however, that the two consumption modes also imply different semantics of composite events and ECA rules.)

- If the `chronicle` consumption mode is used, then garbage collection of old event occurrences is a crucial task. For instance, in ED-11, the initially raised component event occurrences are of no use, since a `same transaction` restriction is specified. Garbage collection would discard these occurrences even before the tests actually start and thus would make SAMOS five times faster for some tests.

Observations on Architectural Styles. Based on our measurements, it is not justified to conclude that integrated architectures are generally more efficient than layered ones. Even integrated architectures use some kind of lower-level platform (e.g., REACH uses Open OODB [WBT92]). In addition to the chosen implementation techniques, the performance of the platform used impacts on the performance of the ADBMS. To put it simply: when a slow platform is chosen, the ADBMS will be slow as well, regardless of its architectural style. For instance, tests ED-03, RE-04, and RE-05 can help to identify the influence of the passive part on performance (commit processing in ED-03 and query processing in RE-04 and RE-05). When compared with other systems, SAMOS performs quite well for these tests.

6.4   Steps Towards Performance Improvement of ADBMS's

Based on the above elaboration, it is an urgent problem how performance of ADBMS might be improved. These improvements can come in two variants:

1. improving and optimizing the ADBMS code, and/or

2. providing database administrators with facilities to improve performance at runtime.

6.4.1   Optimizing ADBMS Implementations

The first possibility to improve ADBMS performance is to optimize the ADBMS implementation or to use techniques that are expected to perform better. Possible optimizations are:

- clustering and indexing event and rule definitions,

- prefetching event detectors,

- indexing component event occurrences,

- garbage collection of event occurrences,

- sophisticated condition evaluation, and

- concurrent rule (action) execution.

Upon event detection, the definition of event types has to be retrieved and brought into main memory. The first optimization thus means that clustered event (and rule) definitions can be retrieved with less I/O. Likewise, if event type definitions are indexed, their retrieval is also accelerated. This optimization has been applied to SAMOS, making it four times as fast [GGD+95b] for some Beast tests.

Prefetching event definitions means that upon session or program start, a set of event detectors is brought into main memory, which then do not have to be retrieved from the database upon event detection. The problem is to determine which event detectors to prefetch, especially if many of them are present. This kind of optimization has been proposed for REACH [BZBW95]. In SAMOS, however, prefetching all event definitions upon database opening has been to little avail [GGD+95b].

As explained above, one of the performance degradations when the consumption mode `chronicle` is used stems from large event histories. Indexing event occurrences could in these cases accelerate the selection of appropriate component events upon event composition. For instance, for composite events with a `same transaction` restriction, the candidates can be indexed by the identifier of their triggering transaction.

Furthermore, garbage collection facilities would remove those event occurrences that can no longer contribute to a composite event from the event history. For SAMOS, this would lead to a tremendous performance improvement (see above).

Especially when conditions are typically complex and may share parts with other conditions, sophisticated condition optimization techniques (as, e.g., proposed in [FRS93]) might improve rule execution performance.

Finally, while most of the current systems execute rules sequentially and block the application program for the rule execution time, concurrent execution of actions can also speed up rule execution [CM95]. This feature requires more work to be done on rule scheduling, and impacts on ADBMS architectures have to be better understood (e.g., multi-threading).

6.4.2   Tuning ADBMS Applications

The second way to improve the performance of ADBMS applications is
tuning [Con96]. Tuning means to perform actions that preserve semantics
(of rules, in our case) while improving runtime performance. Examples for
such actions are enhancements/modifications that affect rule execution or
event detection. Since ADBMS tuning–in contrast to the tuning of (passive)
DBMSs [Sha92]–is still in its infancy, we discuss several initial steps towards
tuning techniques that are potentially helpful for ADBMS applications.

The possibilities for tuning an ADBMS application include:

- appropriate use of consumption modes,

- garbage collection,

- periodically deactivating rules and events,

- decoupling of rules, and

- reordering of rules.

According to the three-level architecture described in [Con96], the first of
these tuning opportunities refers to the conceptual level, because it affects
the semantics of rules. The other ones are performed at the internal level.

We have described why the consumption mode `chronicle` slows down
event composition. Provided that the ADBMS offers a choice among multiple consumption modes, event composition (and event history maintenance) can be tuned in that this consumption mode is used only where
necessary (i.e., in those cases where the semantics of rules requires it).

Second, it has already been mentioned that the size of the event history has a great impact on performance of event consumption, and that
garbage collection can help overcome the inefficiencies of certain consumption modes. However, garbage collection itself requires time, and–when performed too often–is counterproductive. Thus, the first tuning possibility is
to let the database administrator (DBA) specify when and how often to
perform garbage collection. Provided that a service `garbage_collect` is
available, the DBA can specify ECA rules that execute this service. Such
ECA rules can use time events (e.g., on each Saturday at 6 pm) or repeti-
tive events (e.g., after n transactions have been completed) to define when
garbage collection has to be executed.

Third, it might be the case that certain triggers fire only at specific times
(e.g., end of the month). For instance, consider a rule that checks salaries
after each update of an employee object/tuple. If salaries are updated only
at the end of the month, then event detection and condition evaluation
is superfluous during the month. Disabling involved events and rules then
speeds up applications, since they spend less time on event detection and
condition evaluation. Disabling and enabling such events/rules could be
controlled by (meta-)ECA rules (as proposed above for garbage collection).

Fourth, it has been mentioned before that decoupling rule executions decreases transaction size and can lead to smaller response times. Thus, whenever the semantics of a rule allows it, executing rules in independent, separate transactions can improve performance. Thus, the ADBMS should offer the choice among multiple coupling modes, including decoupled.

Finally, reordering rules is in some sense the opposite technique to decoupling. Whenever a set of rules is attached to one event, those that might abort the triggering transaction in their action part should be executed first. Provided that a transaction will be aborted anyway by such a rule, aborting it as soon as possible again decreases transaction size and also minimizes the necessary recovery actions upon abort. This tuning technique requires priorities, and abort rules get high priorities assigned.

While all these tuning techniques are rather intuitive, their benefit still has to be investigated by thorough measurements.

6.5   Related Work

While a bulk of (application domain-specific) benchmarks have been defined for passive DBMSs [CDN93, CS92, Gra93, SFGM93], those for active databases have so far been considered only scarcely. The Beast benchmark has first been proposed in [GGD95a].

Several authors, however, have considered performance issues in some way. In [CJL91], the impact of different coupling schemes on job response time is investigated. In this simulation study, it has been found that rule execution decoupled from the triggering transaction leads to less conflicts and thus to shorter job response times.

This model is adapted in [LS95], which additionally proposes a specific approach for optimizing transactions incorporating rule executions. The major point in this approach is to execute read-only rules (which do not modify the database) at the end of a triggering transaction and to perform a modified multi-version concurrency control scheme for this transaction phase. The expected benefit is less concurrency control conflicts and thus smaller blocking times of transaction.

In [AMC93], different approaches to modeling and storing events and rules are discussed (e.g., as separate database objects, or as parts of class definitions). The impact on performance is also considered, e.g., the authors hypothesize that class-specific rules are more efficient at runtime.

Kersten [Ker95] describes several tests conducted for the ADBMS Monet. This study considers primarily execution of multiple rules, e.g., cascading rule execution, and thus focuses on how an ADBMS can handle large sets of triggered rules.

In [SKD95], it is reported that for some applications, active solutions (applications using triggers) is two to four times slower than the equivalent passive solutions. The authors hypothesize that the addition of rules to transactions leads to worse performance in comparison to optimized, purely passive transactions. They thus state that the global optimization of both rules and transactions is necessary (see also Chapter 20 in this volume).

While Brüchert et al. report performance benefits of an active solution [BZB97], the set of triggers used in this work seems to be rather small, and the measured performance gain seems to stem from the precompilation and optimization of stored procedures used in triggers.

6.6   Conclusion

In this chapter, we have investigated performance assessment of ADBMS's and have presented the Beast benchmark for ADBMS's. So far, measurements with Beast have given insights into the performance characteristics of (object-oriented) ADBMS's, and have helped to identify bottlenecks and to understand performance characteristics of ADBMS implementation techniques more thoroughly.

In our future work, we intend to measure further ADBMS's with Beast (e.g., ROCK & ROLL [DPWF96]). Furthermore, more application-oriented benchmarking is an open issue in two ways:

- proposing a set of typical applications for which a set of benchmarks can be developed (very likely, there will not be a *single* such typical application), and

- comparing active solutions with equivalent passive solutions from a performance perspective.

In addition, considering multi-user mode in Beast is a challenging topic in order to assess performance of event detectors and rule execution components in the presence of concurrent transactions all generating events and triggering rules. Finally, the implementation of the tuning techniques discussed in section 6.4.2 and assessment of their benefit with respect to performance is also subject to future work.

6.7   Acknowledgments

The work on Beast has significantly progressed through the tests of ACOOD, NAOS, Ode, and REACH. We thus are very grateful to Mikael Berndtsson, Claudia Roncancio, Daniel Lieuwen, and Jürgen Zimmermann for their cooperation on Beast. We also thank our colleagues Stella Gatziu and Hans Fritschi for the discussions on performance issues of ADBMS's.

6.8 REFERENCES

[AMC93]   E. Anwar, L. Maugis, and S Chakravarthy. A New Perspective on Rule Support for Object-Oriented Databases. In *Proc. ACM-SIGMOD Intl. Conf. on Management of Data*, pages 99–108, Washington, DC, May 1993.

[Ber94]   M. Berndtsson. Reactive Object-Oriented Databases and CIM. In *Proc. 5th Intl. Conf. on Database and Expert System Applications,*, pages 769–778, Athens, Greece, September 1994.

[BZB97]   L. Brüchert, J. Zimmermann, and A.P. Buchmann. Applications and Performance of Triggers in a Stock Trading Archiving System (short paper, in German). In *Proc. Datenbanksysteme in Büro, Technik und Wissenschaft (BTW)*, Ulm, Germany, March 1997.

[BZBW95]   A. Buchmann, J. Zimmermann, J. Blakely, and D. Wells. Building an Integrated Active OODBMS: Requirements, Architecture, and Design Decisions. In *Proc. 11th Intl. Conf. on Data Engineering*, Taipeh, Taiwan, March 1995.

[CCS94]   C. Collet, T. Coupaye, and T. Svensen. NAOS: Efficient and Modular Reactive Capabilities in an Object-Oriented Database System. In *Proc. 20th Intl. Conf. on Very Large Data Bases, Santiago, Chile*, pages 132–143, September 1994.

[CDN93]   M.J. Carey, D.J. DeWitt, and J.F. Naughton. The OO7 Benchmark. In *Proc. ACM-SIGMOD Intl. Conf. on Management of Data*, pages 12–21, Washington, DC, May 1993.

[CJL91]   M.J. Carey, R. Jauhari, and M. Livny. On Transaction Boundaries in Active Databases: A Performance Perspective. *IEEE Transactions on Data and Knowledge Engineering*, 3(3):320–336, 1991.

[CKAK94]   S. Chakravarthy, V. Krishnaprasad, E. Anwar, and S.-K. Kim. Composite Events for Active Databases: Semantics, Contexts and Detection. In *Proc. 20th Intl. Conf. on Very Large Data Bases*, pages 606–617, Santiago, Chile, September 1994.

[CM95]   C. Collet and J. Machado. Optimization of Active Rules with Parallelism. In *Proc. 1st Intl. Workshop on Active and Real-Time Database Systems (ARTDB-95)*, pages 82–103, Skövde, Sweden, June 1995.

[Con96]   ACT-NET Consortium. The Active Database Management
            System Manifesto: A Rulebase of ADBMS Features. *ACM
            SIGMOD Record*, 25(3):40–49, September 1996.

[CS92]   R.G.G. Cattell and J. Skeen. Object Operations Benchmark.
            ACM Transactions on Database Systems, 17(1):1–31, 1992.

[CW96]   S. Ceri and J. Widom. Applications of Active Databases. In
            J. Widom and S. Ceri, editors, *Active Database Systems*, pages
            259–291. Morgan Kaufmann, 1996.

[Day95]   U. Dayal. Ten Years of Activity in Active Database Systems:
            What Have We Accomplished? In *Proc. 1st Intl. Workshop on
            Active and Real-Time Database Systems (ARTDB-95)*, June
            1995.

[DPWF96]   A. Dinn, N.W. Paton, M.H. Williams, and A.A.A. Fernandes.
            An Active Rule Language for ROCK & ROLL. In *Proc. 14th
            British National Conference on Databases*. Springer-Verlag,
            1996.

[Eri93]   J. Eriksson. CEDE: Composite Event Detector in an Active
            Object-Oriented Database. Master's thesis, Department of
            Computer Science, University of Skövde, 1993.

[FRS93]   F. Fabret, M. Regnier, and E. Simon. An Adaptive Algorithm
            for Incremental Evaluation of Production Rules in Databases.
            In *Proc. 19th Intl. Conf. on Very Large Data Bases*, pages
            455–466, Dublin, Ireland, August 1993.

[GBLR96]   A. Geppert, M. Berndtsson, D. Lieuwen, and C. Roncancio.
            Performance Evaluation of Object-Oriented Active Database
            Management Systems Using the Beast Benchmark. Technical
            Report 96.07, Department of Computer Science, University of
            Zurich, October 1996.

[GD94]   S. Gatziu and K.R. Dittrich. Detecting Composite Events
            in an Active Database Systems Using Petri Nets. In *Proc.
            4th Intl. Workshop on Research Issues in Data Engineering:
            Active Database Systems*, pages 2–9, Houston, TX, February
            1994.

[GGD91]   S. Gatziu, A. Geppert, and K. Dittrich. Integrating Active
            Concepts into an Object-Oriented Database System. In *Proc.
            3rd Workshop on Database Programming Languages*, Nafplion,
            Greece, August 1991.

[GGD95a]   A. Geppert, S. Gatziu, and K. Dittrich. A Designer's Bench-mark for Active Database Management Systems: OO7 Meets the Beast. In *Proc. 2nd Intl. Workshop on Rules in Database Systems*, pages 309–323, Athens, Greece, September 1995.

[GGD+95b] A. Geppert, S. Gatziu, K.R. Dittrich, H. Fritschi, and A. Vaduva. Architecture and Implementation of the Active Object-Oriented Database Management System SAMOS. Technical Report 95.29, Department of Computer Science, University of Zurich, November 1995.

[GJS92]   N.H. Gehani, H.V. Jagadish, and O. Shmueli. Composite Event Specification in Active Databases: Model & Implementation. In *Proc. 18th Intl. Conf. on Very Large Data Bases*, pages 327–338, Barcelona, Spain, August 1992.

[Gra93]   J. Gray, editor. *The Benchmark Handbook for Database and Transaction Processing Systems*. Morgan Kaufmann Publishers, 1993.

[Jai91]   R. Jain. *The Art of Computer Systems Performance Analysis. Techniques for Experimental Design, Measurement, Simulation, and Modeling*. John Wiley & Sons, 1991.

[Ker95]   M. L. Kersten. An Active Component for a Parallel Database Kernel. In *Proc. 2nd Intl. Workshop on Rules In Database Systems*, pages 277–291, Athens, Greece, Springer-Verlag, September 1995.

[LGA96]   D.F. Lieuwen, N. Gehani, and R. Arlein. The Ode Active Database: Trigger Semantics and Implementation. In *Proc. 12th Intl. IEEE Conf. on Data Engineering (ICDE), New Orleans*, pages 412–420, March 1996.

[LS95]   F. Llirbat and E. Simon. Optimizing Active Database Transactions: A New Perspective. In *Proc. 1st Active and Real-Time Database Systems (ARTDB-95)*, pages 23–45, Skövde, Sweden, June 1995.

[SFGM93]   M. Stonebraker, J. Frew, K. Gardels, and J. Meredith. The Sequoia 2000 Benchmark. In *Proc. ACM SIGMOD Intl. Conf. on Management of Data, Washington, DC*, pages 2–11, May 1993.

[Sha92]   D. E. Shasha. *Database Tuning. A Principled Approach*. Prentice Hall, 1992.

[SKD95]   E. Simon and A. Kotz-Dittrich. Promises and Realities of Active Database Systems. In *Proc. 21ˢᵗ Intl. Conf. on Very Large Data Bases*, pages 642–653, Zurich, Switzerland, September 1995.

[SLSV95]   D. Shasha, F. Llirbat, E. Simon, and P. Valduriez. Transaction Chopping: Algorithms and Performance Studies. *ACM Trans. on Database Systems*, 20(3):325–363, September 1995.

[WBT92]   D.L. Wells, J.A. Blakeley, and C.W. Thompson. Architecture of an Open Object-Oriented Database Management System. *IEEE Computer*, 25(10):74–82, October 1992.

[Wid94]   J. Widom. Research Issues in Active Database Systems: Report from the Closing Panel at RIDE-ADS '94. *ACM SIGMOD Record*, 23(3):41–43, September 1994.

7

Tool Support

Oscar Díaz

ABSTRACT
Despite the broad range of applications that can benefit from active database systems, current practice shows that the availability of active mechanisms in most commercial database systems is no guarantee that they will be used. This is partly due to the lack of sophisticated tools to assist in the process of designing, debugging, and administrating large rule sets. This chapter reports advances achieved so far, and identifies areas where enhancements are required.

7.1 Introduction

The need for tools that assist in the process of designing, analyzing, and administrating active rules has been identified in different forums [Wid94, SKD95]. Indeed, the lack of such tools is seen as a main stumbling block for active DBMS'ss usage and dissemination. From a database viewpoint, the introduction of rules as part of the database schema challenges traditional, structure-oriented methodologies. Traditional CASE functionalities need to be extended to support the idiosyncrasies of rule modeling and administration. This chapter addresses these features, and the existing and required tools.

Diverse tools are described in the literature that focus on distinct aspects of rule support. This chapter does not attempt to exhaustively describe all of them, but provides an outline of the distinct tool types that can greatly facilitate rule usage. The classical steps of software development (i.e., analysis and design, implementation and maintenance) are used to pigeonhole these tools, describing their intended aims and how they help in building reliable and usable active databases. The rest of the chapter is organized in five sections. The next three sections address analysis and design, implementation and maintenance support tools, respectively. Section 5 moves a step forward from isolated tools to integrated environments, discussing the central role played by the repository. Some brief conclusions are given in section 6.

7.2   Analysis and Design Support

Analysis refers to the process of identifying and capturing application requirements from the user's point of view. The developer should focus on the semantics of the application rather than the characteristics of the final system. The result is a consistent description (conceptual model) of the expectations the user has about system functionality. As for design, it is concerned with the construction of the proposed system that satisfies the requirements identified during analysis. The outcomes are a logical and a physical model.

Since the requirements identified during this stage impact on the whole life cycle, it is vital that they are error-free and really describe the user's expectations about the system. Validation and verification are aimed at this objective. The purpose of validation is to ensure that the model obtained correctly and adequately describes the user's intended requirements [ABC82]. On the other hand, verification concerns the formal properties of the model, checking for contradictions or inconsistencies. Therefore, this phase can be facilitated by the provision of tools for graphically describing, validating, and verifying rules.

7.2.1   Graphical Description Tools

Rather than natural language, graphical notations are a much better way for capturing requirements and interacting with the user. The employment of formal conceptual models has been encouraged since automatic analysis or execution can easily be conducted, easing the designer's task of interpreting ambiguous specifications. However, increasing formality is commonly achieved at the cost of complicating both the syntax and semantics of the conceptual language, refraining the user from direct participation. Tools that support a graphical representation of the model's notation make the specification more comprehensible and appealing to the end-user, thereby easing model validation.

In [NTMG95], the primitives of the *Entity/Relationship model* are extended to consider events and rules, leading to the $(ER)^2$ *model*. As an example, consider an *account* entity type, described through the customer, branch, and balance attributes, and a *loan* entity type that is qualified by the customer, branch, interest rate and amount of the loan. A bank regulation could be that when a withdrawal is made that exceeds the balance of the account, a loan should be made available to this customer with an amount equal to the surplus at 20 percent interest. This regulation could be reflected using the $(ER)^2$ notation, as shown in Figure 7.1. The regulation is modeled as a modification on *account*, which in turn could lead to inserting the corresponding *loan*. Arc labels indicate the operation to be applied to the entity (e.g., *m* for modification), whereas circles and parallelograms stand for events and rules, respectively. Event sources can be

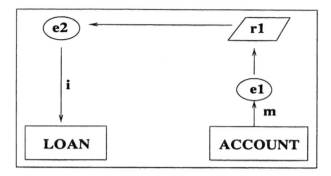

FIGURE 7.1. An $(ER)^2$ schema.

structure operations, interrupts, the clock, or external. As for rules, they
have a primitive event, a condition over the database state, and an action
that is described as a list of database or external operations. Conditions
and actions are described separately from the diagram, using textual descriptions that are displayed through windows when circles or polygons are
clicked on, and in so doing, avoid cluttering the diagrammatic representation [NTMG95]. Composite events are not considered.

Along with the widespread use of ER diagrams, the main advantage of
this approach is that triggers as found in commercial systems can easily be
obtained from the diagram. However, this is also its disadvantage since active behavior is described at a low level, almost in terms of record-oriented
operations. Hence, it does not provide enough abstraction for active behavior description from which low-level triggers could have been generated.

A higher level of abstraction is provided by IFO_2, an extension to the
IFO semantic data model which allows representation of active behavior
[TPC94]. A main feature of IFO_2 is the set of event constructs provided to
build composite events. These constructs are the same as those provided by
the IFO semantic data model for structural modeling, namely: event composition (i.e., event conjunction), event sequencing, event grouping (i.e.,
similar to event closure), and event union (i.e., event disjunction). The
IFO_2 primitives are illustrated in Figure 7.2. Here, a node is an event, and
an arc is a function that links the triggering event (i.e., the domain) with
the triggered event (i.e., the range). This function, which can be described
using an event-based algebraic language [TC94], can be:

- simple or complex (mono or multi-valued), which indicates whether
  a triggering event causes one or several triggered events,

- partial or total, which indicates whether a triggering event can or
  must cause a triggered event,

- deferred or immediate, which indicates whether or not there is a delay

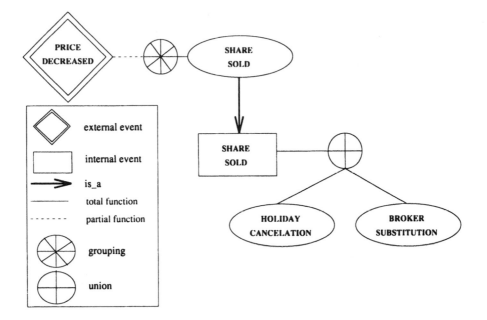

FIGURE 7.2. An IFO$_2$ schema.

between the occurrences of the triggering and triggered events,

System behavior is modeled through event schemas that are connected via *is-a* links. Each event schema represents the triggering caused by a given event known as the *heart* event. In Figure 7.2, two heart events are drawn, an external event *price_decreased* (e.g., coming from the share market), and an internal event *share_sold* caused by an operation. A *price_decreased* event may or may not cause a share to be sold (i.e., it is partial) depending on the condition on the size of the decrease. If this condition is satisfied, then more than one share holder may sell those shares (i.e., event grouping), causing a cascading of *share_sold* events. As for the *share_sold* event, its triggering is described in a different event schema that shows how it causes a union event built upon a *broker_substitution* event and a *holiday_cancellation* event.

As well as uniformity, an advantage of IFO$_2$ schemas is their description of how different objects interact through events, thus giving priority to an overview of the system rather than to individual objects. Furthermore, a derivation process is outlined in [TPC94] where event-condition-action and condition-action rules are obtained from IFO$_2$ schemas. However, the process cannot be completely automated and it imposes significant demands on the underlying DBMS's.

In the object-oriented modeling arena, a first approach to the incorporation of active behavior is presented in [BS94] by means of *activation scripts*. While most previous behavior diagrams (e.g., state-transition diagrams) define *necessary* preconditions for changes to occur, activation scripts allow

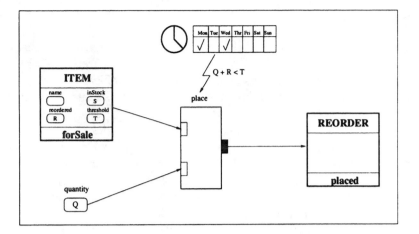

FIGURE 7.3. An activity script for item reordering.

description of *sufficient* conditions for activities to occur. They describe explicitly when changes take place, separating this behavior from application programs.

Using the terminology of Bichler et al. [BS94], an activity script consists of an event, a guard, and an activity. The activity roughly corresponds to a state transition in the life cycle diagram of an object type. An event can be a method invocation or a temporal event, where composite events can be described. The guard is a predicate over event parameters and object states, where input bindings for the activity are stated. Figure 7.3 gives an example of an activity script taken from [BS94]. This script states that on Mondays and Wednesdays at 4 pm (the event), a reorder should be placed (the activity) for each item for which the quantity in stock plus the quantity already reordered is below the item-specific reorder threshold (the condition). The condition is expressed through the object state (i.e., the item should be in state *forSale*) and the current value of the state variables (i.e., *inStock, reordered,* and *threshold*). Notice the expression that obtains the other input parameter of the *place* activity (i.e., the *quantity of items to be ordered*) is also described in the condition part.

This notation offers a thorough description of composite and temporal events, but it could lead to cluttered diagrams for complex rule sets. It assists with the separation of operational and policy aspects of information systems, i.e., operational aspects will be supported using methods, whereas activity scripts that correspond to the policy aspects will be mapped to events and rules. In so doing, it offers a first guideline for active behavior analysis.

7.2.2   Validation Tools

Once the designer has captured the requirements, these have to be checked with the user who has the final decision about their accurateness with respect to the real world. As well as improving the graphical counterpart of the model's constructs, three kinds of techniques are commonly proposed for model validation. The first is to check the model against an expert system that incorporates the experience of both a modeler and a domain expert in the form of condition-action patterns. The second approach, paraphrasing, consists of feeding back to the user natural language sentences obtained from the model. The explanation is given in the user's terms, thereby facilitating user assessment of the accurateness of the model. The third technique is rapid prototyping where the conceptual model is animated so that the user can observe the external behavior of the model (i.e., how the system reacts to stimuli from outside).

An approach is presented in [DP97] where the conceptual model is first described just through stimuli (external events) and business policies (high-level descriptions of rules), and is then animated. Moreover, animation has to be enhanced with explanation facilities that make the user aware of the internal mechanisms responsible for reactions, i.e., the internal system behavior. The user is then guided through the reasoning process and the assumptions or policies that lead to the system's observed behavior. The explanation generated at this level is not related to the active system itself, but to a model of it. The model is validated to make sure that we are implementing a satisfactory information system instead of assessing an active system that is already implemented [Gul96]. This implies that the explanation component should cope with unstable and incomplete conceptual models.

In [DP97], the model is validated by providing explanations of the results of model execution: why a given state has been reached or how a certain property can be satisfied. The system provides explanation in terms of stimuli that can originate from outside or as a result of a policy application. Model execution is achieved by mapping its constructs into the event calculus formalism.

As illustrated in Figure 7.4, stimuli are described in terms of their preconditions and consequences. Consequences describe the resulting state in terms of what becomes valid and invalid through the *initiates* and *terminates* clauses, respectively. These clauses are lists of *property if condition* statements. For instance, the *requesting* postcondition can be described as initiating the fact that the person has the book and that the book is unavailable, whereas it ends the fact that the book is available.

Policy description follows the event-condition-action pattern. For instance, a library regulation could be that a book is bought if three requests for the book have been rejected due to the book being on loan. A definition of this policy is given in Figure 7.4. The policy's event is de-

```
stimulus definition [
        name: requesting([Person,Book]),
        preconditions: [
                property(Book,state,book_available)
                not property(Person,has_books,_) ],
        initiates: [
                property(Person,has_books,Book) if true,
                property(Book,available,fail) if true ],
        terminates: [
                property(Book,available,true) if true ]

policy definition [
        name: r1,
        event:    times(3,request_rejected([_,Book])
        condition: [(true)],
        action: [(
           property(Book,title,Title), % recovers the Book's title
           => nextOid(NextOid),        % obtains next identifier available
           => buying([NextOid,Title])
        )]].
```

FIGURE 7.4. Description of stimuli and the *buying* policy.

fined as *times(3,request_rejected([_,Book]))*, meaning that the three rejected requests should refer to the same book. The action recovers the book's title, requests a new book identifier, and generates the *buying* stimulus. *Request_rejected* is an event generated when the *requesting* stimulus cannot be fulfilled due to the book being on loan.

Now suppose that the state of the system is that members *m1* and *m2* have books *b11* and *b12*, respectively. The system is asked how member *m2* can get book *b11* through the command *how(property(m2, has_books, b11))*. Each answer will correspond to a path of the search tree. Figure 7.5 shows the output for one of the paths where level 0 stands for the root of the search, and subsequent level numbers state the depth of the search. Where stimuli are found at the same level, this means that their order is not significant. The answer shown in figure 7.5 applies the regulation so that instead of having the stimulus *buying* directly issued by the user, the system forces *buying* as a result of three requests for this book being rejected (i.e., the *request_reject* stimulus). In this trace, the three requests have been made by the same borrower, and thus the designer can be made aware of this shortcut that allows a single borrower to cause purchases to take place, and realize how the policy is wrongly defined since the rejection should relate to different users.

7.2.3 Verification Tools

Once each business rule has been validated by the user, checks have to be done to assess the consistency of the rules as a set. Static and dynamic

```
Level: 4  Derived stimulus: request_rejected([_,b11])
   from stimulus: requesting([m1, b11])
Level: 3  Derived stimulus: request_rejected([_,b11])
   from stimulus: requesting([m1, b11])
Level: 2  Derived stimulus: request_rejected([_,b11])
   from stimulus: requesting([m1, b11])
Level: 1  Derived stimulus: buying([NextBookOid,"el-Quixote"]) from rule: r1
   with condition: [true]  and event: times(3,request_rejected([_,b11]))
Level: 1  Stimuli: returning([m2, b12])  with preconditions:
   [property(m2, has_books, b12)]
Level: 0  Stimuli: requesting([m2, b11]) with preconditions:
   [property(b11, state, book_available), not property(m2, has_books, b12)]
```

FIGURE 7.5. Possible outputs to the command *how(property(m2, has_books, b11))*.

analyzers can be used here where the rules are verified without executing the rules (static) or by monitoring rule firing (dynamic).

Static rule analysis has been widely discussed in Chapter 3 where the rule set is checked for termination, confluence and observable determinism. Chimera offers tools to facilitate some of these tasks [BCFP96].

Unfortunately, these properties are not always easy to ascertain for a fully-fledged rule language, and hence research on rule analysis has focused on formal, declarative languages. However, not all authors agree that active rule systems should necessarily be associated with such languages, and many implemented rule systems are integrated with imperative database programming languages [Buc94]. Furthermore, the fact that a rule base exhibits terminating and confluent behavior does not in itself imply that it is correct. Thus, as rule languages become more complicated, thereby increasing the range of applications for which they are suitable, the need for dynamic analyzers will become increasingly pressing. Dynamic analysis can be seen as a complement to static analysis, with rules being informally checked through testing.

VITAL [BGB95] can be classified as a dynamic analyzer where the triggering graph is gradually created as execution proceeds. A color code is used for each event state (i.e., raised or not raised) and each rule state (i.e., inactive, triggered, or executed). As execution continues, the colors change, and a textual trace of the execution is displayed in a separated window.

Thoroughly testing complex rule sets can be tedious, unreliable, and patchy if thoroughness of the testing effort cannot be measured. Systematic testing can be enhanced through test-case generators where database states and event sequences are generated from the set of rules whose behavior is being checked. The usefulness of this approach has been shown for constraint consistency [NML93]. However, ECA rule testing is a more challenging situation, as not only data but significant events have to be generated as well. Besides, the richer description languages commonly used for ECA rule definition make even harder the provision of a systematic mechanism for test generation. Hence, most approaches manually introduce the test data. For instance, in [Beh94], a set of event schedules are generated for each specification (i.e., real-world scenario). As well as the problem of generating relevant event schedules, active behavior depends on the database state (i.e., the database state determines whether a triggered rule is finally executed or not). Hence, this tool allows the user to decide at different points how the execution proceeds (e.g., by defining current event parameters, or by firing rules explicitly even when the condition has evaluated to false).

However, simulation is a forward-looking process, whereas finding bugs or ascertaining the reasons for unclear behavior involves going backwards in time. Questions that arise during the simulation are commonly due to things that occur before the current point in the run. This implies that the designer has to execute the scenario several times with different simulation parameters to clearly identify the causes of the faulty or unexpected behavior. The model is run with breakpoints inserted to detect the deviation from expected behavior. Most systems stop here: they just help to identify the *effect* of the problem. However, *debugging is concerned with searching for causes*. Breakpoints can be used to detect unexpected behavior, but this is not the end of the problem, but the beginning of the search for the cause of the deviation.

Simulation by deduction can help here whereby *the steps in the dynamic behavior of a simulated model are deduced by a reasoning system* [FS93]. This allows the user to question the system as to *why* a given state has (or has not) been reached, an event has (or has not) been signaled, or a rule has (or has not) been fired. In this way, the designer tracks the causes of problem situations. Another useful facility is the *what if* questions, which allow different states to be hypothesized. In this way, users unfamiliar with the system can understand the implications of cause-and-effect links among the distinct components of the system. This facility is especially useful for reactive systems.

This deductive process begins by inserting breakpoints where deviations are suspected. This is not straightforward, and involves a expertise/intuition from the designer. An enhancement could be to build a *model* of the expected faulty behavior and to let the system determine when this situation occurs at runtime. The good news is that this model could be described as a combination of distinct events, i.e., a composite event. In this way, it is the system's responsibility to match the dynamically produced chain of event occurrences with the different models, and when this happens the system can stop, showing the instantiated string of events that lead to the deviation. The user is thus relieved from the burden of tracking the event trace and of backtracking from the effect back to the causes. Breakpoints are no longer introduced by the designer, but by the system itself which knows when it should stop, and how to spot faulty behavior.

7.3   Implementation Support

During implementation, the logical model obtained during design is converted in a working system where the guidelines of the physical model are taken into account. For instance, Chimera allows the mapping of the logical model into five database kernels. In particular, the Pandora tool assists in the translation for the Oracle DBMS's where some interactions with the user are required to choose among distinct implementation options that impact on performance [BCFP96].

The intricacies of rule definition can discourage many users, as well as making rules more error-prone. The availability of high-level description languages has long been recognized as a must, where rules are regarded as an implementation mechanism, hidden from the end-user. ECA rules for integrity constraint maintenance is the area where most studies have been reported (as discussed in Chapter 19). Rule generators will be needed here (e.g., ARGONAUT in Chimera). Precompilers/preprocessors are also required for those active DBMS'ss built on top of existing DBMS'ss using a black-box approach.

When executed, rules are fired in the context of transactions. Runtime debuggers can help in monitoring the combined execution of rules and transactions. Similar to verification during analysis, debuggers should include test-case generators and tracers, but now with fine-grained detail. Also, it is desirable to provide an offline debugging mechanism so that the real data is not affected by the successive dummy executions.

7.3.1   Tracing Tools

Tracing has a long tradition in the programming language area. Unfortunately, traditional tracer models are not adequate for tracing rules. Conventional tracers provide exhaustive information on the state of the execution process (e.g., program variables, subroutines, and the like), thereby allowing the user to monitor the evolution of this state information. By contrast, what makes rule debugging a challenging task is the insidious ways in which rules can interact. Interaction, rather than state, becomes the main source of incorrect or unexpected behavior, and this *context-dependent* control exhibited by active rules imposes new demands on the debugger.

Unlike traditional programming languages, where sequential control is specified both explicitly and statically by the programmer, active rules are fired dynamically by the system based on the previous flow of events. There is thus no way to know in advance which rules will be fired. Rules eligible for firing, as represented by the *conflict set*, depend on the events raised (internal or external to the DBMS's). Hence, it is more appropriate to reveal the context in which rules have been triggered (e.g., the conflict set and the event base) than to present a sequential trace of triggered rules. DEAR, a tracer for the EXACT system, addresses this issue by showing the intertwined cycle of rules and events [DJP94]. Hence, the user can ascertain not only which rules have been triggered, but also whether the event occurrence that triggered the rule originated from a top-level transaction or a rule execution. Furthermore, when an event is raised, such a cycle permits identification of the context in which the event took place in terms of recently triggered rules.

DEAR mainly focuses on displaying the interleaving of events and rules, but is restricted to primitive events. The monitoring of composite event occurrences is a more complicated task due to the large number of occurrences that may need to be shown and the intricate ways in which events are combined to obtain composite event occurrences. A first approach to this issue has been presented as part of the Sentinel system [CTZ95]. Sentinel provides a post-execution debugging tool where information from the execution is stored in log files that are consulted by the debugging tool to simulate runtime activities. An event tree is created where primitive events are leaf nodes and composite events are seen as parents of their component events. A color code is used to represent event status (detected or not detected). This tree grows from primitive events to the root. In addition, a transaction tree describes the triggering rule context: the root node represents the top-level transaction, and child nodes represent rules fired in the context of their parent node (either the user transaction or a rule, as rules are executed as subtransactions). A color code is used to represent the different states of subtransactions: running, suspended or committed. Whenever a rule is fired, a line is drawn connecting the transaction node of the current rule and the triggering event. In the first version of this system, all rules and events produced are shown, which could lead to cluttered visualizations [CTZ95].

Despite the noticeable advances in rule debugging, more remains to be done (e.g., customizable visualization of rule execution, different execution model semantics, automatic generation of test data), and different active rule system functionalities are likely to be most effectively presented to users using different visualizations.

7.4 Maintenance Support

Broadly speaking, maintenance involves any task related to rule administration. Once in production, the active DBMS's can face different problems, from evolution of the policies that regulate the company and which are enforced by means of current database triggers, to user mistrust as to why and how the policies are enforced. Browsers, evolution support tools, and explanation generators can help rule maintenance.

7.4.1   Browsers

Browsers can be available as a kind of online documentation not only about the event, condition, and action rule components, but also about the distinct functionality supported by the rules, be it integrity maintenance, view support, regulation enforcement, etc. Other aspects such as the author or the rationale behind business regulations supported through triggers, can be most valuable during explanation or to assess the applicability of the rule. Browsing can be conducted following potential triggering links between methods and triggers, or among triggers themselves, so that the user can assess the impact of invoking a given method.

7.4.2   Evolution Support Tools

Once in use, the rule set may need to be changed for different reasons: to overcome a failure to realize user requirements (*corrective maintenance*); to enhance accurate system tunning but without impacting its basic functionality (*perfective maintenance*); and to evolve requirements leading to a change in the system's underlying functionality (*adaptive maintenance*) [LST78]. At a first glance, explicit capture of business policies through triggers should certainly help to enforce new corporative regulations in the database system, viewing triggers as chunks of expertise, i.e., self-contained, isolated units that can be enlarged, removed, or updated more easily. However, this is not necessarily so.

Maintenance of large rule sets can be difficult, and ascertaining the effects of rule removal or addition is far from straightforward. It is the insidious ways in which rules can interact that makes adding/deleting a single rule–whose code looks perfectly satisfactory–such a complicated task. A previously correct rule set can stop enjoying this property after the addition or removal of a given rule. Evolution support tools are required to ease smooth migration and to determine the impact of new additions/deletions.

The management of a large rule set can be tackled using a divide-and-conquer approach. As an example, in [BCP96], the *stratification technique* is proposed to partition rules into disjoint strata so that *the designer can abstract rule behavior by reasoning locally on each individual stratum separately, and then reasoning globally on the behavior across strata.* Rather than facing a large set of single rules, the designer should find criteria that serve to partition this rule set into disjoint subsets of independent rules, and then establish the correctness criteria at this higher level of abstraction. Termination is the criteria tackled in [BCP96] where three approaches are proposed for stratification: behavioral, assertional, and event-based, where the former subsumes the other two. *Behavioral stratification* is based on the underlying tasks undertaken by rules. Each stratum contains the rules aimed at a given task, where the designer has to ensure that the task being pursued by one stratum is not affected by rules from other strata. Within each stratum, a convergence metric is defined that measures the distance from the current database state to the quiescent state (i.e., a state where no more rules can be triggered) produced by the execution of rules of this stratum running in isolation. The independence between stratum S_j in relation to S_i is obtained by ensuring that the triggering of any rule from S_j would not decrease the convergence measure of S_i. As pointed out by the authors, stratification helps in organizing and understanding rule sets, as well as in focusing the possible effects of rule addition or removal.

However, preserving correctness is not the end of the problem. Adding or removing an event definition will certainly impact the event history. As event occurrences, particularly those participating in composite events, are recorded as part of the event history, event evolution should also adapt this history to the new state. Deleting an event definition either directly or as a side-effect of removing those rules associated with it, might lead to the disregarding of all its event occurrences. Likewise, a new event type may or may not be instantiated by event occurrences produced prior to its definition. This problem has been addressed by the pioneering work related in [GGD95b], where different alternatives are identified in the context of workflow management systems and process-centered software development environments. For instance, newly introduced rules can be retrospectively enforced so that older event occurrences are used to produce instantiations of the newly created rule. By contrast, other situations are better reflected if previous occurrences are disregarded. Thus, it is up to the designer to choose the model that best fits the semantics of the application at hand.

7.4.3   Explanation Tools

The implicit, dynamic binding between methods and triggers hinders the user from following the control and data flow. The insidious ways that triggers can interact produces a feeling of loss of control, that makes users mistrust and reluctant to apply this technology. The provision of an explanation mechanism which allows users to be aware of the triggers being used has been identified as an urgent need for the success of active databases [Sto92].

Since, by definition, rules are fired automatically without user intervention, the only way to make the user aware of the system's behavior is through explanation. Otherwise, users will be reluctant to rely on a system in which unexpected behavior occurs. Unlike explanations generated during validation and verification, now authorization implications should also be considered (e.g., protected data or regulations used during the process might not be displayed or alternative explanations should be given instead).

Some of the desired capabilities of a rule explanation system are explored in the context of POSTGRES [SHP88] where the keywords *trace* and *explain* are proposed. The keyword *trace* before a command *would cause the corresponding command to be executed and the user to be notified of any rules which are awakened.* A cascading trace, i.e., when tracing is done not only of the rules fired directly by the command but any other rule awakened as a consequence of executing a rule's condition or action, could be achieved inserting *trace**. Finally, if instead of executing the command, the user wants to explore what would happen if the command were run, the keyword *explain* rather than *trace* could be used.

More remains to be done in this area, which can benefit from similar work investigated by the expert system community.

7.4.4   Measurement Tools

Tools to monitor rule execution/event detection, as well as to collect runtime statistics, can be very valuable for assessing both the correctness and performance of system behavior. For ascertaining rule correctness, a statistics manager is suggested in the context of the VITAL tool [BGB95]. This manager calculates and records statistics on the behavior of the rule processor (e.g., the number of tuples inserted, deleted, or modified during a rule execution cycle, the number of times a rule is triggered, etc). This data can be used for *postmortem* analysis to identify potentially infinite cycles, or to help finding erroneous rules. The former can be ascertained by monitoring the size of relevant tables: if the size tends to increase in a uniform way, it suggests that the cycle will not terminate. Erroneous rule condition declarations may be suspected if the number of times a rule is executed is very low compared with the number of times the rule is triggered. Thus, features of statistical data can point to potentially abnormal behavior.

As for assessing performance weaknesses, the Beast benchmark provides some preliminary insights for active object-oriented DBMS's [GGD95a]. Beast helps implementors to evaluate their design decisions against three sensitive functions, namely event detection, rule management (particularly, rule retrieval), and rule execution. The outcomes reported in [GGD95b] point out that *management and retrieval of event information is not yet tolerable.* In particular, composite event detection is observed as degrading considerably the performance of the whole system. It can be envisaged that a fine-grained assessment on the performance penalty for each kind of composite event operator and mask can be most valuable at rule implementation time to determine how business rules will be finally supported.

7.5   From Isolated Tools to Integrated Environments

So far, tool development projects are characterized by their isolated and ad-hoc nature, where each one mainly focuses on one of the tasks involved in active system construction. Table 7.1 gives an overview of the range of

Task	Development process stage
Graphical description	Analysis/Design
Validation	Analysis
Static verification	Analysis/Design
Dynamic verification	Analysis/Design
Test-case generators	Analysis/Design
Model builders	Analysis/Design
Code generators	Implementation
Precompilers/preprocessors	Implementation
Tracers	Implementation/Maintenance
Evolution assistants	Maintenance
Explanation assistants	Maintenance
Browsers	Maintenance
Test managers	Maintenance
Benchmarkings	Maintenance

TABLE 7.1. Tools for rule-based system development.

tools that have been described in previous sections. Each tool focuses on distinct tasks and even on different models of how ECA rules are managed and executed. This is partly due to the lack of both a settled model and a proper methodology. However, and despite the usefulness of each tool, the real breakthrough will come when most of these tools can be encompassed within a single environment. As pointed out in [Fug93], this will achieve presentation and control integration (i.e., a homogeneous and consistent interface where sequencing between tasks is obtained by enforcing control chains among the tools) and, more importantly, provide data and process integration.

Data integration ensures that *all the information in the environment is managed as a consistent whole, regardless of how parts of it are operated on and transformed* [Fug93]. This implies the existence of a repository so that any tool can utilize it for specification storage and retrieval. The repository checks that consistency is preserved during the development life cycle and propagates changes along the distinct stages.

The importance of the repository cannot be underestimated. Indeed, the report on the Chimera support environment [BCFP96] (to the best of our knowledge, the only integrated environment currently at work) reports that *In retrospect, the absence of a global repository is a design error, since now the same application may be associated to two different repositories with potential for inconsistency ... we learned that, when designing a cooperative set of tools, the repository should be designed first and be maximally portable* [BCFP96].

Repository data includes the meta-model, which defines the conceptual model constructs and how they are related. One of the few works reported addressing this issue is [Her96], where a meta-model for information systems is described in terms of business rules.

As well as those elements, the repository should also provide information on other logical or physical aspects. For instance, Herbst's repository [Her96] includes the rule's origin (i.e., the source or reason of the existence of the rule), the organizational unit (i.e., the business unit responsible for the content and maintenance of the rule) and the rule's support (i.e., whether the rule is manually or automatically supported; if automatically, what are the software components, procedures, or triggers that support the rule). The aim is to facilitate easy administration of large rule sets.

In [Etz95], a similar approach is followed, but here the stress is on easing reasoning rather than just storing and retrieving metadata. Reasoning means being able to pose distinct questions to the repository such as which operations (data-elements) are directly or indirectly being activated (updated) as a consequence of detecting a certain event, or whether a given set of rules can be activated together as a result of the same event.

These examples illustrate how the contents of the repository provide the information required for the other tools, and thus it is vital to design and integrate it carefully.

7.6   Conclusion

This chapter presents an outline of current tools that support distinct steps during active database construction and administration.

Unfortunately, there is not yet a proper methodology that guides developers throughout the whole process of building active databases. This partially explains the ad-hoc and isolated nature of most of the tools that are conceived with a given active system in mind, and hence the lack of portability. The movement from isolated tools to integrated environments will necessarily come hand in hand with advances in the methodology for building active databases that consider rules in the wider context of information system support.

7.7   REFERENCES

[ABC82]   W.R. Adrion, M.A. Branstad, and J.C. Cherniavsky. Validation, Verification and Testing of Computer Software. *ACM Computing Surveys*, 14(2):159–192, 1982.

[BCFP96]   E. Baralis, S. Ceri, P. Fraternali, and S. Paraboschi. Support Environment for Active Rule Design. *Journal of Intelligent Information Systems*, (7):129–149, 1996.

[BCP96]   E. Baralis, S. Ceri, and S. Paraboschi. Modularization Techniques for Active Rules Design. *ACM Transactions on Information Systems*, 21(1):1–29, 1996.

[Beh94]   H. Behrends.   Simulation-Based Debugging for Active Databases. In *Proceedings of the 4th Intl. Workshop on Research Issues in Data Engineering (RIDE-ADS'94)*, pages 172–180, 1994.

[BGB95]   E. Benazet, H. Guehl, and M. Bouzebhoub. VITAL: a Visual Tool for Analysis of Rule Behaviour in Active Databases. In *[Sel95]*, pages 182–196, 1995.

[BS94]   P. Bichler and M. Schrefl. Active Object-Oriented Database using Active Object/Behaviour Diagrams. In *Proceedings of the 4th Intl. Workshop on Research Issues in Data Engineering (RIDE-ADS'94)*, pages 163–171, 1994.

[Buc94]   A.P. Buchmann. Current Trends in Active Databases: Are we Solving the Right Problems. In C. Chrisment, editor, *Information Systems Design and Multimedia (Proc. Basque International Workshop on IT)*, pages 121–133. Cepadues Editions, 1994.

[CTZ95]   S. Chakravarthy, Z. Tamizuddin, and J. Zhou. A Visualization and Explanation Tool for Debugging ECA rules in Active Databases. In *[Sel95]*, pages 196–209, 1995.

[DJP94]   O. Diaz, A. Jaime, and N.W. Paton. DEAR: A DEbugger for Active Rules in an Object-Oriented Context. In N.W. Paton and M.H. Williams, editors, *Proc. 1st Intl. Workshop on Rules In Database Systems*, pages 180–193. Springer-Verlag, 1994.

[DP97]   O. Diaz and N. Paton. Stimuli and Business Policies as Modelling Constructs: Their Definition and Validation Through the Event Calculus. In *Proc. 9th. CAiSE*, pages 33–46. LNCS, Springer-Verlag, 1997.

[Etz95]   O. Etzion. Reasoning About the Behavior of Active Database Applications. In *[Sel95]*, pages 86–100, 1995.

[FS93]   Y.A. Feldman and H. Schneider. Simulating Reactive Systems by Deduction. *ACM Transactions on Software Engineering and Methodology*, 2(2):128–175, 1993.

[Fug93]   A. Fuggetta. A Classification of CASE Technology. *Computer*, 26(12):25–38, 1993.

[GGD95a] A. Geppert, S. Gatziu, and K.R. Dittrich. A Designer's Benchmark for Active Database Management Systems: 007 Meets the BEAST. In *[Sel95]*, pages 309–323, 1995.

[GGD95b] A. Geppert, S. Gatziu, and K.R. Dittrich. Rulebase Evolution in Active Object-Oriented Database Systems: Adapting the Past to Future Needs. Technical Report 95.13, Institut fuer Informatik, Winterthurerstr. 190, CH-8047, Zurich, 1995.

[Gul96] J.A. Gulla. A General Explanation Component for Conceptual Modeling in CASE Environments. *ACM Transactions on Information Systems*, 14(3):297–329, 1996.

[Her96] H. Herbst. Business Rules in Systems Analysis: A Meta-Model and Repository System. *Journal of Information Systems*, 21(2):147–166, 1996.

[LST78] B. Lientz, E.B. Swanson, and G.E. Tompkins. Characteristics of Mpplications Software Maintenance. *Communication of ACM*, (21):466–471, 1978.

[NML93] A. Neufeld, G. Moerkotte, and P.C. Lockemann. Generating Consistency Test Data: Restricting the Search Space by a Generator Formula. *VLDB Journal*, 2(2):173–213, 1993.

[NTMG95] S. Navathe, A. Tanaka, R. Madhavan, and Y. H. Gan. A Methodology for Application Design Using Active Database Technology. In *Report RL-TR-95-41 from the Rome Laboratory*, 1995.

[Sel95] T. Sellis, editor. *Proc. 2nd Intl. Workshop on Rules in Database Systems (RIDS'95)*. Lecture Notes in Computer Science, Springer-Verlag, 1995.

[SHP88] M. Stonebraker, E. Hanson, and S. Potamianos. The POSTGRES Rule Manager. *IEEE Transactions on Software Engineering*, 14(7), 1988.

[SKD95] E. Simon and A. Kotz-Dittrich. Promises and Realities of Active Database Systems. In *Proc. 21st VLDB Conference*, pages 642–653. Morgan Kaufmann, 1995.

[Sto92] M. Stonebraker. The Integration of Rule Systems and Database Systems. *IEEE Trans. on Knowledge and Data Engineering*, 4(5):415–423, 1992.

[TC94] M. Teisseire and R. Cichetti. An Algebraic Approach for Event-Driven Modelling. In D. Karagiannis, editor, *Proc. Intl. Conf. on Databases and Expert Systems Applications (DEXA)*, pages 300–309. LNCS, Springer-Verlag, 1994.

[TPC94]   M. Teisseire, P. Poncelet, and R. Cichetti. Towards Event-Driven Modelling for Database Design. In J. Bocca, M. Jarke, and C. Zaniolo, editors, *Proc. 20th Intl. Conf. on VLDB*, pages 1–12. Morgan-Kaufmann, 1994.

[Wid94]   J. Widom. Research Issues in Active Database Systems: Report from Closing Panel at RIDE-ADS 94. In *SIGMOD RECORD*, volume 23 (3), pages 41–43, 1994.

8

ECA Functionality in a Distributed Environment

G. von Bültzingsloewen
A. Koschel
P. C. Lockemann
H.-D. Walter

ABSTRACT

The capabilities of active database systems remain meaningful for distributed applications. However, since the assumptions underlying a distributed active database system differ from those for a centralized active database system, the technical capabilities necessary for supporting active functionality must be revised and extended, and new challenges must be met. In addition, distributed active database systems and distributed rule processing offer new opportunities that make explicit use of the potential of distribution. The goal of this chapter is to provide a systematic overview of the design options for ECA functionality in distributed environments, highlighting the choices from a usage perspective.

8.1 Introduction

8.1.1 Challenges

As Tom Furey put it in 1993: "The vision is nomadic, ubiquitous, client/server computing everywhere" [OH95]. Many take this to mean that future networks will be nothing but a gigantic, global, ubiquitous, ever-present database with associated services. If so, would one not come to expect from such a database system active functionalities similar to those that are familiar in centralized active database systems? And if the answer is yes, how would one provide such a functionality now that:

- system resources such as databases, files, or processing tools are geographically widely dispersed,

- resources are usually heterogeneous,

- events may arise independently at arbitrary locations and times,

- event types may vary over a wider range,

- there is no uniform notion of system time,

- composite events may have to take all these factors into account,

- conditions and actions may consume resources at more than one site or at sites different from the event source, and

- resources often behave autonomously and, for this reason, subject themselves only to a modest amount of common discipline.

Today's sophisticated users will only turn to distributed systems if they see some benefits to be gained by doing so. Such benefits may be better performance, improved fault-tolerance, higher availability, or greater system flexibility due to open system architectures. Certainly a user would expect no loss in functionality from a distributed active database system when compared to non distributed systems. The technical challenge, then, is to provide such benefits despite the numerous new obstacles mentioned above.

8.1.2   Dimensions Revisited

To identify the technical challenges in more detail, it seems only natural to start from the centralized solution for active database systems, more precisely with the models and options of Chapter 1. In that chapter all active functionality was encapsulated within the notion of ECA rule. We will then have to determine how well we can carry over the traditional ECA models into the distributed world of network computing, and which kind of adjustments may become necessary.

To give some sample problems:

Event semantics: In Chapter 1, an event was defined as something that happens at a point in time. What is this point in time in a network without any global time?

Event detection: Think of composite events. An event detector must be able to detect composite events whose component events may occur anywhere in the network.

Condition checking: Condition checking may necessitate accesses to databases at more than one node. The heterogeneity of the nodes as expressed by, e.g., individual interfaces to access their respective states may lead to a more complex specification of the condition part of the rules. The autonomy of the nodes may lead to access restrictions of their states or a lack of coordination which impedes the atomicity of condition evaluation.

Execution model and rule management: If there is more than one rule base and rule engine, ways must be found for them to interoperate if they are heterogeneous and to coordinate them if they act autonomously.

Performance: Under all these conditions, the efficiency of event detection and rule evaluation may suffer due to the need for the exchange of messages and, hence, the added network traffic. Also, distribution breeds new problems of availability and reliability, which can only be overcome by additional precautionary measures.

In the sequel, we concentrate on some of these issues. We assume that if there are several rule systems, they all follow the same rule semantics, i.e., we restrict ourselves to an environment of homogeneous ECA rule systems. However, we tolerate the heterogeneity of the information sources with all its effects on the event types that can be produced by these sources, as well as the effects on the queries to (or invocations of operations on) sources during condition/action processing.

8.1.3   Outline of the Chapter

Distributed active database management systems are a fairly novel area of research. Consequently, few proven techniques are already available. Under these circumstances, the purpose of this chapter cannot be to revisit the individual issues and techniques of the earlier chapters and outline the needed changes again. Rather, the emphasis of this chapter is on a broad outline of issues arising in connection with a networked active database system. Consequently, the chapter takes a primarily architectural approach. Section 8.2 argues that a networked active database system could be seen from two different metaphorical viewpoints and that these views may suggest differences within design decisions. Section 8.3 explores what kind of applications ECA functionality in distributed environments could be useful for. Section 8.4 discusses the impact of distribution on the knowledge model. In Section 8.5, we do the same for the execution model. Section 8.6 introduces several approaches from the literature and relates them to the results of the previous two sections. Section 8.7 concludes the chapter.

8.2   Two Views of the Networked Active Database System

In the centralized case, a client views an active database management system as some sort of service institution that notifies it whenever some event of interest has occurred in the environment. The cause of the event usually remains anonymous because the client has little need for knowing it. Rather, the client's interest is in observing the effects signaled by the event and in being able to react to them. Under such a service view, the client concentrates on solving its problem on the basis of its own strategy and approaches the system only in order to delegate some subproblem to it, which can be expressed in terms of event detection and reaction processing within the database. The client is not interested in whether the system happens to be distributed or not, and who contributes to the solution of the subproblem.

In the service view each application is concentrated in a client that calls upon the active services of the network. The network, then, has the flavor of a centralized active database system and plays the role of the development system of Chapter 1. In essence, the view models the classical client/server system. Figure 8.1 characterizes the view: the client independently pursues its own objectives and while doing so, procures needed and available services and resources from the network which functions as the provider.

We may expect that in this view, the knowledge models which specify rules consisting of events, conditions and actions and the execution models specifying the operational semantics of the rules can be largely carried over from the previous chapters. Some adjustments may be necessary on account of the changed dimensions in Section 8.1.2.

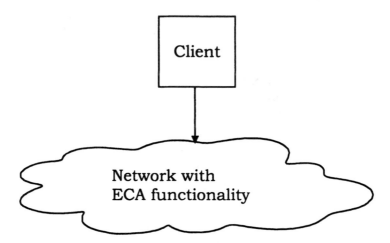

FIGURE 8.1. ECA functionality in a service model of distributed active functionality.

A network offers more potential, though. Problem solving may now be done on a cooperative basis; some client may delegate not only standardized tasks to some server, but may also wish to procure specialized expertise that it does not have itself from another, known resource in the network. Over and above the standard services of the network, several clients should now be in a position to communicate with one another, either synchronously via message exchange, or asynchronously by leaving the effects of actions at the network database. In other words, a client considers itself to be a member in a group of peers that collectively pursue some common objective, i.e., collaboration on a common task. Such a view corresponds to the view of a peer-to-peer system.

Peer-to-peer systems must be supported by a suitable communications infrastructure. Hence, this view places more emphasis on the network acting as a communication channel. We refer to the view as the communications channel view. Figure 8.2 characterizes the view. The technical challenge is in the amalgamation of communication and database functionalities, again augmented with ECA functionality.

Communications channel models are the very essence of distribution. Hence in their case, ECA functionality can be expected to require more pronounced adjustments to the earlier techniques than in the service models. To give a technical example, peer-to-peer systems are message-oriented as opposed to client/server systems, which have the remote procedure call as their underlying communication paradigm. In peer-to-peer systems ECA rules can be used as a coordination mechanism for autonomous communicating partners, e.g., when a message passing between two peers raises an event in the network. In this case, the events are different from those in client/server systems, so that we need a (slightly) revised knowledge model with respect to the semantics of events.

The service view supports more naturally component–based or set of services architectures like OMG's CORBA [Sig96, Obj95], which rely on well-proven classical object-oriented approaches. The communications channel model reflects a more visionary direction, since modern information systems should be open to the attachment and detachment of more or less independent partners that are distributed across local or global networks. These partners must maintain their independence by entering into voluntary cooperations. The service model could certainly support collaboration as well, but it can only do so in a rather indirect way, by building up and providing status information to each client so that each can draw its own conclusions. The communications channel model may appear more natural to a partner and give him or her better control over which partners to collaborate with.

8.3   Applications for ECA Rules in Distributed Environments

Chapter 1 distinguished three different categories of applications for active rules: database system extensions where active rules serve as a primitive mechanism for supporting the implementation of other database system functions; closed database applications which determine their behavior solely on the basis of database-internal events; and open database applications which also respond to situations observed outside of the system.

Since we expect the functionality of the centralized system to be preserved in the distributed case, these categories remain the same except that the technical solutions for them may become more elaborate and expensive. Consequently, our major interest in this section must be in the

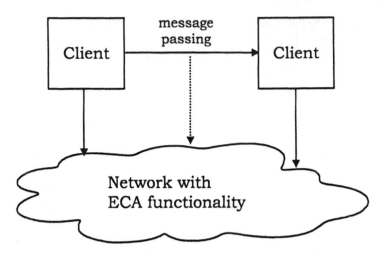

FIGURE 8.2. ECA functionality in a communications channel model of distributed active functionality.

added benefits that the distributed active database management system provides to the outside world.

8.3.1 Service View

In the simplest case, events are nothing but a purely internal instrument for the database system to offer certain functionalities to the clients. For example, in centralized systems, active rules have long been known to support integrity constraints, materialized views, derived data, and the coordination of tasks within database systems, to name just a few. This functionality remains relevant to a distributed database, though it may pose novel technical challenges. A prominent example is the maintenance of materialized views in data warehousing systems [Wid95, ZHKF95] that have been derived from data kept by other sources, or distributed constraint maintenance [RSK91, CW92]. ECA rules can also be used to implement services required for network management, e.g., mail services or firewalls.

The events just referred to are an internal matter of the system. Externally observable events under the service view are those that can be directly traced to the database system, thus in our case potentially all of the heterogeneous event sources in the whole network. Either the client raises an event by submitting a standard request to the network database services, and this is indeed the only kind of external event that the system can recognize, or the database system raises an event with a client by noting a particular change in the network database and seeing a need to notify this client. The changes causing the event must clearly be a consequence of someone else's request to the database. Hence, the notified client is put in a position to observe an event within the network, though only indirectly.

For an indication of the events originator, passing of context information to the notified client is necessary. Those external events that lead to network database internal events are observable, e.g., by means of monitoring wrappers.

The service model allows one to restrict the context of ECA rules for condition checking and action execution to these inside the network cloud of Figure 8.1. This has several advantages. First, the distributed database system has full control over the types of events that take place, the conditions to be evaluated, and the actions to be invoked. It may thus impose certain (external or internal) standards. Second, the system has a good chance to provide each client with a homogeneous view of its functionality even though the network includes a number of possibly heterogeneous data or even non data sources, each generating its own events on certain updates. In other words, the system can hide the composition of and the heterogeneities within the network.

Take as an example a scientific or environmental information system, which is usually distributed over a range of network nodes. If a client's request needs information from several nodes, the associated event triggers a number of rules, each converting the information to the format expected by one of the providers. To collect the results from the providers, the system registers the event associated with the reply to each of them and then uses its active functionality of complex situation monitoring to assemble the combined result into a homogeneous reply to the client [vBKK96]. The system may also act on its own by signaling an unexpected event to the client. Take a civil servant who may need to be informed whenever a measured air quality parameter exceeds a certain threshold. Detection of such a critical situation requires monitoring of several data sources (e.g., a database that records measurement values and a second database with parameterized threshold values) combined with data analysis (e.g., for calculating the spread of pollutants under the current wind direction).

8.3.2 Communications Channel View

This view stresses the equality of both internal and external events. Hence, the active database system, in our case the network, may observe events outside the system and as a consequence may present itself to the clients in the form of actions other than pure database services. An important class of such events are those that can be traced to the direct interaction between clients.

Take distributed workflow management [TGD95, SEM97, MSKW96]. Consider a workflow consisting of a number of steps, a number of distributed processing entities (tools) for executing one or more of these steps, and a number of constraints that enforce or prohibit the execution of steps in certain situations. Let the network monitor the state of the workflow, thus providing some sort of coordination. Active functionality can be used to observe events that originate with the beginning or termination of steps by tools, to update or check the state, and to enforce and/or prohibit processing steps accordingly. Clearly, only some of the events bear any relationship to classical database functionality. If we take, as we have so far, a database perspective of the network, then the observable or available functionality of the network exceeds that of a classical database system.

As a second example, consider events by clients that concern requests for message transfers to other clients. They play an essential role for peer-to-peer systems. Take complex planning and control tasks that require cooperation amongst a number of autonomous peers. For example, transport logistics involve the scheduling of resources at different locations, while overall optimization of resource usage remains a global objective. A similar kind of application is distributed production planning and control. The common objective underlying the need for coordination, or here even cooperation, can be formulated as constraints that govern the way peers act and interact with one another. Because peers act autonomously and (as seen from the outside) unpredictably, the actions must be captured by events. Consequently, ECA rules are an ideal means to reflect reactions and complex events, relating several actions and reactions to reflect constraints.

The two examples seem to indicate a number of possibilities for how the network may get involved, i.e., what kind of added benefits it may provide. Involvement may range from a highly distributed solution, whereby the rules are part of the clients' implementations to a more centralized solution where the rules are collected into a shared construct. The first is the usual way cooperation is realized in pure object-oriented systems, whereas the second is the traditional approach for telecommunication systems, where communication constraints are collected in a protocol [AGP94, CDK94, LW95]. Correspondingly, the added functionality may range from pure event transmission all the way through state monitoring up to the properly augmented event control regimes of active databases.

In the communication channels view, applications are usually heterogeneous and because the distribution now becomes at least somewhat visible to the clients, they may themselves have to deal with heterogeneity. However, one could still use ECA rules in order to hide the heterogeneity arising within the network from clients.

8.4   How Distribution Affects the Knowledge Model

In this section, we discuss the impact of distribution on each of the dimensions for the knowledge model identified in Chapter 1. Table 8.1 summarizes the results. In order to distinguish the currently considered dimensions from those of Chapter 1 and to stress the resulting differences, we annotate them with $_D$.

Event source: The potential event sources mentioned for the centralized case remain the same. However, while for the centralized case most non database internal event-sources are simply classified as external event sources, mostly without further distinction, more detailed classifications are often extremely useful. This is due to the fact that in the distributed case, many highly heterogeneous event sources are often involved. Also the complexity arising from the distribution of possibly heterogeneous events, given the network database is distributed, adds a new quality to ECA rule processing. The event sources of the communications channel view must be added to these. Events like the arrival of a truck at a certain location or the completion of a production step occur outside the networked system and have to be raised explicitly by some client. Similarly, events related to communication amongst clients must be considered (see Figure 8.2).

Granularity, type, and role of events, role of conditions: Distribution itself has no effect on granularity, type of events, role of events, and conditions in ECA rules. Heterogeneity, however, does. It may give rise to a deeper hierarchy of external event types. Event sources can be classified by the support they offer for monitoring, e.g., triggers, log files, or query interfaces. Different sources may support only certain event granularities, e.g., only instance-oriented event signaling. (See [Wid95, ZHKF95, vBKK96, FD95, vBKK97] for more detailed classifications.)

Context of condition and action; state: The context of condition evaluation and action execution is a very critical issue in distributed systems. First, there is no single database. As a consequence, the state of a distributed system, which condition evaluation refers to, may be ill-defined. In large distributed and highly concurrent systems, defining the overall state of the system would require the availability of all nodes at all times and instantaneous access to them. Traditionally, these requirements are simulated by transactions. However, in a system of heterogeneous resources and originators of external events, there may not exist a current transaction relative to which event detection, condition evaluation, and action execution are defined (see also next section). Consequently, DB_T, DB_E, DB_C, DB_A (see Chapter 1) must be redefined.

Instead, one may have to narrow the system state scope in order to make it possible to implement the knowledge model. One possible scheme for narrowing this scope would introduce two levels of state information: local states and a global state, where an explicit mapping between both levels is required. Events on the global level refer to the global state, events on the local level to the local state. The latter are not visible at the global level. This approach implies that clients must offer appropriate interfaces that allow them to export their local state to some higher distribution level. An alternative scheme for narrowing this scope would have event detection, condition evaluation, and action execution refer to a state separate from the state of the clients, i.e., the rule base has its own database in which it maintains state information. This is especially necessary, if one expects nodes without interfaces for transactional (or even any) access to their state.

Whatever notion of context a knowledge model applies in a distributed environment, this notion significantly influences the expressiveness of the rule language.

Rules: In the service view, it appears that ECA rules are stored in a single global rule base. A possible distribution of the rule base that is used to optimize the system remains invisible to applications. In the communications channel view, there may be reasons, though, to associate some rules with the peers, e.g., because of a far larger rule base, increased system complexity, specialized event detection, condition evaluation, and action execution capabilities in the clients, or autonomous control over rules by some clients. Hence, the network may not be entirely able to hide the heterogeneity and distribution of the rule base. If the structure of the rule base has to become visible to the clients, it should somehow be represented in the knowledge model. Options are:

- a global rule base,

- a set of local rule bases, e.g., one rule base per node,

- a structure of rule bases that is determined by application semantics, e.g., all rules relevant to a specific task could be collected into a dedicated rule base.

Perhaps the options may be used in some combination. For example, application-specific structuring of rules may be combined with location-specific structuring ("Where do we best install the rules for a specific task?") of rules.

8.5   How Distribution Affects the Execution Model

8.5.1   Architectural Model of the Network System

Distribution impacts the execution model of ECA rules. To discuss the impact, we introduce an architectural model that characterizes the internal structure of the network system in general terms.

A network system consists of loosely coupled autonomous nodes. If two or more nodes work on a common task, they have to cooperate with each other by doing some local computations and communicating with one another. Consequently, the internal structure of a network is always of the kind depicted in Figure 8.2. A set of (more or less) autonomous peers or agents, that contribute to the overall functionality of the distributed system. They specifically contribute to the active functionality, which we

Event	$\textbf{Source}_D \subset$	$\textbf{Source} \cup \{ \text{ Interaction } \}$
	$\textbf{Granularity}_D =$	$\textbf{Granularity}$
	$\textbf{Type}_D =$	$\textbf{Type}$
	$\textbf{Role}_D =$	$\textbf{Role}$
Condition	$\textbf{Role}_D =$	$\textbf{Role}$
	$\textbf{Context}_D \subset$	$\{ \text{ DB}_T, \text{ Bind}_E, \text{ DB}_E, \text{ DB}_C \}$
		where DB is a $\textbf{Database}_D$
		(see below, sec. 8.5.4)
Action	$\textbf{Options}_D =$	$\textbf{Options}$
	$\textbf{Context}_D \subset$	$\{ \text{ DB}_T, \text{ Bind}_E, \text{ Bind}_C, \text{ DB}_E, \text{ DB}_C,$
		$\text{DB}_A \}$ where DB is a $\textbf{Database}_D$
		(see below, sec. 8.5.4)
State	$\textbf{Database}_D \subset$	Global, Local, $\textbf{Rule Base}_D$
Rules	$\textbf{Rule Base}_D \subset$	Global, Local, Task

TABLE 8.1. Additional or modified dimensions of the ECA knowledge model in distributed environments.

discuss here, together with a network system, now of a lower-level functionality. This structuring process may be applied recursively along the lines of the ISO/OSI model.

Agents interact with one another by means of messages. Regulations to constrain interaction are captured by *contracts* among a set of agents.

In an active network system, we can identify the following types of agents.
Clients: Clearly, clients are agents. They may access the active database, e.g., start a transaction or read or write a database tuple. Second, they may raise events indicating some occurrence of interest (explicit or external events). Third, they may modify the rule base.

Database or information managers: Database managers are the targets of clients' requests for access to relations or objects. They evaluate queries against the database they maintain and check for given database conditions. They synchronize concurrent accesses to databases by clients and by other agents within the system (see below). In a distributed environment, there may be a single database manager or several, possibly heterogeneous, database managers. If we allow for non data sources, we refer to the recipients of requests more generally as information managers.

Rule managers: Rule managers are responsible for the maintenance and utilization of a set of ECA rules (a rule base). They accept requests, both to modify the rule base and to interrogate it for condition evaluation and action execution. Note that the single-threaded execution model of a centralized active DBMS becomes inappropriate as the number of nodes in the distributed system grows. From an application perspective, the signaling of one situation is independent from the signaling of a second

Event Signaling	Event Visibility $\subset$	Global, Local
	Detection Method $\subset$	Reactive, Proactive
	Event Manager $\in$	Central, Distributed
Rule Triggering	Communication Method $\in$	Reactive, Proactive
	Rule Manager $\in$	Central, Distributed
Scheduling	Rule Manager $\in$	Global, Local, Directed
	Rule Set $\in$	Global, Local
	Rule Distribution $\in$	Transparent, Visible
Condition Evaluation and Action Execution	State Access $\in$	Global, Local
	Database or $\in$	Distributed DB,
	Information Manager	Federated DB,
		Federation of Sources
	Coordination $\in$	Global Transactions,
		TP Monitor, Local
		Transactions, None

TABLE 8.2. Architectural design options.

situation and consequently, execution of one action may often be scheduled independently of the execution of some other action. Hence, in contrast to monolithic active systems, it makes good sense to have more than one rule manager, and more than one rule base, in a network.

Event managers: An event manager records events and maintains an event history. It is accessed by clients and database managers, both of which produce events, and rule managers which consume events. In the peer-to-peer case, clients may also be event consumers. Again, more than one event manager may be found in an active network.

Each step that takes place during rule execution, i.e., event detection, scheduling, condition evaluation, and finally action execution (cf. Figure 4, Chapter 1) requires a contract between those agents that contribute to a step. To examine these contracts more closely, we study the various agent configurations conceivable for each step below. Table 8.2 summarizes the results.

8.5.2   Event Detection

Event detection involves the event sources, event managers and rule managers in a contract. It consists of two phases; the signaling of events, and the triggering of rules.

Event signaling: Event signaling requires a (sub-)contract between event managers and an event source, either a client or a database manager. The contract determines the kind of events the sources may produce, the kind of events the event managers subscribe to, the visibility of events, and the method for detecting events. The spectrum of visibility ranges from global visibility, i.e., all events are visible throughout the entire network, to purely local visibility, i.e., events are only visible at the node where they occur.

Global visibility is required if event managers must recognize composite events that consist of component events arising at different nodes in the network. Global visibility of events can be achieved either by letting event sources communicate their events to some central event manager, or by the cooperation of local event managers that aggregate their local event histories to a (logically) global event history in order to detect composite events, possibly by using some form of replication/fragmentation policy. The trade-off is between the well-known disadvantages of centralized solutions with respect to reliability and performance bottlenecks, vs. the communication overhead for the coordination among several event managers. In both cases, the lack of a global clock introduces uncertainties into the order of events.

Local visibility suffices if events are not deemed relevant outside a node, e.g., events are raised within some GUI object. Here, the installation of an event manager at each node avoids costly communication overhead. If an application does not have any notion of a global event history, it will be satisfied with this solution.

The detection of events follows one of two approaches:

1. a reactive event manager where event producers communicate events to an event manager, and

2. a proactive event manager where the manager polls clients and database managers for new events, or generates internal events unrelated to the activities of the network, e.g., internal clock settings or external events outside the boundaries of the system considered.

Reactive models are useful for central event managers provided it is known that every event bears some relevance within the overall system. Otherwise, the model may lead to a tremendous communication load because in its pure form, every "tiny" event must be communicated to the event manager. If event managers are distributed, a proactive behavior may instead be in order, due to the lighter load. The same is true if the managers can statically preselect the set of relevant events. Pro-active models, however, pay the price of consuming additional processing resources.

Rule triggering: Triggering of rules requires a contract between event managers and rule managers. The contract determines the events that may fire rules and the method for communicating events. While the events covered by the contracts between event sources and event managers are primitive, the events passed between event managers and rule managers may be primitive or composite. The event managers must be capable of constructing composite events and of recognizing when one has occurred.

The communication between the managers may again follow a reactive or a proactive approach, with similar advantages and disadvantages:

1. Reactive rule managers are those where all primitive as well as composite events are passed from the event managers on to the rule managers. Since an event manager must know what constitutes a composite event, it makes sense to economize on the communication of events by some kind of subscription mechanism, i.e., rule managers explicitly declare what kind of events they are interested in. An event manager now communicates to a given rule manager just those events to which this rule manager has subscribed.

2. Proactive rule managers poll the set of known event managers for events they are interested in at a certain point in time.

Common to both subscription and polling is that only those events that actually contribute to certain rules are communicated across the network. The difference is that subscription event managers must provide a subscription interface. Consequently, polling seems to offer better scalability, since new rule managers can be added to the system dynamically without any modifications to and communication with event managers. This may be useful in cases where the addition of rule managers occurs frequently. On the other hand, upon adding new event managers, polling requires the existing rule managers be notified, but since in a distributed system, we can assume that there are far fewer rule managers than event managers, this does not seem to be a major disadvantage. Note, incidentally, that similar considerations apply to the relationship between event sources and event managers.

While polling seems superior at system management time, subscription is often superior at runtime. Polling causes a runtime overhead at the event consumers sites. In large distributed systems with only a few event consumers, this overhead may prove negligible, but not in small systems or in systems consisting of a large number of event consumers.

The choice of event detection and event communication model is orthogonal to the decisions on the distribution of event and rule managers. Both managers may be central, though perhaps at different nodes, or one of the two may be central while the other is distributed, or both may be distributed. This degree of freedom is particularly important in light of the criteria for centralization or distribution, which differ for event managers whose primary influence is the distribution of event sources and event visibility, and for rule managers where the major factor is the distribution of data that is subjected to condition checking and the effect of actions.

8.5.3 Scheduling

Rule managers schedule the execution of all rules. Scheduling regulates the time at which the conditions of rules are to be evaluated and when their actions are to be executed. If more than one rule manager exists in the distributed environment, the rule managers must cooperate with one another and, consequently, enter into a scheduling contract. The main design parameters for such a contract are the number of rule managers and rule bases in the system, the event detection mechanism, and the scheduling policy defined by the execution model. Options for the first two parameters are:

- a central rule manager maintaining a global rule base (which would reduce the problem of scheduling to that used in monolithic systems),

- a set of rule managers distributed in the network maintaining their local rule bases,

- a set of rule managers distributed in the network together with a global set of rules.

Dimensions of the scheduling policy are the coupling modes, the priorities, and the number of rules to be fired in parallel. Depending on the rule system, either the user controls the scheduling by selecting specific settings within these dimensions, or the rule system uses predefined settings.

Coupling modes are generally defined relative to transactions. Consequently, common scheduling policies from active DBMS require either that the agents offer a distributed transaction interface (2PC), or that a separate transaction facility such as a TP-Monitor is available. If transactions are not present, this restricts itself with respect to supported coupling modes.

A set of rule managers gives rise to communication overhead because in order to enforce a scheduling policy, the cooperation among the managers must be organized. Such a set is necessary, though, if one allows some form of parallel rule firing. Priorities and the number of rules to be fired in parallel have a direct impact on the cooperation overhead among the rule managers. Global priorities force the rule managers to agree on a corresponding global partial order among the triggered rules. On the other hand, a central rule manager may easily become a bottleneck and may degrade overall system performance and availability. A combination of both may overcome some of the drawbacks, for instance, by installing local rule managers for local rule bases together with a global rule manager maintaining rules that span more than one site (directed approach).

8.5.4   Condition Evaluation and Action Execution

For condition evaluation and action execution, rule managers and database managers must cooperate and, hence, establish contracts. If condition evaluation appraises the state of clients, or rules are used to coordinate clients (see Section 8.3), clients are also part of the contract.

For the purpose of coordination, the contract should have the traits of a transaction:

- If condition evaluation appraises the states of clients, the transaction semantics for rule execution require that clients offer transactional access to their states. The same holds for actions if they access some client's state.

- If the scope of conditions and/or actions reaches beyond a single agent (client or database manager), distributed transaction facilities are required either by the agent itself or by a separate TP monitor, since in order to abort some action, agents must first offer transactions. Secondly, the transaction models must be compatible because otherwise no unique semantics could be defined at the global level.

Transaction management is needed for other reasons as well: coupling modes are defined in relation to transaction boundaries, and parallel firing of rules must be controlled such that the serializability of rule actions can be guaranteed. For example, if all agents (clients and database managers) offer a transactional interface, we can largely carry the coupling modes over from centralized systems.

Otherwise, we either have to give up the high level of consistency that transactions systems are offering, or we have to exclude agents (clients, information managers) from the contract. Conceivable approaches can be found among the techniques of distributed, federated database and multi-database technology [BHP92, SL90].

NCL / NIIIP	*Service View* rules compiled into method calls at nodes
Coffein	*Service View* separately usable components for event detection, rule processing etc. for CORBA-based distributed systems
Oracle	*Service View* central rule processing, separate gateway servers for data source access
Wide	*Communication Channel View* distributed components for workflow execution, active rules, transactions, and event detection
Alliances	*Communication Channel View* rules regulating communication between autonomous objects are collected into a separate construct

TABLE 8.3. System model–architecture

NCL / NIIIP	*System Extension* ECAA rules for security, constraints, negotiation, ...
Coffein	*Supervision* complex situation monitoring, active information delivery, ...
Oracle	*System Extension* Triggers for database constraints, negotiation, ...
Wide	*Control* Execution of workflows
Alliances	*Supervision* rules enforce an inter-object communication protocol

TABLE 8.4. Application characteristics.

8.6 Classification of Existing Approaches

The previous sections have been of a somewhat speculative character. We identified major issues and related them to the classification scheme of Chapter 1. However, little was presented in terms of hard techniques. The reason is that distributed ADBMS-style ECA rule processing, let alone distributed ADBMS themselves, have only recently become the subject of more intense interest to researchers. Nonetheless, some approaches do exist. To give examples with no attempt to list them all, we shall pick out five in order to relate them to our classification scheme. We give short descriptions of their main purposes and then classify them in comparison tables based on the criteria from tables 8.1 and 8.2. These comparisons are in tables 8.3 to 8.11. What we hope for is that the examples clearly show the usefulness of our identified issues and parameters, and also that they provide some insight into which combinations of system parameters have been successfully tested and which techniques were employed.

NCL/K3, NIIIP   In the NCL approach of NIIIP [NII95, SLY+95, SLAF+95], a high-level ECA (ECAA: Event Condition Action Alternate Action) rule approach for the virtual enterprise is introduced. Integration of sources into the virtual enterprise is based on CORBA as a communication layer. NCL allows for view definitions on arbitrary encapsulated (wrapped) sources from those enterprises, but is restricted in event types, since only method event types are supported.

The methods of CORBA objects can be associated with NCL rules. This means the invocation of such an associated method is the event, which gives, as usual, method parameters as the event binding. A precompiler approach is used to compile the definitions into CORBA-IDL. Each object method that is associated with a rule is surrounded with code, which first does the processing of the ECAA rule and then calls the original method.

Thus, after the rule definition phase, the systems consists of a (now hard-coded) set of distributed local-per-node rules.

Coffein, FZI   The approach described in [vBKK96] allows for ECA-like rule definitions, e.g., for online monitoring of complex situations in distributed, heterogeneous information systems. It especially allows for arbitrary (not only data) information sources as event producers, and it is also possible to revert to such sources (read access) during condition processing.

The architecture of the system consists of wrappers enabling primitive event detection, an event history for capturing primitive events that arise at different places in the distributed systems, and a component for complex event detection and rule processing based on the expert system shell CLIPS. While wrappers for information sources (event monitoring and reversion to sources in conditions) are hard-coded but parameterizable, the CA parts of the rules are interpreted during runtime, allowing for flexible rule changes. All system components are integrated using CORBA as a middleware layer. They are by themselves CORBA objects. Thus, they can also be distributed and replicated. The overall system is part of a federation architecture for heterogeneous information systems [KKN+96] consisting of CORBA and WWW technology. Environmental information systems are used as an application background. The system is currently extended to a widely configurable CORBA-based set of services for active functionality, the C^2offein system. The system provides services ranging from pure event monitoring up to full ECA rule processing. It allows for, e.g., different qualities of communication protocols between services, several kinds of event monitoring techniques, and customizable use of CORBA features.

Oracle, Oracle Cooperation   As another example, we take a commercial database system, the RDBMS Oracle. Oracle, with its distributed database option [Ora96], allows for (limited) ECA rule definition (Oracle triggers) across distributed databases.

The Oracle distributed database appears to the user as a single database server, a global database, but is, in fact, a set of two or more database servers. The data on each database server can be distributed across a network (using Oracle's SQL-Net). Each local database has to cooperate, e.g., in transaction protocols, to maintain the global databases consistency.

With Oracle's Open Gateway technology, access to several other database systems and data sources (like flat files) is provided by so-called gateway servers, which directly access these sources. These gateway servers are tightly integrated with the global Oracle server. Clients therefore only need to communicate with the integrating global server.

WIDE, WIDE Consortium   The WIDE system [SEM97, CCPP96] is a prototype for distributed workflow management. Its architecture basically consists of a workflow management environment and a work task execution (or agent) environment. In our terminology, this corresponds to a communication channel model: the workflow agents act as peers that implicitly

communicate asynchronously via the workflow management environment–
in our case the communication channel. The workflow management environment comprises a workflow execution engine, which is bundled with
components for active rules, transaction processing, and a basic access layer
to provide an object-oriented view to data sources (Oracle in the current
system). Components may be distributed by means of CORBA. The system
supports ECA rules for workflow specification, which are processed in decoupled mode. Event types distinguish data, external, workflow, and time
events. Two transaction layers are used; global transactions based on the
Saga model [GMS87], and local ones based on classical nested transactions.

Alliances   An almost pure communication channel view is provided by
the concept of alliances [LW95]. Alliances define a relationship between a set
of cooperating objects, which communicate explicitly and synchronously.
They implement a task-specific cooperation protocol. In order to do so,
they use rules that enforce constraints on the communication behavior of
the participating objects. Their execution model is based on proactive event
detection (polling of sources). Rules are processed per task. The rule set
of a task can be distributed across the set of nodes that provide a location
for the participating objects.

8.7   Conclusion

Distributed ECA functionality is a rather novel field of research. As such, it
poses a large number of scientific challenges that will have to be explored in
some depth before such functionality can find its way into commercial products. Some of the issues are also examined in other (non database) fields
of computer science, like telecommunications and distributed AI, which
can give valuable input to distributed ADBMS-style ECA rule processing. Many of the overall research issues have been raised in the previous
sections. Here they are summarized, and a few more have been added.

The first area of issues is concerned with the strategic influences in distributed ECA rule processing, namely temporal and spatial distribution,
autonomy, and heterogeneity of sources and system components. This comprises definition and exploration of:

- appropriate system, knowledge, and execution models that take the
  strategic influences into account and support applications with different characteristics,

- meaningful semantics for distributed rule systems, to cope with issues
  like context for rule processing without global state.

The second area is concerned with the event and rule processing engine.

Besides the investigation of architectural options about how to really build a distributed ECA rule system, the following issues need to be addressed:

- Develop and transfer techniques to deal with the strategic influences in distributed ECA rule processing, namely temporal and spatial distribution, autonomy, and heterogeneity of sources and system components.

- Event monitoring service: Find policies/mechanisms for detecting and composing events across individual subsystem boundaries in the absence of global time and universal scope.

- Rule execution service: Consumption of events signaled by the event monitoring service, and execution of ECA-style rules in an environment with distributed condition checking and action execution.

- Rule execution policies for consumption of events, for parameter passing from event monitoring service and event sources to the rule execution service.

- Strategies for rule processing under various transaction models or the lack thereof.

- Unbundling the Active DBMS, that means separation of functional components of Active DBMS into several units, to provide ADBMS-style active functionality as a set of services [KGvBF97].

Finally, distribution adds a new dimension to the reliability of the overall system:

- Dealing with the distribution and unreliability in the network, and the unpredictability of participants' behaviors.

- Distribution and reliability strategies for placement of information sources and for handling replication and fragmentation of data and ECA rules.

In summary, full ADBMS-style distributed ECA rule functionality is far from being available in products and offers a promising area for further research.

8.8 References

[AGP94]   J.-M. Andreoli, H. Gallaire, and R. Pareschi. Rule-Based Object Coordination. In A. Yonezawa P. Ciancarini, O. Nierstrasz, editor, *Object-Based Models and Languages for Concurrent Systems: Proceedings of ECOOP'94 Workshop on Models and Languages for Coordination of Parallelism and Distribution*, volume 924 of *Lecture Notes in Computer Science*, pages 1–13, July 1994.

[BHP92]   M.W. Bright, A.R. Hurson, and S. H. Pakzad. A Taxonomy
             and Current Issues in Multidatabase Systems. *IEEE Computer*, pages 50–60, March 1992.

[CCPP96]   F. Casati, S. Ceri, B. Pernici, and G. Pozzi. Deriving Active
             Rules for Workflow Enactment. In *Proc. 7th DEXA*, Springer-Verlag, 1996.

[CDK94]   G. Coulouris, J. Dollimore, and T. Kindberg. *Distributed Systems: Concepts and Design.* Addision-Wesley, second edition,
             1994.

[CW92]   S. Ceri and J. Widom. Production Rules in Parallel and Distributed Database Environments. In *Proc 18th Int'l. Conf. on
             Very Large Data Base*, Vancouver, Canada, August 1992.

[FD95]   R. Fernandez and O. Diaz. Reactive Behaviour Support:
             Themes and Variations. In Timos Sellis, editor, *Proc. Second
             Intl. Workshop on Rules in Database Systems*, Lecture Notes
             on Computer Science, No. 985, pages 69–85. Springer-Verlag,
             Athens, Greece, September 1995.

[GMS87]   H. Garcia-Molina and K. Salem. Sagas. In *Proc. 1987 ACM
             SIGMOD*, 1987.

[KGvBF97]   Arne Koschel, Stella Gatziu, Günter von Bültzingsloewen,
             and Hans Fritschi. Applying the Unbundling Process on
             Active Database Systems. FZI-DBS-Report DBS.97.415,
             Forschungszentrum Informatik (FZI), Karlsruhe, Germany,
             April 1997.

[KKN+96]   Arne Koschel, Ralf Kramer, Ralf Nikolai, Wilhelm
             Hagg, and Joachim Wiesel. A Federation Architecture
             for an Environmental Informaton System Incorporat-
             ing GIS, the World-Wide Web, and CORBA. In *3rd
             Intl. Conference/Workshop Integrating GIS and Envi-
             ronmental Modeling*, Santa Fe, New Mexico, USA, Jan-
             uary 1996. http://ncgia.ucsb.edu/conf/SANTA_FE_CD-
             ROM/sf_papers/nikolai_ralf/fedarch.html.

[LW95]   P.C. Lockemann and H.D. Walter. Object-Oriented Protocol
             Hierachies in Distributed Workflow Systems. *TAPOS: Theory
             and Practice of Object Systems*, 1(4), 1995.

[MSKW96]   J.A. Miller, A.P. Sheth, K.J. Kochut, and X. Wang. CORBA-
             Based Run-Time Architectures for Workflow Management.
             *Journal of Database Management, Special Issue on Multi-
             databases*, 7(1):16–27, 1996.

[NII95]   NIIIP Consortium. NIIIP Reference Architecture - Concept
             and Guidelines. Technical Report NTR95-01, National In-
             dustrial Information Infrastructure Protocols (NIIIP) Consor-
             tium, http://www.niiip.org, January 1995.

[Obj95]   Object Management Group. The Common Object Request
             Broker: Architecture and Specification, Version 2.0. OMG
             Document, Object Management Group, Inc. (OMG), July
             1995.

[OH95]   R. Orfali and D. Harkey. *The Essential Client/Server Survival
             Guide*. Addison-Wesley, New York, USA, 1995.

[Ora96]   Oracle. *Oracle7 Server Distributed Systems, Volume I: Dis-
             tributed Data*, release 7.3, part no. a32543-1 edition, 1996.

[RSK91]   M. Rusenkiewicz, A. Sheth, and G. Karabatis. Specifying In-
             terdatabase Dependencies in a Multidatabase Environment.
             IEEE Computer, 24(12):46–54, December 1991.

[SEM97]   SEMA Group. Wide newsletter number 05, March 1997.
             http://www.sema.es/projects/WIDE.

[Sig96]   J. Sigel. *CORBA Fundamentals and Programming*. John Wi-
             ley & Sons, Inc., New York, USA, 1996.

[SL90]   Amit P. Sheth and James A. Larson. Federated Database
             Systems for Managing Distributed, Heterogenous, and Au-
             tonomous Databases. *ACM Computing Surveys*, 22(3):183–
             236, September 1990.

[SLAF+95]   S.Y.W. Su, H. Lam, J. Arroyo-Figueroa, T. Yu, and Z. Yang.
             An Extensible Knowledge Base Management System for Sup-
             porting Rule-Based Interoperability among Heterogeneous
             Systems. In *Conference on Information and Knowledge Man-
             agement, CIKM'95*, Baltimore, MD, U.S.A, November 1995.

[SLY+95]   S. Su, H. Lam, T. Yu, S. Lee, and J. Arroyo. On Bridging
             and Extending OMG/IDL and STEP/EXPRESS for Achiev-
             ing Information Sharing and System Interoperability . In *5th
             Annual Express User Group Infernational Conference (EUG
             '95)*, Grenoble, France, October 1995.

[TGD95]   D. Tombros, A. Geppert, and K.R. Dittrich. Brokers and
             Services: Constructs for the Design and Implementation of
             Process-Oriented Environments.   Technical Report 95.26,
             Computer Science Department, University of Zurich, October
             1995.

[vBKK96]   Günter von Bültzingsloewen, Arne Koschel, and Ralf Kramer. Active Information Delivery in a CORBA-Based Distributed Information System. In Karl Aberer and Abdelsalam Helal, editors, *Proc. 1st IFCIS International Conference on Cooperative Information Systems (CoopIS'96)*, pages 218–227, Brussels, Belgium, June 1996. IFCIS, IEEE Computer Society Press, Los Alamitos, California.

[vBKK97]   Günter von Bültzingsloewen, Arne Koschel, and Ralf Kramer. Poster on Accept Heterogeneity: An Event Monitoring Service for CORBA-Based Heterogeneous Information Systems. In *Proc. 2nd IFCIS Conference on Cooperative Information Systems (CoopIS'97)*, South Carolina, U.S.A, June 1997.

[Wid95]   Jennifer Widom. Research Problems in Data Warehousing. In *Proceedings of 4th Intl. Conference of Information and Knowledge Management (CIKM'95)*, November 1995.

[ZHKF95]   G. Zhou, R. Hull, R. King, and J. Franchitti. Supporting Data Integration and Warehousing Using H₂O. *Data Engineering*, 18(2):29–40, June 1995.

	Event Sources, Event Types	Granularity
NCL / NIIIP	Method events (before, after) for encapsulated arbitrary sources (via CORBA-wrappers). Examples for predefined types include *system defined* (retrieve, update, delete, insert) and *user-defined* (check-out-design, display-part) types	
Coffein	Events may arise from any CORBA object in the system, especially arbitrary heterogeneous wrapped event sources. Event types include *RDBMS* (transaction and DML events based on triggers), *CORBA-level* (method events, exception events), and *time events*	source-specific granularity supported
Oracle	Event types are DML events including before/after triggers at row/statement level for insert, update, and delete operations	row and statement level triggers
Wide	Event types are: *data events* insert, update, delete in shared data tables; *workflow events* start, end, etc.; *external events* from applications; and *time events*	set-oriented
Alliances	Event sources are objects and alliances. Event types include request for a message (raised by objects), the indication of a message (raised by alliances), and alarms	

TABLE 8.5. Knowledge model–event.

	Context	State
NCL / NIIIP	method parameters via event binding	*local* actual state for conditions and actions
Coffein	actual state and (some) older event states via event binding	*local* actual state for conditions and actions
Oracle	actual event parameters via event binding	*local* coupled processing
Wide	inserted/deleted tables	*old/new values*
Alliances	message and protocol state	a separate protocol state that is maintained by an alliance

TABLE 8.6. Knowledge model–condition/action.

	Rule base distribution
NCL / NIIIP	*local; task possible* several node local rule bases
Coffein	*global* one (or several independent) (distributed) global rule base(s)
Oracle	*distributed* one global rule base
Wide	*distributed* workflow hierarchy; rule bases may be distributed accordingly
Alliances	*task* one logical rule base per task (may be also physically distributed)

TABLE 8.7. Knowledge model–rules.

	Event Signaling		
	Visibility	Detection Method	Event Manager
NCL / NIIIP	*local* no event history, no complex events	*reactive*	*no event manager* direct calls to rule manager (compiled-distributed approach ⇒ rules are directly triggered)
Coffein	*global* event history for complex events	*reactive* event sources signal events to "their" event history, which calls rules processing	*distributed* one central/several independent event managers/histories
Oracle	*local* no event history, no complex events	*reactive*	*central*
Wide	*local* no event history, no complex events	*reactive*	*central*
Alliances	*local* event histories per task (alliance)	*proactive*	*distributed*

TABLE 8.8. Execution model–event signalling.

	Communication Method	Rule Manager
NCL / NIIIP	*reactive* event sources directly trigger rule processing	*distributed* rules are not local but may include access to other nodes
Coffein	*reactive* event manager triggers rule processing	*central* (not fully implemented)
Oracle	*reactive*	*central*
Wide	*reactive*	*central*
Alliances	*proactive* alliances are polling message queues	*distributed*

TABLE 8.9. Execution model–rule triggering.

	Rule Manager (Execution)	Rule Set	Rule Distr.
NCL / NIIIP	*local* no real scheduling; rules are evaluated at nodes inside "incoming" method calls	*local* rule set per node; compiled-distributed approach	*visible*
Coffein	*global* one (or several independent) global rule manager(s); conflicts resolved, e.g., via prioritization	*global* one (or several sets in independent) rule manager(s)	*not visible*
Oracle	*global* one global rule manager; no conflicts, since only the four mentioned trigger types are allowed per event type	*global* one rule manager	*not visible*
Wide	*global* one global rule manager	*global* one rule manager	*not visible*
Alliances	*local per task*	*local per task*	*visible*

TABLE 8.10. Execution model–scheduling.

	State Access	DB or Inform. Mgr.	Coordination
NCL / NIIIP	*local*	*federation of sources* method calls to sources possible; KBMS (Knowledge Base Management System) used for query processing	*no transaction* no transaction manager
Coffein	*local*	*federation of sources* arbitrary information sources (also non data sources) can be queried in conditions using wrappers	*no transactions* arbitrary heterogeneous information sources; no transaction manager
Oracle	*global*	*distributed database* data source access via gateways	*global transactions* across distributed databases; distributed (XA) transaction manager
Wide	*global*	*federation of sources* sources specific to workflow processing	*mixed global and local transactions* Saga (global) and nested transactions (local)
Alliances	*local*		*no transactions*

TABLE 8.11. Execution model–condition evaluation and action execution.

9

Comparing Deductive and Active Databases

Alvaro A.A. Fernandes

ABSTRACT
This chapter compares the use of *rules* in deductive and in active databases. Syntactic similarities notwithstanding, deductive rules and active rules express quite different knowledge models and induce quite distinct execution models. In the last few years, there has been a strong research interest in unifying the two uses of rules by means of a language that either reconciles or, at least, encompasses the more distinctive aspects of their expected combined functionality. After a discussion of the most salient differences between deductive and active rules, an overview is given of different approaches to characterize a rule language providing some level of support for the knowledge and execution models that underlie deductive and active rules. The chapter includes a brief survey of rule languages that attempt to bridge the divide.

9.1 Introduction

9.1.1 Main Classes of Rule-Based Database Systems

The use of rule sets to express application semantics has spawned two classes of database systems: deductive databases and active databases. This chapter has the main objective of discussing the differences between these two classes and surveying recent research efforts applied to the problem of unifying them.

Rules in database systems have been deployed as specifications of different kinds of functionality. On the one hand, rules have been used to specify schemas, derived data, views, and integrity constraints, and on the other, rules have been used to specify events of interest along with the automatic, but conditional, response of the database system to the occurrence of such events. The first deployment of rules as a specification language gave rise to deductive databases, the second to active databases.

The starting point for this comparison of deductive and active databases is the observation that, syntactic similarities notwithstanding, the different knowledge and execution models of deductive and active rules are difficult to reconcile, let alone unify. Many attempts find themselves forced to adopt a controversial, because reductionist, view of one or the other kind of rule.

9.1.2   Some Pragmatic Issues to Confront

The facts that any unification attempt must confront include:

- *Deductive and active database technologies target different aspects of application functionality.*

  While deductive databases major at providing database designers with a unified language to define schemas, integrity constraints, views, and (certain classes of) derived data, active databases major at allowing application programmers to delegate to the database management system parts of the application's functionality that would otherwise be scattered across many modules and many programs.

  Although this generalization is no doubt too broad, it is supported by the fact that deductive database research has suffered from a dearth of clearly defined applications that could be argued to benefit from its results. In contrast, much active database research is targeted at, and sometimes driven by, specific application areas, and would, in any case, find it less difficult to list beneficiaries of its results.

- *Deductive and active databases have different, formally distinct, theoretical foundations.*

  Although both deductive and active databases could be said to have origins in artificial intelligence research, while the former have emerged from research into automated theorem proving via logic programming, the latter are closer to research into expert systems based on production rules.

  Thus, deductive databases spring from a tradition in which there is little concern with modeling state transition because only the static aspects of applications are of concern, whereas active databases spring from a tradition in which one of the main concerns of the system is to model state transitions, insofar as the focus is markedly on the dynamic aspects of applications.

- *Research efforts into deductive and active databases have long evolved independently and with different overall objectives.*

  Deductive database research has been mainly driven by metalogical development, i.e., by the exploitation of the fact that deductive databases form a class of very constrained formal systems based on classical first-order predicate logic. Concentration has been on studying useful techniques for query optimization and evaluation, integrity-constraint checking and view maintenance, while at the same time exploring issues of expressiveness and computational complexity of particular classes of logic-based query languages. Deductive database research has, therefore, followed the pattern of relational database research in first tackling the development of formal foundations before engaging in the implementation of prototype systems.

Active database research has followed the different pattern of experimenting with prototype systems before pondering the formal properties that such systems may be formally shown to have. Thus, an implementation-driven approach to issues such as the design of very expressive event specification languages, subtle and refined coupling modes, and very powerful execution models, has dominated research activity with much less attention being given to formal theories with which the results of this activity could be studied in abstraction from their concrete realizations.

Thus, much of the attractiveness of deductive database systems lies in their formal underpinnings, which rely crucially on languages with carefully controlled expressiveness and on an assumption of a static model of reality, whereas active databases are often attractive mainly because of their largely unconstrained expressiveness and of their potential effectiveness as a tool for modeling an important class of phenomena implicit in a dynamic model of reality.

In the context of this chapter, the main questions posed by these observations include whether, to what extent and, broadly, how a class of database systems can be characterized that reconciles, or more ambitiously, unifies deductive and active databases.

9.1.3 Possible Directions for Unification Efforts

Two possible approaches suggest themselves: either one starts from the framework underlying deductive rules and works towards encompassing active database technology under that framework or else one starts from the framework underlying active rules and works towards encompassing deductive database technology. It comes as no surprise that the literature contains records of attempts following each of these approaches.

There has been a great deal more research activity in the deductive-to-active direction than in the opposite one. This seems to stem from the following implicit assumptions. Firstly, that there is functionality that active databases deliver that deductive databases cannot deliver unless they are extended, and that such extensions require reconsidering the very logical basis which underlies current deductive databases. Secondly, that active databases could be made to support any functionality delivered by deductive databases if suitably constrained. These assumptions lead to the view that there are more, and more challenging, research issues in the deductive-to-active direction than in the opposite one.

Whereas the first assumption is trivially true, insofar as classical deductive databases cannot effect state transitions as can active ones, it is more difficult to agree without qualifications on the truth of the second. Even if one assumes an active database whose knowledge model is constrained to effect no state transition and to not monitor events (other than user requests reflecting the activation of deductive database services, e.g., evaluate a query, check integrity, etc.), it remains the case that the execution model of (pure) active databases would have to be extended with a theorem-proving procedure if they were to deliver the functionality of deductive databases as currently construed.

9.1.4 Main Requirements for Unification Efforts

Adopting a somewhat simplifying stance to what is in fact a complex web of issues, the following observations (to which labels are attached for further reference) seem to lie at the start of any enterprise aimed at integrating or unifying deductive and active databases:

(R1) a logic-based view of a dynamic reality: Supporting active functionality in deductive databases involves supporting, at least, a logic-based view of a dynamic reality, e.g., one that is modeled as a sequence of states. A logic-based account of event specification and detection, of the interleaving of event detection, condition verification and action execution, and of action specification and execution must emerge.

(R2) a declarative semantics for rule sets: Supporting deductive functionality in active databases requires, at least, the execution model to support automated theorem-proving in the adopted system of logic. The knowledge model must allow behavior invocations that request the initiation of the tasks typically supported by a deductive database and must allow action execution to have its ability to effect state transitions curtailed.

The remainder of this chapter is structured as follows. Section 9.2 discusses the syntactic similarities and the semantic differences between the deductive- and the active-rule paradigms. Section 9.3 is aimed at delineating the specific issues that an attempt to unify deductive and active rules must aim at. Section 9.4 is a brief survey of proposals for a unifying rule language that provides some level of support for the knowledge and execution models that underlie deductive and active rules. Finally, Section 9.5 draws some conclusions.

9.2   Deductive Rules Compared with Active Rules

A rule in a deductive database system can be viewed as a closed formula of first-order predicate logic or as a state-preserving production rule. The former is a logic-based view, and the latter a production view of what a deductive rule specifies.

9.2.1   Semantic Dissimilarities

In the simpler cases, the two views are equivalent, in the sense that the information that can be extracted through rule processing from a database state in either view is the same and, since no state transitions are allowed, so is the unique database state resulting from rule processing. This equivalence means that the semantics of a deductive rule can be formally described from three different, but equivalent, viewpoints [vEK76]: the first two stem from the logic-based view and are referred to as the model-theoretic and the proof-theoretic semantics, respectively, while the third stems from the production view and is typically referred to as the fixpoint semantics.

The model-theoretic approach is purely declarative. It does not rely on any algorithm to define formally the meaning of a deductive rule set, nor does it suggest how such an algorithm might be constructed, e.g., to be used in extracting information from the database using the deductive rule set. The proof-theoretic approach is also declarative insofar as it does not rely on an algorithm to define the meaning of a rule set either; however, it does suggest one or more proof procedures, i.e., proof-constructing algorithms, one of which would stand at the core of an automated theorem-prover by means of which information can be extracted from the database using the deductive rule set. Crucially, what is common to these two approaches to the assignment of meaning to deductive rule sets in a formal way is the fact that both view the union of a deductive rule set with the database state underlying it as the set of axioms of a logical theory [Men87, Rei84].

The production view is not at all dependent on viewing rule sets and database states as axioms of a logical theory. The semantic account that underlies the production view of deductive rule sets relies on, and precisely defines, an algorithm by means of which information can be extracted from the database. This account is referred to as a fixpoint semantics because the algorithm computes the fixpoint of a pattern-matching operator, sometimes referred to as *elementary production* [CGT90].

The production view faces comparatively simple problems to extend the rule language towards allowing rules to effect state transitions, i.e., to insert and delete facts as a result of computations. In contrast, the logic-based view faces, from the outset, a fundamental dilemma: either to provide an account of state transitions within the framework of first-order logic, or else to reconstruct somewhat from scratch the foundations of deductive rule processing. This dilemma stems from the fact that first-order logic views the reality from which semantic models are drawn as essentially static, and hence the logic-based view may need to switch to using as root a logical system that intrinsically models a dynamic reality (e.g., an intensional, perhaps modal, logic of time or of state).

The crucial difference between deductive and active rules is that the latter only supports a production view of deductive rule processing if no state transitions are allowed, i.e., if actions are constrained not to transform, but merely report on, the state of the database.[1] This leads to the conclusion that, in their pure form, deductive rules and active rules have irreconcilable purposes, insofar as, by definition, the very purpose of active rules makes it impossible for deductive rules to retain their semantic foundations.

9.2.2 Syntactic Similarities

There is a deceptive syntactic similarity between deductive and active rules, further fostered by the fact that the logic-based and the production views agree if rules are prevented from expressing state transitions. If one only considers active rules with no event specification part, both deductive and active rules can be read as *if–then* expressions. However, for deductive rules the intended reading interprets the rule in a declarative, truth-denoting way, whereas for active rules the intended reading is altogether different, insofar as it interprets the rule in an imperative, transition-effecting way.

While the whole of a deductive rule expresses a condition, only the condition part of an active rule does so, insofar as the whole of an active rule, in general, denotes instead a state transition. Furthermore, the antecedent of an active rule is indeed truth-valued, but it is only interpreted as a guard on the execution of the consequent, which may cause a state transition (e.g., via a simple destructive assignment, or via the invocation of a procedure capable, in principle, of expressing any computation whatsoever). In contrast, the entire deductive rule is truth-valued, being equivalent to asserting that either the antecedent is false or the consequent is true, or both. The bridge that is typically built in extensions of deductive databases towards encompassing active functionality is one that changes this purely declarative, truth-functional interpretation and views the antecedent as a guard. The problem, of course, is that this change of interpretation may require a far-reaching reconstruction of the semantic foundations of deductive rule sets.

---

[1] In terms of the dimensions proposed in the introduction to this book this is equivalent to constraining the options dimension of the action component of the knowledge model to be the singleton {Inform}.

9.2.3   A Dimensional Analysis of Deductive Rule Sets

Clearly, the knowledge models that can be expressed by an active rule set and by a deductive rule set have, in principle, only a small intersection. Only the deceptive syntactic similarity between deductive and active rules somewhat obscures this realization. The application to Datalog of the framework adopted in this book to describe active rule systems highlights how an attempt to view a pure deductive rule system as an active one reveals a severely limited functionality and throws light, therefore, on the areas where extensions should be sought in any unification effort.

For the purpose of illustrating some of the observations above, Table 9.1 describes deductive rules along the dimensions proposed in the introduction to this book.

Knowledge Model:

Event	Source	[not applicable]
	Granularity	[not applicable]
	Type	[not applicable]
	Role	None
Condition	Role	Mandatory
	Context	$DB_T = DB_C$
Action	Options	[not applicable]
	Context	$DB_T = DB_C = DB_A$

Execution Model:

Condition-Mode	Immediate
Action-Mode	Immediate
Transition granularity	[not applicable]
Net-effect policy	[not applicable]
Cycle policy	[not applicable]
Priorities	None
Scheduling	Saturation
Error handling	[not applicable]

Management Model:

Description	Query Language
Operations	$\emptyset$
Adaptability	Compile Time
Data Model	Deductive

TABLE 9.1. Dimensions for (pure) deductive rules.

Notice that deductive rules do not monitor events. Conditions are mandatory, insofar as a fact, i.e., a consequent-only rule is understood to have a vacuously true antecedent. The contexts for processing both conditions and actions arc, and must remain, the same as they were at the start of the transaction.

Notice also that actions are not specifiable; in particular, notice that in pure deductive rule systems the consequent of a rule is *not* the specification of an action. Rule processing culminates in an answer set to the query that initiated that processing cycle, although one might choose to view the processing of each individual rule as yielding a set of bindings, and the processing of the entire set as yielding the final set of bindings as an answer to a query that is then returned to the caller. The condition and action modes are said to be immediate in the sense that deductive rule processing does not interact with the caller transaction in any more sophisticated manner. This also explains why the error handling dimension is typically not applicable to deductive rule processing.

Deductive rule processing can be carried out without any conflict resolution in a purely declarative language such as Datalog. However, if stratification is used to allow negation in bodies [CGT90], then the strata defined by the occurrence of negative literals impose an ordering on rules that the evaluation algorithms take into account. Scheduling is typically by saturation, but there are evaluation schemes that process rules with an all-parallel scheduling.

Notice, finally, that no operations on the rule set are allowed, and the mandatory creation and deletion operations are only allowed at compile time. This means that the requirement that no state transition occurs is extended to the rule set itself and is consistent with the view that a database state is the union of the rule set and the set of extensionally asserted facts, and not just the latter.

9.3   Bringing Deductive and Active Rules Together

9.3.1   Issues and Targets

As section 9.2 suggested, the differences between deductive rule systems and active rule systems give rise to, at least, the following broad questions (to which labels are attached for further reference):

(Q1) *How to support events in deductive rule processing?* Deductive rule systems neither detect nor react to events. From this it follows that they are, in the terminology introduced in the introduction to this book, *call-driven systems.*

(Q2) *How to support state transition in deductive rule processing?*

(Q3) *How to support interaction with the transaction manager in deductive rule processing?* Deductive rule systems neither effect state transitions nor interact with the transaction management system in any significant way.

(Q4) *How to support a logic-based view of the database in active rule processing?* Active rule systems do not support a logic-based view (i.e., model- and proof-theoretic) of rule processing.

Questions **Q1**, **Q2**, and **Q3** stem from requirement **R1** from Section 9.1.4, viz., that a logic-based view of a dynamic reality must emerge from a deductive database that is extended to support active database functionality. Question **Q4** stems from requirement **R2** from Section 9.1.4, viz., that a declarative semantics for rule sets must be provided by an active database that is extended to support deductive database functionality.

These questions, therefore, implicitly set targets for any endeavor to extend support for active behavior in deductive databases and for deductive behavior in active databases. For the former, more complex case, Table 9.2 shows, in terms of the dimensions proposed in the introduction to this book, what have been typical targets in attempts to support active behavior in deductive rule processing.

Thus, attempts so far have, in general, confined themselves to supporting primitive, structure-operation events without an explicit specification and a limited ability to support actions denoting structure operations only, with bindings from the condition evaluation stage being propagated to the action execution stage.

9.3.2   Basic Research Stances

Apart from specific proposals, of which a small subset is described later in this chapter, there has been some interest from both the deductive database and the active database research areas in investigating whether a broad, general framework that reconciles the two kinds of rules in a single database system can be devised in an intuitive and clean way. Apart from their intrinsic interest, attempts to formulate such broad views are useful in characterizing basic research stances.

Two somewhat symmetrical positions can be discerned. The first position, reported in [Wid94], stems from the active-rule research area and proposes that active rules subsume (the important aspects of) deductive rules. It presents as evidence a framework from which a characterization of both deductive and active rule systems can be derived in a straightforward way. Under this approach, active rules and deductive rules are construed as lying at opposite ends of a spectrum in which one can move from purely declarative to totally imperative rule-based expression of behavior in discrete incremental steps, each of which relinquishes some declarativeness and encompasses more imperativeness.

The second position [Zan94] stems from the deductive-rule research area and proposes that deductive rules subsume (important aspects of) active

Knowledge Model:

Event	Source	Structure Operation
	Granularity	Set
	Type	Primitive
	Role	Optional
Condition	Role	Mandatory
	Context	$DB_T=DB_C$
Action	Options	Structure Operation
	Context	$= \{Bind_C, DB_C=DB_A\}$

Execution Model:

Condition-Mode	$\subset \{$ Immediate, Deferred $\}$
Action-Mode	$\subset \{$ Immediate, Deferred $\}$
Transition granularity	Set
Net-effect policy	No
Cycle policy	$\subset \{$ Iterative, Recursive $\}$
Priorities	Relative
Scheduling	Saturation
Error handling	[not applicable]

Management Model:

Description	Query Language
Operations	$\emptyset$
Adaptability	Compile Time
Data Model	Deductive

TABLE 9.2. Typical targets for an active extension of deductive databases.

rules. It argues that the fixpoint interpretation of deductive rule sets can be extended to compute strata that emulate the notion of database states. In addition to this crucial first step, [Zan94] defines four predicates (to be understood as built-ins): these are referred to as **quevt**, **add**, **del**, and **evt**. Intuitively, **quevt** characterizes an intensional relation that models an event queue; **add** and **del** characterize intensional relations that model the set of inserted and deleted facts, respectively, and, finally, **evt** characterizes an intensional relation that models the log of raised events. These extensions open the way for the development of an account of active rules in which the semantics of event detection and state transition is declaratively specified, which allows [Zan94] to remain firmly within the semantic framework of deductive rules. Both [Wid94] and [Zan94] are further discussed later in this chapter.

It seems that the respective stances taken by [Wid94] and [Zan94] can only be sustained if one judiciously arbitrates which features of deductive rules (in the case of [Wid94]) or of active rules (in the case of [Zan94]) are important and need supporting in the extended framework. Thus, it is not clear that certain of the implementation technologies associated with deductive-rule processing (especially optimization) can be so easily assimilated in the active-rule setting as implicitly assumed in [Wid94]. Similarly, the framework proposed in [Zan94] falls short of achieving the expressiveness of active rules, in particular with respect to interactions with the transaction manager. In terms of the questions put forward in Section 9.3.1, it is arguable that under the stance taken in [Wid94] certain implications of **(Q4)** would be difficult to support, and the stance taken in [Zan94] does not address **(Q3)** and takes a limiting view of both **(Q1)** and **(Q2)**.

The stances taken by [Wid94] and [Zan94] can be characterized as favoring a tight coupling between the deductive and the active rule processing components. A third stance emerges from considering a looser coupling. This is the view taken by [FWP97]. It is founded on the perception that paradigm-merging enterprises are only justified if they deliver more than is provided by each paradigm in isolation and if the original paradigms retain their distinctive strengths in the resulting merger.

The basic idea is to use a history of events as the basis for the characterization of all deductive and active database functionality. First, over the event history, occurrences of primary and composite events are declaratively characterized by deductive rules, thereby allowing event detection to be given a logical semantics. Second, over the same event history, a Kowalski-Sergot event calculus [Kow92] models the successive states of the database as time-stamped intensional relations, and over these, in turn, application-specific deductive rules can be written. This means that condition verification retains its classical logical semantics. Finally, the events caused by the execution of the action component in an active rule need only be appended to the event history for the logical framework to reflect it both in event detection and condition verification. This makes the semantics of action execution very simple in comparison to other approaches.

In contrast with [Wid94], in [FWP97], deductive functionality of the database is fully supported. In contrast with [Zan94], in [FWP97] a logical framework is provided from which a natural formalization of those aspects of active behavior that are necessary to address **(Q1)** and **(Q2)** more directly emerge in the form of more expressive event and action specification languages than are possible in the approach taken by [Zan94]. Although **(Q3)** is also not addressed by [FWP97], there is no strong impediment for extending the approach so that it does so. ROCK & ROLL, an implemented system whose ADB functionality is based on the foundations laid in [FWP97], is further discussed later in this chapter.

9.4   A Brief Survey of Proposals for Languages with Deductive and Active Capabilities

9.4.1   The Widom Spectrum

The proposal in [Wid94] is not of a language, but rather of a spectrum within which the execution models of existing rule languages exist as points. The central argument is that there is a basic computational engine for rule processing that can be gradually extended, thereby giving rise to a discrete number of points in a spectrum, so as to characterize the execution model of a number of rule languages from purely deductive Datalog to very active POSTGRES. Only the production view of deductive rules is considered, and there is no attempt to view deductive rules as axioms of a logical theory. Hence, (**Q4**) is not addressed.

As a result, unless one is prepared to accept a more restricted perspective of deductive database technology than currently embodied in existing prototypes, [Wid94] falls short of the unification ideal. Also, it is arguable that some of the extension steps from one point to another are not as small, intuitive and well-understood as one would wish, i.e., the distance between any two adjacent pair of languages in the spectrum is far from constant and can indeed reflect quite complex extension steps.

The important contribution of [Wid94] is to demonstrate that there exists a level of abstraction that allows the description of a subsumption relationship in which deductive rules are active rules. It seems, however, that the level of abstraction in which the description is viable is far too high to explain the actual practice of deductive databases (DDB's) and of active databases (ADB's) as embodied in concrete prototypes and systems.

9.4.2   DDB-Oriented Proposals

The proposals discussed in this subsection are grouped together by their origins and allegiance to the deductive approach to database programming. The proposals discussed below are DLP [MW88], $\mathcal{LDL}$ [NT89], U-Datalog [BCG$^+$94, BGM95], $\mathcal{T_R}$ [BK93], and   that of [Zan94].[2] Since this survey does not aim at completeness, it should not be assumed that the above are the only proposals for active extensions to the deductive approach.

DLP (for Dynamic Logic Programming) follows a top-down, left-to-right approach to evaluation that leads naturally to the specification of updates in the antecedents of rules. DLP casts a Harel-style modal logic of programs into the logic programming framework. Thus, it provides a logic-based view of a dynamic reality via the classical semantics for modal logics based on

---

[2]Unfortunately, space restrictions prevent a wider coverage. In particular, the reader might wish to consider the interesting work reported in [BJ94] and in [HD94].

Kripke structures. As a consequence, update operators (+ for insertion and – for deletion) are interpreted as modal operators. Updates are performed immediately, and update atoms can be preceded or followed in the evaluation order by a query-only atom. If a query atom following an update atom evaluates to false in the updated state, then changes are rolled back. Updates can only be specified on the extensional part of the database. There are other restrictions on the expressiveness of DLP programs (e.g., negation is not handled, recursive rules with update operators are disallowed).

$\mathcal{LDL}$ is in many ways similar to DLP, but rule antecedents are more clearly structured into a query part and a procedure part. The former is executed first and must ground all atoms in the procedure part. $\mathcal{LDL}$ can detect that the procedure part yields the same final state irrespective of the order of evaluation and hence is capable of optimizing its execution plan. Another important distinction between DLP and $\mathcal{LDL}$ is characterized by the tuple-at-a-time approach of the former and the set-at-a-time approach of the latter. The DLP approach can lead to nondeterminism, while the $\mathcal{LDL}$ approach allows an all-parallel scheduling policy.

Both DLP and $\mathcal{LDL}$ are representative of the first wave of deductive languages extended with active functionality. They remain close to the top-down evaluation approach of traditional logic programming proof procedures. They face up to the ideal of having a model- and a proof-theoretic semantics for transition-effecting languages, too. However, while they address (Q2), the effecting of state transitions, they are also totally oblivious to (Q1), the support for events, and fall short of addressing (Q3), the integration with transaction management. This last question is picked up by the second wave of logic-programming-based deductive rule languages extended with active functionality.

U-Datalog relinquishes the immediate-update approach first proposed by DLP (which implies the loss of declarativeness under most circumstances) and incorporates into the evaluation mechanisms an awareness of transaction management, going as far as allowing constructors into the rule language to form composite transactions. U-Datalog is an extension of Datalog supporting the declarative specification of updates. The execution model of U-Datalog consists of two phases: the marking phase and the update phase. In the marking phase, the updates specified as a result of the evaluation process are collected but not carried out; the update phase carries out the updates provided there are no conflicting pairs and all update specifications are ground. This is in contrast with DLP and $\mathcal{LDL}$, in which updates are also specified in the antecedent of rules but are carried out as an immediate side effect of the evaluation process. The semantic framework underlying U-Datalog is that of constraint logic programming, which is a generalization of the classical logic programming framework based on first-order term unification. In U-Datalog, updates are specified as constraints. This gives U-Datalog a more general semantic setting than DLP or $\mathcal{LDL}$. Also, a bottom-up evaluation strategy exists for U-Datalog, where none has been provided for DLP.

$\mathcal{T}_{\mathcal{R}}$ (Transaction Logic) is, in some sense, the confluence of DLP and U-Datalog, insofar as its logical foundations are, like those of DLP but not U-Datalog, in a Harel-style modal logic of programs, and it formalizes, like U-Datalog but not DLP, the relationship between a transaction model and rule evaluation.

Thus, U-Datalog and $\mathcal{T}_{\mathcal{R}}$ address (**Q2**), the effecting of state transitions, as do DLP and $\mathcal{LDL}$, and go beyond the latter by also addressing (**Q3**), the integration with transaction management. However, none of these languages tackles (**Q1**), the support for events. This question is picked up by the most recent proposal for a logic-programming-based deductive rule language extended with active functionality.

The main contribution of [Zan94] is an approach to unifying aspects of deductive and active databases that encompasses event specification, thereby addressing (**Q1**). The approach is founded on a model of state transition that identifies distinct states with different strata of a fixpoint computation. Not only does this enable [Zan94] to model state transitions non-destructively, it also yields a model of an event queue, thereby opening the way for the explicit specification of events in a deductive rule context. Unfortunately, [Zan94] does not include an account of how deductive rule evaluation integrates with a transaction manager as do U-Datalog and $\mathcal{T}_{\mathcal{R}}$.

It is interesting to note that by explicitly naming states, [Zan94] seems to stand in the same relation with the modal approaches of DLP and $\mathcal{T}_{\mathcal{R}}$ as a tensed logic (i.e., a logic that can quantify over time-denoting terms) to a temporal logic (in which, rather then explicit quantification, modal operators are used to talk about formulas that hold, or not, over more than one point in time).

9.4.3   ADB-Oriented Proposals

The proposals discussed in this subsection are grouped together by the fact that their users primarily see them as instances of the active approach to database programming. The proposals discussed are A-RDL [SK96], Chimera [CM93, CFPT96], and ROCK & ROLL [DPWF96]. Since this survey does not aim at completeness, it should not be assumed that the above are the only proposals for the integration of deductive features with the active approach.

A-RDL is an extension of RDL1 [KdMS90]. RDL1 only supported deductive rules, but it already had the ability to express state transitions (via update operators on rule consequents). A-RDL supports active rules that react to events modifying the state of the database. A-RDL active rules are production rules, i.e., they do not allow event specification. They allow the specification of coupling modes and can command the rule not to fire again. The condition and action specification languages are richer than any of the deductive-oriented proposals discussed above. However, A-RDL rigidly adheres to a production view of rule processing. Thus, it does not answer **(Q4)**, the support of a logic-based view of the database, insofar as a model- and proof-theoretic semantics for A-RDL rule sets has not yet been provided.

Chimera, like ROCK & ROLL, integrates active and deductive databases in an object-oriented context. Chimera supports a comparatively sophisticated transaction model. Deductive rules (called passive in Chimera) must be, as in practical implementations of Datalog, both range-restricted and stratifiable. Active rules are event-condition-action rules. Conditions are queries, equivalent to passive-rule bodies augmented with special facilities to query the event history. While there are no restrictions on specifiable actions (within the manipulation capabilities of Chimera and of the externally-defined procedures into which the system has an interface), only query and manipulation events are specifiable. Moreover, there is no possibility of specifying complex events, although Chimera does support alternative consumption modes. The formal semantics of the rule-language components of Chimera has yet to be made publicly available. Gauging from publicly available documents, there is reason to suppose that Chimera does support all of **(Q1)** to **(Q4)**, subject to reasonable restrictions.

ROCK & ROLL shares many similarities with Chimera. It extends with active rules the deductive object-oriented database system described in [BFP+95]. The design of the extension is such that deductive rule processing is not disturbed syntactically or semantically. Since ROLL (the deductive language of ROCK & ROLL) is reducible to Datalog with range restriction and stratification, this implies that the active version of ROCK & ROLL supports **(Q4)**, i.e., a logic-based view of the database. With regard to **(Q1)**, i.e., support for events, ROCK & ROLL is comparable to Chimera, allowing the specification of a rich set of primitive events and providing a rich set of operators to compose events. With respect to **(Q2)**, support for state transitions, ROCK & ROLL allows unrestricted use of ROCK (the imperative language of ROCK & ROLL) in the action specification part of an active rule. Finally, ROCK & ROLL supports immediate and deferred coupling modes but is mostly dependent for its transaction management facilities on those provided by the implementation platform, viz., EXODUS [CDG+90]. The formal semantics of the active extensions of ROCK & ROLL builds on the foundations laid in [FWP97].

9.5 Conclusion

The first conclusion to be drawn is that the Widom spectrum mentioned in Section 9.4.1 and discussed in more detail in [Wid94] seems to deserve further development. Independently, this is already happening, to a certain degree and under different motivations, in the explorations of the foundations of rule-based languages reported in [PV95] and [Via96]. These explorations could still yield the formal underpinnings for the Widom spectrum that a position paper such as [Wid94] is not expected to address.

The second conclusion, for which the survey in section 9.4 provides the evidence, is that following a DDB-oriented approach has not yet led to as comprehensive and satisfying results as those yielded by an ADB-oriented approach.

Seen as a group, the DDB-oriented proposals mentioned in Section 9.4.2 address **(Q1)**, the support for events **(Q2)**, the effecting of state transitions, and **(Q3)**, the integration with transaction management. However, no single proposal has answers for all three questions. Even if the expressiveness of the event and action specification languages in this group is limited in comparison with state-of-the-art active database systems, as are the possibilities of integrating rule processing and transaction management, the time seems ripe to attempt a convergence of proposals, such as those surveyed above, into a clean, powerful, unifying, rule-based database language following a DDB-oriented approach.

In contrast, two of the three ADB-oriented proposals mentioned in section 9.4.3, viz., Chimera and ROCK & ROLL, yield a fully fledged active database with deductive capabilities. Both these proposals provide answers for all of **(Q1)** to **(Q4)**, the differences between them being few and not substantial in what concerns the topic of this chapter.

A final conclusion is that while Chimera and ROCK & ROLL suggest that adopting an ADB-oriented approach to the unification of the two classes of rule processing tends naturally to converge, this convergence seems possible but must be actively sought in the case of a DDB-oriented approach. There seems to be enough evidence to suggest that the body of research dispersed throughout the many proposals in section 9.4.2 is ripe for consolidation and unification at a foundational level.

9.6   Acknowledgments

The author's understanding of the subjects discussed in this chapter is due in great part to his joint work with the members, past and present, of the Database Research Group at Heriot-Watt University, and in particular, Dr. Norman Paton, Andrew Dinn, and Prof. M. Howard Williams. Any error, however, is unquestionably the author's own.

9.7   References

[BCG+94]   E. Bertino, B. Catania, G. Guerrini, M. Martelli, and D. Montesi. A Bottom-Up Interpreter for Database Languages with Updates and Transactions. In *Proceedings Joint Conference on Declarative Programming Gulp-Prode*, pages 207–220. 1994.

[BFP+95] M.L. Barja, A.A.A. Fernandes, N.W. Paton, M.H. Williams, A. Dinn, and A.I. Abdelmoty. Design and Implementation of ROCK & ROLL: A Deductive Object-Oriented Database System. *Information Systems*, 20(3):185–211, 1995.

[BGM95] E. Bertino, G. Guerrini, and D. Montesi. Towards Deductive Object Databases. *Theory and Practice of Object Systems*, 1(1):19–39, 1995.

[BJ94] P. Bayer and W. Jonker. A Framework for Supporting Triggers in Deductive Databases. In N.W. Paton and M.H. Williams, editors, *Proc. 1st Intl. Workshop on Rules In Database Systems*, pages 316–330. Springer-Verlag, 1994.

[BK93] A.J. Bonner and M. Kifer. Transaction Logic Programming. In *Proceedings of 10th ICLP*, pages 257–279. MIT Press, 1993.

[CDG+90] M.J. Carey, D.J. DeWitt, G. Graefe, D.M. Haight, J.E. Richardson, D.T. Schuh, E.J. Shekita, and S.L. Vanderberg. The EXODUS Extensible DBMS Project: An Overview. In S. Zdonik and D. Maier, editors, *Readings in Object-Oriented Database Systems*, pages 474–499. Morgan Kaufmann, 1990.

[CFPT96] S. Ceri, P. Fraternali, S. Paraboschi, and L. Tanca. Active Rule Management in Chimera. In J. Widom and S. Ceri, editors, *Active Database Systems*, pages 151–176. Morgan Kaufmann, 1996.

[CGT90] S. Ceri, G. Gottlob, and L. Tanca. *Logic Programming and Databases*. Springer-Verlag, 1990.

[CM93] S. Ceri and R. Manthey. Chimera: A Model and Language for Active DOOD Systems. In *Proceedings of the 2nd East-West Database Workshop*, pages 3–16. Springer-Verlag, 1993.

[DPWF96] A. Dinn, N.W. Paton, M.H. Williams, and A.A.A. Fernandes. An Active Rule Language for ROCK & ROLL. In *Proc. 14th British National Conference on Databases*. Springer-Verlag, 1996.

[FWP97] A.A.A. Fernandes, M.H. Williams, and N.W. Paton. A Logic-Based Integration of Active and Deductive Databases. *New Generation Computing*, 15(2):205–244, 1997.

[HD94] J.V. Harrison and S.W. Dietrich. Integrating Active and Deductive Rules. In N.W. Paton and M.H. Williams, editors, *Proc. 1st Int. Workshop on Rules In Database Systems*, pages 288–305. Springer-Verlag, 1994.

[KdMS90] G. Kiernan, C. de Maindreville, and E. Simon. Making Deductive Databases a Practical Technology: A Step Forward. In *Proceedings 1990 ACM SIGMOD*, pages 237–246. ACM Press, 1990.

[Kow92] R. Kowalski. Database Updates in the Event Calculus. *Journal of Logic Programming*, 12:121–146, 1992.

[Men87] E. Mendelson. *Introduction to Mathematical Logic*. Wadsworth & Brooks/Cole, 3rd. edition, 1987.

[MW88] S. Manchanda and D.S. Warren. A Logic-Based Language for Database Updates. In J. Minker, editor, *Foundations of Deductive Databases and Logic Programming*, pages 363–394. Morgan Kaufmann, 1988.

[NT89] S. Naqvi and S. Tsur. *A Logical Language for Data and Knowledge Bases*. Computer Science Press, 1989.

[PV95] P. Picouet and V. Vianu. Semantics and Expressiveness Issues in Active Databases, 1995. To appear in *Journal of Computer and System Sciences*. Shorter version in *Proceedings PODS 95*, pp. 126-138.

[Rei84] R. Reiter. Towards a Logical Reconstruction of Relational Database Theory. In M.L. Brodie, J. Mylopoulos, and J.W. Schmidt, editors, *On Conceptual Modelling: Perspectives from Artificial Intelligence, Databases, and Programming Languages*, pages 191–233. Springer-Verlag, 1984.

[SK96] E. Simon and J. Kiernan. The A-RDL System. In J. Widom and S. Ceri, editors, *Active Database Systems*, pages 111–149. Morgan Kaufmann, 1996.

[vEK76] M.H. van Emden and R.A. Kowalski. The Semantics of Predicate Logic as a Programming Language. *Journal of the ACM*, 23(4):733–742, 1976.

[Via96] V. Vianu. Rule-Based Languages, 1996. To appear in *Annals of Mathematics and Artificial Intelligence*.

[Wid94] J. Widom. Deductive and Active Databases: Two Paradigms or Ends of a Spectrum? In N.W. Paton and M.H. Williams, editors, *Rules in Database Systems*, pages 306–315. Springer-Verlag, 1994.

[Zan94] C. Zaniolo. A Unified Semantics for Active and Deductive Databases. In N.W. Paton and M.H. Williams, editors, *Rules in Database Systems*. Springer-Verlag, 1994.

Part III

Systems

10

Active Database Features in SQL3

Krishna Kulkarni, Nelson Mattos
Roberta Cochrane

ABSTRACT Many commercial relational database systems provide support for active rules, which are generally referred to as triggers. However, these facilities have been developed independently by different vendors, and triggers developed for one system generally do not work with another. This chapter describes how triggers are supported in the SQL3 standard, and in particular how the triggers relate to other features of the standard.

10.1   Introduction

In this chapter, we focus on the active database features being introduced into SQL3 [ISO96], the intended replacement for the current database language standard, SQL-92 [ISO92]. The database language SQL is now firmly established as the predominant *de jure* language standard for database access. Because of its nonprocedural nature, SQL has gained tremendous popularity for developing data-intensive applications. The number of implementations claiming conformance to SQL has been growing over the last few years. Correspondingly, the number of applications built using SQL has also grown rapidly.

The first version of the SQL standard, SQL-86, was published in 1986. In 1989, a revised version of the standard, SQL-89, was published; this version enhanced SQL-86 with the notion of *referential integrity*. A substantial revision of the standard appeared in 1992 as SQL-92. Among other significant extensions, SQL-92 introduced the notion of *referential actions*, which can be considered as a limited form of rule support. More recently, significant active database functionality is being incorporated into SQL3 in the form of *triggers*.

In parallel to the standards work, there has been a significant commercial interest in supporting active features from the relational database vendors as well. Most SQL products support SQL-92 declarative constraints. Some have also implemented triggers (roughly based on the SQL3 specification), though there is a tremendous variation among the products. [CW95] provide a recent survey of the features supported by various products.

[CW95] also describe briefly the specification of triggers as it existed in SQL3 at the time of their writing. As they point out, the specification suffered from many shortcomings. First, the SQL3 draft existing at that time failed to specify a well-defined execution semantics for triggers. Second, it did not deal with the interaction between triggers and referential actions that are performed during the enforcement of referential integrity constraints. In fact, the SQL3 specification existing at that time prohibited the definition of triggers on a table that was the target of a cascading referential action. Since then, a series of change proposals addressing these deficiencies (mostly written by two of the authors of this chapter) have been accepted into SQL3. Though some problems still remain, we believe SQL3 now has a well-defined execution semantics for triggers.

We describe in this chapter the specification of triggers as it exists currently in the SQL3 specification. It is to be noted that SQL3 is still an ongoing effort, and the trigger facility as described in this chapter may change as SQL3 goes through its final steps. The SQL3 specification is expected to replace SQL-92 sometime in 1998. It is hoped that the emergence of a standard syntax and semantics will spur the vendors to offer a clean notion of triggers with a standard execution semantics.

The rest of this chapter is organized as follows: we introduce the notion of triggers in section 10.2, provide a brief description of SQL3 constraints in section 10.2.1, the detailed description of triggers in section 10.2.2, the execution model of triggers in section 10.2.3, followed by a brief description of the execution model in section 10.2.4. Section 10.3 provides some examples. Section 10.4 compares SQL3 triggers to the active database framework introduced in Chapter 1. We offer some concluding remarks in section 10.5.

10.2   Triggers in SQL3

The notion of triggers is one of the main extensions being introduced into SQL3. A *trigger* in SQL3 is a named event-condition-action rule that is activated by a database state transition. Every trigger is associated with a particular table and is activated whenever that table is modified and an optional condition, specified as part of the trigger definition, evaluates to *true*. Once activated, a trigger can execute SQL statements that are part of the trigger's action, which can in turn activate other triggers. A trigger can be either a BEFORE trigger or an AFTER trigger. A BEFORE trigger is activated before the operation that modifies a table executes, while an AFTER trigger is activated after the modifying operation executes.

There are two major issues that complicate the specification of execution semantics for triggers in SQL3. One is the interaction between triggers and declarative constraints, and the other is the notion of BEFORE and AFTER triggers. Since SQL supports both declarative constraints and triggers,

SQL needs to specify clearly the precise timing of constraint enforcement and of trigger execution. SQL also needs to take into account the interaction between referential action executions and trigger executions. Another issue with SQL3 triggers is the notion of BEFORE and AFTER triggers. It is important to ensure that both BEFORE and AFTER triggers see consistent database states. Hence, SQL needs to specify precisely when the triggers should execute with respect to the application of modifications to the database and constraint checking.

The only two previous publications that deal with both the above issues are [Hor94] and [CaNM96]. While [Hor94] describes some of the issues that arise with BEFORE triggers and with the interaction of triggers and declarative constraints and proposes some tentative solutions, [CaNM96] provides a comprehensive execution model for triggers that takes into account the existence of both BEFORE and AFTER triggers and is well-integrated with the execution model of declarative constraints. In fact, much of the trigger execution model that is currently in SQL3 (and hence, much of the material in this chapter) is based on the model described in [CaNM96].

Before we delve into the intricacies of triggers in SQL3, we provide a brief description of declarative constraints in SQL3.

10.2.1 Constraints in SQL3

Constraints in SQL3 are predicates on database states that a SQL-conformant system must ensure evaluate to *true*.[1] There are three types of constraints: *column constraints*, *table constraints* and *assertions*. Table constraints are associated with a particular table while column constraints are associated with a particular column of a particular table.[2] Assertions are simply multitable constraints.

There are three forms of table constraints: *unique/primary key, check,* and *referential constraints,* and there are four forms of column constraints: *NOT NULL, unique/primary key, check,* and *referential constraints.* Assertions can only be check constraints. All these constraints fall into the category of so-called *static constraints,* as they only define what are consistent database states, not what are consistent database transitions.

An unique/primary key constraint on a column or on a table specifies that no two rows in that table can have the same combinations of values for the specified column or the specified combinations of columns. A check constraint on a column or on a table specifies an arbitrary predicate that must evaluate to *true* for every row in that table. A referential constraint specifies that a combination of column values (*foreign key*) of a table (*ref-*

---

[1] Actually, because of SQL's 3-valued logic, constraints are satisfied if the predicates evaluate to either *true* or *unknown*.

[2] Actually, column constraints are internally treated as table constraints.

erencing table) must be present as unique/primary key values in another table (*referenced table*). A NOT NULL constraint on a column specifies that the value of that column for every row in that table must always be a non-null value. An assertion is an arbitrary predicate that must evaluate to *true* for every row of every table referenced in that assertion.

Both constraints and assertions are normally checked at the end of every statement execution (*immediate* mode), unless they are deferred, in which case they are checked just before the transaction commits (*deferred* mode). If any of the constraints or assertions are found violated, either the modifications done by the statement are undone (in immediate mode) or the entire transaction is rolled back (in deferred mode).

Referential constraints are somewhat special, in that users can specify one of five actions (called *referential actions*) to deal with violations whenever the referenced table of a referential constraint is modified: NO ACTION, RESTRICT, SET NULL, SET DEFAULT, and CASCADE. (In contrast, the user has no control over violations due to modifications to the referencing table of a referential constraint; in this case, either the effects of the statement are undone, or the transaction is rolled back.) The NO ACTION and RESTRICT options prohibit constraint violations, the SET NULL option sets the nullable columns of the foreign key columns in the matching rows of the referencing table to the null value, the SET DEFAULT option sets the values to the default value declared for those columns, and the CASCADE option cascades the referenced table changes (updates or deletes) to the matching rows of the referencing table.

According to SQL3, the constraints must effectively be processed only after all modifications of the original statement are applied. SQL3 also employs a fixpoint computation model for enforcement of constraints, which results in a deterministic result in the presence of cascaded referential actions. Consequently, the result of a statement execution neither depends on the order in which the rows are modified, nor on the order in which constraints are processed.

Briefly, the execution of SQL3 statements (in the absence of triggers) proceeds in the following sequence:

1. Apply all modifications caused by the statement's action to the database.

2. Evaluate all applicable constraints with RESTRICT semantics. If any are violated, return an error and restore the database to the state that existed prior to the execution of the statement.

3. Execute all cascaded referential update actions. As modifications caused by these actions are applied to the database, evaluate all applicable constraints with RESTRICT semantics. If any are violated, return an error and restore the database to the state that existed prior to the execution of the statement.

4. Execute all cascaded referential delete actions. As modifications caused by these actions are applied to the database, evaluate all applicable constraints with RESTRICT semantics. If any are violated, return an error and restore the database to the state that existed prior to the execution of the statement.

5. Evaluate all applicable check constraints, unique constraints, NOT NULL constraints, and referential constraints with NO ACTION semantics. If any are violated, return an error and restore the database to the state that existed prior to the execution of the statement.

10.2.2 Overview of SQL3 Triggers

A trigger consists of four components: a *subject table*, a *triggering operation*, a *trigger condition*, and a *trigger action*. Each trigger is specific to its subject table. A trigger TR is said to be *activated* whenever a triggering operation on its subject table is initiated and the trigger condition of TR evaluates to *true*. When a trigger is activated, its trigger action is executed as part of the execution of its triggering operation.

Users (or database administrators) must explicitly create triggers using CREATE TRIGGER statements. Triggers can be created either during the creation of a schema or any time after a schema is created. The current SQL3 syntax for the creation of a trigger is as follows:

```
<trigger definition> ::=
      CREATE TRIGGER <trigger name>
      <trigger action time>
      <trigger event> ON < table name>
      [ REFERENCING <old or new values alias list> ]
      <trigger action>

<trigger action time> ::= BEFORE | AFTER

<trigger event> ::= INSERT | DELETE | UPDATE [ OF <column name
list> ]

<old or new values alias list> ::= <old or new values alias> ...


<old or new values alias> ::=
      OLD [AS] <identifier>
      | NEW [AS] <identifier>
      | OLD_TABLE [AS] <identifier>
      | NEW_TABLE [AS] <identifier>

< trigger action> ::=
```

```
[ FOR EACH { ROW | STATEMENT } ]
[ <trigger condition> ]
<triggered SQL statement>
```

< trigger condition> ::=
    WHEN <left paren> <search condition> <right paren>

<triggered SQL statement> ::=
    <SQL procedure statement>
    | BEGIN ATOMIC
    { <SQL procedure statement> <semicolon> } ...
    END

The name of a trigger must be unique among all trigger names in a given schema. The subject table of a trigger has to be a base table. (SQL3 does not support triggers on views.) The triggering operation of a trigger can only be an INSERT, DELETE, or an UPDATE statement. If the triggering operation is an UPDATE operation, an optional column list can be specified to further restrict the set of update operations that activate the trigger.

A trigger defined on a table T is activated whenever

1. an INSERT, UPDATE, or DELETE statement executes on T, or

2. an INSERT, UPDATE, or DELETE statement executes on an updatable view defined on T, or

3. a referential action (e.g., ON UPDATE CASCADE, ON DELETE SET DEFAULT, etc.) is initiated on T as a result of an INSERT, UPDATE, or DELETE operation on table S. Note that S and T may be the same table.

The trigger condition can be any arbitrarily complex SQL predicate. The predicates may include subqueries, user-defined functions, etc. The specification of the trigger condition is optional. If omitted, a trigger condition that specifies WHEN (TRUE) is implicit.

The trigger action is a list of SQL statements within a BEGIN/END block. (Note that the BEGIN/END block must behave as an atomic block, hence the mandatory ATOMIC keyword following BEGIN.) All SQL3 statements, except those dealing with schemas, connections, sessions, and transactions (i.e., COMMIT, ROLLBACK, etc.), are allowed in the trigger action. The trigger action may also include SQL/PSM procedural constructs (i.e., IF, CASE, WHILE, assignment statements, etc.), calls to stored procedures, and invocation of user-defined functions.

When a trigger is activated, every statement in the trigger action is executed in order. The execution of the triggering operation and the trigger actions of every trigger that gets activated is treated as atomic, i.e., if any one of them fails, the triggering operation together with all trigger and referential constraint actions are undone.

The execution of trigger actions of a trigger may activate other triggers (including the same trigger) and/or referential actions. Because of this, it is possible for the execution of a statement involving triggers to never terminate. Earlier versions of the SQL3 draft used to specify a set of restrictions on trigger definitions using a so-called *trigger action graph* to ensure that the execution always terminated. However, the set of restrictions proved to be overly restrictive and resulted in prohibiting many useful trigger definitions. Consequently, the concept of trigger action graph and the set of restrictions on trigger definitions have now been removed from SQL3. It is up to the users to make sure that cascaded triggers do not lead to nonterminating statement executions.

BEFORE and AFTER Triggers

Each trigger is associated with a *trigger activation time*, which determines whether the trigger is activated before or after the triggering operation. A trigger that is activated before the triggering operation is referred to as a *BEFORE trigger*, and a trigger that is activated after the triggering operation is referred to as an *AFTER trigger*. BEFORE triggers are specified by associating the keyword BEFORE with a trigger definition, while AFTER triggers are specified by associating the keyword AFTER. The specification of the trigger activation time as either BEFORE or AFTER is mandatory.

The two kinds of triggers offer different benefits. Since AFTER triggers execute after the triggering operation, they are especially useful for performing follow-on updates to other tables, or for invoking functions that perform useful follow-on tasks outside the database. In contrast, because BEFORE triggers execute before the triggering operation, they are especially useful for enforcing transitional constraints. For example, a BEFORE trigger may be employed to reject any update to an employee database that causes a change to the salary of an employee to exceed 10 percent.

FOR EACH ROW and FOR EACH STATEMENT Triggers

Each trigger is also associated with a *trigger granularity*, which determines how many times a trigger is activated when its triggering operation executes. (Note that trigger granularity is referred to as "transition granularity" in Chapter 1.) SQL3 allows for two levels of trigger granularity: *row-level triggers* and *statement-level triggers*. For row-level triggers, users need to specify FOR EACH ROW with a trigger definition, while for statement-level triggers, they need to specify FOR EACH STATEMENT. The specification of trigger granularity is optional; if neither is specified, FOR EACH STATEMENT is implicit.

A statement-level trigger executes once for a triggering operation, whereas a row-level trigger executes as many times as the number of rows in the *set of affected rows* of the triggering operation. The set of affected rows of a triggering operation is defined as follows:

1. If the triggering operation is an INSERT operation, then a set containing copies of all rows to be inserted;

2. If the triggering operation is a DELETE operation, then a set containing copies of all rows to be deleted; (Note: Because of referential delete actions, this set contains not only the copies of rows to be deleted by the triggering operation, but also copies of all rows of the subject table to be deleted because of referential actions.)

3. If the triggering operation is an UPDATE statement, then a set containing copies of all rows to be updated. (Note: Because of referential update actions, this set contains not only the copies of rows to be updated by the triggering operation, but also copies of all rows of the subject table to be updated because of referential actions.)

The set of affected rows of a triggering operation may sometimes be empty. For example, during the execution of an update statement of the form UPDATE T SET C = 10 WHERE ...;, the evaluation of the WHERE clause may result in an empty result table. A row-level trigger does not execute if the set of affected rows is empty. However, a statement-level trigger always executes once, even if the set of affected rows is empty.

Transition Tables and Transition Variables

Both the trigger action and the trigger condition of a trigger have access to the "current" state of the database, as well as the old and new values of each row in the set of affected rows of the triggering operation. Being able to refer to both the old and new values of the affected rows is important if, say, the trigger defined for an INSERT operation wants to refer to just the newly inserted rows in its trigger condition or if the trigger action needs to apply aggregations over the set of affected rows, (for example, MAX, MIN, or AVG of some column values).

A trigger condition or a trigger action may refer to the set of affected rows by means of two *transition tables*. One of the transition tables corresponds to the old values of the affected rows, and the other corresponds to the new values of the affected rows. They are accessible to the trigger condition and trigger action only when explicitly named in the REFERENCING clause of a trigger definition. The table identified by OLD_TABLE captures the original state of the set of affected rows (that is, before the triggering operation's modifications are applied to the database); the table identified by NEW_TABLE captures the new values of all rows that would result immediately after the modifications are applied to the database. Both transition tables are read-only tables.

During the execution of row-level triggers, one may also need to refer to the values of columns of a particular row in a transition table. This can be achieved by using two transition variables that can be specified in the

REFERENCING clause of a trigger definition. SQL3 supports two kinds of transition variables, OLD and NEW, each of which must be identified by a unique name in the REFERENCING clause. These transition variables represent correlation names over the transition tables. OLD defines a correlation name over the OLD_TABLE transition table, whereas NEW defines a correlation name over the NEW_TABLE transition table. Hence, OLD and NEW transition variables have exactly the same semantics as the correlation names used in SQL query statements.

Note that not all types of transition variables and transition tables are valid for all types of triggers. While triggers defined for INSERT operations can only see new values, triggers defined for DELETE operations can only see old values, and triggers defined for UPDATE operations can see both old and new values. Furthermore, transition variables can be specified only for row-level triggers.

Order of Trigger Execution when Multiple Triggers Become Eligible

SQL3 allows the definition of several triggers that have the same subject table, the same triggering operation, and the same activation time (BEFORE or AFTER). Hence, multiple triggers can be simultaneously eligible for execution. Also, because of referential actions, additional updates may be carried out during the execution of a triggering operation and hence, additional triggers may get added to the list of eligible triggers. Another situation where multiple triggers become eligible for execution is when the user requests deferred checking of constraints. In this case, constraints are checked when the transaction is ready to commit. This may result in the execution of multiple referential actions on multiple tables, which in turn might activate multiple triggers at the same time.

When multiple triggers become eligible for execution, there needs to be a strategy for ordering the execution of those triggers. Previously, SQL3 allowed users to specify a numeric order for triggers defined on the same table using an ORDER clause. However, the user-defined ordering could only supply partial ordering; SQL3 still needed a mechanism to specify global ordering. Also, the previous specification did not deal well with the collisions in user-specified order numbers. Hence, SQL3 has recently eliminated the ORDER clause for triggers. Instead, SQL3 now chooses the ordering based on the ascending order of the creation time of triggers. Thus, a trigger that is newly added to a database executes after all the other triggers that are previously defined. Note that this scheme does guarantee global ordering.

The standards committees may, sometime in the future, reintroduce explicit language constructs to let users specify ordering for triggers. It is important to note that the execution model as specified currently in SQL3 is not dependent on the mechanism used for ordering triggers. It only requires that there always be a global ordering when multiple triggers become eligible for activation. Therefore, it is likely that the standards committees will continue to base the default ordering on the creation time of triggers. The creation time of triggers may also be used as a means of guaranteeing global ordering when the users specify only partial orderings.

10.2.3   Execution Model for Triggers in SQL3

There are two major requirements on the execution model of triggers:

1. The execution model must ensure that the trigger actions see a consistent database state when they execute.

2. The execution model must ensure that all BEFORE triggers appear to execute entirely before the triggering operation's modifications are applied to the database, and all AFTER triggers appear to execute entirely after the triggering operation's modifications are applied to the database.

The main reason for the above restrictions is to ensure the deterministic execution of SQL statements. Furthermore, many semantic optimizations can only be applied if the declarative constraints are enforced at all times. This is particularly important for AFTER triggers because they are being used extensively in the market place to support automatic execution of application logic. SQL3 now allows calls to stored procedures and invocations of user-defined functions from the body of triggers. These functions and procedures can be specified using the procedural extensions made to SQL such as BEGIN and END blocks with local variables, IF/THEN/ELSE statements, CASE statements, different forms of loops, etc. It is important to ensure that a stored procedure executes under the same circumstances irrespective of whether it is called from an application program or from a trigger body. Such a stored procedure could have been compiled using semantic optimization techniques that can only be applied if the declarative constraints defined on the database are enforced. Otherwise, the resulting plans may yield erroneous results.

In the case of AFTER triggers, the above requirements imply that all AFTER triggers must execute only after the modifications of their triggering operation are applied to the database and all declarative constraints are enforced. In the case of BEFORE triggers, the above requirements imply that trigger actions of BEFORE triggers should not be allowed to modify the database. If BEFORE triggers are allowed to modify the database, an endless chain of unapplied modifications will build up during the execution of such triggers. Since these modifications will not be visible to the nested invocations of other triggers, it may result in an ambiguity as to what persists in the database when the BEFORE triggers and any cascaded actions due to their trigger actions complete.

The current trigger execution model of SQL3 is designed keeping in mind the above two requirements. Note that for the purpose of describing the execution model, we will assume the trigger actions of BEFORE triggers do not update the database. (Though SQL3 has no such restrictions currently, we plan to propose such restrictions in the near future.) Because of this, all BEFORE triggers see the database state that existed prior to the execution of the triggering operation and that is guaranteed to be consistent. Also, in the current execution model, all AFTER triggers execute after the modifications caused by the triggering operation are applied to the database and all applicable constraints are checked. Thus, an AFTER trigger sees the database state that existed prior to the triggering operation's execution as modified by the triggering operation (including modifications due to referential actions), followed by the modifications of all the AFTER triggers that were activated before its activation. Since constraints are checked every time the database is modified, the database state seen by every AFTER trigger is also guaranteed to be consistent.

Description of the Trigger Execution Model

Assume the database engine is starting the execution of a SQL statement Si. Assume Si is modifying (INSERT, DELETE, or UPDATE) a table Ti. Let the set of affected rows of Si be SARi. The execution of Si is said to create a new *trigger execution context* TECi. This trigger execution context TECi remains active until the completion of Si. Any other SQL statement Sj that is executed before the completion of Si (e.g., Sj may be one of the SQL statements contained in the body of an AFTER trigger activated by Si) preserves TECi and creates a new trigger execution context TECj that remains active until the completion of Sj. At the completion of Sj, the trigger execution context TECi is restored. At any given time, there is only one trigger execution context active, which is the trigger execution context that was created by the SQL statement that is currently being executed.

During the processing of SQL statements, data is conceptually maintained in two different repositories: the database and the trigger execution context. The database represents the persistent repository of the enterprise data that is shared among applications and whose visibility is protected by the authorization and locking mechanisms of the DBMS. On the other hand, the trigger execution context is local and contains transitions computed during the execution of the triggering SQL statement and cascaded referential actions.

Every trigger execution context contains a *set of state changes*, where each state change corresponds to a 3-tuple: (table-name, event-type, set-of-transitions).[3] Each transition in the *set-of-transitions* corresponds to a

---

[3] Actually, in the case of updates, a state change may contain additional information if the trigger definition specifies a list of columns. To keep the description simple, this

2-tuple: (old-row, new-row). If T is a transition representing a modification of a row for some event E, then T.new-row (applicable for insert and update events) is the value of the row to be applied to the database, and T.old-row (applicable for delete and update events) is the value of the row in the database before E is executed.

When a trigger execution context TECi comes into existence, the set of state changes SSCi contains a single element that captures the table name of Ti and the INSERT, DELETE, or UPDATE event specified in Si. The number of transitions in the set of transitions, STNi, for this state change corresponds to the number of rows in SARi, with appropriate old and new values for each transition derived from the data in the database and the user-supplied input data.

As the modifications caused by Si are applied to the database and the constraints checked, one or more referential actions may be initiated. In the current execution model, all referential actions initiated by Si execute under Si's trigger execution context, i.e., the execution of referential actions does not lead to nested execution. Consequently, each referential action caused by Si results in the creation of a new state change, and insertion of the newly created state change into SSCi, unless SSCi already contains an element corresponding to the state change caused by that referential action. In that case, the set of transitions for the particular state change in SSCi is suitably modified.

A trigger is activated by a state change if the event type of the trigger is the same as the event type of the state change and if the subject table of the trigger is the same as the subject table of the state change. As discussed before, multiple triggers may be activated for a given state change, and the ordering of these trigger executions is based on the ascending order of the creation times of these triggers. The contents of OLD_TABLE and NEW_TABLE transition tables required for the executions of statement-level triggers activated by a state change are derived from the set of transitions for that state change.

The procedure EXECUTE_STATEMENT, given below, describes the sequence of actions that take place when Si executes. Note that, according to the current specification, if an exception is raised at any stage during the execution of Si, the execution of Si is terminated immediately and the database is restored to the state that existed before the execution of Si.

PROCEDURE EXECUTE_STATEMENT (S statement)

1. Save the current trigger execution context (if any) and create a new trigger execution context, TEC.

2. Determine the set of affected rows, SAR.

---

level of detail is omitted.

3. Create the set of state changes, SSC, with one state change, SC, whose table name is the name of the table referenced in S, event type is one of INSERT, DELETE, or UPDATE referenced in S, and the set of transitions, STN, derived from SAR.

4. Call PROCESS_BEFORE_TRIGGERS with (SC, TRUE) as its arguments.

5. Apply the modifications caused by S to the database.

6. Evaluate all applicable constraints according to the execution model described in section 10.2.1. For each referential action resulting from this step, do the following:

   (a) If SSC contains a state change SCi corresponding to the state change of the referential action, insert the transitions caused by the referential action to the set of transitions of SCi. Create a dummy state change, SCk, which is identical to SCi except for the fact that the set of transitions for SCk contains only those transitions caused by the referential action. Then proceed to call PROCESS_BEFORE_TRIGGERS with (SCk, FALSE) as arguments.

   (b) otherwise, create a new state change SCj and insert it into SSC. Call PROCESS_BEFORE_TRIGGERS with (SCj, TRUE) as arguments.

7. For each state change SC in SSC, call PROCESS_AFTER_TRIGGERS with SC as the argument.

8. Restore the saved trigger execution context (if any).

PROCEDURE PROCESS_BEFORE_TRIGGERS
    (SC state_change, FLAG boolean)

1. Compute the set of eligible row-level and statement-level BEFORE triggers activated by the state change in SC. Let (B1, B2, ... Bn) be the sequence of BEFORE triggers, ordered according to their global ordering. Let BTS be the resulting sequence.

2. If the set of transitions contained in SC is empty, remove all row-level triggers from BTS.

3. If FLAG is set to FALSE, remove all statement-level triggers from BTS. (Note: Since the execution of referential actions happens under the trigger execution context of the original statement, statement-level BEFORE triggers need to be activated only once per state change.)

4. Populate the contents of OLD_TABLE and NEW_TABLE transition tables from the set of transitions contained in SC.

5. For each trigger TR in BTS, do the following:

   (a) If TR is a statement-level trigger, evaluate TR's trigger condition. If the trigger condition evaluates to *true*, then execute sequentially each of the statements in TR's trigger action.

   (b) If TR is a row-level trigger,

        i. Order each transition in SC's set of transitions in an arbitrary order.
        ii. For each transition, set the values for OLD and NEW transition variables. Evaluate TR's trigger condition. If the trigger condition evaluates to *true*, execute sequentially each of the statements in TR's trigger action.

(Note: We are assuming the trigger actions of BEFORE triggers do not update the database, so no new state changes will be caused by the execution of BEFORE triggers, and hence no new triggers will be activated.)

PROCEDURE PROCESS_AFTER_TRIGGERS (SC state_change)

1. Compute the set of eligible row-level and statement-level AFTER triggers activated by the state change in SC. Let (A1, A2, ... An) be the sequence of AFTER triggers, ordered according to their global ordering. Let ATS be the resulting sequence.

2. If the set of transitions contained in SC is empty, remove all row-level triggers from ATS.

3. Populate the contents of OLD_TABLE and NEW_TABLE transition tables from the set of transitions contained in SC.

4. For each trigger TR in ATS, do the following:

   (a) If TR is a statement-level trigger, evaluate TR's trigger condition. If the trigger condition evaluates to *true*, then execute sequentially each of the statements in TR's trigger action. For each statement Sj in the trigger action that is either an INSERT, an UPDATE, or a DELETE statement, call EXECUTE_STATEMENT (Sj).

   (b) If TR is a row-level trigger,

        i. Order each transition in SC's set of transitions in an arbitrary order.

ii. For each transition, set the values for OLD and NEW transition variables. Evaluate TR's trigger condition. If the trigger condition evaluates to *true*, execute sequentially each of the statements in TR's trigger action. For each statement Sj in the trigger action that is either an INSERT, an UPDATE, or a DELETE statement, call EXECUTE_STATEMENT (Sj).

10.2.4 Discussion of SQL3's Execution Model

One of the main contributions of the SQL3's execution model for triggers is the integration of triggers with the fixpoint semantics that describes the semantics of SQL's declarative constraints. Such integration has been achieved with full compatibility with SQL-92, the current international SQL standard to which commercial SQL databases conform. Several other models developed previously were either incompatible with SQL-92 or ignored important aspects of the SQL language (see [CaNM96]).

As we mentioned before, allowing SQL update operations within the body of BEFORE triggers leads to nondeterministic and/or nonmonotonic behavior. It is important to observe that such changes could also cause further triggers to be activated by changes that are yet to be applied to the database, yielding quite untrackable results. For this reason, the SQL committee is considering restrictions regarding the SQL operations that can occur within the body of BEFORE triggers.

In addition, because BEFORE triggers are part of the fixpoint computation of declarative constraints, they participate in the computation of the set of affected rows for AFTER triggers, and as such in the computation of the transition tables. Consequently, BEFORE triggers cannot perform certain operations on transition tables because they will yield wrong results. For example, selecting the total number of employees being deleted cannot be given until the fixpoint computation (including the DELETE statement and delete cascade actions) is complete. Since BEFORE triggers must execute before the triggering statement and constraints are checked at the end of SQL statements, it is clear that accessing transition tables in BEFORE triggers may lead to incorrect results because the contents of the transition tables will not reflect the results of the evaluation of constraints. For this reason, the SQL committee is also considering restrictions on the access of transition tables within BEFORE triggers.

It should be clear that these restrictions are quite conservative. Identifying situations in which access to transition tables or update operations within BEFORE triggers do not cause nondeterministic behavior or incorrect results is likely to be a topic of further work in the version of the SQL standard following SQL3.

During the execution of AFTER triggers, each of the UPDATE, DELETE, or INSERT statements that is part of the trigger action invokes the EXECUTE_STATEMENT procedure recursively. SQL3 users defining AF-

TER triggers must take this recursive evaluation into account when specifying the body of triggers in order to avoid the definition of triggers whose execution may never terminate. For example, if an SQL statement S activates an AFTER trigger T, and the execution of T causes the execution of an SQL statement S' that, in turn, activates a new instantiation of T, then execution of S may never terminate. Currently, the SQL3 standard does not address this problem, leaving it open to implementations to decide how such issues are handled.

Note that it may sometimes be efficient to process all row-level triggers in-flight, i.e., as each row is processed. However, if any of the constraints to be evaluated require access to either the subject table or any other table modified by the trigger action or the constraints, then row-level triggers can only be processed in a set-oriented fashion. For example, if a row-level trigger with a subject table T accesses the average of a column of T, then the average must not be computed in the middle of the triggering operation; it must be processed completely either before or after the triggering operation (according to its activation time).

Finally, the current SQL3 execution model for triggers does not address the inherent nondeterministic behavior of row-level triggers. Since row-level triggers execute once for each transition contained in the set of transitions, and since sets have no order associated with them, it is possible to get different answers depending on the order in which the row-level triggers are processed. Unfortunately, no restrictions to the language or refinement to the trigger execution model can remove this particular flavor of nondeterministic behavior.

10.3   Examples

In this section, we discuss a few simple examples that demonstrate the trigger functionality in SQL3. The tables used in these examples are:

```
create table MAIN
    (mainPrimKey integer primary key,
    textlen integer,
    text char(100))
```

```
create table REPLICA
    (replPrimKey integer primary key,
    textlen integer,
    text char(100))
```

```
create table WHOUPDATED
    (opType char(1),
    updated_by VARCHAR(8),
    updated_on DATE)
```

where REPLICA is a replica of MAIN, and WHOUPDATED records the operation, date, and userid of any operation that modifies MAIN.

Example 1:
Consider the following trigger:

```
create trigger propDelMain
  after delete on MAIN
  referencing old as OLDREC
  for each row
  begin atomic
    delete from REPLICA where replPrimKey = OLDREC.mainPrimKey;
    insert into WHOUPDATED values('D', USER, CURRENT DATE);
end
```

This trigger propagates deletions from MAIN to the replica REPLICA and records the operation in WHOUPDATED. Suppose user MATTOS deletes three records from MAIN on July 3 with a single DELETE statement. Trigger propDelMain will execute once for each of the records. Suppose the first such record is r1. The row in REPLICA corresponding to r1 will be deleted and a row ('D', MATTOS, July 3) will be added to WHOUPDATED. Similar operations will occur for the other two rows, resulting in three records being deleted from REPLICA and three rows being inserted into WHOUPDATED (assuming REPLICA is identical to MAIN before the deletion).

Example 2:

Using a FOR EACH ROW trigger to record access to MAIN in the above example causes many duplicates to be added to WHOUPDATED. Suppose instead we replace the above trigger with the following two triggers:

```
create trigger replDelMain
  after delete on MAIN
  referencing old as OLDREC
  for each row
  begin atomic
    delete from REPLICA where replPrimKey = OLDREC.mainPrimKey;
  end

create trigger recordDelMain
  after delete on MAIN
  for each statement
  begin atomic
    insert into WHOUPDATED values('D', USER, CURRENT DATE);
  end
```

Suppose, again, user MATTOS deletes three records from MAIN on July 3 with a single DELETE statement. Trigger replDelMain will be executed first, since it was defined before recordDelMain. It executes once for each row deleted from MAIN and hence, deletes three records from REPLICA. Then recordDelMain will be executed exactly once, inserting a single record ('D', MATTOS, July 3) into WHOUPDATED.

Example 3:

Consider the triggers in example 2 with the following additional constraint that there is some table that is referentially dependent on MAIN:

```
create table CHILD
  (childPrimKey integer primary key,
   childForKey integer constraint FKMAIN references MAIN)
```

Again, assume user MATTOS deletes three records from MAIN on July 3 with a single DELETE statement. Before either trigger is executed, the constraint FKMAIN is checked. If there are any records in CHILD that would be orphaned by the operation, then an error is raised, any modifications made are rolled back, and processing terminates. If the constraint is satisfied, then processing continues as described in example 2, i.e., replDel-Main executes once for each of the deleted records, and recordDelMain is then executed once.

Example 4:

Consider, now, if FKMAIN were defined with a delete rule of cascade. In this case, when records in CHILD are orphaned, the orphaned records are deleted rather than raising an error. Then processing continues as described in example 2.

Example 5:

Suppose there is yet another table that maintains replicas of CHILD:

```
create table CHILD_REPLICA
  (childReplPrimKey integer primary key,
   childReplForKey integer);
```

To maintain this replica when records are deleted from CHILD, the following trigger is defined:

```
create trigger replDelChild
  after delete on CHILD
  referencing old as OLDREC
  for each row
```

```
begin atomic
  delete from CHILD_REPLICA where childReplPrimKey =
  OLDREC.childPrimKey;
end
```

Suppose also that there is another table that is a copy of REPLICA.

```
create table REPLICACOPY
  (replPrimKey integer primary key,
    textlen integer,
    text char(100))
```

The following trigger is created to maintain this copy when records are deleted from REPLICA:

```
create trigger copyDelReplica
  after delete on REPLICA
  referencing old as REPLICAOLDREC
  for each row
  begin atomic
    delete from REPLICACOPY
          where replPrimKey = REPLICAOLDREC.replPrimKey;
  end
```

In this case, deletion of three records from MAIN by MATTOS on July 3 proceeds as follows:

1. Perform the deletion of the three records from MAIN.

2. Perform constraint processing for the deletes from MAIN. Suppose this results in the deletion of six child records from CHILD. At this point, three triggers are selected for execution: replDelMain, recordDelMain, and replDelChild. Order these according to the total order. Suppose this results in replDelChild first, recordDelMain second, replDelMain last. (Note that we reverse the order of recordDelMain and replDelMain just to demonstrate that the user has the ability to specify any order, even between FOR EACH STATEMENT triggers and FOR EACH ROW triggers).

   (a) Execute replDelChild once for each of the six child records deleted from CHILD. This will delete the six corresponding records from CHILD_REPLICA.

   (b) Execute recordDelMain exactly once for the entire statement, recording that MATTOS performed a DELETE on July 3.

   (c) Execute replDelMain once for each of the three records deleted from MAIN.

      i. When replDelMain processes the first row, it will delete a row from REPLICA. This will then cause trigger copyDelReplica to be executed.

     ii. Then, replDelMain processes the second row, deleting another row from REPLICA, and causing trigger copyDelReplica to be executed again.

    iii. Finally, replDelMain will process the third row, deleting another row from REPLICA, and causing trigger copyDelReplica to be executed again.

After the original DELETE statement completes, three rows are deleted from MAIN, six rows are deleted from CHILD because of an ON DELETE CASCADE <referential triggered action>. Rows in REPLICA that correspond to the three rows deleted from MAIN, and rows in CHILD_REPLICA corresponding to the six rows deleted from CHILD are deleted because of triggers, and rows in REPLICACOPY that correspond to the rows deleted from REPLICA are deleted because of cascade trigger invocations.

10.4   Comparison of SQL3 Triggers to the Active Database Framework

The tabular summary of the SQL3 trigger system according to the framework in Chapter 1 is given in Tables 10.1, 10.2, and 10.3. Distinctive features are discussed below.

10.4.1   Knowledge Model

Although SQL3 supports only structure-oriented primitive events, events on other kinds of operations or composite in nature may be supported in a future version of the standard.

    The context in which rule conditions and actions are evaluated depends on the trigger activation time. BEFORE triggers always evaluate their condition against DB_E (state of the database when the event took place), whereas AFTER triggers always evaluate them against DB_A (the state of the database when the action is executed).

    SQL3 currently does not support updating the structure of the database or do-instead triggers. As for the context, the execution of trigger actions follow the same context as the trigger condition, which may be either DB_E or DB_A.

10.4.2   Execution Model

The condition mode and action mode of all triggers are immediate and executed in the same transaction as the triggering operation. SQL3 supports

Event	Source	Structure Operation
	Granularity	Member, Subset, Set
	Type	Primitive
	Role	Mandatory
Condition	Role	Optional
	Context	$Bind_E$, DB_E, DB_A,
Action	Options	Structure Operation, Behavior
		Invocation, External
	Context	$Bind_E$, DB_E, DB_A

TABLE 10.1. Knowledge model for SQL3.

both tuple and set transition granularity. In fact, the relationship between event occurrences and rule instantiations in SQL3 could be 1:1, 1:many, many:1, or many:many.

SQL3 does not follow the net effect policy, i.e., triggers are executed according to their global ordering such that each trigger sees the database as modified by all triggering operations, integrity constraints, and/or triggers executed previously. Since SQL3 does not follow a net-effect policy, FOR EACH ROW triggers that both read and modify the database may result in nondeterministic behavior since the standard does not specify in which order the rows in the set of affect rows are considered for execution.

SQL3 follows a static priority scheme determined by the system based on the trigger creation time to determine the order of trigger executions when multiple triggers are activated at the same time.

The error handling mechanism in SQL3 is to undo the effects of the triggering operation and the trigger actions that have already executed, but not abort the transaction itself.

Condition Mode	Immediate
Action Mode	Immediate
Transition granularity	Tuple, Set
Net-effect policy	No
Cycle policy	Recursive
Priorities	None
Scheduling	All Sequential
Error handling	Backtrack

TABLE 10.2. Execution model for SQL3.

10.4.3 Management

SQL3 triggers are expressed in the SQL query language extended with the procedural constructs and routine invocations. SQL3 provides for creation and deletion of triggers only; no other actions are supported on triggers. Once created, SQL3 does not allow trigger definitions to be modified. Finally, the data model supported by SQL3 can be classified either as Extended Relational or Object Relational.

Description	Query/Programming Language
Operations	
Adaptability	Compile Time
Data Model	Extended Relational

TABLE 10.3. Management model for SQL3.

10.5   Conclusion

In this chapter, we described the active functionality that is currently supported in SQL3. We described how users can define triggers that are activated whenever the database is modified and the execution semantics of those triggers.

It is probably still true that the active features supported by the SQL standard and the current commercial products are somewhat limited compared to the active features found in the current research prototypes. However, we believe that the SQL standard has dealt with fairly tricky problems that have not received much attention from the research community at all. For example, the interaction between the execution of triggers and the enforcement of declarative constraints and the complexities due to BEFORE triggers have hardly received any attention form the research community.

10.6   REFERENCES

[CaNM96] Roberta Cochrane and Hamid Pirahesh anhd Nelson Mattos. Integrating Triggers and Declarative Constraints in SQL Database Systems. In *Proc. 22th VLDB Conference, Mumbai, India*, 1996.

[CW95]   Stefano Ceri and Jennifer Widom. Standards and Commercial Systems. In S. Ceri J. Widom and U. Dayal (eds), editors, *Active Database Systems: Triggers and Rules for Advanced Database Processing*. Morgan Kaufman, 1995.

[Hor94]   Bruce Horowitz.   Intermediate States as a Source of Nondeterministic Behavior of Triggers. In *Proc. 4th Int. Workshop on Research Issues in Data Engineering: Active Database Systems*, 1994.

[ISO92]   Database Language SQL. ISO/IEC 9075:1992, 1992.

[ISO96]   Working draft: Database Language SQL (SQL3). ISO/IEC DBL MAD-007, June 1996.

11

Ariel

Eric N. Hanson

ABSTRACT
This chapter gives an overview of the design and implementation of the
Ariel active DBMS. The query language of Ariel is a subset of POST-
QUEL, extended with a new production-rule sublanguage. The Ariel rule
system is tightly coupled with query and update processing. Ariel rules can
have conditions based on a mix of selections, joins, events, and transitions.
For testing rule conditions, Ariel makes use of a discrimination network
composed of a special data structure for testing single-relation selection
conditions efficiently, and a modified version of the TREAT algorithm,
called A-TREAT, for testing join conditions.

11.1   Introduction

The Ariel system is an active relational DBMS with a rule (trigger) system based on the production system model [For82]. The approach taken in
the design of Ariel has been to adopt as much as possible from previous
work on main-memory production systems such as OPS5 [For81], but make
changes where necessary to improve the functionality and performance of
a production system in a database environment. These changes include a
rule language extension to POSTQUEL [SRH90] with a query-language-
like syntax, a discrimination network for rule condition testing tailored to
the database environment, and measures to integrate rule processing with
set-oriented database update commands and transactions. A distinguishing feature of Ariel is that it is a complete implementation of a relational
DBMS with a rule system that is tightly coupled with the query processor.
Ariel's rule condition testing mechanism, called A-TREAT, is a variation
of the TREAT algorithm [Mir87] enhanced with features to speed up testing of selection predicates in rule conditions, reduce the amount of state
information kept in the network, and handle event, transition, and pattern-
based conditions in a uniform way. A more complete discussion of Ariel can
be found in [Han96].

11.2   The Ariel Query and Rule Languages

Ariel is based on the relational data model and provides a subset of the POSTQUEL query language of POSTGRES for specifying data definition commands, queries, and updates [SRH90]. POSTQUEL commands **retrieve**, **append**, **delete**, and **replace** are supported, along with other commands for creating and destroying relations and indexes, and performing utility functions such as loading relations, gathering statistics on data in relations, and so forth.

The Ariel rule language (ARL) is a production rule language with enhancements for defining rules with conditions that can contain relational selections and joins, as well as specifications of events and transitions. The ARL syntax is based on the syntax of the query language. Hence, the syntax of a rule condition is nearly identical to that of the **where** clause of a query. The general form of an ARL rule is the following:

> **define rule** *rule-name* [**in** *ruleset-name*]
> [**priority** *priority-val*]
> [**on** *event*]
> [**if** *condition*]
> **then** *action*

The optional **priority** clause allows specification of a numeric priority to control the order of rule execution.[1] The priority can be a floating-point number in the range -1000 to 1000. If the priority clause is not present, priority defaults to 0. Priorities are used to help the system order the execution of rules when multiple rules are eligible to run.

The **on** clause allows specification of an event that will trigger the rule. The following types of events can be specified after an **on** clause:

- **append** [**to**] *relation-name*

- **delete** [**from**] *relation-name*

- **replace** [**to**] *relation-name* [(*attribute-list*)]

The **on** clause is optional since potential triggering events are normally inferred based on the relations used in the **if** clause, simplifying rule specification.

The *condition* after the **if** clause has the following form:

> *qualification* [**from** *from-list*]

The *qualification* part of a rule's **if** condition has the same form as the qualification of a **where** clause in a query, with some exceptions. A rule's

---

[1] PRS and some main-memory production systems support numeric priorities.

qualification clause can contain only selection and join conditions. Aggregates and the relational projection operation are not allowed. This design was chosen to simplify rule condition testing. The **from** clause is for specifying bindings of tuple variables to relations. Relation names can be used as default tuple variables.

Transition conditions are important in a database rule language because application developers often wish to specify transition integrity constraints and alerting conditions. For example, it may be that in a particular application, it is important that no one ever be given more than a 10 percent raise. To allow transition conditions to be specified in Ariel, a special keyword **previous** lets a condition refer to the previous value of an attribute. The value that a tuple attribute had at the beginning of a transition can be accessed using the following notation:

> **previous** *tuple-variable.attribute*

The **then** part of the rule contains the action to be performed when the rule fires. The action can be a single data manipulation command, or a *compound command* which is a **do** ... **end** block surrounding a list of commands.

The binding between the condition and the action of a rule is specified by using the same tuple variable(s) in both. This means a tuple variable appearing in both the rule condition and action ranges in the action only over the data that has matched the rule condition since the last execution of the rule.

ARL rule conditions are similar to OPS5 conditions in expressive power. The main differences are that unlike OPS5, ARL supports event and transition conditions. However, OPS5 supports negated conditions and ARL does not. Negated conditions are important for the expressive power of a production rule language, and would be a worthwhile feature in an extended version of ARL. ARL also does not include some relational operations, including negation, union, projection, and containment. These were intentionally left out to allow a streamlined implementation.

11.2.1 Semantics of Rule Execution

The Ariel rule system uses a production system model. Execution of rules is governed by a *recognize-act cycle* similar to that used in OPS5 [For82]. Ariel rule instantiations are *set-oriented*, which means that when a rule fires, all combinations of tuples that have matched the rule condition since the last time the rule fired are processed at once. Ariel rules are processed after each database *transition*. A transition in Ariel is defined to be the changes in the database induced by either a single command, or a **do** ... **end** block containing a list of simple commands. Blocks may not be nested. The programmer designing a database transaction thus has control over where transitions occur.

initial match
while (*rules left to run*) {
    conflict resolution
    act
    match

}

FIGURE 11.1. The recognize-act cycle.

The Rule Execution Cycle

Rules in Ariel are processed using a control strategy called the *recognize-act cycle*, shown in Figure 11.1, which is commonly used in production systems [For81].

The *match* step finds the set of rules that are eligible to run. The *conflict resolution* step selects a single rule for execution from the set of eligible rules. Finally, the *act* step executes the statements in the rule action. The cycle repeats until no rules are eligible to run.

Ariel picks a rule to execute during the conflict resolution phase using the following criteria (after each of the steps, shown below, if there is only one rule still being considered, that rule is scheduled for execution; otherwise, the set of rules still under consideration is passed to the next step):

- *Select the rule(s) with the highest priority.*

- *Select the rule(s) most recently awakened.* If two or more different rules with the highest priority had their conditions satisfied by the same database transition, then those rules would be tied at this point. If two or more different rules with the highest priority had their conditions satisfied by different transitions, then only the ones that had their conditions satisfied by the *latest* transition would still be considered after this point.

- *Select the rule(s) whose condition is the most selective.* The selectivity is estimated by the query optimizer at the time the rule is compiled. This is possible because the rule condition has the same form as the **where** clause of a query.

- If more than one rule remains, select one arbitrarily.

11.3 Examples

Some examples are presented below using these relations:

    emp(eno, name, age, salary, dno, jno)
    dept(dno, name, building)
    job(jno, title, paygrade, description)

define rule SalesClerkRule
if emp.sal > 30000
and emp.dno = dept.dno
and dept.name = "Sales"
and emp.jno = job.jno
and job.title = "Clerk"
then append salaryErrorLog("salary too high",emp.eno)

FIGURE 11.2. Example rule with a join condition.

Simple conditions and Condition-action binding: This rule illustrates
a simple, one-table condition, and condition-action binding based on
common tuple variables in the rule condition and action:

define rule FritzRule
if emp.name = "Fritz"
then delete emp **where** emp.sal > 30000

The above rule deletes people named Fritz from the emp relation
if they earn more than $30,000 a year. It does *not* delete everyone
earning more then $30,000 a year if there is someone named Fritz.
The rule will be triggered if an updated emp tuple has name field
Fritz.

Join conditions: The rule shown in Figure 11.2 illustrates use of a join
condition.

Transition conditions: This rule illustrates use of a transition condition:

define rule raiseLimit
if emp.sal > 1.1 * **previous** emp.sal
then append to salaryError(emp.name, **previous** emp.sal,
emp.sal)

The effect of this rule is to place the name and new/old salary pair
of every employee that received a raise of greater than 10 percent in
a relation salaryError.

11.4   Architectural Overview

The architecture of Ariel, shown in Figure 11.3, is similar to that of System
R [ABC+76] with additional components attached for rule processing. Ariel
has a front-end consisting of a lexer, parser, semantic analyzer, and query
optimizer.

In addition to the standard front- and back-end components, Ariel has a
rule catalog for maintaining the definitions of rules, a *discrimination network* for testing rule conditions, a *rule execution monitor* for managing rule

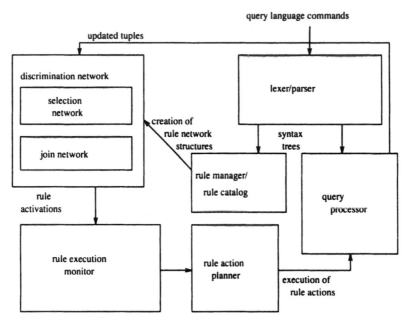

FIGURE 11.3. Diagram of the Ariel system architecture.

execution, and a *rule action planner* for binding the data matching a rule condition with the rule action and producing an execution plan for that action.

11.4.1   The Discrimination Network

An efficient strategy for incrementally testing rule conditions as small changes in the database occur is critical for fast rule processing. Ariel uses a variation of the TREAT [Mir87] discrimination network, called A-TREAT, to incrementally test rule conditions. The A-TREAT network in Ariel is a persistent data structure subject to database concurrency control and recovery.

At an abstract level, the A-TREAT algorithm implemented in Ariel works as follows. Logically, an A-TREAT network consists of the following components:

- a **root** node that accepts tokens describing changes to the database,

- a set of **select** nodes[2] that test single-relation selection conditions,

- a set of α-**memory** nodes, one per select node, that logically contain the tuples matching the condition in the associated select node,

---

[2]In the production systems literature, select nodes are called *t*-const nodes, but the more self-explanatory term borrowed from relational algebra is used here.

- a set of **P-nodes** that contain tuples or combinations of tuples that have recently matched rule conditions.

An α-memory node may be either *stored*, in which case it contains the tuples matching the associated select node, or *virtual*, in which case it contains a predicate but not the stored tuples. Relevant portions of virtual α nodes are materialized on demand. The α-memory nodes are connected by join edges labeled with join predicates. Logically, for each transaction there is one P-node for each rule. All types of nodes except P-nodes are persistent. P-nodes are volatile objects that are created on a per-transaction basis for a rule whenever a transaction first causes data to match that rule. The P-nodes created for a transaction are destroyed at the end of the transaction.

Changes to the database are packaged as "+" tokens and "−" tokens, representing inserts and deletes, respectively. Condition matching is performed by propagating tokens through the A-TREAT network. Modifications of existing records are modeled as deletes followed by inserts.

When a tuple is inserted into the database, a + token is created containing the tuple value and passed to the root node. The root logically broadcasts it to all the select nodes. If a token matches the condition of a select node, it is inserted into the associated α-memory node. Next, the token is "joined across" the other α-memory nodes. A set of zero or more tuple combinations may be found that match all the selection and join conditions of the rule. If this set has one or more tuple combinations in it, those tuple combinations are inserted in the P-node for the rule. At the end of the current database transition, the rule will be run for the tuple combinations in the P-node. Deletion of a tuple from the database causes a − token to be propagated through the A-TREAT network, which removes the deleted tuple from α-memory nodes, and removes tuples from the P-node that have the deleted tuple as a component.

An example of an A-TREAT network for the SalesClerkRule rule in Figure 11.2 is shown in Figure 11.4. Pattern matching for SalesClerkRule can be done using the network shown in Figure 11.4. The middle α-memory node (alpha2) is virtual (the contents are not stored, only the selection predicate), as indicated by the dashed box around it. If the predicate sal>30000 is not very selective, then making alpha2 be virtual may be a reasonable choice for SalesClerkRule, since it can save a significant amount of storage. The use of virtual alpha memories allows trading space for time in an A-TREAT network. Moreover, if there is an index on the relation underlying the virtual alpha memory that can support access via either the memory's join or selection access path, then the system can find the tuples in the memory that join to a particular token quickly via the index.

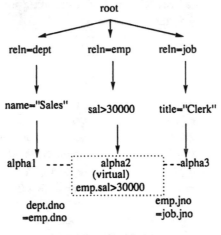

FIGURE 11.4. Example A-TREAT network.

The Selection Predicate Index

An important performance optimization in A-TREAT is the use of a special selection predicate index for testing selection conditions of rules [HCKW90]. Each tuple variable (relation) that appears in a rule's **if** condition can have zero or more selection predicates defined on it. In order to speed up rule condition testing, Ariel filters out tokens (descriptions of updated tuples) as soon as possible. To speed up the filtering process, Ariel uses a special *selection predicate index* (SPI). An overview of the SPI is given in Figure 11.5. Ariel indexes selection predicates of the form "attribute=constant" and "constant1 < attribute < constant2", which are found in rule conditions, by treating predicates of this type as intervals and building a special interval index from them. The index, called an interval binary search tree (IBS tree) [HCKW90], can efficiently find all intervals that overlap a point. Another interval index the author has developed, but which has not been implemented in Ariel, is called the interval skip list (IS list) [HJ96]. The IS list is as efficient as the IBS tree but is much easier to implement.

Only the most selective component of a selection predicate consisting of the **and** of two or more predicates is indexed. When a token enters Ariel's discrimination network, the appropriate interval indexes, and a list of non-indexable predicates are searched to find a set of partial matches. For each predicate for which a partial match is found, the whole predicate is tested against the token. If a complete match is found, the token is propagated forward in the discrimination network.

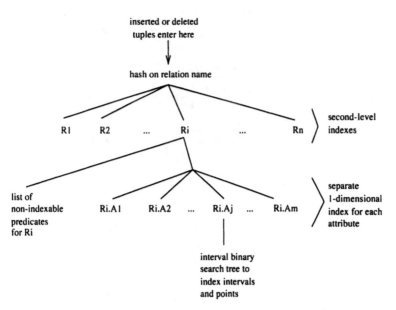

FIGURE 11.5. High-level diagram of predicate indexing scheme.

11.4.2   The Rule Execution Monitor

The rule execution monitor maintains the rule agenda, firing rules as required. The rule agenda is a priority queue, with one entry, called a *priority group*, for each group of rules with equal priority. Within a priority group, rules are ordered such that the one whose condition was most recently matched is first. Before a rule action is executed, query modification is performed on the rule action, so that the rule action runs only for the data currently in the P-node for the rule [Han96].

11.5   System Properties and Relationship to Other Work

Ariel uses a pattern-driven, production-rule-style approach to active rules, which makes it quite different from most other active database prototype, which are based on a pure ECA model and are fundamentally event-driven. In Ariel, an explicit attempt has been made to make rule condition expression nonprocedural. Nonprocedural specification has benefits for rule systems, just as it does for relation database query processing systems. The **where** clause of an Ariel rule is a pattern. In the case when no event is specified in the rule condition (which may be often), Ariel implicitly checks any relevant insert, delete, and update events as needed. The designers of Ariel feel that over-reliance on event specification may be harmful, since it is procedural in nature. It may make applications that use triggers less flex-

Knowledge Model:

Event	Source	Structure Operation, Clock
	Granularity	Set
	Type	Primitive
	Role	Optional
Condition	Role	Optional
	Context	DB_A
Action	Options	Structure Operation, Behavior Invocation, Abort
	Context	$Bind_E$, $Bind_C$, DB_A

Execution Model:

Condition-Mode	Deferred
Action-Mode	Deferred
Transition granularity	Set
Net-effect policy	Yes
Cycle policy	Iterative
Priorities	Numerical
Scheduling	All Sequential
Error handling	Abort

Management Model:

Description	Query Language
Operations	Activate, Deactivate
Adaptability	Runtime
Data Model	Relational

FIGURE 11.6. Ariel's dimensions of active database behavior.

ible than they could be. Also, when treating a rule condition as a pattern, rather than an event-condition sequence, opportunities for optimization of rule condition testing performance may arise that would have been unavailable otherwise.

For purposes of comparison with other systems described in this book, Figure 11.6 shows where Ariel fits regarding the different dimensions of active database behavior that were outlined in Chapter 1.

11.6 Conclusion

The Ariel project has shown that a database system can be built with an active rule system that (1) is based on the production system model, (2) is set-oriented, (3) is tightly integrated with the DBMS, (4) provides condition-action binding based on shared tuple variables, (5) supports event, transition, and ordinary conditions in a uniform way, and (6) is implemented in an efficient fashion using a specially designed discrimination network, and a rule-action planner that takes advantage of the existing query optimizer.

Changes have recently been made to Ariel that are beyond the scope of this chapter. One involves optimization of discrimination network structure to provide good performance given the database update pattern, size of relations and memory nodes, join relationships in the rule condition, etc. using generalized TREAT/Rete (Gator) networks [HBH+95]. Another considers support for streamlined development of reliable, recoverable applications that can receive notification messages from database trigger actions [HCD+97]. In addition, in an attempt to develop technology that will broaden the use of trigger systems that can efficiently support sophisticated trigger conditions, the author has initiated a research project to develop an asynchronous, external trigger system called TriggerMan [HK97]. An asynchronous trigger processor can allow processing of many types of complex triggers and alerters without slowing down online update transactions. It can also allow triggers to be defined on heterogeneous and legacy data sources. TriggerMan will use a parallel variation of a discrimination network similar in many ways to the one used in Ariel.

11.7   References

[ABC+76]   M.M. Astrahan, M.W. Blasgen, D.D. Chamberlin, K.P. Eswaran, J.N. Gray, P.P. Griffiths, W.F. King, R.A. Lorie, P.R. McJones, J.W. Mehl, G.R. Putzolu, I.L. Traiger, B.W. Wade, and V.Watson. System R: Relational Approach to Database Management. *ACM Transactions on Database Systems*, 1(2):97–137, June 1976.

[For81]   C.L. Forgy. OPS5 User's Manual. Technical Report CMU-CS-81-135, Carnegie-Mellon University, Pittsburgh, PA 15213, July 1981.

[For82]   C. L. Forgy. Rete: A Fast Algorithm for the Many Pattern/Many Object Pattern Match Problem. *Artificial Intelligence*, 19:17–37, 1982.

[Han96]   E.N. Hanson. The Design and Implementation of the Ariel Active Database Rule System. *IEEE Transactions on Knowledge and Data Engineering*, 8(1):157–172, February 1996.

[HBH+95]   E.N. Hanson, S. Bodagala, M. Hasan, G. Kulkarni, and J. Rangarajan.   Optimized Rule Condition Testing in Ariel Using Gator Betworks.   Technical Report TR-95-027, University of Florida CIS Dept., October 1995. http://www.cis.ufl.edu/cis/tech-reports/.

[HCD+97]   E.N. Hanson, I-C. Chen, R. Dastur, K. Engel, V. Ramaswamy, C. Xu, and W. Tan. Flexible and Recoverable Interaction Between Applications and Active Databases. *VLDB Journal*, 1997. Accepted.

[HCKW90]   E.N. Hanson, M. Chaabouni, C. Kim, and Y. Wang. A Predicate Matching Algorithm for Database Rule Systems. In *Proc. of the ACM SIGMOD Intl. Conference on Management of Data*, pages 271–280, May 1990.

[HJ96]   E.N. Hanson and T. Johnson. Selection Predicate Indexing for Active Databases Using Interval Skip Lists. *Information Systems*, 21(3):269–298, 1996.

[HK97]   E.N. Hanson and S. Khosla. An Introduction to the TriggerMan Asynchronous Trigger Processor. In *Proc. of the 3rd Intl. Workshop on Rules in Database Systems*, pages 51–66. Springer Verlag, June 1997.

[Mir87]   D.P. Miranker. TREAT: A Better Match Algorithm for AI Production Systems. In *Proc. AAAI National Conference on Artificial Intelligence*, pages 42–47, August 1987.

[SRH90]   M. Stonebraker, L. Rowe, and M. Hirohama. The Implementation of POSTGRES. *IEEE Transactions on Knowledge and Data Engineering*, 2(7):125–142, March 1990.

12

SAMOS

Stella Gatziu
Klaus R. Dittrich

ABSTRACT
This chapter gives a brief overview of the SAMOS project which has been underway since 1991 at the Database Technology Research Group at the University of Zurich, the main goal of which is the development of an active object-oriented database system supporting advanced active functionality. The first implementation of the SAMOS prototype (release SAMOS 1.0) was completed in 1995 and is available in the public domain (http://www.ifi.unizh.ch/DBTG/SAMOS/release.html).

12.1 Introduction

The main objective of the SAMOS[1] project was the development of an active object-oriented database management system supporting advanced active functionality. In SAMOS, we focussed on the proposal of a powerful and easy-to-use event definition language. Together with the languages proposed in the Sentinel [CKEA94] and in the Ode project [GJS92], the SAMOS language was among the first expressive event definition languages. It concentrates on the definition of complex events and offers a small number of event constructors which in combination with the concept of monitoring intervals allow expressive event definitions[GD93].[2]

SAMOS also investigates the coexistence of active and object-oriented features in one system. In this context, issues are addressed concerning the nature of events specified on database operations and the association between rules and classes [GGD91].

Moreover, SAMOS deals with the detection of complex events based on colored Petri-nets [GD94]. Petri-nets are a promising model that allows powerful but also succinct descriptions of many complex systems in general. In our case, Petri-nets describe how a number of event occurrences lead to the signaling of a complex event occurrence. Besides the support

---

[1]SAMOS is an acronym for Swiss Active Mechanism Based Object-Oriented Database Systems. If not used as an acronym, Samos is a Greek island known from the philosopher and mathematician Pythagoras who lived there.

[2]A detailed description of many of the aspects handled in SAMOS is given in [Gat95].

of event detection, Petri-nets allow the precise specification of the semantics of complex events from the appropriate Petri-net structures. Colored Petri-nets are well suited for the modeling and detection of complex events because they enable a distinction between the modeling of event definitions and event occurrences. Thus, concepts like event history or event parameters are supported by the model and are not hidden in the programs implementing the event detection like in other approaches (e.g., automata in Ode [GJS92] and trees in Sentinel [CKEA94] and REACH (see also Chapter 13)).

The SAMOS prototype follows a layered architecture. All components implementing the active behavior are built "on top" of the passive object-oriented DBMS ObjectStore, which is left unmodified [GGD+95c]. In spite of the restrictions imposed by the layered architecture, it was possible to implement in the SAMOS prototype the advanced active mechanisms proposed in the SAMOS project. SAMOS 1.0 was completed in 1995 and is available in the public domain [GFV96]. Now, it has been installed at several places and is used for experimentation with an active object-oriented DBMS.

In the SAMOS project, we have also investigated tools for supporting users during the development and maintenance of active applications. Tools are essential particularly for large rule sets, defined by different persons at different points in time. Potential conflicts and dependencies among rules are hard to predict and rule behavior is difficult to control. The SAMOS tools provide for graphical interfaces supporting both, build-time activities (performed during rule specification) such as rule editing, browsing, rule termination analysis [VGD97], and runtime activities (performed during the execution of an application) such as the explanation of rule behavior.

This chapter is organized as follows. Section 12.2 discusses the main features of the SAMOS rule language. Section 12.3 presents the SAMOS system and shows how it works. We conclude this chapter with future directions and an overview of the SAMOS features according to the classification presented in Chapter 1.

12.2   ECA Rules in SAMOS

SAMOS integrates active features into an object-oriented data model. Concepts like classes, object identity, modeling of behavior, and inheritance are exploited [GGD91]. In addition to the data definition language of the underlying DBMS, SAMOS provides a rule definition language as a means to specify ECA rules. A rule in SAMOS has the following form:

```
DEFINE RULE rulename
ON eventclause
IF condition
DO action
COUPLING MODE (coupling, coupling)
PRIORITIES (BEFORE | AFTER) rulename
```

A rule definition specifies an event description (also called *event type*[3]), a condition, an action, and execution constraints (priorities and coupling modes). The definition of an event and an action are mandatory, while the definition of a condition is optional, i.e., as well as ECA rules SAMOS also supports EA rules. Events, conditions, and actions may be named and defined separately (outside rule definitions).

SAMOS proposes *class-external rules* that are defined independently from class definitions and are global in the sense that they may refer to arbitrary classes. *Class-internal rules* are defined as part of class definitions. Their events may also be defined on operations that modify the value of an object without violating encapsulation.

Events can be either *primitive* or *composite*. Primitive events in SAMOS can be time events (which occur at a specific point in time or periodically), message sending events (which occur at the beginning or the end of a method execution), value events (which occur at the beginning or the end of a data modification operation), transaction events (which occur before or after a transaction operation), or abstract events (which are not detected by SAMOS, but have to be signaled explicitly by the application or the user). Composite events are constructed out of primitive or other composite events (called component events). The event constructors supported by SAMOS are sequence, conjunction, disjunction, negation, and reduction. The reduction constructors allow the signaling of the repeated occurrence of an event E only once. For example, in case of the closure constructor *E, the event E is signaled only after its first occurrence, or, in case of the TIMES-constructor TIMES(n, E), it is signaled after each n occurrences.

In some cases, component events have to occur during a specific interval in order to let the composite event occur. Such an interval is called a *monitoring interval* and is defined through a start and an end point in time (which can be absolute, periodical, or specified as the occurrence time of any predefined event). Every composite event in SAMOS can be specified in connection with a monitoring interval, whenever required. Negative events always require a time interval to be specified.

A condition in SAMOS is an expression written in the query language of the underlying DBMS (ObjectStore in the case of the current prototype implementation of SAMOS). Actions are programmed in the data manip-

---

[3]We distinguish between event types and event occurrences.

ulation language (DML) of the underlying DBMS. The range of tasks that can be performed by an action is as follows: behavior invocation, abort of a transaction, and user notification.

SAMOS supports event parameters for passing information about the database state to the action and condition. The set of event parameters is fixed (except for abstract events), as described in what follows. Each event (except a time event) has so-called *environment parameters*, like the occurrence point or the identifier of the transaction that triggered an event. Method events also have the object identifier of the object executing the method as a parameter. Thus, rule execution can refer to the actual database state, i.e., to the state when the condition is evaluated or the action is executed. For example, in the case of a value event defined as the end of an update operation, rule execution may refer to the new object value. To also provide the old value, SAMOS offers a versioning mechanism.

Event parameters can be used to further restrict composite events to actually interesting ones. For example, the *same transaction* restriction attached to a composite event requires that all component events have to be triggered by the same transaction.

The event history in SAMOS consists of all occurrences of the defined event descriptions. Each signaled event occurrence is persistently stored in the event history as long as required, i.e., until it is consumed for composite event detection and/or rule execution. Event occurrences are ordered based on their occurrence time and are consumed in a first come, first served basis, i.e., events are taken into account in the chronological order they occur. Thus, SAMOS supports the chronicle consumption mode. The continuous consumption mode can be modeled in SAMOS as a composite event defined with a monitoring interval.

The event history begins at the point in time when the first event description is defined and ends when all event descriptions are deleted (i.e., when the rulebase is deleted). Usually, the history lasts over many sessions and obviously over several transactions. Thus, it is possible to signal a composite event based on events that have occurred in different application sessions or transactions.

SAMOS supports the coupling modes *immediate* (directly after the event has been detected), *deferred* (at the end of the triggering transaction), and *decoupled* (in a separate, independent transaction). It may be that multiple rules are defined for the same event and with the same coupling mode. In this case, priorities specify the order to be imposed on the execution of the rules. Priorities form a partial order on rules. Rules that are not ordered (transitively) by priorities are executed in an arbitrary (system-determined) order.

SAMOS offers a set of operations on rules, events, conditions, and actions. Beyond the DEFINE RULE operation shown above for the definition of rules, further operations like MODIFY RULE, MODIFY EVENT and DELETE RULE are supported. We have investigated in [GGD95b] event modification in detail. Each time an event definition E is deleted or modified, it has to be considered what happens with the occurrences of E that are still in the event history. We offer several options like deleting old occurrences of E as well, or further using them for the triggering of rules. Furthermore, rules in SAMOS can be activated and deactivated.

12.3   The SAMOS Prototype

In the prototype implementation of SAMOS, all components implementing the active behavior are built "on top" of the passive object-oriented database system ObjectStore [Obj93], which is left unmodified and is a black box for SAMOS. This is the major feature of layered architectures in contrast to integrated architectures, where the kernel DBMS is internally modified. ObjectStore is a commercial object-oriented database management system developed by Object Design as a persistent extension of C++. SAMOS currently runs on SUN machines under UNIX. The SAMOS prototype consists of three building blocks (Figure 12.1):

- the object-oriented DBMS ObjectStore,

- a layer on top of ObjectStore implementing the active functionality which consists of a number of active components including a rule manager, a detector for composite events, and a rule execution component, and

- a set of tools comprising a compiler, a rule analyzer, a rule editor, and a rule explanation component.

To show how SAMOS works, we describe in the following how rule and event definitions are performed in SAMOS, what exactly SAMOS does after a rule/event definition, and how it treats a primitive or composite event occurrence.

12.3.1   Defining Rules and Events

SAMOS users define or modify ECA rules either by using the graphical *rule editor* of SAMOS, or by writing (based on the syntax of SAMOS' rule definition language) all rule definitions or modifications into a text file. The rule editor provides a user-friendly graphical interface using pop-up menus and visual representations that facilitate the editing of rule definitions.

During rule definition or modification, users can select information about rules defined so far using the *rule browser*, which allows navigating in the rulebase. The rule browser shows individual rules, events, actions, and conditions, and allows the selection of items that meet various criteria, e.g., for

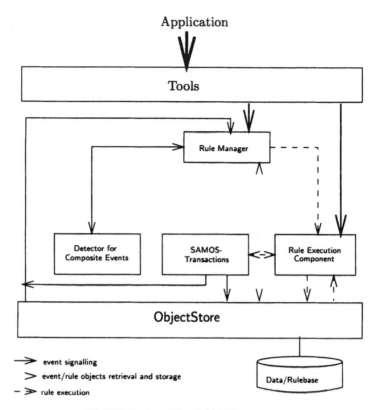

FIGURE 12.1. The SAMOS architecture.

a primitive event it indicates the list of composite events it is participating in.

All rule definitions are first syntactically and semantically analyzed and in a second step persistently stored. In a third step, for each event defined, the appropriate event detector is initialized.

Compiling and analyzing rule definitions: Rule definitions are compiled using the *rule compiler* and analyzed using the *rule analyzer*. The rule compiler is responsible for the syntactic and part of the semantic analysis of rule definitions. The rule analyzer investigates the termination of the rule execution. It determines whether rules could potentially trigger each other indefinitely. Thus, it detects and visualizes potential cycles that could occur during the execution of an application. The rule designer then decides whether the rule set must be changed. Our approach to termination analysis is discussed in [VGD97].

Storage of rule and event definitions: If syntactic and semantic analysis have been completed successfully, the compiler uses the interface offered by the rule manager to store the information about rule definitions as part of the rulebase. SAMOS uses the underlying DBMS to provide persistence of the rulebase. Thus, event descriptions, rules, conditions, and actions are represented as objects. This allows inspection of the rulebase using the retrieval facilities of the underlying DBMS. Furthermore, atomicity and durability are supported for operations on the rulebase. A detailed description of the class hierarchy can be found in [GD94].

In addition, the condition and the action body of each defined rule are compiled, resulting in two executable C++ code fragments. These executable code fragments are linked to the program code of SAMOS, and references of rule objects to these fragments are defined. This allows condition evaluation and action execution at runtime. Note that this linkage must be done each time a new condition or action is defined.

Initializing event detection: The system (actually the rule manager) "knows" about the occurrence of an event only after it has received the message *raiseEvent* that is sent from the appropriate event detector. Thus, the event detector must be initialized to detect occurrences of each defined event. Note that SAMOS signals only events of interest, i.e., event occurrences of predefined event types.

The initialization of the event detector depends on the event type. In case of method events, the original method needs to be modified as follows: the operation *raiseEvent(event-name)* is added at the beginning and/or at the end (before the return statement) of the method body. In case of time events, appropriate entries are inserted into the *crontab* system file provided by the UNIX operating system. These entries are generated automatically from time event definitions, and are inserted into the *crontab* file by the compiler.

Concerning the detection of composite events, step-by-step (or incremental) detection is required. The event detector needs to know for each composite event the ordered sequence of all primitive events that need to occur in order for the composite one to happen. Thus, each time a primitive event occurs, the detector can check if a step forward in any of these ordered sequences can be made. If so, it marks the attained positions. As a consequence, we can talk about the actual state of detection processes that is represented by the marked positions. The event detector can signal the occurrence of a composite event (by sending the message *raiseEvent*) as soon as the last element of the appropriate sequence order gets marked. The step-by-step detection requires a model that allows the representation of sequences of primitive events and of detection states in the system. As mentioned above, in SAMOS we use colored Petri-nets. We have defined Petri-net types for all constructors of the event algebra. Based on these types, SAMOS builds the Petri-net instance for each user-defined composite event description. All these Petri-net instances together form the event detector for composite events. A detailed description of the detection of composite events can be found in [Gat95, GD94].

12.3.2 Rule Processing

After a primitive event has occurred, SAMOS starts rule processing, which can be split into four phases:

- *the signaling phase*: After the rule manager has received the message *raiseEvent* from a primitive event detector, it retrieves the appropriate event object. If one or more rules are defined on this event type, the event occurrence (a reference to the event object) is entered into the event history.[4] Recall that the event occurrences in the event history are ordered based on their occurrence time. In a second step, the rule manager checks whether this primitive event is used in an event composition. Each event object contains an instance variable *compositeEvent* which stores the composite event(s) in which it participates. If the event is used in composite event definitions, the composite event detector is notified. The Petri-net begins to play the "token game".[5] As a result, one or more composite events may be signaled. The token game continues until no more composite events can be signaled. Then, each signaled composite event for which a rule definition exists is also entered into the event history. This means that at the end of a signaling phase, the event history is updated with the primitive event signaled at the beginning and all composite events signaled as a consequence.

- *the triggering phase* corresponds to the processing of the event history and the construction of the set of triggered rules. The set of triggered rules is split into three subsets: one for rules with immediate coupling mode, one for deferred, and one for decoupled. During the triggering phase, *each* element of the event history is processed in a first come first served order. Thus, the oldest event occurrence is removed from

---

[4]Note that in the current SAMOS implementation, the event history only consists of event occurrences on which rules are defined. Event occurrences used for composite event detection are directly passed to the Petri-net component which creates the appropriate tokens.

[5]In general, this is the moving of tokens through the Petri-net; one or more transitions whose input places are marked with tokens are fired, and as a result tokens are added to their output places. In case of SAMOS, the token game implements the way composite events are detected. Composite events represented as output places can be signaled as soon as the output places are marked, i.e., the signaling is the consequence of the occurrence of component events represented as the input places.

the event history and its associated rule(s) is/are triggered, i.e., inserted into the appropriate set of triggered rules. Since one event at a time is processed, SAMOS follows a tuple-oriented execution in contrast to a set-oriented execution where only one rule for a set of events is triggered, e.g., those signaled in the same transition.

- *the scheduling phase*: During the scheduling phase, *one* rule is selected from the set of triggered rules. The first come, first served scheduling applies again. Rules are selected in the same sequence as they have been inserted into the set of triggered rules, i.e., as their events have been entered into the event history. If there is more than one rule defined for an event, then several rules are triggered at the same point in time. The selection of one rule is now based on the user-defined priorities, i.e., rules with higher priority are executed first. If no priority is specified, SAMOS arbitrarily chooses a rule.

- *the execution phase*: Each rule selected during the scheduling phase is executed during the execution phase. First, the condition is evaluated in order to determine which actions must actually be executed. While evaluating a query, SAMOS refers to recent database states based on the information held in the event parameters (e.g., in the case of a method event, it may refer to the object on which the method is executed). During the action execution, further events may be signaled producing *nested rule execution*. In this case, the action execution is interrupted due to the processing of the nested rules. Ensuring the termination of nested rule execution is supported by the rule analyzer discussed above.

To implement rule execution in the framework of the transaction model of ObjectStore, we have defined a new class *samTransaction*. Each instance of *samTransaction* contains a reference to an ObjectStore transaction and further information required by rule execution, like a rule register that implements the set of triggered rules. This class defines methods for the transaction operations start, commit, and abort which must be used in the application programs for SAMOS instead of the transaction operations proposed by ObjectStore.

12.3.3   Evaluation of the SAMOS Prototype

The reason for applying the layered approach in SAMOS is the shorter implementation time in comparison to the integrated architecture, since the passive part can be reused in its entirety. The layered approach of SAMOS is thus construction-efficient. The current implementation of the SAMOS prototype comprises approximately 20,000 lines of C++ code. Many components providing tasks like recovery or concurrency control, that are critical parts in from-scratch implementations, come for free in the layered approach.

With the SAMOS prototype, we show that advanced active functionality can be implemented through a layered architecture, under the assumption that sufficient support is provided by the underlying system. Especially, the provision of nested transactions in ObjectStore allowed support of the immediate and deferred coupling modes as well as the implementation of the nested rule execution. However, since ObjectStore was a black box for our implementation, it has not been possible to extend the transaction model to be able to support more sophisticated concurrency control techniques for the Petri-net component. Furthermore, the lack of parent/child and sibling parallelism in ObjectStore leads to performance drawbacks during rule execution. Further restrictions concern the detection of method and value events. ObjectStore does not support the dynamic modification and recompilation of methods. Hence, the body of the methods for which an event is defined must be modified by inserting a call to the operation *raiseEvent*. The program that contains the method body has to be subsequently recompiled.

12.3.4   An Example

Using a very simplified banking application for stock management we briefly show how an active application is programmed with SAMOS 1.0. The passive part of the application includes the definition of the class **stock** and the method implementations.

```
class stock {
persistent<stockDB> os_Set<stock*> *extent; //the extension
void setPrice(int, samTransaction*); // update stock price
void sell(int); //sell stocks
char *companyName;
int price; // the price of the stock
};

void stock::setPrice(int pr) {price = pr;}

void stock::sell(int quant) {quantity -= quant;}
```

The active part of the application is described by rule **R1** with the following semantics: After each modification of the stock price for a company, it must be checked whether this company is IBM and whether the new stock price is greater than the stock price of the company HP. If this condition is satisfied (i.e., if the value returned is 1), 1,000 stocks of IBM must be sold.

```
DEFINE EVENT StockSetPrice AFTER.stock.setPrice
```

```
DEFINE RULE R1
ON StockSetPrice
IF
   stock *HP_Stock = (*stock::extent)[% companyName == "HP" %];
   if (oid->companyName=="IBM" && oid->price > HP_Stock->price)
      return 1;
   else
      return 0;
DO
   oid->sell(1000);
COUPLING (immediate, immediate);
```

A simplified sample application program for updating the price for stocks of a given company by calling the method setPrice is as follows:

```
main( int argc, char **argv) {
   ...
   samTransaction* stx = samTransaction::begin();
   cout << "Please enter the company name: "; cin >> name;
   cout << "\n\nPlease enter the new price for the stock.\n"
   cin >> newprice;
   stck->setPrice(newprice, stx);
   samTransaction::commit(stx);
   ...
}
```

After the price modification, the event detector signals the method event StockSetPrice and the rule execution is started. Note that the user of SAMOS has to make use of methods of the class samTransaction for the transaction operations. The programming of the event detector for the method event StockSetPrice is achieved by modifying the method setPrice as follows:

```
void stock::setPrice(int pr, samTransaction *st) {
price = pr;
raiseEvent("StockSetPrice", st, this); }
```

The modified method has now a pointer to the current SAMOS transaction (in which the method is called) as a further argument.

12.4 Future Directions

In this section, we briefly overview our current and future work in SAMOS and in the area of active databases in general, influenced by our experiences made in the SAMOS project.

We have already identified performance drawbacks of SAMOS 1.0 using the BEAST benchmark.[6] As a consequence, we investigate, e.g., the efficient management of the rulebase of SAMOS, and in particular of the event history, using advanced indexing and clustering strategies. A step in this direction has already been taken for the efficient retrieval of event objects using the indexing and clustering facilities of ObjectStore.

Furthermore, we continue our work on tools supporting the user during the development and maintenance of active applications. Our main guideline is to fulfill the requirements set by expressive rule languages as they are supported by almost all research systems. Such rule languages allow the specification of more application semantics in the form of rules; however, they complicate the rule analysis or rule browsing [VGD97].

Following the idea of the layered architecture, where active components reside in a module built on top of a conventional DBMS and are not directly incorporated into the DBMS, we go a step further. We consider in our current work on active mechanisms the total separation of active functionality from a DBMS. In [GKvBF97], we propose the provision of active database mechanisms as an individual service. In other words, we unbundle active functionality from the DBMS. Thus, we follow a general direction that database research is currently about to take, namely to provide individual database management services that can be used and combined in a variety of ways and in a variety of environments. This allows the use of active capabilities with arbitrary DBMS's and in broader contexts.

In our FRAMBOISE project [FGD97], we focus on a construction system that can be used to build so-called ECAS (ECA-Services) supporting active database functionality as known from active database systems. Each ECAS is constructed for a particular commercial DBMS. FRAMBOISE follows the idea of unbundling active functionality since active components, merged in an ECAS, are decoupled from the particular DBMS. It comprises specification mechanisms, construction tools, and an object-oriented framework that provides implemented active components and a generic system architecture.

12.5   Conclusion

This chapter has presented the active object-oriented DBMS SAMOS. We have discussed the contributions, the rule language, and the prototype implementation of SAMOS. We conclude with an overview of the features of SAMOS applying the dimensions introduced in Chapter 1. This is illus-

---

[6]A description of BEAST can be found in Chapter 6. BEAST is intended for performance measurements of the active functionality of an object-oriented DBMS [GGD95a, GBLR96].

trated in the following tables.

Execution Model:

Condition-Mode	Immediate, Deferred, Decoupled
Action-Mode	Immediate, Decoupled
Transition granularity	Tuple
Net-effect policy	No
Cycle policy	Recursive
Priorities	Relative
Scheduling	All Sequential
Error handling	Backtrack

Knowledge Model:

Event	Source	Structure Operation, Transaction, Abstract, Behavior Invocation, Clock
	Granularity	Set, Member
	Type	Primitive, Composite
	Operators	or, and, seq, closure, times, not
	Consumption	Chronicle, Continuous
	Role	Mandatory
Condition	Role	Optional
	Context	DB_E, DB_C
Action	Options	Structure Operation, Behavior Invocation, Abort, External
	Context	DB_E, DB_A

Management Model:

Description	Objects
Operations	Activate, Deactivate, Signal
Adaptability	Compile Time
Data Model	Object-Oriented
Programmer Support	Query, Analyse

12.6 Acknowledgments

Many persons have worked or are still working in the SAMOS project. Several aspects discussed in this chapter have been developed in cooperation with our colleagues Hans Fritschi, Andreas Geppert, and Anca Vaduva. Furthermore, many students have contributed to the implementation of the SAMOS prototype. We also thank the UBS Information Technology

Laboratory for funding the work of S. Gatziu until the end of 1995.

12.7 REFERENCES

[CKEA94]   S. Chakravarthy, V. Krishnaprasad, S.-K. Kim and E. Anwar. Composite Events for Active Databases: Semantics, Contexts, and Detection. In *Proc. of the 20th Intl. Conf. on Very Large Data Bases*, Santiago, Chile, 1994.

[FGD97]   H. Fritschi, S. Gatziu, and K.R. Dittrich. FRAMBOISE - an Approach to Construct Active Database Mechanisms. Technical Report 97.04, Department of Computer Science, University of Zurich, 1997.

[Gat95]   S. Gatziu. *Events in an Active Object-Oriented Database System (Doctoral Dissertation*, Department of Computer Science, University of Zurich). Dr. Kovac Verlag, Hamburg, 1995.

[GBLR96]   A. Geppert, M. Berndtsson, D. Lieuwen, and C. Roncancio. Performance Evaluation of Object-Oriented Active Database Management Systems Using the Beast Benchmark. Technical Report 96.07, Department of Computer Science, University of Zurich, 1996.

[GD93]   S. Gatziu and K.R. Dittrich. Events in an Active Object-Oriented Database System. In *Proceedings 1st Intl. Workshop on Rules in Database Systems (RIDS)*, Edinburgh, UK, 1993.

[GD94]   S. Gatziu and K.R. Dittrich. Detecting Composite Events in Active Database Systems Using Petri Nets. In *Proc. 4th Intl. Workshop on Research Issues in Data Engineering: Active Database Systems (RIDE-ADS)*, Houston, TX, 1994.

[GFV96]   S. Gatziu, H. Fritschi, and A. Vaduva. Samos an Active Object-Oriented Database System: Manual. Technical Report 96.02, Department of Computer Science, University of Zurich, 1996.

[GGD91]   S. Gatziu, A. Geppert, and K.R. Dittrich. Events in an Active Object-Oriented Database System. In *Proceedings 3. Intl. Workshop on Database Programming Languages (DBPL)*, Nafplion, Greece, 1991.

[GGD95a]   A. Geppert, S. Gatziu, and K.R. Dittrich. A Designer's Benchmark for Active Database Management Systems: 007 Meets the Beast. In *Proc. 2nd Intl. Workshop on Rules in Database Systems (RIDS)*, Athens, Greece, 1995.

[GGD95b]   A. Geppert, S. Gatziu, and K.R. Dittrich. Rulebase Evolution
in Active Object-Oriented Database Systems: Adapting the
Past to Future Needs. Technical Report 95.13, Department of
Computer Science, University of Zurich, 1995.

[GGD+95c]   A. Geppert, S. Gatziu, K.R. Dittrich, H. Fritschi, and
A. Vaduva. Architecture and Implementation of the Ac-
tive Object-Oriented Database Management System SAMOS.
Technical Report 95.29, Department of Computer Science,
University of Zurich, 1995.

[GJS92]   N.H. Gehani, H.V. Jagadish, and O. Shmueli. Composite
Event Specification in Active Databases: Model and Imple-
mentation. In *Proc. of the 18th Intl. Conf. on Very Large
Databases*, Vancouver, 1992.

[GKvBF97]   S. Gatziu, A. Koschel, G. von Bueltzingsloewen, and
H. Fritschi. Unbundling Active Functionality. Technical Re-
port 97.11, Department of Computer Science, University of
Zurich, 1997.

[Obj93]   *ObjectStore–Manuals for Release 3.0 Sun.* Object Design,
1993.

[VGD97]   A. Vaduva, S. Gatziu, and K.R. Dittrich. Investigating Termination Analysis for Expressive Rule Languages. In *Proc. 3rd
Intl. Workshop on Rules in Database Systems (RIDS)*, Sko-
evde, Sweden, 1997.

13

EXACT: An Approach to Coping with Heterogeneous Rule Execution Models

Oscar Díaz

ABSTRACT
The large and heterogeneous range of applications that are being supported through rules requires the availability of flexible rule systems that are easy to tailor to application requirements. Such requirements affect not only how rules are described, but also how rules are handled at execution time. Indeed, a substantial part of the application semantics is realized through the rule execution model. While flexible knowledge models can be accomplished by supporting rules as first-class objects, it has been far from clear how to obtain flexible execution models. This chapter describes the EXACT approach, an active DBMS where the execution model is defined as part of the rule class definition, so that the designer can choose the rule execution strategy that best fits the application at hand.

13.1   Introduction

A broad range of applications have been enumerated as benefiting from active database management systems (DBMS), as described in Part IV of this book. Rules can support traditional database functionality (e.g., integrity constraint maintenance, support for derived data, monitoring of data access and evolution, access control) as well as application-based tasks (e.g., network management, air-traffic control, tracking, etc). Making DBMS active allows a broad range of applications to be moved from user programs or some sort of polling mechanism to the database. However, this diversity makes it difficult to find a common execution strategy that is suitable no matter what application is to be supported. Indeed, requirements can greatly vary depending on the concept supported by the rule. The semantics of this concept will influence, for example, whether all rules reacting to a given event should be fired when this event is detected, or what reaction follows once a rule fails.

Thus, as the number of applications requiring rule behavior increases, and this seems to be the tendency, flexible rule execution strategies become an essential feature of future active DBMS. However, this aspect has not received enough attention, and most systems only provide a *fixed* execution model for rules. This can lead to ad-hoc solutions or even worse, to complicating the conditions of rules with elements whose only purpose is to achieve the required solution.

EXACT, an EXtensible approach to ACTive object-oriented DBMS, focuses on this aspect, allowing the rule designer to choose the execution model that best fits the semantics of the concept to be supported. Two contentions support this work, namely:

1. It is the user who, as well as defining the rules, should specify how these rules have to be executed. The user knows the semantics of the concept to be supported which includes not only the definition of the basic rules, but also control information about how these rules have to be exploited.

2. Control information rarely refers to individual rules. Rather, it is shared by a set of rules supporting the same concept or functionality (e.g., integrity constraint maintenance, derived data, etc). Hence, this control information should be removed from single rules and abstracted higher out.

The following sections describe how these ideas have been realized in EXACT, a fully-developed system built on top of ADAM [Pat89], an OODBMS implemented in ECLiPSe Prolog[1] with disk-resident and multiuser features provided through MegaLog [Boc91]. The knowledge model follows the event-condition-action approach where rules are supported as first-class objects. However, the main asset of EXACT does not rest with the knowledge model, but with how heterogeneous execution models can be accomplished. This is achieved by using metaclasses. Metaclasses allow the advantages of the OO paradigm to be applied to the DBMS since the system itself is described using classes and methods. In this way, not only are rules described using an OO approach, but so is the rule processing strategy. Describing rule processing using an OO approach, allows a hierarchy of execution models to be available from which the user can choose the one that best fits the semantics of the application at hand. Moreover, skillful users can easily extend this hierarchy by refining already provided methods or introducing new ones.

The rest of this chapter is organized as follows. For completeness sake, section 13.2 briefly describes the EXACT knowledge model. However, the main emphasis of this system lies in the execution model, which is described in section 13.3. Some examples are shown in section 13.4. Conclusions are presented in section 13.5.

---

[1] ECLiPSe is a trademark from ECRC (European Computer-Industry Research Center).

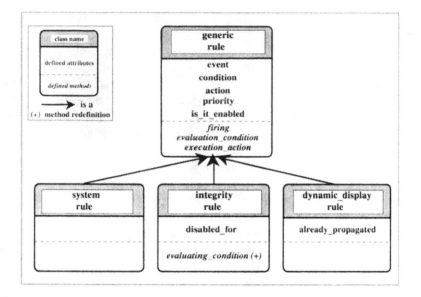

FIGURE 13.1. The rule hierarchy in EXACT.

13.2   The Knowledge Model

EXACT follows an event-condition-action approach for the description of active behavior, where rules are supported as first-class objects. Being objects, rule classes can be arranged in hierarchies like the one shown in Figure 13.1. The *generic_rule* class keeps the common description of a rule through the attributes *event, condition, action, priority*, and *is_it_enabled*, the latter being a boolean attribute that describes whether the rule is activated or not. This class can subsequently be specialized to account for new requirements: subclasses *system_rule, integrity_rule*, and *dynamic_display_rule* are introduced where method (e.g., *evaluating_condition*) and/or attributes (e.g., *already_propagated*) are added or specialized.

As for events, they are also supported as objects, where their definition depends on their sources (e.g., events that result from message sending, exception raising, clock signals, and the like). Composite events are supported in EXACT only in a limited way, and only the sequence construct is provided.

13.3   The Execution Model

Whereas the previous section tackled how isolated rules can be described, this section addresses how a set of rules is handled at execution time. So far, most of the systems encompass all triggered rules in the same set so that only one execution strategy is available. However, our assumption is that such a homogeneous approach does not match the diversity exhibited by the wide range of applications that benefit from active DBMS.

The EXACT approach is to split the conflict set according to the class to which the triggered rule belongs. Each class realizes a rule usage, a way to support a given application (e.g., integrity maintenance or air-traffic control), and this usage includes not only the description of the rules, but also how these rules are handled at execution time. Application semantics dictate both rule description and rule execution. EXACT attempts to face this fact first by using an OO approach to describe the execution model, and second by identifying a number of parameters that can be used to characterize the execution model. These roughly correspond to the ones presented in Chapter 1. Instead of providing code, the user can declaratively specify the required execution model by choosing from a set of pre-established alternatives. If none of these alternatives accommodates the problem, extensions at the behavioral level (i.e., specialization of methods) will be required.

Implementation-wise, the idea of *set* is supported in OO systems by the concept of *class*. A class has a twofold definition. On the one hand, it describes the common features shared by its instances (the class as a template), and on the other hand, a class can be seen as collecting together a set of instances and their properties (e.g. the *average_age* of people). It is worth noticing that these properties of the set-as-a-unit apply not only to the structural features of the set–as is commonly found in semantic data models such as SDM [HM81]–but also to its behavioral features. Hence, in the same way that the common description shared by a set of instances is abstracted at a higher level to form the class, the common description shared by a set of classes, now seen as the unit set-of-instances, can be abstracted at a higher level: *the metaclass*. A metaclass is a class, the instances of which are all classes. Metaclasses not only permit classes to be stored and accessed using the facilities of the data model, but make it possible to refine the default behavior for class creation using specialization and inheritance.

The DBMS underlying EXACT, ADAM, supports metaclasses [DP94], and the metaclass *rule_manager* is defined. In the same way that the *generic_rule* class holds how to describe single rules, the *rule_manager* metaclass records how the execution model for a rule class is described. Such a description is achieved through a set of attributes (better said, meta-attributes): the *e-c_coupling* attribute which stands for the event-condition coupling mode; the *c-a_coupling* attribute which represents the condition-action coupling mode; the *scheduling_mode* attribute; the *error_recovery_mode* attribute; the *conflict_resolution_mode* attribute, which holds the function and parameters to be used to decide the next rule instantiation to be fired from the conflict set; the *priority_function* attribute, which holds the function to be followed to assign the priority of instance rules[2]; and the *before* attribute whose value is another rule class, and which supports a relative class-based priority (e.g., all occurrences of integrity rules are fired before any occurrence of auditing rules). Notice that unlike previous approaches, coupling modes are specified at the class level rather than at the rule instance level. This is consistent with our contention that control information rarely refers to single rules but rather depends on the concept being considered, which is reflected in the rule class.

Besides these meta-attributes, *rule_manager* keeps the description of three main methods, namely *new*, *triggering*, and *scheduling*. The former is used to create rule instances, and is a specialization of the standard creation procedure provided by ADAM. As for *triggering* and *scheduling*, they support the corresponding phases of the rule evaluation process. Details of how these methods are implemented are out of the scope of this paper (see [DJ97] for further details).

A rule instance provides values for the attributes described in its class (e.g., the rule's priority). Likewise, a rule class provides the values for the meta-attributes described in its meta-class (e.g., the class's scheduling mode). Therefore, there is a three-level definition, as shown in figure 13.2:

1. the metaclass level where the dimensions of the execution model shared by the rule classes are factored out in metaclasses such as *rule_manager*,

2. the class level where the characteristics of single rules are factored out (i.e., the knowledge model) and their execution model is defined (e.g., the *generic_rule* class),

3. the instance level where rule instances are defined (e.g., *1#generic_rule*).

Notice that whereas the knowledge model is inherited from the superclass to its subclasses, this is not the case for the execution model which must be specified for each class, regardless of its superclass. The execution model of class *C* only affects the rule instances that have *C* as its immediate class, in the same way that the value of the *average_age* for the *person* class is not inherited by its subclass *student*, which would have its own *average_age*.

A parameterized execution model is provided by the core of EXACT. When a new rule class is created, a customized version of this standard model is generated from the above meta-attributes by the system. This version overrides the standard execution model for this new rule class.

---

[2]This function, defined by the user, is invoked at rule creation time to establish priorities based on structural features of the rule (i.e., attribute values).This function can be supported as an attribute due to the features of Prolog, the underlying language. In other environments, it can be supported as a method.

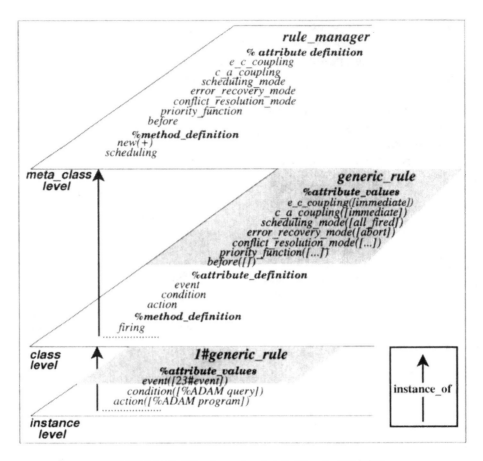

FIGURE 13.2. The three-level definition in EXACT.

If these meta-attributes do not convey the functionality required, the user can specialize the methods that support the execution model. In implementation terms, new sub-metaclasses can be defined where inherited methods can be specialized or overridden. Despite the burden to the user, this approach allows the possibility of specializing the standard execution model to accommodate the special requirements of the concept to be supported using rules.

13.4   Some Examples

This section outlines how applications that require different execution models can be supported in EXACT. The point to note is not the accurateness of the proposed models as such, but how different execution strategies can coexist, and most importantly, illustrating how a substantial part of the application characteristics are realized through the execution model chosen. Integrity constraint maintenance, dynamic display support, and relationship semantic support are used to illustrate this point. For the sake of brevity, rule description is left out, and we focus on the application semantics that influence the rule execution strategy.

13.4.1   Dynamic Display Support

Graphical database interfaces allow some portion of the data stored in the database to be displayed for browsing or manipulation. However, there is no guarantee that while this data is presented on screen, the extension of the database will remain unchanged. Thus, changes to database objects that are depicted on screen can lead to inconsistencies between the data that is stored and that which is displayed. Dynamic displays remove such inconsistencies by propagating changes to the state of the database to the different interfaces where the affected data is being displayed. In [DJPaQ94], an approach is presented to support this application by using active rules. Aspects that influence the execution model include:

1. The semantics of the displayed data determines the frequency of display updating: for critical data (e.g., stock market), updates on the display should be made immediately once the data has been modified; for noncritical data (e.g., booking applications), display updating can be delayed until the end of the transaction. Here, the final result is provided rather than keeping the screen updated as changes happen. Another alternative is to acknowledge at the end of the transaction any significant change that is produced during the transaction i.e., if a sensible gap exists between the new value and the old value at the time of the update (i.e., immediate event-condition coupling), the screen is updated at the end of the transaction (i.e., deferred condition-action coupling).

   If displaying is a slow process, concurrency can be enhanced by running this process in a separate but commit-dependent transaction (i.e., the displaying transaction commits only if the updating transaction ends successfully). However, since this separate transaction has some effects visible from outside, the user should be warned somehow that the update is not permanent till the updating transaction commits (e.g., by showing transient and committed data in different colors). If the transaction finally fails, a contingency action should follow where the data formerly on the display is restored.

2. As data updating fires only one rule, the conflict set contains one triggered rule of the *data_display_rule* class. Hence, the *scheduling_mode* is of no use here. However, this does not imply that the conflict set con-

tains a single rule occurrence; other rule occurrences that belong to other classes can compete to obtain control. The *before* meta-attribute supports a partial order among rule classes.

3. If the update on the display is achieved within the initial transaction, a failure during this update (e.g., due to communication problems) does not cause an interruption of the whole process: a message can be issued, and the propagation process continues with the next display. Of course, this approach depends on the sensibility of the data being displayed, that is, how important it is for the display to accurately reflect the data content at any time.

A possible definition of the *data_display_rule* class is described next:

```
new([data_display_rule,[
        is_a([generic_rule]),
        e-c_coupling([immediate]),
        c-a_coupling([deferred]),
        scheduling_mode([all_fire]),
        before([recording_rule]),
        error_recovery_mode([ignore]),
        – Attribute and method definition
]]) => rule_manager.
```

13.4.2 Relationship Semantic Support

Rules have been used to implement modeling constructs that are not directly supported by a given data model. In semantic data models, abstract relationship (e.g., generalization, aggregation, etc.) semantics are defined, specifying how insertion, deletion, and modification operations made at a higher level of abstraction can affect the objects abstracted over, and vice versa. These semantics, also known as *structural constraints*, are expressed through so-called *update rules*. This perspective can be applied not only to abstract relationships, but also to user-defined relationships (e.g., *marriage*, *working_in*, and the like). In [Dia95], an approach is presented where relationship definition includes how operations made on an object can affect a related object by virtue of the relationship itself. As an example, consider the *part_of* relationship between *parts* and *wholes*. Copying a *whole* can lead to copying all its *parts*, i.e., the *copy* operation is propagated from the whole to the parts. It is worth pointing out that such propagation reflects the *part_of* semantics, and not the operation *copy*: the copy operation should be propagated over the *part_of* but not over the *made_by* relationship. As the operation itself must ignore the links along which it has to be propagated, such propagation has to be supported by an independent mechanism: the rules. For instance, the previous example can be supported by a rule such as: *on* deleting an object, *when* this object is composite, *do* deletion of its components. The following aspects should be considered when defining the execution model for relationship rules:

1. Propagations can be seen as side-effects of operations. Hence, an operation ends once all its side effects are accomplished. This imposes an immediate coupling mode.

2. As an object can be related to several objects, an operation could require to be propagated along different relationships, i.e, several propagation rules can be triggered. In which order are these rules fired? Is there any precedence among propagations? As the final result is influenced by rule order, rule priority must be considered.

3. As an object can be reached from different links (i.e., the sets of objects affected by each propagation are not disjoint), propagations should be considered sequentially.

4. As propagations are seen as side effects, an error during the propagation stage is not seen as an operation error. Some backtracking or contingency action could be attempted, if available.

A possible definition of the *relationship_rule* class could be:

```
new([relationship_rule,[
      is_a([generic_rule]),
      e-c_coupling([immediate]),
      c-a_coupling([immediate]),
      scheduling_mode([all_fire]),
      before([recording_rule]),
      error_recovery_mode([contingency]),
      - Attribute and method definition
]]) => rule_manager.
```

13.4.3 Integrity Constraint Maintenance

Aspects of this application that influence the execution model include:

1. Once a database update occurs which affects one or more constraints, the integrity checking can begin either immediately, be deferred until the transaction ends, or both. The appropriate option depends on the kind of constraint to be maintained.

2. *All* integrity constraints affected by a database update should be checked in turn *until one is falsified.* Once a constraint is violated, there is no point in prolonging the checking process.

3. Due to the former point, if different integrity constraints have to be checked, an order can be established based on the complexity of each

constraint: the higher its complexity is, the lower its priority is. This assumes that each false check aborts the transaction.

4. If a constraint is violated and no repair action is available, the transaction must be aborted.

The definition of a rule class for integrity maintenance thus includes not only attribute and method definitions (i.e., the knowledge model), but the set of values of the meta-attributes that describe the execution model. A possible description of such a rule class in EXACT could be as follows:

```
new([integrity_rule,[
        is_a([generic_rule]),
        e-c_coupling([immediate]),
        c-a_coupling([immediate]),
        scheduling_mode([all_fire]),
        priority_function([( ... )]),
        before([relationship_rule]),
        error_recovery_mode([abort]),
        - Attribute and method definition
]]) => rule_manager.
```

As implied by the value of the *before* attribute, relationship rule occurrences are fired once all integrity rule occurrences have been fired. If any error occurs during integrity validation, the whole process is aborted. Moreover, if deferred integrity constraints are also required, the following subclass can be defined:

```
new([deferred_integrity_rule,[
        is_a([integrity_rule]),
        e-c_coupling([deferred]),
        c-a_coupling([immediate]),
        scheduling_mode([all_fire]),
        priority_function([( ... )]),
        before([recording_rule]),
        error_recovery_mode([abort]) ]]) => rule_manager.
```

This class exhibits the same knowledge model and most of the features of the execution model of the previous integrity rules. The only difference stems from the event-condition coupling mode (i.e., the *e-c_coupling* parameter) which now is *deferred*. Notice that the condition-action coupling mode (i.e., the *c-a_coupling* attribute) is *immediate,* as the condition evaluation is already deferred. Also, the concept-based priority (i.e., the *before* attribute) has been changed since now the potentially conflicting rules are those also evaluated at the end of the transaction (e.g., *recording rules* that keep track of changes).

Knowledge Model		
Event	Source	Structure Operation, Transaction, Abstract, Behavior Invocation
	Granularity	Member, Set
	Type	Primitive, Composite
	Role	Mandatory
Condition	Role	Mandatory
	Context	$Bind_E$, DB_C
Action	Options	Structure Operation, Behavior Invocation, Abort
	Context	$Bind_E$, $Bind_C$, DB_A
Execution Model		
	Condition-Mode	Immediate, Deferred
	Action-Mode	Immediate, Deferred
	Transition granularity	Tuple
	Net-effect policy	No
	Cycle policy	Recursive
	Priorities	Numerical, Relative
	Scheduling	All Sequential, Some
	Error handling	Abort, Ignore
Management Model		
	Description	Objects
	Operations	Activate, Deactivate, Signal
	Adaptability	Runtime
	Data Model	Object-Oriented

FIGURE 13.3. Knowledge, execution, and management models for EXACT.

13.5 Conclusion

Whereas the support of rules as objects accounts for flexible definitions, this is not the case for rule execution strategies that are commonly fixed in the system code where the rule designer has little control over the strategy that best fits the application at hand.

EXACT attempts to tackle heterogeneous execution models by using metaclasses. Three main advantages stem from this approach:

- *flexibility:* different sets of rules can have different execution strategies, where each set supports a distinct application (e.g., integrity constraint maintenance).

- *declarativeness:* ease of use is enhanced by describing the rule execution model through a set of meta-attributes. In this way, the user just provides the values that best fit the application requirements, and the system customizes the appropriate methods to support this execution model.

- *extensibility:* being supported as methods, the rule execution strategy can be easily extended by refining already provided methods or introducing new ones.

Modularity can be seen as a by-product of this approach. Active DBMS can be jeopardized if appropriate structuring mechanisms are not available to handle the increasing complexity and number of rules that future active systems expect to hold. Similar problems to those found in Artificial Intelligence can be encountered where disappointment among production system practitioners is largely due to the lack of structuring mechanisms available to cope with large rule sets. The approach presented in this chapter provides some help as active rules are grouped according to the functionality supported, where control can be customized to obtain the desired requirements.

Table 13.3 summarizes the main features of EXACT according to the dimensions introduced in Chapter 1. So far, EXACT does not support the detached coupling mode, and the cycle policy is always recursive. However, it is our experience that the approach presented in this paper greatly enhances the rule system's ability to cope with heterogeneous applications in active DBMS.

13.6   REFERENCES

[Boc91]   J. Bocca. MegaLog: A Platform for Developing Knowledge Base Management Systems. In *Proc. 2nd. Intl. Symposium on Database Systems for Advanced Applications (DASFAA'91)*, 1991.

[Dia95]   O. Diaz. The Operational Semantics of User-Defined Relationships in Object-Oriented databases. *Journal of Data and Knowledge Engineering*, (16):223–240, 1995.

[DJ97]   O. Diaz and A. Jaime. EXACT: an EXtensible Approach to ACTive Object-Oriented Databases. *VLDB Journal*, 6(4), 1997.

[DJPaQ94] O. Diaz, A. Jaime, N. Paton, and G. al Qaimari. Supporting Dynamic Displays Using Active Rules. *SIGMOD RECORD*, 23(1):21–26, 1994.

[DP94]   O. Diaz and N. Paton. Extending ODBMS Using Metaclasses. *IEEE Software*, 11(3):40–47, 1994.

[HM81]   M. Hammer and D. McLeod. Database Description with SDM: A Semantic Database Model. *ACM Transactions on Database Systems*, 6(3):351–386, 1981.

[Pat89]   N. Paton. ADAM: An Object-Oriented Database System Implemented in Prolog. In M.H. Williams, editor, *Proc. British National Conference on Databases*, pages 147–161. Cambridge University Press, 1989.

14

REACH

Jürgen Zimmermann
Alejandro P. Buchmann

ABSTRACT

REACH is an active OODBMS that was developed as a platform to experiment both with the issues arising from the implementation of advanced active functionalities, and as a platform for the development of applications that are potential beneficiaries of active database technology. To achieve the former, we chose an experimental OODBMS, Texas Instruments' OpenOODB, for which the source code was available to us, and tried to implement the full range of active functionality with multiple coupling modes, a complete event algebra, full transaction management, and support features, such as garbage collection of events. To achieve the latter goal, a rich set of tools was implemented to facilitate the use of the system by application programmers. This chapter gives a brief overview of the REACH system implemented on OpenOODB. Currently, efforts are underway to port the REACH functionality to ObjectStore.

14.1 Introduction

The REACH project set out to build an active OODBMS with full active functionality [BBKZ93, BBKZ92, BZBW95]. This was considered important since previous projects had set ambitious goals and specified a broad range of functionality [DBB+88], but no robust system with full active functionality that could be used for actual implementation of applications was available. The initial goal was to use a commercial OODBMS and build REACH on top of it to speed up development and to benefit from the stability of a commercial platform. However, soon the limitations of building on top of a closed system became evident. Problems appeared when trying to implement some of the coupling modes, and when modifying the pre-processor. Therefore, it was decided in 1993 to begin a new implementation on top of Texas Instruments' OpenOODB [WBT92]. OpenOODB is an experimental platform that was conceived as an extendible OODBMS in which individual functions are specified in a modular way as policy managers that can be exchanged or extended as needed. The policy managers can be invoked in response to low-level events. This appeared to be philosophically very close to the paradigm proposed by active databases and it was decided to use OpenOODB as the implementation platform. This was particularly attractive, as we were able to obtain the source code and were included in the list of Alpha test sites. The use of OpenOODB proved to be a fortunate choice in that it gave us a good head start. It was particularly useful to have access to the source code of the precompiler that was modified to include the wrappings for method events. However, OpenOODB was built on top of the Exodus storage manager 2.2 [CDRS86], and since Open OODB used extensively the Exodus transaction manager with its page locking and recovery mechanisms, it turned out quite difficult to implement necessary changes to the transaction manager, especially parallel nested transactions. In addition, since OpenOODB is implemented as a client to the Exodus server, the whole REACH functionality is only available on the client side. On balance, the use of OpenOODB gave us a significant initial boost but did not live up completely to our expectations, in part also because of the growing pains of an experimental system.

In spite of the limitations encountered, REACH implements a fairly complete range of active functionality. The event algebra is a superset of the HiPAC event algebra and was adapted from the SAMOS project [GD93a, GD93b]. The six coupling modes provided are also a superset of the HiPAC modes [HLM88] and the most comprehensive set of coupling modes implemented to our knowledge. Special emphasis was placed in the efficient and specialized implementation of event detectors, the correct composition of events relative to transaction boundaries, the passing of events and parameters, the garbage collection of semi-composed events, and the possibility for future distribution, i.e., no design decision should preclude future use in a distributed environment.

The second major area of concern was to provide a set of tools for the administration of rules and as a support for the application programmer. These tools include static termination checkers, detailed event histories, rule browsers, a graphical interface for rule specification by the naive user, and the organization of the rule space in analogy to the directory structure of the UNIX file system [ZBB+96].

In this chapter section 14.2 briefly describes OpenOODB and its philosophy. Section 14.3 describes the functionality of REACH and how it was realized, section 14.4 describes the tools, and section 14.5 summarizes the features of REACH in accordance with the criteria formulated in Chapter 1. Section 14.6 presents conclusions and lessons learned.

14.2   The OpenOODB Platform

Texas Instruments' OpenOODB is an extensible OODBMS whose computational model transparently extends the behavior of operations in application programming languages. Invocations of these operations are examples

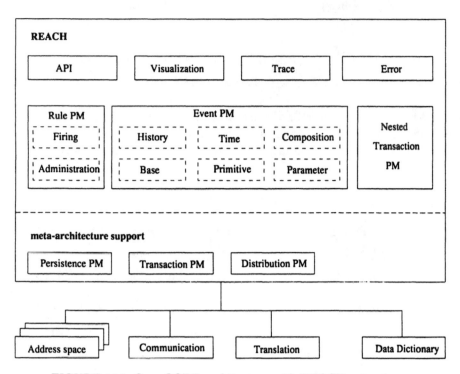

FIGURE 14.1. OpenOODB architecture with REACH extensions.

of primitive method events. OpenOODB uses the C++ type system.

OpenOODB consists of two layers: the lower layer consists of support modules for address space management, communication, translation, and the data dictionary. The upper level is the meta-architecture module that implements the computational model by providing events, sentries, and policy manager interfaces. The meta-architecture module provides the extensibility mechanisms for OpenOODB and plays the role of a software bus into which the database components can be plugged. Each database component is realized as a policy manager. Figure 14.1 shows the OpenOODB architecture with the REACH extensions.

The meta-architecture is philosophically close to the active database paradigm. Any operation performed within the context of a programming language can be an event. A sentry mechanism tracks primitive events and invokes the appropriate policy manager (PM) which implements the extended behavior. There must be at least one policy manager for each database function, and the Open OODB architecture provides for the possibility of exchanging a given policy manager, e.g., the flat transaction PM in favor of a nested transaction PM. While philosophically clean and attractive, it is not easy to exchange policy managers because of interactions and dependence on functionality of the Exodus storage manager or to add a new policy manager to OpenOODB, e.g., for distribution.

14.3   REACH Goals, Design Principles, and Implementation Decisions

The long-term goal of REACH was to support complex applications and to provide a stable testbed for applications using active capabilities, to be extendible to open environments, and to allow for applications with timing constraints.

To satisfy the goals that were set for REACH, we formulated some design principles that can be summarized as follows:

- provide dynamic rule specification through orthogonality of monitoring and type,

- provide a rich event set with a clear definition of event semantics,

- provide flexible rule execution through a rich set of coupling modes,

- provide efficient rule invocation through fast basic event detection and low composition overhead,

- do not preclude future use in a distributed environment through central components that can become bottlenecks, and

- provide the necessary maintenance mechanisms for long-term stable operation.

Dynamic rule specification is essential in making an active OODBMS useful for application development. The orthogonality of monitoring and type makes it possible to treat all classes and their methods in a uniform manner. Therefore, it is not necessary to know at the time a class is defined which method event will eventually be relevant for a rule. Rules can be defined independently of the object classes and subscribe to a given event type. Since all methods are uniformly wrapped by the precompiler, no recompilation is needed when a new rule is defined.

14.3.1   Event Detection and Composition

It was not a goal of the REACH project to define new event types and event algebras. Therefore, the event hierarchy that was used is similar to that of Sentinel [CKAK94] and SAMOS [GD93a, GD93b, GD94]. It includes method events; flow-control events that include Begin, End, Commit and Abort of transactions; and absolute, relative, periodic, and aperiodic time events. State change events are not implemented, as they would require a different basic event detection mechanism. However, in an attempt to allow for time-constrained processing in an inherently non-real-time environment, we defined the notion of milestone events. A milestone event is raised when a transaction passes a certain point. If the corresponding milestone is not reached by a certain time relative to a deadline, a rule specifying an alternative action can be invoked. Detached exclusive coupling is required to avoid two different results from becoming valid. In detached exclusive coupling mode, the rule is executed in a separate transaction that commits and thus becomes visible only when the triggering transaction aborts. As to event algebra, REACH implements the three operators proposed in HiPAC, sequence, disjunction, and closure—with their original semantics [DBM88]. In addition, it implements conjunction, negation, and history as defined in the SAMOS project with the same semantics [GD93a, GD93b, GD94].

To allow for future use in a distributed environment, no single central component should act as a bottleneck. This is particularly true for event detectors/composers and the logging of event histories. Therefore, specialized event detectors exist for each type of composite event, and for each instance of a composite event, a separate event hierarchy is constructed. The event detectors create an event object. Logging of event histories occurs in parallel by writing the event objects into partial logs with asynchronous merging of the partial logs.

A stable active DBMS requires maintenance facilities, such as garbage collection, to remove semicomposed events or event-log consolidation. Through the implementation of a separate event graph for each composite event, it is relatively easy to eliminate events for which it becomes obvious that they will not be completed. Through careful definition of the scope of an event, it is possible to eliminate useless events and their parameters.

14.3.2   Rule Execution and Coupling Modes

To provide an adequate support for a wide variety of applications, it was decided to implement as complete a set of coupling modes as possible. REACH implements the coupling modes immediate, deferred, detached, and three variants of detached with causal dependencies, parallel, sequential, and exclusive [BBKZ93]. Detached parallel allows for parallel evaluation of a rule, but termination of rule execution depends on the commit of the spawning transaction. Detached sequential requires the beginning of rule execution to be delayed until the spawning transaction commits. Detached exclusive allows for parallel execution of a rule, but the rule may only commit if the spawning transaction aborts. This coupling mode is intended for the implementation of contingency plans through ECA rules. The coupling of the condition and of the action part are specified separately.

To speed up rule invocation, the event detectors are specialized. A separate event detector exists for each event type. The event detectors for primitive events know which rules are directly fired by that event and whether a

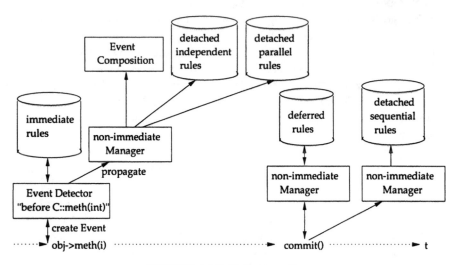

FIGURE 14.2. Rule execution.

complex event detector consumes a primitive event. This reduces the number of indirections. A specialized event detector exists also for each type of composite event, and for each instance of a composite event a separate event hierarchy is constructed. Whenever a new rule is defined and compiled, the corresponding event detector is created. An event detector also includes the necessary data structures for the parameters of the event and the necessary instructions for copying the state of the relevant objects depending on the coupling mode. If an event detector already exists because the triggering event of the new rule already is used to trigger an existing rule, the new rule only subscribes to that event detector. Subscription means that the corresponding rule is added to the set of rules that need to be fired by that event detector. For the condition and the action, two functions are generated and stored in a shared library.

Figure 14.2 illustrates the processing of events and execution of the triggered rules at runtime. A method detector traps a method event. Rules that are fireable by the method event in immediate coupling mode are fired, and the trapped method event is propagated to the non-immediate manager. The non-immediate manager either passes the method event to the corresponding composite event detector for composition, or fires the rules that are to execute in detached or detached parallel coupling modes. REACH does not allow composite events to trigger rules in immediate mode. The reason is that a composite event contains several basic events with different timestamps and parameters (see section 14.3.3). Since the parameters of the older events could be invalid or out of scope, immediate event composition could result in runtime errors during rule execution when the event parameters are accessed. There also exists a performance reason. If rules that are triggered by a composite event can be executed in immediate coupling mode, the execution of any transaction must be interrupted while event composition occurs. This interruption lasts until it is clear that no rule must be fired by a just-completed composite event. Detached independent and detached parallel rules are executed in separate child processes. Whenever the transaction manager raises the End-Of-Transaction (EOT) event, i.e., wants to begin the commit process, the EOT event is signaled to the non-immediate manager to trigger the deferred rules. After execution of the deferred rules and completion of the commit process, the non-immediate manager is invoked once more by passing it the commit event to fire the detached sequential rules.

A separate temporal event detector handles the detection of temporal events and the firing of the corresponding rules and passing of temporal events to the event composers.

In REACH, the rules that are executed in immediate or in deferred coupling mode are executed as closed nested transactions. The subtransactions commit through the top with the commit and abort dependencies of Moss-style closed nested transactions [Mos85]. Subtransactions execute sequentially. When rules are executed in a detached coupling mode the possibility of a locking conflict between the spawning transaction and the rule transaction exists. In particular, if the rule is executed in a detached parallel mode that requires the spawning transaction to commit for the detached rule to commit, hidden deadlocks are possible. Since the underlying Exodus storage system doesn't know how to handle rule transactions, this must be solved at the REACH level.

Conflicts between the spawning transaction and a detached transaction are solved in REACH through the introduction of the notion of strong and weak transactions [Mar95]. Weak transactions are not allowed to wait for a lock. They are aborted as soon as a conflict occurs. Strong transactions are allowed to wait for resources and locks. Rule transactions are always started as weak transactions and therefore cannot cause a deadlock before finishing. However, they may be involved in a hidden deadlock where the rule transaction has finished and is waiting for the spawning transaction to commit. Since a rule transaction could have gained a lock on a resource later needed by the spawning transaction which is waiting for the resource, a hidden deadlock could occur. Since the underlying Exodus storage system cannot handle this situation and recognize a rule transaction, REACH solves the problem by timing out the rule transaction. Detached sequential rules can be executed as strong transactions.

14.3.3 Events: Scoping, Composition, and Parameter Passing

Special attention was given to the correct scoping of events and to the composition of events relative to transaction boundaries. Rules triggered by a single method event can be executed in any coupling mode. Rules fired by a purely temporal event may be executed only as independent detached rules. If all the events that participate in a composite event originate in a single transaction, all coupling modes are acceptable, but for the runtime handling of parameters mentioned above, immediate coupling mode is disallowed. If the events that make up a composite event originate in multiple transactions, neither immediate nor deferred couplings are allowed since no identification of the spawning transaction is possible. The other four coupling modes are legal with the restriction that all transactions from which primitive events originate must commit in the detached parallel and sequential cases, and all must abort in the detached exclusive mode.

Events are consumed according to one of two consumption policies: chronologically or most recent. In chronologic consumption, the first possible event of a type participates in a composition. Under a most recent policy it is the latest occurrence of an event that participates in a composition. Which policy is used depends on the semantics of an application.

One of the more difficult problems is the correct passing of parameters, particularly the state of objects that must be acted upon. The detectors that detect the events also are responsible for passing the appropriate parameters. These include the object reference to be acted upon, timestamp, and the arguments that make up the signature of the method. Correct parameter passing depends on the transaction execution model.

The condition and action parts of a rule are mapped as ordinary functions that may have parameters of various types. In the case of a method event the parameters are, in addition to the timestamp, a reference to the object on which the method was invoked, all the arguments of the method invocation, and in the case of an after-event, the return value. Pointer variables are always valid for the case of immediate execution. For deferred and detached execution, the pointers may not be valid at the time the condition or action is executed, and dereferencing of the pointer may cause a runtime error. Therefore, in any non-immediate case, the referenced values must be saved. This leads to a copy semantic for parameters that goes beyond the copying of single values. This copy semantic must also be used for event composition since the events that participate in the composition may be raised separately and the composite event is raised at a different time than the component events.

The goal in parameter passing is to support as many data types as possible (ideally all the C++ data types), produce as little overhead as possible at runtime, and provide a simple interface to the rule compiler. These three goals are contradictory and require a compromise. The compromise implemented in REACH consists in supporting simple values (integers, enumerated types, floats, and single characters), pointers to simple values, strings, and persistent objects. Parameters are stored in an object called a non-immediate parameter object that consists of a parameter bag and a pointer array indicating the position of the parameter in the bag.

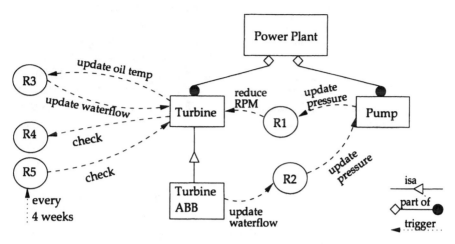

FIGURE 14.3. An OMT+ diagram.

14.4   REACH Environment and Tools

Application developers will use active DBMS technology only if the active DBMS's offer a clean interface and a set of support tools. Since REACH was conceived as a testbed for application development, emphasis was placed on integrating a set of tools [ZBB+96] into the REACH platform. The three main objectives were to provide

- a well-understood design methodology for rules in an active DBMS,

- a user-friendly interface, and

- a toolset to manage and maintain the rules and events.

14.4.1   Modeling Rules with OMT+

Rather than inventing yet another design methodology, we considered it more appropriate to extend a well-known and widely used methodology with a rule component. Therefore, OMT [RBP+91] was extended with the concept of ECA rules, resulting in OMT+ [ZBB+96]. This methodology guarantees an integral approach to modelling objects and rules while minimizing the effort required on the part of the database and application designers to learn new concepts. Figure 14.3 shows an OMT+ diagram.

A rule in an active OODBMS can be viewed as an n-ary relationship between the objects in the event part and those in the action part. The condition part is a constraint. Hence, OMT+ introduces only the notion of a rule (represented as an oval) and a triggering relationship between the classes. The input slots of a rule represent the (composite) events that trigger the rule, and the output slots refer to the effects resulting from the rule execution. These output slots refer to methods invoked for other object classes, and the name of the method appears next to the edge connecting the rule to the object that is invoked. Every rule must have at least one input slot, but there may be rules without an output slot if the rule does not invoke a method. If the input to a rule is a method event, it will originate in another class represented by a box. However, events may also be temporal events or system events, in which case the triggering event is not connected to any application class.

14.4.2 Rule Language REAL

OMT+ serves as the starting point for rule definition in REAL, the rule language of REACH. REAL treats a rule as an atomic unit with the respective clauses for event, condition, and action. Below, we illustrate a rule from a demonstration scenario of a power plant that was implemented in REACH:

```
#include "Reactor.hh"
rule /powerplant/reactor/r1 {
    prio    5
    decl    River*   river;
            int      level;
            Reactor* reactor named "BlockA";
    event   after river->updateWaterLevel(level);
    cond    imm    level < 3 &&
                   river->getTEMP() > 24.5 &&
                   reactor->getHeatOutput() > 1000000;
    action  imm    reactor->reducePlannedPower(0.05);
};
```

The object for which the method was invoked and all the arguments of the method call are passed. Therefore, these parameters are declared in the `decl` clause, and their types have to be provided in C++ include files. For objects that are not directly referenced in the event clause to be accessible in the condition and/or action part of the rule (e.g., `reactor` in our example), they must be uniquely identifiable. REAL requires these objects to be root objects (with a unique name) in the database system. The example above also shows the declaration of the priority of the rule and the individual coupling modes between event and condition and condition and action.

REAL offers a structured name space modeled along the lines of the UNIX directory structure. This is an advantage when dealing with applications that may have hundreds of rules. In such a case, it becomes difficult to assign manageable, self-explaining names to the rules, and it is even harder to find the rules. In a structured name space, the rules that belong to the same context can be stored in the same rule directory that is reachable through a hierarchical path. Since rules may not always be attached to exactly one directory, REACH offers the possibility of creating UNIX-like links to create multiple paths to a rule.

14.4.3 Administration Tools

REACH provides a command line interface for managing rule directories. These commands are styled in analogy with their counterparts in UNIX, and include commands for rule manipulation, such as copying, enabling, disabling, changing protection mode, etc.; commands for rule inspection, such as listing, displaying, or plotting; commands for handling of include files and paths, such as appending or removing files and paths; and commands for handling events.

A rather useful tool is the graphical rule browser that displays the whole directory tree or it can be qualified to display only parts of the directory tree. Through clicking on the corresponding rule name, this can be displayed in detail.

In the same graphical manner, a static analysis of the triggering graph can be displayed. The triggering graph is a pessimistic approach that considers potential cycles of rule firings based on the methods invoked in the action part of a rule and the events that trigger the rules defined in the system. REACH exploits the fact that all the necessary information is available explicitly in the event detectors which know which rules are fired by an event. By extracting the method calls from the action part and the corresponding pointers from event detector to the fired rules, one can construct the triggering graph.

Two additional tools that have proven quite useful deserve mention: the trace mode and the event history browser. The static information provided by the triggering graph is not very helpful in understanding the dynamics of applications when rules are fired. The trace mode allows the application designer to step through the execution of rules for debugging purposes. However, since tracing is quite expensive, two modes were implemented with macros: a tracing and debugging mode for developing applications, and an optimized mode without tracing that runs up to twenty times faster. The event history browser is a useful support in tracking errors or unexpected system behavior and allows the system administrator or application developer to retrace the history of events and the rules that were fired by them.

14.5   Summary of Features

The features of the REACH system can be organized according to the parameters outlined in Chapter 1, and are shown in the following tables:

Knowledge Model:

Event	Source	Structure Operation, Transaction, Clock, Behavior Invocation
	Granularity	Member, Subset, Set
	Type	Primitive, Composite
	Role	Mandatory
Condition	Role	Optional
	Context	$Bind_E$, DB_E, DB_C, DB_A
Action	Options	Structure Operation, Behavior Invocation, Abort, Do Instead, Inform
	Context	$Bind_E$, DB_E, $Bind_C$, DB_A

Execution Model:

Condition-Mode	Immediate, Deferred, Detached
Action-Mode	Immediate, Deferred, Detached
Transition granularity	Tuple
Net-effect policy	No
Cycle policy	Recursive, Iterative
Priorities	Numerical
Scheduling	All Sequential
Error handling	Abort, Contingency

Management Model:

Description	Programming Language (OO)
Operations	Activate, Deactivate
Adaptability	Runtime (limited)
Data Model	Object-Oriented

14.6   Conclusion

A prototype of REACH with a demonstration application showing the control of a small subsection of a powerplant was demonstrated during SIG-MOD95, CeBIT96, and EDBT96. The development of even such a small application illustrated many of the difficulties that will be faced until active database systems mature. However, the small application scenario clearly showed that the active database paradigm is well-suited to handling such diverse applications requirements as those posed by plant control and work-flow management. Both kinds of applications could be modeled within the same system and could coexist. This indicates that the expressive power of the events, the rule language, and the execution model are adequate.

The passing of parameters is a critical area both for the semantics as well as the performance of REACH. Performance gains for non-immediate rules and event composition are expected through further tuning of the parameter-passing mechanism.

During the development phase of the application, the trace mode and the event history were particularly useful. It was also during this phase that extensive testing of the rule compiler took place and many modifications had to be made.

The use of OpenOODB gave us an initial head start since we could integrate the REACH functionality well into the overall concept. It was also a great help to have a precompiler available that could be modified instead of having to write one from scratch. It turned out to be less than ideal as far as the concurrency control mechanism. Particularly problematic were the Open OODB write-back mechanism of every object that was fetched in a transaction, the duplication of shared objects if they are not root objects, and the restriction to open only one database.

The basic ideas developed in REACH were used to expand the functionality of the commercial middleware Persistence. This system offers a C++ interface to relational databases. Active database functionality was integrated into Persistence to provide an active object-oriented mediator system for consistency enforcement in heterogeneous legacy systems.

Currently efforts are underway to implement the REACH ideas on top of ObjectStore. We are convinced that the design principles described in this chapter are the right approach. At the same time, we are humbled by the detailed work that is still needed to make active OODBMS's into robust tools capable of exploiting the full potential of the technology.

14.7   Acknowledgments

A large project such as the REACH active OODBMS could not be carried out without the help of many people. Special thanks are due to A. Deutsch, who modified the precompiler, wrote the first event detector, and spent many hours testing and debugging. Many students provided valuable input and contributed to portions of REACH in their Diplom-thesis: G. Arens, C. Türker, J. Marschner, W. Dürholt, T. Simon, and T. Kröhl. Other members of the Group who contributed in early discussions are H. Branding and T. Kudraß. J. Blakeley, S. Ford, C. Thompson, and D. Wells, all formerly at

Texas Instruments, were instrumental in helping us to obtain OpenOODB. Last but not least, the input from members of the ACT-NET research network on active databases, funded by the European Union, was always appreciated.

14.8 REFERENCES

[BBKZ92] A.P. Buchmann, H. Branding, T. Kudraß, and J. Zimmermann. Reach: A Real-Time Active and Heterogeneous Mediator System. *Bulletin of the TC on Database Engineering*, 15, December 1992.

[BBKZ93] H. Branding, A.P. Buchmann, T. Kudraß, and J. Zimmermann. Rules in an Open System: The Reach Rule System. In M. Williams N. Paton, editor, *Rules in Database Systems, Proc. 1st Intl. Workshop on Rules in Database Systems*, Edinburgh, 1993.

[BZBW95] A.P. Buchmann, J. Zimmermann, J. Blakeley, and D. Wells. Building an Integrated Active OODBMS: Requirements, Architecture, and Design Decisions. In *Proc. 11th Intl. Conference on Data Engineering*, Taipei, Taiwan, March 1995.

[CDRS86] M.J. Carey, D.J. DeWitt, J.E. Richardson, and E.J. Shekita. Object and File Management in the Exodus Extensible Database System. In *Proc. 12th VLDB*, Kyoto, Japan, August 1986.

[CKAK94] S. Chakravarthy, V. Krishnaprasad, E. Anwar, and S.-K. Kim. Composite Events for Active Databases: Semantics, Contexts, and Detection. In *Proc. 20th Intl. Conf. on Very Large Databases*, Santiago, Chile, September 1994.

[DBB+88] U. Dayal, B. Blaustein, A.P. Buchmann, S. Chakravarthy, D. Goldhirsch, M. Hsu, R. Ladin, D. McCarthy, and A. Rosenthal. The Hipac Project: Combining Active Databases and Timing Constraints. *SIGMOD Record*, 17(1), March 1988.

[DBM88] U. Dayal, A.P. Buchmann, and D. McCarthy. Rules Are Objects Too: A Knowledge Model for an Active Object-Oriented Database System. In *2nd Intl. Workshop on Object-Oriented Database Systems*, Bad Münster am Stein, Germany, September 1988.

[GD93a] S. Gatziu and K.R. Dittrich. Eine Ereignissprache für das Aktive, Objektorientierte Datenbanksystem Samos. In *Proc. BTW*, Braunschweig, Germany, 1993.

[GD93b]   S. Gatziu and K.R. Dittrich.   Events in an Active Object-Oriented Database System. In M. Williams N. Paton, editor, *Rules in Database Systems, Proc. 1st Intl. Workshop on Rules in Database Systems*, Edinburgh, 1993.

[GD94]   S. Gatziu and K.R. Dittrich. Detecting Composite Events in Active Database Systems Using Petri Nets. In *Proc. 4th Intl. Workshop on Research Issues in Data Engineering: Active Database Systems (RIDE-ADS)*, Houston, TX, February 1994.

[HLM88]   M. Hsu, R. Ladin, and D. McCarthy. An Execution Model For Active Database Management Systems. In *Proc. 3rd Intl. Conf. on Data and Knowledge Bases*, Jerusalem, June 1988.

[Mar95]   J. Marschner. Non-Standard Transaktionsmanagement in inem Aktiven Objektorientierten Datenbanksystem. Master's thesis, Dept. of Computer Science, Technical University Darmstadt, 1995.

[Mos85]   E. Moss. *Nested Transactions*. MIT Press, Cambridge, MA, 1985.

[RBP⁺91] J. Rumbaugh, M. Blaha, W. Permerlani, F. Eddy, and W. Lorensen. *Object-Oriented Modelling and Design*. Prentice-Hall, 1991.

[WBT92]   D.L. Wells, J.A. Blakeley, and C.W. Thompson. Architecture of an Open Object-Oriented Database Management System. *IEEE Computer*, 25(10), October 1992.

[ZBB⁺96] J. Zimmermann, H. Branding, A.P. Buchmann, A. Deutsch, and A. Geppert. Design, Implementation and Management of Rules in an Active Database System. In *Proc. DEXA*, September 1996.

15

NAOS

Christine Collet

ABSTRACT
This chapter presents the NAOS rule system developed at the LSR-IMAG
laboratory, University Joseph Fourier–Grenoble. This system incorporates
active capabilities into the O_2 object-oriented DBMS. It is able to manage
and detect various types of events. The detection process is based on a
subscription mechanism plus an event graph for composite event detection.
NAOS provides immediate and deferred rules. Execution of these rules takes
place in nested (recursive) and consecutive (iterative) cycles, respectively.
Both kinds of cycles belong to the triggering transaction.

15.1   Introduction

NAOS (Native Active Object System) [CCS94, Col96] builds on O_2 [BDK92]
as the kernel for data management and applications processing. It is integrated with the modular architecture of O_2 and might be considered as
a new component alongside other components such as O_2C, C++, OQL,
etc.[1] The NAOS component may be used for defining ECA rules that will
be executed when processing O_2 applications, especially software engineering applications [CHCA94].

The NAOS model supports primitive and composite events [CC96a,
CC96b] and provides delta structures for managing data related to events.
Such structures are also used for passing data between components of a
rule. The primitive event detector detects events produced during an application processing, from operation processing, explicit signaling, or clock
interrupts. For efficiency reasons, it has been integrated into the kernel
of the database system. The event manager detects composite events and
uses a graph built from event type expressions. This graph includes detection contexts for events, and therefore has a way to know exactly the time
interval during which it has to consider component events for producing
composite events.

When considering NAOS rule processing, the issues relate to event consumption, net effect calculation, multiple and cascading rule execution,

---

[1] O_2 and all product names derived from it (OQL, O_2C, O_2 API) are registered trade-
marks of O_2 Technology, Versailles, France.

coupling modes between components of a rule, and scheduling. NAOS rules consume events and consider the net effect of operations. Immediate and deferred coupling modes are supported. An immediate rule is processed right after the triggering event, while a deferred rule is executed at the end of the triggering transaction, i.e., the transaction in which the triggering event occurs. Priorities are used for ordering a set of triggered rules, and execution cycles are provided for managing nested execution of immediate rules and as synchronization boundaries for deferred rules. Such rules are processed in consecutive cycles at the end of the triggering transaction but before its validation.

This chapter is organized as follows. Section 15.2 introduces the NAOS knowledge model. It also discusses rule management. Section 15.3 complements the previous section while giving some details on the event expression semantics. Section 15.4 presents the NAOS rule execution model. For every one of these sections, we compared our propositions with the dimensions of Chapter 1, given in bold. Then, section 15.5 concentrates on the resulting architecture of the prototype we developed. Finally, section 15.6 presents conclusions and introduces some research directions.

15.2   Rules in NAOS

15.2.1   Rules and O_2

Rules and schemas: NAOS rules are ECA rules defined at the same level as classes and applications of an O_2 schema. This provides a flexible approach for expressing some reactions to different kinds of operations (low-level operations, methods, programs). Rules are isolated from programs and methods, and this provides some programming guidelines. As rules are not components of classes, they are not (a priori) concerned with inheritance. However, O_2 inheritance is based on substitution. Therefore, one may use an instance of Employee when an instance of Person is expected (assuming Employee inherits Person). Rules triggered by operations on Person instances may also be triggered by operations on Employee instances.

Rules, encapsulation, and persistence: Rules respect encapsulation, i.e., only authorized operations on entities can produce valid events. Entities are objects and values that become persistent if they are directly or indirectly attached to names (persistent roots). Persistent entities are stored in bases. An O_2 base groups together entities that have been created in compliance with a schema. Rules are transparent to persistence, i.e., rules may be triggered by events on entities that may be persistent or not.

In order to increase reusability, O_2 provides an import/export mechanism. This approach has also been considered in NAOS: a rule of a schema S can be exported and reused in another schema S' assuming the elements of its definition are imported as well. This means that one may have to import (in S') classes from S as well.

Rules, programs, and transactions: An O_2 application is a set of programs whose execution takes place in reference to a schema and to one or more associated databases. When an application starts up, it opens a *read-only transaction*. Programs can manipulate transient entities (apply methods, modify values, etc.) but are restricted to read-only access to persistent entities. To ensure consistency of the bases, a *(read-write) transaction* must be initiated before updating persistent entities. Transactions in O_2 are atomic and classical commands such as `transaction` (creation), `validate`, `commit`, and `abort` are provided for managing such transactions. The `validate` command validates updates requested during the current transaction, allowing the execution of the code in which the transaction was initiated to continue, while the `commit` command validates the updates but stops the triggering code.

Generally speaking, rules are triggered by events produced by an application, either during the execution of a program when events concern transient entities, or during the execution of a transaction. For the time being, the processing of triggered rules and transactions are strongly related. Triggering events are produced within a (read-only or a read-write) transaction, and the processing of rules interrupts the current transaction. Rules may be executed immediately in a program or a (read-write) transaction, or at the end of a triggering transaction.

15.2.2 Rule Definition

The overall structure of a NAOS rule definition is as follows:

```
[create] rule <rule name>
[precedes <list of rule names>]
[coupling <coupling mode>]
on <event type> [ with <name of associated delta structure>]
[if <condition>]
do [instead] <action>
```

Examples of rules are given below, considering a schema containing an Employee class. Each employee has a name, an age, a profile, and a salary.

```
create rule IC_Employee_salary
coupling immediate
on before update Employee->salary  with e
if new(e)->salary > 1.5 *  current(e)->salary
do instead { notify_increase_salary(Project_Manager, e); }
```

The immediate IC_Employee_salary rule is defined for controlling the update of the salary of an Employee. The on clause defines the event type before update(Employee, salary). An event of this type occurs when the salary attribute of an Employee's instance is updated. The condition of IC_Employee_salary holds if the updated salary increased with more than 50 percent. In that case, Project_Manager is notified instead of updating the salary of e.

```
create rule IC_Employees_salaries
coupling deferred
on after update Employee->salary  with set_e
if   ( sum(select emp->salary from emp in set_e)
       - sum(select emp->salary from emp in old(set_e))) /count(set_e) > 750
do { display("Salary updates refused: average raise cannot exceed 750");
     abort; }
```

The IC_Employees_salaries rule checks that "the average salary increases of a set of employees cannot exceed 750." It is a deferred rule executed once at the end of the current transaction in which updates of salaries were made.

As shown in the above examples, a rule has a name, which is unique within the O_2 schema to which the rule belongs. It has ECA parts described in the remainder of this section and other characteristics introduced through the precedes and coupling clauses. These characteristics are related to rule execution and specify that a rule (i) may precede a list of rules in the case that multiple rules are triggered at the same time (see section 15.4.2), and (ii) may be *immediate* or *deferred* (see section 15.4.1).

15.2.3 Event Part

The event part of a NAOS rule specifies an event type, i.e., an expression describing occurrences of interest (events) that may trigger the rule. It is *mandatory* and is used for characterizing *primitive and composite events.* Primitive event types characterize entity manipulation events (*structure operation*), method events (*behavior invocation*), applicative (transaction and program invocation) events (*transaction*), and also temporal (*clock*) and user-defined (*abstract*) events. Composite event types characterize events that are sequences of events, unions of events, negations of events, etc. Event types are detailed in section 15.3. Note that time cannot be dissociated from events [CM93], and a NAOS event is always associated to a point in time belonging to the *validity time interval* of the corresponding event type [Col96]. Such an interval, also called a monitoring interval in more classical works on time, defines the interval during which occurrences of that type may be recognized. NAOS validity time intervals are not explicit. They depend on the *unit of production* for events. Except for user events and temporal events, this unit of production is a transaction as NAOS detects events produced within the framework of an O_2 transaction.

15.2.4 Condition

The condition part of a rule is *optional*. It specifies predicates over persistent or transient entities. These predicates are defined as O_2SQL/OQL queries. A predicate holds if the result of the corresponding query is not empty. Queries may use method calls as well. We ensure that the evaluation of a condition cannot trigger another rule. This is done by deactivating the detection of all events while evaluating a rule condition. The target of a query is the actual database (DB_C) or the data associated with the triggering event/operation (an entity or the parameters of a method call) $(Bind_E)$. The result of a query evaluated in the condition of a rule is visible to the action part.

15.2.5 Action

The action part is *mandatory*. It is made of O_2C statements that may operate on persistent and transient entities (update the *structure* of the database or perform some *method/program invocation*), *inform* the user, and *abort* the current transaction. Action parts are not allowed to start or commit transactions. Also, operations for controlling the cascading execution of rules may be used (see section 15.2.7). Information available when processing the action comes from the actual database (DB_A), the condition evaluation $(Bind_C)$, and the triggering events $(Bind_E)$. As the coupling mode between the condition and the action is immediate, the action also has context of DB_C.

The *instead* keyword may be used in the do clause for indicating that the triggering operation is suppressed and replaced by the action. This is only possible for immediate rule executed before the operation.

15.2.6 Event-Condition-Action Binding

At runtime, a rule is associated with a *delta structure* containing data related to the triggering event(s). Such a structure is used for binding data between components of the rule. A delta structure associated to an immediate rule is known as a *delta element*. It contains (i) the entity that is subject to the operation producing the event and, (ii) the inserted, deleted, or updated data, or the actual parameters of a method or a program. A deferred rule responds to cumulative changes to entities. When a deferred

rule with event type E is executed, the system considers every event of
type E that has occurred during the triggering transaction or an execution
cycle. These events may concern the same or different entities. Therefore,
the delta structure of a deferred rule reflects the operations performed on a
set of entities, all necessarily of the same type. To each entity is associated
the modified, inserted, or deleted data. The resulting *delta collection* is in
other words a set of delta elements.

15.2.7   Management of Rules

NAOS offers specific operations for manipulating rules. By means of the
`create`, `delete`, `modify`, `display`, `rename` commands, rules can be manipulated in a similar way to other elements of an O_2 schema. This also means
that we do not support runtime rule modification. However, when changing
a rule, we do not have to recompile the applications codes defined in the
schema the rule belongs to. The `enable` and `disable` operations allow a rule
to be activated or deactivated, respectively. Such operations can be used
to control the cascading execution of rules and the definition of a pertinent
set of rules for an application. However, rules and programs are well separated, i.e., it is impossible to manage rules from programs, and vice versa.
Therefore, in order to treat only events of interest for an application, a rule
may have to be triggered `after` the start of the application to deactivate
some other rules of the actual schema.

15.2.8   Conclusion

Table 15.1 summarizes the knowledge model of our rules. As we already
said, events can occur when an object attribute is updated, or when a
method is applied to an object, or when a program or a transaction is
triggered. Also, events may come from time and explicit invocation (user-
defined events). Table 15.1 shows the source of our events. There exists
others, and the next section will give more details on the way events are
described and produced, and explain the granularity of our events. As explained in section 15.2.4, a condition has a context of DB_C, and $Bind_E$.
The action's context is $Bind_E$, $Bind_C$, DB_C and DB_A (see section 15.2.5).
Note that in case of immediate rules, the condition and action also have a
context of DB_E.

Table 15.2 summarizes our rule management capabilities. As we explained in section 15.2.7, rules are defined and manipulated using specific
commands of a *programming language*. The *Activate* (`enable`) and *Deactivate* (`disable`) operations are provided. User-defined events are explicitly
produced using the *Signal*(`signal`) function (see section 15.3.1).

Event	Source	Structure Operation, Behavior Invocation, Transaction, Abstract, Clock
	Granularity	Member, Subset, Set
	Type	Primitive, Composite
	Role	Mandatory
Condition	Role	Optional
	Context	$Bind_E$, DB_C, DB_E
Action	Options	Structure Operation, Behavior Invocation, Abort, Inform, Do Instead
	Context	$Bind_E$, $Bind_C$, DB_C, DB_A, DB_E

TABLE 15.1. Dimensions of the NAOS knowledge model.

Description	Programming Language
Operations	Activate, Deactivate, Signal
Adaptability	Compile Time
Data Model	Object-Oriented

TABLE 15.2. Dimensions of NAOS rule management.

15.3   Event Types

15.3.1   Primitive Event Types

Operations that may produce events are the creation of an entity, deletion of an entity, access to an entity, update of an entity, a change to an entity's persistence or transience, the insertion and deletion in a collection attribute of the entity, and method calls. All these operations correspond to *structure operations* or *behavior invocations*. The moment of production (i.e., when an event occurs) can be either **before** or **after** the actual operation depending on the type of the event. When dealing with event granularity, it is possible to define an event expression using persistent roots characterizing a *set* of instances, i.e., all the instances of a class or a given *subset*, or a specific instance (*member*). One may notice that such a granularity does not explicitly appear at the event language level but is related to the way persistency is managed in O_2.

Applicative events may be produced by the beginning or the end of a transaction, a program, or an application. NAOS also supports *user-defined* events as well as *temporal events*. Let **spy** be the user event type defined as **create event spy(name: string, type: string)**. This type can be used to define a rule having the on clause on **spy(n,t)**, and the statement **spy->signal("f","function");** produces a spy event.

Temporal events may be *absolute*, *periodic*, or *relative*. Instances of absolute temporal event types are absolute points in time. Instances of periodic temporal event types are periodically reappearing events. Periodical temporal events allows, a rule to be triggered periodically. Relative temporal events are relative to occurring events. This kind of event allows delays to the execution of a rule (triggered by any event, eventually a temporal one).

15.3.2   Composite Event Types

As with primitive events, composite events are described by event types. A composite event type expression is comprised of other event types (primitive or composite) and some of the following constructors: Disjunction (||), Strict Disjunction (^), Sequence (,), Strict Sequence (;), Negation (!), Conjunction (&&), Iteration (n()), Strict Iteration (n.()), or a specific operator called *Restriction*. As an example of a composite event type, let us introduce the negation constructor considering the event type E. !E is a composite event type expression: the negation of E. An instance of !E occurs if and only if an instance of E does not occur in the current transaction.

15.3.3   Validity Time Interval

As we already said, NAOS detects events produced within the framework of a transaction. Therefore, the *validity time interval* during which an event may occur is [*transaction_begin*, *transaction_end*], or more simply [TB,TE]. When dealing with composite events, the occurrence time of a composite event e is the occurrence time of the last primitive event that makes e happen, and the validity interval is also [TB,TE], as we do not manage inter-application events. However, this interval has to be calculated more precisely if we want to have a clear and precise semantics of composite event expressions. This calculation is based on the definition of a *context of detection* for an event expression. [CC96b] gives details on the way we determine *contexts* (of component events) from which we infer intervals. To illustrate our proposal, let us consider the composite event type expression (E1,(!E2 || E3), (E4 || E5)). From this expression, the system generates several contexts, one for each subexpression. For !E2, the context is (E1, !E2, (E4 || E5)) and the corresponding interval is [E1, (E4 || E5)]. This means that an instance of !E2 occurs if an instance of E2 does not occur after an instance of E1 and before an instance of (E4 || E5).

15.3.4   With Clause

As we already said, when rules are processed, the system builds runtime structures whose type depends on the related event types (see section 15.2.6). For example, when rule IC_Employee_salary is processed, i.e., when the salary of an employee is updated, the system builds a delta element tuple(ENTITY: E , COMPONENT: 10000) where E identifies the employee and 10,000 is the new value for salary.

As there might be as many delta structure types as event types, it would be very hard for the programmer to use such structures. Therefore, we provide a mechanism for naming delta structures (the with clause). In rule IC_Employee_salary, the delta element is named e. We also provide some operators current, new, old, delta, and arg for constructing views giving a simplified description of the binding data. In our example, e identifies the above tuple value, current(e) is E, and new(E)->salary is 10,000.

A delta structure is associated to each (primitive) event type. For a composite event type, we do not provide one global delta structure but only component delta structures, one for each component event type. Thus, the environment of a composite event type is a list of delta structures.

15.4   Rule Execution

15.4.1   Coupling Modes

NAOS supports *immediate* and *deferred* rules; Detached mode is not considered. Immediate rules have their Condition and Action modes defined as *immediate*. They are scheduled for immediate execution and respond to operations on a single entity. Therefore, immediate rules run with a *transition granularity* of *tuple*. The deferred rules have their Condition and Action modes defined as *deferred* and *immediate*, respectively: the condition evaluation and action execution take place after the last operation of the triggering transaction, but before it validates or commits. A deferred rule is always executed within a transaction and accumulates events until the end of this transaction. Therefore, deferred rules run with a *transition granularity* of *set*.

15.4.2   Multiple Rule Execution

Multiple rules are executed according to their priorities. Rules of a schema are associated to *relative priorities* considering a default total ordering (i.e., the order in which the rules have been declared) and an explicit *precedence relationship* defined between rules at definition time. Components of a rule are always scheduled for *sequential execution*, and yet one after the other. A rule condition evaluation is either followed by the execution of its corresponding action, or the action is not executed at all. That means that rules are considered as a unique block of execution and executed in a synchronous way. Section 15.4.5 presents our work for supporting the processing of rules in an asynchronous way.

15.4.3   Cascading Execution

The execution of the action part of a rule may generate new events that may trigger other rules and so on. To manage cascading execution of rules, we adopt the notion of *execution cycle* from [DBM88, DHL90]. Operations

of a transaction, a program, or a rule that may produce events constitute
a cycle.

Triggered rules are always executed in a new execution cycle distinct
from the one in which the triggering events were produced, whatever the
coupling mode under consideration. The following introduces characteristics of execution cycles depending on the kind of rules r_1, r_2, r_{1a}, and r_{1b}
(see Figure 15.1). r_1 and r_2 have the same event type E1, and r_{1a} and r_{1b}
the event type E2.

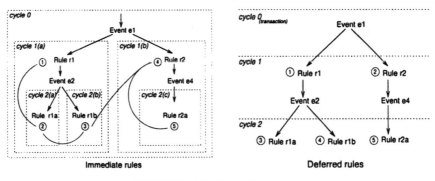

FIGURE 15.1. Execution cycles.

Immediate triggered rules are executed depth first. Every rule triggered
in a cycle (rules r_1 and r_2) will be executed in a new nested execution
cycle (cycles 1(a) and 1(b), respectively). The final execution order for the
immediate rules of Figure 15.1 is: r_1, r_{1a}, r_{1b}, and r_2, assuming r_1 precedes
r_2 and r_{1a} precedes r_{1b}. Events produced in an execution cycle are treated
without considering rules already triggered but still to be executed. This is
why in Figure 15.1, rules r_{1a} and r_{1b} are executed before rule r_2. The cycle
policy of immediate rules is *recursive*.

Deferred rules are executed at the end of the transaction in which the
triggering event occurs but before it commits or validates. Deferred rules
triggered in *cycle n* are executed in a new cycle *cycle n+1* after the complete
processing of rules of the current *cycle n*. This enforces the breadth-first
execution order of deferred rules. Deferred rules of a cycle see the effect of
operations performed since the beginning of the transaction. The processing
of the triggering transaction continues until there are no more deferred rules
to process. The cycle policy of deferred rules is *iterative*.

15.4.4   Net Effect Policy and Error Handling

NAOS does not consider each individual event occurrence: it computes the
net effect of events based on the composition of pairs of operations applied
on the same entities and executed in the triggering transaction (or rule
execution). For instance, if a rule is triggered by the creation of an entity,
but this same entity happens to be deleted before the actual execution of

the rule, the rule is not executed. Further, during a cascading execution of rules, such as the one in Figure 15.1, the execution of a rule (e.g., r_{1b}) may nullify the effect of an event (e1) having triggered a rule (r_2) so that the latter no longer has reason to execute. Also, the execution of a rule may change the value of the entity on which the triggering event occurred. For example, when rule r_2 in Figure 15.1 is executed, it sees the net effect of all operations executed on the entity in previous execution cycles. This shows that NAOS considers the net effect for the triggering of rules but also for the construction of delta structures. This allows us to provide rule execution environments more robust and consistent. Therefore, before processing a triggered rule, NAOS checks if it is really necessary to process it, i.e., if there is still at least a triggering event for that rule.

During rule execution, NAOS aborts the current transaction if a rule raises an error.

15.4.5 Asynchronous Rule Execution

NAOS rules are always executed in an execution cycle that completely includes the control flow among rules of the cycle. [CM95] presents our approach to providing parallel execution of rules inside an execution cycle and without user-defined control structures. Optimization is based on rule compatibility, which is automatically determined at the rule compilation phase. Rule execution plans are dynamically and efficiently built as far as execution cycles are processed and without creating a new transaction. Our approach differs from previous works already proposed for asynchronous rule execution [HLM88, GGD91, GJS92]. Such works are not only interested in performance, as they proposed decoupled or detached transactions for allowing rules to be executed under all circumstances (even if the triggering transaction aborts later on). Thus, transaction creation has to be specified within the rule definition explicitly in [HLM88, GGD91] or using composite and transaction events in [GJS92]. In [SJC+94], rule associations define execution order between rules. Our approach does not respond to the same concern for expressing semantics of rules. However, coupled with detached transactions, it should give better performance, as detached transactions may also be optimized based on the same principles [MC97].

15.4.6 Conclusion

Table 15.3 summarizes our execution model. The Event-condition coupling mode determines the immediate and deferred rules. As already stated, the action is executed immediately after the condition. A single event triggers an immediate rule, while a set of events are used together to trigger a deferred rule. Actions of an immediate rule may be suspended to allow rules to be triggered and executed by events produced by this action. Immediate rules have a recursive cycle, while deferred rules have an iterative one.

Both kind of rules consider the net effect of event occurrences. After each recursive execution of an immediate rule, the set of triggering (immediate) rules is recalculated, as during the execution of the rule we may have an event that nullifies the triggering event. For deferred rules, the set of triggering rules of each cycle is calculated based on the composition of events produced during the previous cycle. When a set of (multiple) rules have to be executed, relative priorities are used to order rules of the set; all of these rules are then fired sequentially. During rule firing, if an error occurs the triggering transaction is aborted.

Condition-Mode	Immediate, Deferred
Action-Mode	Immediate
Transition granularity	Tuple, Set
Net-effect policy	Yes
Cycle policy	Recursive, Iterative
Priorities	Relative
Scheduling	All Sequential
Error handling	Abort

TABLE 15.3. Dimensions of the NAOS execution model.

15.5   Implementation

Figure 15.2 shows the main components of the NAOS prototype (version 2.2). The components represent 35,000 lines of C and C++ that are compiled into a library and can be linked to O_2. The processing of rule definitions is done by the Analyser and the Constructor. The Event Manager in collaboration with the Event Detectors detects and signal events to the Executor that triggers and processes the corresponding rules. Details on the integrated architecture and implementation of NAOS may be found in [CC97a].

15.5.1   Analyser

The Analyser is able to communicate with programmers who want to define and manipulate rules in an easy way, i.e., using the *Rule Language*. It principally analyzes a rule definition and produces (i) an intermediate representation of the rule sent to the Constructor, and (ii) O_2C methods implementing the condition and action of the rule.

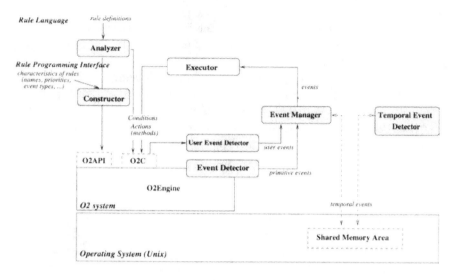

FIGURE 15.2. NAOS 2.2 architecture.

15.5.2 Constructor

The communication protocol used to communicate with the Constructor is a low-level one: the *Rule Programming Interface*, which is a set of C functions through which the main characteristics of a rule (its name, priorities, coupling modes, and event type) can be defined. These functions build the persistent objects representing rules. At that level, the conditions and actions of rules are defined directly as methods. The constructor is well adapted for software integrators and developers who need basic reactive capabilities for supporting some functions of the system they want to implement and do not need a high-level rule definition language. For example, such a module can be used when choosing an active rules approach for evaluating integrity constraints. Constraints defined in a specific language have to be compiled into rule definitions that are then handled by the constructor.

15.5.3 Event Detectors and Event Manager

The NAOS event detection process is based on two principles:

- as primitive event detection must be efficient and fine-grained, it is therefore placed within the database it is supposed to monitor.

- detection is based on a subscription mechanism; only events for which an event type subscription has been submitted are signaled.

The Event Detector detects events and signals them to the Event Manager. The User Event Detector is in charge of signaling user events (with their parameters) to the Event Manager. The Temporal Event Detector is implemented as a system process distinct from the NAOS process. These two processes communicate via a UNIX shared memory. The Event Manager does the possible compositions and sends the resulting event(s) to the Executor. The composite event detection process depends on the semantics of event expressions and also on which events have to be considered for producing composite events. The production mode for events is the *continuous* one, and the process is modeled by an *event graph*. [CC96a] details the way such a graph is built and presents the principle for recognizing events.

15.5.4   Executor

The Executor selects the rules to trigger, evaluates conditions, and executes actions taking into account the coupling modes, rule cascading, rule priorities, and the calculation of net effect. It also consumes events. When a client process is launched, the O_2 system calls the executor that creates several C++ objects for managing event type objects, rule objects, and logs of events. Then, when an O_2 schema is chosen for application execution, C++ instances are created from persistent objects representing rules and event types of the actual schema. Using such a C++ approach speeds up rule execution. For every (active) primitive event type, expressions subscriptions are sent to the O_2 engine, while using composite event type expressions subscriptions are sent to the Event Manager that builds its event graph for further detection.

15.6   Conclusion

NAOS covers all mandatory aspects of a complete rule system in a logical and consistent manner. Rules have been introduced within the framework of the O_2 system as a new concept independent from the others and well separated from methods and programs. When looking at the expressiveness of the rule languages, it is clear that we took advantage of the power of O_2 languages. The notion of delta structure has been defined for ECA binding, and operators have been proposed for a simple manipulation of these structures. Such an approach giving a clear structuring and semantics for binding information is unique of its kind (as far as I know).

NAOS provides a fine-grained event detection process. It supports primitive event types of different levels and allows for the control of other operations than just method calls, i.e., database updates, program execution, etc. *Disjunction, Strict Disjunction, Conjunction, Sequence, Strict Sequence, Iteration, Strict Iteration,* and *Negation* are operators for composing events. To deal with negative events, we introduce *contexts of detection* that allow computation of *validity intervals* which thus do not have to be given explicitly. The detection process is based on a dynamic subscription mechanism.

Immediate and Deferred rules have a clear semantics as described in [CC95]. Rule processing is based on execution cycles: synchronous execution of rules, within the triggering transaction. Such a model can be easily adapted to a more sophisticated transaction model.

In developing NAOS, performance has been taken into account, as it is an important issue. The event detector has been made an integral part of the kernel of the database system. It treats only events for which an event type subscription has been submitted. Also runtime structures are built to avoid multiple accesses to the object manager when rules are executed: the executor module works with C++ snapshots of the persistent objects representing rules (information on rules, event types) and uses indexing to improve accessibility. This approach makes it possible to alter rule definitions of a schema without interfering with the execution of applications. We enhanced the performance of the system by providing parallel execution of rules [CM95]. This proposal has not been incorporated within the current prototype mainly because the proposed scheduling algorithm is really pessimistic, and we proposed a new one in [CG97]: all immediate rules are scheduled in parallel and if conflicts are detected, some rule executions may be rolled back. More research is needed on these aspects. Recently, we extended our rule language to allow the definition of event types distinct from rule definitions. This provides more reusability and event types sharing between rules.

We are working on some extensions to improve the efficiency and the modularity of the event manager that implements the composite event detection process. Also, we will have to improve performance in condition evaluation as shown in the BEAST [GGD95] results for NAOS [GBLR96], avoiding repeated execution of the same condition as discussed in Chapter 4. Having the condition and action of a rule stored as compiled methods is not sufficient for efficient execution.

When looking at current proposals, we can see that there are as many rule execution models as systems mainly because the execution model is most of the time adapted to one kind of application having its characteristics and its specificity [FRG96] (see also Chapter 13 on the EXACT system). Therefore, some aspects of the execution model are fixed, like in NAOS. The advantage of this approach is that it facilitates the understanding of the system behavior but the model might not be well suited for another kind of application. We do think it is interesting to provide a rule execution model that supports various strategies based on a rich taxonomy characterizing execution models [CC98]. We proposed FL'ARE, such a FLexible Active Rule Execution model [CC97b]. It allows adaptation to the (NAOS) rule executor for processing different modules of rules (of the same application or not), each of them having its own semantics or execution model.

Further research directions include (i) investigating the introduction of a new dimension in the execution model, related to advanced transaction processing, and (ii) considering the distribution of data, programs, events and rules. We are currently designing and implementing an event service and a reaction service well-adapted to active distributed database applications. We want these services to be as flexible as possible, as they should be adaptable to applications.

15.7   Acknowledgments

I would like to thank A. Chabert, T. Coupaye, P. Habraken, L. Fayolle, S. Grießer, J. Machado, T. Svensen, and C. Roncancio for their contribution in designing, implementing, and benchmarking NAOS. Special thanks to T. Coupaye for his fruitful collaboration on NAOS. NAOS has been partially funded by the Esprit-III project GOODSTEP No 6115 (92-95). Developments based on NAOS are now continuing in the framework of the STORM project (http://www-lsr.imag.fr/storm.html).

15.8   REFERENCES

[BDK92]   F. Bancilhon, C. Delobel, and P. Kanellakis. *Building an Object-Oriented Database–The Story of O_2*. Morgan Kaufmann, 1992.

[CC95]   T. Coupaye and C. Collet. Denotational Semantics for an Active Rule Execution Model. In T. Sellis, editor, *Proc. 2nd Intl. Workshop on Rules in Database Systems*, pages 36–50. Springer-Verlag, 1995.

[CC96a]   C. Collet and T. Coupaye. Composite Events in NAOS. In *Proc. of the 7th Intl. Conf. on Database and Expert Systems Applications (DEXA'96)*, Zurich, Switzerland, September 9-13, 1996.

[CC96b]   C. Collet and T. Coupaye. Primitive and Composite Events in NAOS. In *Actes des 12ièmes Journées Bases de Données Avancées*, Cassis, France, August 27-30, 1996.

[CC97a]   C. Collet and T. Coupaye. Architecture and Implementation of the NAOS Active Rule System. In *In Preparation*, 1997.

[CC97b]   T. Coupaye and C. Collet. FL'ARE: a Flexible Active Rule Execution Model. Technical report, LSR–IMAG, Université Joseph Fourier, Grenoble, France, July 1997.

[CC98]   T. Coupaye and C. Collet. Modèles de Comportement des SGBD Actifs : Caractérisation et Comparaison. *Techniques des Systèmes d'Information (TSI)*, 1998. To be published.

[CCS94]   C. Collet, T. Coupaye, and T. Svensen. NAOS Efficient and Modular Reactive Capabilities in an Object-Oriented Database System. In *Proc. of the 20th Intl. Conf. on Very Large Databases*, pages 132–143, Santiago, Chile, September 12-15, 1994.

[CG97]   C. Collet and S. Grießer. An Optimistic Approach to Parallel Rule Execution in Active DBMS. Technical report, Université Joseph Fourier, Grenoble, France, January 1997.

[CHCA94] C. Collet, P. Habraken, T. Coupaye, and M. Adiba. Active Rules for the GOODSTEP Software Engineering Platform. In *Proc. of the 2nd Intl. Workshop on Database and Software engineering, 16th Int. Conference on Software Engineering*, Sorrento, Italy, May 16-17, 1994.

[CM93]   S. Chakravarthy and D. Mishra. Snoop: An Expressive Event Specification Language For Active Databases. Technical Report UF-CIS-TR-93-007, University of Florida, Gainesville, USA, March 1993.

[CM95]   C. Collet and J. Machado. Optimization of Active Rules with Parallelism. In *Proc. of the Intl. Workshop on Active and Real-Time Database Systems (ARTDB-95)*, Skövde, Sweden, June 9-11, 1995.

[Col96]   C. Collet. Bases de Données Actives : des Systèmes Relationnels aux Systèmes à Objets. Diplôme d'Habilitation à Diriger les Recherches (DHDR) RR 965-I-LSR 4, LSR–IMAG, Université Joseph Fourier, Grenoble, October 1996.

[DBM88]   U. Dayal, A.P. Buchmann, and D.R. McCarthy. Rules are Objects Too: A Knowledge Model for an Active Object Oriented Database System. In K.R. Dittrich, editor, *Proc. 2nd Intl. Workshop on OODBS*, volume 334, pages 129–143. Springer-Verlag, 1988. Lecture Notes in Computer Science.

[DHL90]   A. Dayal, M. Hsu, and R. Ladin. Organizing Long-Running Activities with Triggers and Transactions. In *Proc. of the 1990 ACM SIGMOD Intl. Conf. on Management of Data*, pages 204–214, Atlantic City, USA, May 1990.

[FRG96]   A. Front, C. Roncancio, and J-P. Giraudin. Behavioral Situations and Active Database Systems. In *Proc. of the Intl. Workshop on Databases: Active & Real-Time (DART'96)*, pages 293–305, Rockville, Maryland, USA, November 1996.

[GBLR96] A. Geppert, M. Berndtsson, D. Lieuwen, and C. Roncancio. Performance Evaluation of Active Database Management Systems Using the BEAST Benchmark. Technical report 96-07, University of Zurich, October 1996.

[GGD91] S. Gatziu, A. Geppert, and K. Dittrich. Integrating Active Concepts into an Object-Oriented Database System. In P. Kanellakis and J.W. Schmidt, editors, *Proc. 3rd Workshop on Database Programming Languages*. Morgan-Kaufmann, 1991.

[GGD95] A. Geppert, S. Gatziu, and K.R. Dittrich. A Designer's Benchmark for Active Database Management Systems: 007 meets the Beast. In T. Sellis, editor, *Proc. of the Second Intl. Workshop on Rules in Database Systems, (RIDS-95)*, pages 309–323, Athens, Greece, September, 25-27 1995.

[GJS92] N.H. Gehani, H.V. Jagadish, and O. Shmueli. Event Specification in an Active Object-Oriented Database. *ACM SIGMOD*, pages 81–90, 1992.

[HLM88] M. Hsu, R. Ladin, and D. McCarthy. An execution model for active data base management systems. In *Proc. Int. Conf. on Data and Knowledge Bases*, pages 171–179, 1988.

[MC97] J. Machado and C. Collet. A Parallel Execution Model for Database Transactions. In *Proc of the 5th International Conference on Database Systems for Advanced Applications (DASFAA'97)*, Melbourne, Australia, April 1 - 4, 1997.

[SJC+94] S.Y.W. Su, R. Jawadi, P. Cherukuri, Q. Li, and R. Nartey. OSAK*.KBMS/P: A Parallel, Active, Object-Oriented Knowledge Base Server. Technical Report TR94-031, University of Florida, Gainesville, 1994.

16

PFL: An Active Functional DBPL

Swarup Reddi
Alexandra Poulovassilis
Carol Small

ABSTRACT
This chapter describes the active subsystem of PFL, a functional database
programming language (DBPL). We discuss how PFL has been extended
with transactions and ECA rules without compromising the confluence of
expression evaluation. We describe the support for primitive and composite
events, the definition and semantics of ECA rules, and the execution model.
To our knowledge, this is the first time that an active subsystem has been
added to a functional DBPL.

16.1   Introduction

PFL is a functional database programming language (DBPL). It is a *deductive* language in the sense that it supports extensionally defined relations
and also functions that play the role of intentional relations [PS91, SP91].
A key feature of PFL, and of functional languages in general, is that expression evaluation is *confluent*, meaning that the value of an expression
is independent of the order in which its subexpressions are evaluated (this
usage of the term *confluent* is distinct from, but related to, its normal usage in active databases in which it denotes a rule set that is deterministic).
Confluence means that properties of expressions such as termination and
equivalence with other expressions can be formally proven. Also, coarse-grained optimizations, such as those discussed in [PS94] and [PS96], can
be applied to expressions.

This chapter describes the salient features of PFL and its active subsystem. In section 16.2, we introduce PFL, including its type system and
facilities for defining functions, relations, transactions, and user-defined
primitive events. In section 16.3, we focus on the active subsystem, including the support for primitive events, the definition and semantics of ECA
rules, the execution model, and abort handling. We give our concluding
remarks and identify directions of further work in section 16.4.

16.2   PFL

PFL is a polymorphic, statically typed, functional DBPL. It supports commands to

- declare new types (as described in section 16.2.1),

- define equations for user-defined functions (section 16.2.2),

- declare relations (section 16.2.3),

- evaluate queries and transactions (section 16.2.4),

- declare user-defined primitive events (section 16.2.5), and

- define ECA rules, which we address in more detail in section 16.3.2 below.

In this chapter we use `teletype` font for PFL code and *italic* font for syntactic variables. We use $e, e_1, \ldots, e_n$ to denote expressions, $t, t_1, \ldots, t_n$ to denote types, and $e_1, \ldots, e_n :: t$ to indicate that the expressions $e_1, \ldots, e_n$ all have type t.

16.2.1   Types

PFL's built-in primitive types include `Num`, `Chr`, and `Str`, which are respectively populated by numbers, characters, and strings.

The built-in structured types include list, product, and function types. In particular, for any types $t, t_1, \ldots, t_n$,

- the type $[t]$ consists of lists of elements of type t,

- the type $(t_1, \ldots, t_n)$ consists of n-tuples of the form $(e_1, \ldots, e_n)$ where each e_i is of type t_i, and

- the type $t_1 \rightarrow t_2$ consists of functions that map values of type t_1 to values of type t_2.

The list constructors are [] and (:) where, for all types t, [ ] is of type $[t]$, and (:) $e_1\, e_2$ is of type $[t]$ if e_1 is of type t and e_2 is of type $[t]$. Some syntactic sugar is provided for lists in that (:) can be written infix and unbracketed. Also, an enumerated list $[e_1, e_2, \ldots, e_n]$ is synonymous with $e_1 : [e_2, \ldots, e_n]$.

New types and their constructors can be declared by the user. For example, ECA rules (described in section 16.3.2 below) require two enumerated types, `SMode` (scheduling mode) and `AMode` (abort mode), for their definition. These types are defined as follows:

```
SMode    ::= Imm | Def;
AMode    ::= ParentChild | ChildParent | Mutual | Independent;
```

16.2.2   Expressions and Functions

An *expression* can be a variable, an operator, a constructor, or an application of one expression to another. Variables start with a lower case letter and constructors with an upper case letter c.f. the constructors for SMode and AMode above.

The built-in functions include the usual arithmetic and relational operators. User-defined functions are defined by means of equations, and we give an example below. The symbol == is used for equation definitions, while the symbol = is the equality operator. ++ is the list-append operator:

```
flatmap f []        == []
flatmap f (x:xs)    == (f x) ++ (flatmap f xs)
```

Thus, flatmap applies a list-valued function f to each element of a list in turn and concatenates the resulting lists.

A further syntactic construct supported in PFL is list comprehensions. A list comprehension takes the form $[e \mid q_1; \ldots; q_n]$, where each q_i is either a *filter* or a *generator*. For example, the list comprehension

$$[(x,y) \mid x<-xs; \; y<-ys; \; f \; (x,y)]$$

returns the elements of the cartesian product of xs and ys for which the filter f (x,y) is true. List comprehensions add no expressiveness to our language and are simply syntactic sugar for successive applications of flatmap (see [PRS96] for details).

16.2.3   Bulk Data

Bulk data are stored in 0-argument, list-valued functions termed *relations*. For example, the following commands declare three relations that respectively store accident identifiers and the grid references at which the accident occurred, grid references of all accident black spots (a black spot being a grid reference where more than five accidents have occurred), and the grid references of all accident black spots on motorways:

```
_rel accSite::[(Acc,(Num,Num))];
_rel blackSpots::[(Num,Num)];
_rel mWayBlackSpots::[(Num,Num)];
```

The extent of a relation r is initially the empty list. It can be updated by the built-in functions inc and exc. These take as arguments the name of a relation, r, and a value, e. inc adds e to the head of r, provided e is not already present there, and returns r. exc removes e from the extent of r and returns r. The name of a relation and its extent are distinguished by prefixing the name with "&". Although inc and exc update relations by side-effect, PFL's type checker will reject any query that would compromise the confluence of the language. [SS95] gives details of how this is achieved. For example, if blackSpots is initially empty, then the expression

$$(\text{blackSpots, inc } (10,5) \text{ \&blackSpots})$$

evaluates either to ([(10,5)],&blackSpots) or to ([],&blackSpots), depending on which component of the pair is evaluated first. Thus, the above expression is not confluent and would be rejected by the type checker.

16.2.4   Queries and Transactions

A *query* is simply an expression. Since expressions may invoke the built-in functions inc and exc, queries may update the database by side-effect provided confluence is not compromised.

A *transaction* is a sequence of expressions of the form:

$$tranStart;\ e_1;\ e_2;\ \ldots;\ e_n;\ tranEnd;$$

where $n > 0$, *tranStart* and *tranEnd* are built-in functions, and $e_1,\ldots,e_n$ are arbitrary expressions.

The $n+2$ expressions of a transaction are evaluated in turn. The evaluation of an expression may cause the occurrence of one or more *primitive events*. In particular, the invocation of inc, exc, tranStart, or tranEnd constitutes a primitive event, as also does the invocation of any function so declared by the user (see section 16.2.5 below).

A *schedule* is a list of transactions. The transaction that is at the head of the schedule is termed the *current transaction*, and the expression that is at the head of the current transaction is termed the *current expression*.

16.2.5   User-Defined Events

The invocation of any user-defined function can be declared to be a primitive event. This facility allows users to define new events according to the application semantics and corresponds to designating method invocation as an event in active object-oriented systems. In our approach, such events are deemed to occur after the function has been evaluated — extending this to support before events would give no extra expressiveness since ECA rules are executed only after the evaluation of the current expression has terminated.

The following command declares the invocation of a function f to be a primitive event:

$$\_makeEvent\ f\ v_1\ \ldots\ v_n\ ==\ [action_1,\ldots,action_m];$$

where $v_1,\ldots,v_n$ are variables and $action_1$, ..., $action_m$ are expressions to be executed in order to compensate an aborted invocation of f. For example, the declaration of foo::Num->Num as a primitive event and goo as its compensating event is given by

```
_makeEvent foo x == [goo x];
```

We note that any primitive events that occur during the evaluation of a function will automatically be compensated in the event of an abort. Consequently, the evaluation of the inverse function (goo in the above example) is a do instead activity.

16.3   The Active Subsystem

16.3.1   Primitive Events

Each class of primitive event has associated with it two relations, a *history* relation and a *delta* relation. The history relation contains a tuple for each event occurrence since the database was last committed (database commit is an explicit command in PFL). The delta relation contains a tuple for each event occurrence during the evaluation of the current expression. Each tuple in a history or delta relation contains the transaction identifier, a unique event identifier, and possibly further information, as defined below.

The names and types of the history and delta relations are as follows:

- tranStartH, tranStartD, tranEndH, tranEndD :: [(EventId, TranId)] record the cumulative and delta transaction start and transaction end events.

- For each relation r:: [t], the relations rIncH, rIncD, rExcH, and rExcD all of type [(EventId,TranId,t)] respectively record the cumulative and delta inclusions and the cumulative and delta exclusions with respect to r.

- For each function f of type $t_1 \rightarrow t_2 \rightarrow \ldots \rightarrow t_n \rightarrow t$ that has been cast as a primitive event, a history relation fH and a delta relation fD of type $[(\text{EventId}, \text{TranId}, t_1, \ldots, t_n)]$ are available. Each time f is evaluated, a tuple containing the event and transaction identifiers and the arguments to which the function was applied is added to fH and fD. This requires the function's arguments to be evaluated, and hence casting a function as a primitive event renders it strict in all its arguments (a function is *strict* in an argument if that argument needs to be evaluated in order for the function to return its result).

16.3.2   ECA rules

ECA rules are defined by a command of the form:

$$\text{\_ecaRule } i \quad == \quad (events, condition, [action_1, \ldots, action_m], sm, am);$$

where i is a unique number that determines the priority of the ECA rule. We discuss each of the components of the 5-tuple comprising an ECA rule in turn.

events is an expression of type $[t]$ for some type t. *events* must not update the database, i.e., it may not call inc, exc, or any function that has been cast as a primitive event. Subject to these provisos, *events* can be an arbitrary expression. It can interrogate the history and delta relations associated with each primitive event and can compose arbitrarily complex composite events from these primitive events. The evaluation of *events* will yield a list of expressions $[ev_1, \ldots, ev_n]$, where each ev_j represents the occurrence of an event during the evaluation of the current expression.

condition is an expression of type $t \rightarrow Bool$ and must also not update the database. It is applied to each ev_j and only those for which *condition* ev_j is *true* are retained. Thus, the ECA rule specifies the following sequence of events:

$$[e \mid e \leftarrow events;\ condition\ e]$$

We term this expression the rule's *parameter list*. A rule is triggered when its parameter list is non-empty.

Each $action_i$ is a function to be applied to the parameter list; it can, and usually will, update the database. Thus, overall, the user can regard the ECA rule as specifying the following *reaction transaction* provided the parameter list, *evs*, is non-empty:

$$tranStart;\ action_1\ evs;\ \ldots;\ action_m\ evs;\ tranEnd;$$

sm is an expression of type SMode. The above reaction transaction is run immediately before resuming the current transaction if *sm* is Imm, and is deferred until the end of the schedule if *sm* is Def.

Finally, *am* is an expression of type AMode representing the abort dependency between the original transaction, $tran_o$, and the reaction transaction, $tran_r$, as follows:

> ParentChild - if $tran_o$ aborts, then $tran_r$ is to abort;
> ChildParent - if $tran_r$ aborts, then $tran_o$ is to abort;
> Mutual - if either $tran_o$ or $tran_r$ aborts, then so must the other;
> Independent - no abort dependency between $tran_o$ and $tran_r$.

To illustrate, ECA rule 1 below enforces the constraint that accidents must occur on roads, while ECA rule 2 materializes blackSpots and mWay-BlackSpots from accSite:

```
_ecaRule 1  == (e1,c1,[a1],Imm,ChildParent);
_ecaRule 2  == (e2,c2,[a2,a3],Def,Mutual);
```

```
e1              == [(acc,gr) | (eId,tId,(acc,gr))<-accSiteIncD];
c1 (acc,gr)     == roadClassAt gr = None;
a1 x            == error "accident not located on road";

e2              == [gr | (eId,tId)<-tranEndD;
                         (eId2,tId2,(acc,gr))<-accSiteIncH;
                         tId = tId2];
c2 gr           == length [a | (a,gr2)<-accSite; gr = gr2] > 5;
a2 grs          == inclist grs &blackSpots;
a3 grs          == inclist [gr | gr<-grs; roadClassAt gr = MWay]
                           &mWayBlackSpots;
```

For ECA rule 1, the event query e1 retrieves the tuples inserted into
accSite during the evaluation of the current expression, the condition c1
tests for each of these tuples whether there is a road class recorded for its
grid reference component, and the action a1 invokes the error function —
this prints its argument and aborts the evaluation of the current expression,
which in turn causes the evaluation of the current transaction to be aborted
(see section 16.3.4 below). The Imm scheduling mode and ChildParent
abort mode cause the immediate abort of any transaction violating the
constraint.

For ECA rule 2, the event query e2 retrieves all the tuples inserted into
accSite during the evaluation of the current transaction, the condition c2
tests for each of the updated grid references whether there are more than
five accidents occurring at it, the action a2 inserts such grid references
into blackSpots, and the action a3 inserts such grid references that occur
on motorways into mWayBlackSpots (where inclist adds a list of tuples
to a relation). The Def scheduling mode causes the rematerialization of
blackSpots and mWayBlackSpots at the end of transactions that update
accSite. The Mutual abort mode causes the rematerialization transaction
to be aborted if the original transaction is aborted, and vice versa.

We note that no implicit event consumption occurs and that all primitive events that have occurred since the last commit are accessible via the
history relations.

Table 16.1 summarizes the knowledge model of our ECA rules. Primitive
events are those for which history and delta relations are automatically
maintained, as described in section 16.3.1. Allowing functions to be cast
as primitive events provides both Behavior Invocation and Abstract event
sources. Composite events are specified by event queries, which can be any
list-valued expression that does not update the database. Thus, for example, an event can be defined to occur whenever a relation is updated, when
a subset of a relation is updated, or when a particular tuple is updated. The
condition has a context of $Bind_E$ since it has access to the history and delta
relations both directly and via its application to the values returned by the
event query. As seen in section 16.3.2, the argument to which the actions

Event	Type	Primitive, Composite
	Source	Structure Operation, Transaction, Abstract, Behavior Invocation
	Granularity	Member, Subset, Set
	Role	Mandatory
Condition	Role	Optional
	Context	$Bind_E$, DB_C
Action	Context	$Bind_E$, $Bind_C$, DB_A
	Options	Structure Operation, Behavior Invocation, Abort, Do Instead

TABLE 16.1. Dimensions of the knowledge model.

Description	Programming Language (= Query Language)
Operations	
Adaptability	Runtime
Data Model	Relational

TABLE 16.2. Dimensions of rule management.

in a reaction transaction are applied is the parameter list. Thus, the reaction transaction is bound to an argument that is evaluated at the time of event detection. However, a parameter list can contain items retrieved from the history and delta relations, thereby also binding the actions to items evaluated at the time that the event occurred. Consequently, an action's context is $Bind_E$, $Bind_C$, and DB_A.

Table 16.2 summarizes our rule management capabilities. We note that since PFL is a computationally complete DBPL, the programming language and the query language are one and the same. We also note that although we do not provide explicit operations to dynamically activate and deactivate rules, this can be simulated by checking the value of a switch in an event query and by turning the switch on or off in an action. The rule remains active until the reaction transaction executes, so deactivating a deferred rule requires an extra immediate rule, with identical event and condition, to turn the switch off.

16.3.3 Execution Model

As stated above, a *schedule* is a list of transactions, and a *transaction* is a list of expressions. The transaction that is at the head of the schedule is termed the *current transaction*, and the expression that is at the head of the current transaction is termed the *current expression*.

Expressions are removed from transactions once they have been evaluated. Thus, the schedule may contain partially executed transactions, and every transaction on the schedule contains only expressions that have not yet been evaluated. The schedule contains no empty transactions.

Our execution model can be viewed as a cycle of three phases:

1. evaluation of the current expression,

2. event detection,

3. scheduling.

In practice, phases (2) and (3) are combined into one but we separate them here to facilitate the explanation. These three phases are repeated until the schedule is empty.

The expression evaluation phase comprises clearing the delta relations, evaluating the current expression, and then removing it from the schedule. Each primitive event that occurs during the evaluation of the current expression is automatically logged in the appropriate history and delta relations, along with the id of the current transaction and a unique event id. If the evaluation terminates normally, then the processing cycle moves on to the event detection and scheduling phases; otherwise, the abort handler is invoked (see section 16.3.4 below).

Event detection simply entails evaluating the parameter lists of all the ECA rules. An ECA rule is triggered if its parameter list is not empty. We note that since neither event queries nor conditions are allowed to update the database, all parameter lists are evaluated with respect to the same database state.

During the scheduling phase of the processing cycle, the reaction transactions are added to the schedule and the *abort graph* is updated. This graph is a directed graph whose nodes represent transactions. An arc from transaction T to transaction T' means that if transaction T aborts, then transaction T' must be aborted also. The abort graph is updated for each reaction transaction according to the abort mode of the associated ECA rule, where the the current transaction and the reaction transaction are respectively regarded as the parent and child transactions ($tran_o$ and $tran_r$ in section 16.3.2 above).

The scheduler partitions the reaction transactions into two lists according to whether the scheduling mode of the associated rule is deferred or immediate. The reaction transactions in both lists are ordered according to their rule's priority. The lists of immediate and deferred reactions are added to the front and the end of the schedule, respectively. Thus, the immediate reactions correspond to a recursive cycle policy, whilst the deferred reactions correspond to an iterative one. Table 16.3 summarizes our execution model.

16.3.4   Abort Handling

When an expression invokes the built-in **error** function, then the transaction containing it is aborted. This may require other transactions to be

Condition-Mode	Immediate, Deferred, Detached
Action-Mode	Immediate, Detached
Transition granularity	Set
Net-effect policy	No
Cycle policy	Iterative, Recursive
Priorities	Numerical
Scheduling	All Sequential
Error handling	Abort, Contingency

TABLE 16.3. Dimensions of the execution model.

aborted as well. These transactions may be interspersed with transactions, and contain nested transactions that should not be aborted. Due to this interleaving and nesting of normal and aborted transactions and the consequent interleaving of wanted and unwanted primitive event-occurrences, an aborted transaction is not rolled back. Instead, it is *compensated* by compensating each of its constituent primitive events in the reverse order of their occurrence. A single transaction compensates all the aborted transactions. Rather than log this compensating transaction, we remove the events being compensated from the history relations.

The abort handler's task can be subdivided into five stages:

1. All the transactions to be aborted are identified by starting from the current transaction node in the abort graph and computing the set of nodes reachable from it.

2. Events in aborted transactions that have already occurred (and which consequently need to be compensated) are retrieved from the history relations, and for each a sequence of compensating inverse events is determined.

3. The aborted transactions that have either not started or not completed execution are removed from the schedule.

4. Primitive events that occurred during aborted transactions are removed from the history relations.

5. The compensating transaction is executed.

16.4   Conclusion

This chapter has described the active subsystem of PFL, a functional database programming language. Extending PFL with an active subsystem has been achieved without introducing any impedance mismatch since PFL itself is used for the specification of events, conditions, and actions. Also, the computation model and type system remain unchanged.

In order for the evaluation of each expression to remain confluent, ECA rules are fired only upon the termination of the evaluation of the expression. Also, clock and external events that would need to be detected and acted upon during expression evaluation are not supported.

Our aim in extending PFL with an active subsystem has been to provide a general-purpose tool for handling constraints, default rules, and view materialization, and the extended PFL is currently being used for the analysis of road accident data at the Centre for Transport Studies, University College London.

In [RPS95] and [PRS96], we show how PFL has been used to specify the semantics of its own active subsystem, and we discuss the resulting benefits. In [PRS96], we also discuss the expressiveness of PFL as an event specification language, and we show how event detection can be optimized by optimizing the event query, or optimizing the event query and the condition query in tandem, using the query transformation techniques developed in [PS94] and [PS96]. We are currently implementing a query optimizer that will automate these optimizations. We are also investigating using our functional specification of PFL's active subsystem as the formal foundation for ECA rule analysis.

16.5   Acknowledgments

This work has been supported by EPSRC grants GR/J 98134 and GR/L 26872. It was undertaken while Swarup Reddi was Research Fellow at Birkbeck College and subsequently at King's College London, and Carol Small was Senior Lecturer at Birkbeck College and subsequently Visiting Senior Research Fellow at King's College London.

16.6   References

[PRS96] A. Poulovassilis, S. Reddi, and C. Small. A Formal Semantics for an Active Functional DBPL. *Journal of Intelligent Information Systems*, 7(2):151–172, 1996.

[PS91]   A. Poulovassilis and C. Small. A Functional Approach to Deductive Databases. In G. Lohman, A. Sernadas, and R. Camps, editors, *Proc. 17th VLDB*, pages 479–487. Morgan-Kaufmann, 1991.

[PS94]   A. Poulovassilis and C. Small. Investigation of Algebraic Query Optimisation in Database Programming Languages. In J. Bocca, M. Jarke, and C. Zaniolo, editors, *Proc. 20th VLDB*, pages 415–426. Morgan-Kaufmann, 1994.

[PS96]   A. Poulovassilis and C. Small. Algebraic Query Optimisation in Database Programming Languages. *The VLDB Journal*, 5(2):119–132, 1996.

[RPS95] S. Reddi, A. Poulovassilis, and C. Small. Extending a Functional DBPL With ECA-Rules. In T. Sellis, editor, *Proc. 2nd Intl. Workshop. on Rules in Database Systems*, pages 101–115. Springer-Verlag, 1995.

[SP91]   C. Small and A. Poulovassilis. An Overview of PFL. In P. Kanellakis and J. W. Schmidt, editors, *Proc. 3rd Intl. Workshop on Database Programming Languages (DBPL-3)*, pages 479–487. Morgan-Kaufmann, 1991.

[SS95]   D. Sutton and C. Small. Extending Functional Database Languages to Update Completeness. In C.Goble and J.Keane, editors, *Proc. 13th British National Conference on Databases (BNCOD-13)*, pages 47–63. Springer-Verlag, 1995.

17

Chimera: A Language for Designing Rule Applications

Piero Fraternali
Stefano Paraboschi

ABSTRACT

Chimera is a conceptual model and language for active databases, developed in the context of the Esprit project P6333 IDEA. In this chapter, we discuss its essential features and describe the tool environment assisting the use of Chimera in the design of active database applications according to the IDEA Methodology, a novel approach to information system development.

17.1 Introduction

Chimera [CM93, CM94] is a conceptual database language based on an object-oriented data model and offering active and deductive functionalities. The language has been developed in the context of the Esprit project P6333 IDEA, from June 1992 to March 1997.

The language draws its name from the Chimera, an imaginary creature of Greek mythology with a lion's head, a goat's body, and a serpent's tail, which well represents the integration of three different paradigms, object-orientation, active rules, and deductive rules, into a single powerful body.

The Chimera language has been the object of two distinct implementation efforts by the partners of the IDEA project. The *Chimera Prototyping Tool (CPT)* developed at the University of Bonn is a lightweight, Prolog-based implementation covering the entire spectrum of the language. The *Algres Testbed of Chimera*, developed by Politecnico di Milano, focuses only on the object-oriented and active features of Chimera and is built on top of the extended relational system Algres. A novel version of the Politecnico Testbed of Chimera has recently been produced which targets a commercial relational product (Oracle v. 7).

All the software mentioned, as well as a significant fraction of the project documentation, can be downloaded from the IDEA Project official Web site, http://www.txt.it/idea.

The initial definition of the Chimera language has been extended in a number of directions, including support for management of composite events [MPC96], temporal capabilities [BFG96], and trigger inheritance and overriding [BG96].

Finally, Chimera has been adopted in the context of the Esprit project WIDE, to be used as a modeling language for the active component of workflow management systems.

This chapter is organized as follows: section 17.2 discusses the main features of Chimera according to the classification model presented in Chapter 1; section 17.3 illustrates the role of Chimera as a conceptual specification language for the IDEA Methodology and presents the set of tools supporting the IDEA development process.

17.2   The Chimera Model and Language

Chimera consists of a data model and a conceptual language [CM93]. The Chimera model is object-oriented, featuring classes and value types.

Classes are collections of persistent objects, possibly organized into inheritance hierarchies; multiple inheritance is permitted. A class has a signature and an implementation, which can be compiled separately.

A class signature includes ancestor classes, typed attributes, the signature of operations with typed input and output parameters, built-in constraints (key, unique, not null), and the names of integrity constraints and triggers targeted to the class.

A class implementation gives a body to the operations, constraints, and triggers listed in the signature, using the declarative and procedural expressions offered by the Chimera language.

Differently from classes, value types represent domains of printable elements. Value types are used to define the structure of class attributes and operation parameters; they may be simple or built from the usual record, set, and list constructors.

The Chimera language offers expressive features to specify the implementation of classes and other schema elements not defined in the context of a class, like views, untargeted constraints, and untargeted triggers.

Basically, the language permits the definition of declarative and procedural expressions. Declarative expressions are logical formulas used to specify Datalog-like deductive rules for views, constraints, queries, and the condition parts of triggers. Procedural expressions are imperative statements used to specify database manipulations. They appear in user transactions and in the action parts of triggers.

In the sequel, we concentrate only on the active part of the Chimera language and discuss the features of Chimera triggers.

```
define event_consuming deferred trigger EmpSalary
        for employee
events modify(Salary), create
condition Employee(E), Manager(M),
          occurred(modify(Salary),create,E),
          E.ManagedBy = M, E.Salary > M.Salary
actions modify(Employee.Salary,E,M.Salary)
after EmpDept, EmpManager
end
```

FIGURE 17.1. A Chimera trigger targeted to class employee .

Event	Source	Structure Operation, Abstract (in [CCPP96]), Exception (in [CCPP96]), Clock (in [CCPP96]), External (in [CCPP96])
	Granularity	Set
	Type	Primitive, Composite (in [MPC96])
	Role	Mandatory
Condition	Role	Optional
	Context	DB_T, $Bind_E$, DB_C
Action	Options	Structure Operation, Behavior Invocation, Abort, Inform (in [CCPP96]), External (in [CCPP96])
	Context	DB_T, $Bind_E$, DB_C, $Bind_C$, DB_A

TABLE 17.1. Features of Chimera knowledge model.

17.2.1 The Chimera Trigger Language

The flavor of the active portion of the Chimera language is illustrated by the trigger in Figure 17.1, defined in the context of class employee. The trigger is deferred (is evaluated at transaction commit) and reacts to the insertion of an employee into the database or to updates of his or her salary. When the employee's salary is greater than that of the employee's manager, the employee's salary is decreased to the level of the manager. The trigger has a lower priority than triggers EmpDept and EmpManager.

Tables 17.1 and 17.2 report the classification of the characteristics of Chimera along the dimensions described in Chapter 1. In these tables, we refer by default to the original definition of the Chimera language [CM93, CM94]; features added in later language versions are explicitly pointed out by adding the reference where the extension is defined.

17.2.2   Events

Events in Chimera refer to object manipulations (query, creation, update, and deletion), and to the migration of objects along class hierarchies (generalization and specialization).

The event part of a trigger lists all the events that may activate it. For example, the rule in Figure 17.1 is triggered by event `create` on class employee, or by event `modify` on employee's attribute `Salary`.

Event granularity is set-oriented: a Chimera trigger is considered only once for the set of objects affected by its triggering event(s).

The basic event types of Chimera have been extended in two directions: event composition [MPC96], and abstract and exception events [CCPP96].

17.2.3   Conditions

The condition of a Chimera trigger is a declarative expression, that is, a conjunctive formula of a logical language. The terms permitted in a declarative expression are constants of atomic or structured types, variables ranging over class extensions or value type domains, and evaluable terms like object attribute selectors, arithmetic and aggregate operators, and operators on structured types.

Formulas are either atomic or complex. Complex formulas are composed from atomic formulas by means of connectives expressing conjunction and negation; negation is only applicable to atomic formulas. Atomic formulas include class and type formulas respectively built from class and type names (e.g., `employee(E)`, `integer(I)`), comparison formulas (e.g., X=3), membership formulas (e.g., Y in X.children), external formulas built from n-ary predicates defined externally to Chimera (e.g., `asciiToInteger(S,I)`), and view formulas built from view definitions (e.g., `marriage([X,Y])`).

Two special types of atomic formulas are also defined: constraint and event formulas.

Constraint formulas are built from constraint predicates defined by deductive rules; they are satisfied when the database contains violations of the constraint, and their variable substitutions usually identify the objects that cause the constraint violation(s).

Event formulas, used only in the context of trigger conditions, permit the retrieval of the objects affected by the triggering event(s) of a rule. They are built from the predicates *occurred* and *holds*, which have as first arguments a subset of the rule's triggering events defined on a single class, and as last argument a variable ranging over such class. When the predicate is satisfied, the variable at the last argument gets bound to the objects affected by the events listed in the previous arguments. For example, in the trigger of Figure 17.1, predicate `occurred(modify(salary),create,E)` binds to variable E only the employees whose creation or salary update has triggered the rule.

The sequence of event instances to use in the evaluation of the event predicates is determined by the so-called *event consumption mode* of the trigger. When the *event consuming* option is adopted (like in the trigger of Figure 17.1), if a rule has already been evaluated in the course of the transaction, then only those events are considered that have occurred after the last rule consideration (we say that triggering events are consumed by condition evaluation); if the trigger is *event preserving*, all the events since transaction start are considered.

Orthogonal to the trigger's consumption mode is the difference between the predicates *occurred* and *holds*, which is determined by the treatment of *net effect*: the former considers all the objects affected by the triggering event(s), whereas the latter restricts the binding to only those objects that satisfy the net effect criteria, e.g., those employees whose creation has triggered the rule that has not been successively deleted.

In addition to event predicates, the condition may contain terms evaluated on past database states. These terms are prefixed by the function *old* (e.g., old(E.Salary)). The evaluation of past state terms is particularly flexible, since it varies based on the consumption mode of the trigger: if the trigger is defined as *event consuming*, then the past database state is the one preceding the last consideration of the rule; if the trigger is *event preserving*, the term is evaluated in the before state of the entire transaction.

17.2.4   Actions

The action part of a Chimera trigger contains an arbitrary Chimera procedural expression. A procedural expression is a sequence of queries, updates, and operation invocations, which is executed in a set-oriented way. Procedural expressions are used to write *transaction lines*, i.e., sequence of updates atomic with respect to rule processing. In turn, transaction lines are assembled into transactions, whose execution interleaves with rule processing at points defined by the boundaries of transaction lines.

A Chimera trigger is executed as a special transaction line, considering the condition as a select statement in front of the action part statement sequence. The statements in the action may share variables, and the action as a whole may use variables introduced in the condition. Note that the action can access values from past database states by referencing a variable introduced in the condition via the function *old*.

In the example in Figure 17.1, all the employee-manager pairs satisfying the condition are retrieved and passed down to the action, where the employee's salary is decreased to that of his or her manager.

Condition-Mode	Immediate, Deferred, Detached (in [CCPP96])
Action-Mode	Immediate
Transition granularity	Set
Net-effect policy	Active, Disabled
Cycle policy	Iterative
Priorities	Numerical (in [CCPP96]), Relative
Scheduling	All Sequential
Error handling	Abort, Backtrack (Oracle implementation)

TABLE 17.2. Features of the execution model of Chimera triggers.

17.2.5 Execution Model

The execution of a Chimera trigger follows the traditional stages of execution for ECA rules with the immediate action mode.

When its triggering events occur, the rule is triggered and enters the conflict set; when selected for execution from the conflict set, the rule is considered, i.e., its condition part is evaluated; if the condition is satisfied then the action is immediately executed.

Chimera triggers may have *deferred* or *immediate* condition modes. Immediate rules are evaluated at the end of the transaction line containing the command that triggers them, while deferred rules are evaluated at transaction commit. In both cases, the same transaction context is retained.

The WIDE extension of Chimera [CCPP96] is adding the detached execution mode, where rules are executed as separate transactions under the surveillance of the concurrency control manager of the underlying passive database system.

Chimera has been designed to be a set-oriented language, and this choice is reflected both in the execution semantics of procedural expressions, which is based on the flow of sets of bindings along transaction lines, and in the granularity of triggers, which react once per set-oriented update.

Net effect computation is optional and can be specified rule by rule. It must be noted that, for efficiency reasons and due to the set-oriented nature of Chimera triggers, net effect is not computed during triggering (all events are used for determining triggered rules), but only in the evaluation of event formulas built from the predicate *holds* in rule conditions. As a consequence, rules are never untriggered by the occurrence of an event (say, a deletion after a creation).

The cycle policy is strictly iterative to preserve the set-orientation of the language.

Priorities are defined specifying a relative order among rules, using the *after* and *before* clause. For example, the rule in Figure 17.1 has a lower priority than rules EmpDept and EmpManager. The Chimera compiler analyses the priority relationship among rules and builds a corresponding priority graph, which must be acyclic. The Wide extension of Chimera [CCPP96] permits to specify priorities as integer values, with a considerable simplification of their management.

Finally, little emphasis has been dedicated to error handling. In the Algres Testbed, errors caused by rule execution are treated as errors in the transaction, requiring a rollback, whereas the Oracle implementation relies on the error handling capabilities provided by the Oracle system.

17.3   Chimera as a Conceptual Specification Language

The experience gained during the IDEA project in the design of active database applications demonstrated that the major obstacle toward an effective use of advanced database technology was the absence of methods and tools for the designers. This consideration shifted the emphasis of the project toward the construction of support tools and the definition of a methodology. The Chimera model and language has become only one ingredient, although fundamental, of a wider proposal for the development of data-intensive systems based on the object-oriented and rule-based technologies, known as the *IDEA Methodology*.

The IDEA Methodology, described in the book [CF97], addresses the analysis, design, prototyping, and implementation of modern database systems applications, taking advantage of classical approaches developed in the context of database design, but also of techniques and methods from object-oriented software engineering.

The distinguishing goal of the IDEA Methodology is *knowledge independence*, that is, the ability to extract from applications semantic knowledge normally encoded in a procedural format, and place it into the database schema, expressed declaratively in the form of object definitions and rules.

Knowledge independence is primarily achieved by using Chimera as a conceptual language for knowledge design. Application requirements, stated during analysis by means of semi-formal models, are turned into a set of Chimera design specifications describing the main entities of the domain and their declarative properties and reactive behavior in terms of Chimera classes, deductive and active rules. It is in this process that most features that in traditional information systems must be coded into application programs, like integrity constraints and business rules, find their place in the shared knowledge directly supported by the DBMS.

Using Chimera as a design language has further purposes besides knowledge independence. First, since Chimera definitions are computer processable. Design results constitute a first-cut system prototype, which fosters the early assessment of the adherence of the application to the user's requirements. Second, the existence of a sound formal semantics allows the verification of a number of fundamental properties, like stratification and satisfiability of deductive rules, and termination and confluence of active rules; [FT95] presents a procedural formalization of the active rules of Chimera. Finally, Chimera specifications can be semiautomatically mapped to most commercial database platforms, which ensures a direct path from design to implementation.[1]

The IDEA development process is supported by a number of CASE tools that constitute the *IDEA Environment*. Each tool is described in the next sections.

17.3.1   Generation of Chimera Triggers from High-Level Declarative Specifications

An underlying assumption of the IDEA approach is that the designer should be able to specify as many properties of the system as possible in a declarative way, leaving the burden of mapping them into executable procedural specifications to semiautomated tools. This approach is applied in the most important tasks of the IDEA development process.

During analysis, the designer uses high-level graphical models (the object model, which is an advanced entity-relationship model, and the dynamic model, based on statecharts) to express declaratively the structural and reactive features of objects in the application domain. In the passage to design, declarative features are translated into procedural Chimera specifications. For example, referential integrity links and relationships in the Object Model are transformed into Chimera triggers that maintain the correct links among objects after database operations. Similarly, graphical state transitions in the Dynamic Model are mapped into Chimera triggers targeted to the classes that exhibit the dynamic behavior. The editing and translation of the Object Model is supported by *Iade*, a CASE tool serving the upper phases of the development lifecycle.

Another facet of the mapping from declarative to procedural specifications is the transformation of deductive rules into active rules performing equivalent functions. This transformation is mandatory when the target implementation platform does not support deduction, but offers some form of active behavior, as do most commercial products.

The transformation of deductive rules into triggers is performed by a tool of the IDEA Environment called *Argonaut*. Argonaut has two components: *Arg-V* translates a possibly recursive Chimera view definition into a set of Chimera materialization triggers; *Arg-C* generates integrity maintenance triggers from Chimera constraints and assists the designer in the choice of

---

[1]In [CF97], five different commercial implementation targets are considered: Oracle, DB2, Illustra, Ode, and Validity.

the best mix of repair actions.

17.3.2 Chimera Rule Analysis and Debugging

The IDEA Environment offers rather unique tools for the analysis and debugging of Chimera active rules.

Rule analysis evaluates the properties of active rules at compile-time, i.e., when rules are created; it is a static technique (in contrast with debugging, a runtime technique). The most relevant properties to be checked are termination, confluence, and observable determinism (see Chapter 3).

Analysis of Chimera active rules is performed by a tool named *Arachne*, an Active Rules Analyzer for Chimera, which focuses on termination analysis.

Arachne accepts as input a set of Chimera triggers and detects rules that may exhibit non-terminating behavior. Rules are guaranteed to terminate if their *triggering graph*, defined, e.g., in [CW90], is acyclic, because in this case it is easy to prove that the number of rules that can be transitively triggered is bound by some upper limit.

Arachne supports event-based analysis, which performs a simple, syntax-based analysis of the triggering graph, and condition-based analysis, which refines event-based analysis by discarding superfluous arcs from the triggering graph after more sophisticated verification. Condition-based analysis consists in testing, for each edge $\langle r_i, r_j \rangle$ in the triggering graph, whether it is possible to conclude that the condition of r_j is not made true by the execution of r_i, even if r_j is triggered by r_i's action; in this case, the edge can be removed from the graph.

After either event- or condition-based analysis, Arachne displays a graphical representation of active rules and highlights all cycles in the triggering graph. It is the responsibility of the designer either to modify the active rule set, or to manually verify that a particular set of rules involved in a cycle has a terminating behavior.

Figure 17.2 shows Arachne applied to a sizeable rule set consisting of over fifty triggers; the large number of rules produces a very intricate triggering graph with many interactions, which it would be almost impossible to analyze manually. However, Arachne is very effective in highlighting the critical parts of the triggering graph and makes termination analysis effective in such conditions. Cycle analysis in this case reveals that twenty four cycles are caused by only four rules.

To support the manual assessment of cycle termination, Arachne lets the designer isolate a cluster of rules from the entire rule set, filtering the noise induced by the remaining triggers. Any cycle may be displayed on a separate window as a chain of event/action pairs. Rules and events in the window can be easily inspected by clicking on the respective icon.

Besides termination analysis, Arachne supports also *active rule modularization*, which is a novel concept introduced in [BCP96] and adopted by

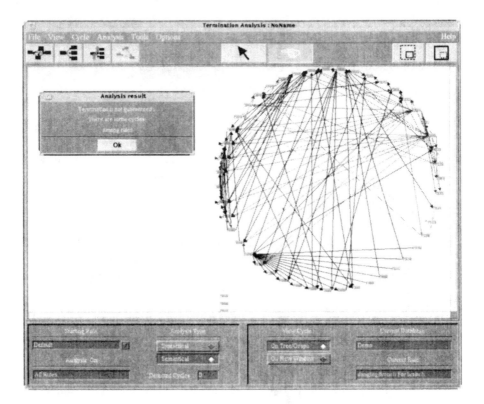

FIGURE 17.2. Arachne at work on a rule set.

the IDEA Methodology.

Active rule modularization enables the designer to focus on subsets of the rule set, thus partitioning a large design space. *Stratification* is the key design principle for providing the modularization and control of active rules. Informally, stratification consists of partitioning rules into disjoint strata so that the designer can abstract rule behavior by reasoning locally on each stratum separately, and then globally on the behavior across strata.

Three forms of stratification are proposed, each with a different way of characterizing rule interaction: behavioral, assertional, and event-based stratification [BCP96].

With the help of Arachne, it is possible to cluster rules into modules, give each module a name, and perform rule analysis in the small (within one module) and in the large (across modules). Although there is no automatic support to the choice of a modularization structure, the tool comprises options for documenting the modularization criteria, such as textual descriptions of the rationale associated with a module (for example, the kind of stratification applied to obtain the module).

Rule debugging is supported by the *Algres Testbed of Chimera*. This tool implements a significant subset of Chimera, the most important omission concerning deductive rules.[2] The Algres Testbed provides a sophisticated runtime environment for the debugging of the reactive process, which may be invoked during the execution of transactions. When the debugger is active, the designer can observe the step-by-step evolution of rule processing; this enables the evaluation of rule interactions at execution time, thus complementing compile-time analysis. A user-friendly interface allows the designer to obtain a trace of the execution, as well as to access the current database state and recently occurred events.

The debugger can be invoked after a given number of rule executions, or be activated at spy-points set by the user. Once the debugger is active, it enables execution to stop at inspection points set either when the choice is made of the next rule to be considered, or after the condition of a rule has been evaluated and before its execution. The designer can obtain from the system a variety of useful information displayed in appropriate windows of the debugger interface:

- the *conflict set*, containing all rules that are triggered at the time when the debugger is activated,

- the *trace*, illustrating the sequence of events and consequent trigger activations since the start of the transaction,

- the *event instances*, i.c., the oids of objects affected by events, and

- the *content of specific objects*, chosen among the tvent instances.

17.3.3 Implementation of Chimera on Top of Commercial Systems

Implementation is the process of mapping Chimera specifications into schemata, objects, and rules of existing database platforms; this process is obviously influenced by the features of the specific target environment selected. In the IDEA Methodology, five products have been chosen to demonstrate the feasibility of mapping a Chimera design onto existing database technology. These include Oracle and DB2, two classic relational products supporting triggers; Illustra, a powerful object-relational product; Ode, an active object-oriented database available on the Internet to universities and research institutes; and Validity [FLV96], a deductive and object-oriented database system.

One of the above mappings (the one to Oracle) has been selected for the development of a computer-based support tool. The result is *Pandora*, a tool of the IDEA Environment that can be seen both as a fully fledged

---

[2]As already mentioned, a second tool, called *Chimera Prototyping Tool (CPT)*, implements both the active and deductive components of Chimera. However, advanced rule debugging facilities at present are available in the Algres Testbed only.

implementation of Chimera on top of Oracle Version 7, or as an *implementation assistant* supporting the (quite tedious) generation of Oracle code from design specifications written in Chimera.

The present version of Pandora consists of three different compilers supporting the mapping of Chimera schemata, triggers, and transactions, respectively. The schema compiler processes Chimera class definitions and produces equivalent SQL DDL statements. Oids, inheritance, set-valued attributes, referential integrity, and the semantics of deletion are supported.

The trigger compiler accepts any legal Chimera trigger and produces its implementation in PL/SQL. The present version of Pandora uses a technique called meta-triggering (defined in [CF97]), which permits the reproduction of the full semantics of Chimera triggers in spite of the limitations of the Oracle trigger system.

According to meta-triggering, each Chimera rule is compiled into a stored procedure, and execution is managed by a set of ad-hoc native Oracle triggers capable of implementing features like deferred activation and priorities, which are not offered by Oracle.

Finally, Pandora's transaction compiler accepts any stream of Chimera transaction lines and generates equivalent SQL DML statements preserving the Chimera execution semantics, which requires set-orientation, atomicity of transaction lines with respect to immediate triggers, and atomicity of entire transactions with respect to deferred triggers.

In the present phase, efforts of the Chimera development team are mostly concentrated on porting the IDEA tools to the Web for letting remote users experience the development of applications using Chimera as a conceptual design language. As a result of this activity, the so-called IDEA Web Lab is now open at address http://www.elet.polimi.it/idea.

In the Web Lab, users find a Java-enabled implementation of the most important tools of IDEA architecture, namely IADE, Arachne, and Pandora, which permit the development of an application from analysis to the production of code running on Oracle 7. Users are offered shared resources, like technical documentation and demos, and an individual protected environment where they can create and evolve their own testcases.

17.4   Acknowledgments

The creators of Chimera are Stefano Ceri, Rainer Manthey, and Elisa Bertino. Several other researchers have contributed to the design of Chimera and its tool environment. The implementation of the tools is the result of the thesis work of more than forty students at the Database Laboratory of Politecnico di Milano.

17.5 REFERENCES

[BCP95] Elena Baralis, Stefano Ceri, and Stefano Paraboschi. Arachne: A Tool for the Analysis of Active Rules. In *Proc. of the 2nd Intl. Conf. on Applications of Databases–ADB'95*, pages 68–81, Santa Clara, California, December 1995.

[BCP96] Elena Baralis, Stefano Ceri, and Stefano Paraboschi. Modularization Techniques for Active Rules Design. *ACM Transactions on Database Systems*, 21(1):1–29, March 1996.

[BFG96] Elisa Bertino, Elena Ferrari, and Giovanna Guerrini. A Formal Temporal Object-Oriented Data Model. In *Proc. Extending Database Technology (EDBT)*, pages 342–356, Avignon, March 1996.

[BG96] Elisa Bertino and Giovanna Guerrini. Trigger Inheritance and Overriding in an Active Object Database System. Technical report, Università di Genova, 1996.

[CBFP95] Stefano Ceri, Elena Baralis, Piero Fraternali, and Stefano Paraboschi. Design of Active Rule Applications: Issues and Approaches. In *Proc. of the Intl. Conf. on Deductive and Object-Oriented Databases*, Singapore, 1–18, December 1995.

[CCPP96] Fabio Casati, Stefano Ceri, Barbara Pernici, and Giuseppe Pozzi. Specification of the Rule Language and Active Engine for FORO v.1. Technical Report 3008-4, Esprit Project WIDE, Politecnico di Milano, October 1996.

[CF97] Stefano Ceri and Piero Fraternali. *The IDEA Methodology*. Addison-Wesley Publisher Ltd., May 1997. "Series on Database Systems and Applications."

[CFPT94] Stefano Ceri, Piero Fraternali, Stefano Paraboschi, and Letizia Tanca. Automatic Generation of Production Rules for Integrity Maintenance. *ACM Transactions on Database Systems*, 19(3):367–422, September 1994.

[CM93] Stefano Ceri and Rainer Manthey. Consolidated Specification of Chimera, the Conceptual Interface of Idea. Technical Report IDEA.DD.2P.004, ESPRIT Project n. 6333 Idea, June 1993.

[CM94] Stefano Ceri and Rainer Manthey. Chimera: A Model and Language for Active DOOD Systems. *East/West Database Workshop*, pages 3–16, 1994.

[CW90] Stefano Ceri and Jennifer Widom. Deriving Production Rules for Constraint Maintenance. In *16th Intl. Conf. in Very Large Databases, Brisbane*, pages 567–577. Morgan Kaufman, 1990.

[FLV96]   Oris Friesen, Alexandre Lefebvre, and Laurent Vieille. VALID-
           ITY: Applications of a DOOD System. In *Proc. Extending
           Database Technology (EDBT)*, pages 131–134, Avignon, March
           1996.

[FT95]   Piero Fraternali and Letizia Tanca. A Structured Approach
           for the Definition of the Semantics of Active databases. *ACM
           Transactions on Database Systems*, 20(4):414–471, December
           1995.

[MPC96]   Rosa Meo, Giuseppe Psaila, and Stefano Ceri. Composite
           Events in Chimera. In *Proc. Extending Database Technology
           (EDBT)*, pages 56–76, Avignon, March 1996.

18

RAP: The ROCK & ROLL Active Programming System

Andrew Dinn
Norman W. Paton
M. Howard Williams

ABSTRACT
This chapter describes RAP (ROCK & ROLL Active Programming system), an active rule system embedded within the ROCK & ROLL deductive object-oriented database system. A brief description of ROCK & ROLL is followed by an overview of RAP and a categorization of its Knowledge and Execution Models according to the dimensions introduced in Chapter 1.

18.1   Introduction

The ROCK & ROLL deductive-object-oriented database (DOOD) system [BPF+94, BFP+95] supports an expressive object-oriented data model, a deductive language in which to write queries and rules, and an imperative database programming language. As such, it provides a comprehensive collection of passive facilities for defining database functionality. However, in the same way as the imperative and deductive mechanisms in ROCK & ROLL are complementary, an active extension can itself be seen as adding to the range of facilities available to a programmer. For example, there is no built-in mechanism for integrity checking in ROCK & ROLL, and while certain checks can be implemented using methods in the context of strict encapsulation, it is sometimes the case that the checking of integrity should not be done immediately an update is executed, but rather later, when any temporary inconsistencies should have been overcome. Essentially, active capabilities in a system such as ROCK & ROLL allow nonintrusive monitoring of activities in the database, with a view to enforcing integrity, maintaining derived information, keeping users informed of activities, or refreshing displays.

The ROCK & ROLL Active Programming system (RAP) provides both an expressive language for describing active behavior and a comprehensive execution model. The emphasis in the design of RAP has been on exploiting declarative features as much as possible, but without trying to support the complex semantics of active rule execution models within a purely deduc-

```
type part:                          type composite_part:
   properties:                          specialises: part;
     public:                            properties:
       name : string,                     public:
       partid : int,                        assem_cost : real,
       lifetime : int,                      assem_quality: real;
       quality : real,                  public {part};
       cost : real;                     ROCK:
end_type                                    update_quality();
                                            update_cost();
type base_part:                          new(n:string,l:int,
   specialises: part;                        q:real,c:real,id:int);
   ROCK:                               ROLL:
      new(n:string,l:int,                 contains(part);
          q:real,c:real,id:int);   end_type
end_type
```

FIGURE 18.1. Example ROCK & ROLL type declarations.

tive context. The declarative language features of RAP have been useful in enabling more comprehensive work on rule analysis and optimization than has previously been possible with such a powerful rule language [DPW96].

18.2   ROCK & ROLL

18.2.1   Data Model

The ROCK & ROLL data model supports built-in primary types – integers, reals, booleans, and strings – and user-defined secondary types. Secondary types may be either aliases for existing types, or may be constructed from existing types.

As well as having attributes, a type may also be constructed as either an association, a sequentiation, or an aggregation. Associations and sequentiations are collection types that correspond to sets and sequences, respectively. Associations store a collection of objects without duplicates. Sequentiations store a collection of objects (possibly sparsely) indexed by an integer position. Sequentiations may be appended to like a list but may also be accessed or updated by index like an array. Aggregations are record types, with a fixed number of typed fields. Constructions may also be public or private.

Types may be specialized by subtypes, in which case the subtype inherits attributes and, possibly, a construction from its (direct or indirect) supertypes. Multiple supertypes are allowed, as are joins in the subtype graph so long as they do not result in cycles. Example ROCK & ROLL type definitions are given in Figure 18.1.

The example types implement the bill of materials problem. Type **part** is a generic type that defines attributes associated with all parts, a name, a unique id, a lifetime for which the part can be expected to survive, a quality level, and a cost. Type **base_part** is a subtype of part that does not add any extra structure to that inherited from **part**.

Type **composite_part** also specializes **part**. It includes two extra attributes, a cost and a quality for the assembly, in addition to the costs and qualities of the parts that make up the composite. **composite_part** also has a construction as an association of **part** objects (represented by naming **part** between curly braces). This allows a hierarchy of parts to be constructed using base and composite parts.

The definitions for **base_part** and **composite_part** also include an interface declaration specifying methods associated with the type. Methods are implemented using either the imperative language ROCK or the declarative language ROLL. ROCK is an imperative, object-oriented programming language that can be used to implement methods or the main body of a ROCK & ROLL program. ROLL is a Horn clause logic language similar to Datalog [CGT90]. Implementations of a method are not provided in the type but in a separate class definition.

In the ROCK interfaces for both **part** and **composite_part** a **new** method is defined, allowing a part to be initialized when it is created. The class **composite_part** defines two other ROCK methods, **update_cost** and **update_quality**, which are used to compute the cost and quality of the composite part by combining the cost and quality of the components and the assembly cost/quality, respectively. **composite_part** also implements a deductive method **contains**, which can be used to identify parts that are members of a composite part, either directly or by recursive inclusion via other composite parts.

18.2.2   ROCK

ROCK is an imperative programming language used to implement user-defined methods and program bodies. ROCK provides a variety of built-in operations on primitive types plus control constructs and I/O facilities.

System-generated methods are created automatically whenever a type is defined, enabling attributes and/or the construction of the type to be accessed and updated. So, for example, the methods **get_name** and **put_name** are automatically provided on class **part**, allowing the attribute **name** to be read or written. Since **name** is a public attribute, the methods are publicly accessible.

Several system-generated methods are provided to access or update the members of a **composite_part**. For example, the message **is_in** can be sent to a composite_part with a **part** as argument. If the part is a member of the composite, it returns **true**, otherwise **false**. Once again, access to the construction depends on whether the construction is declared public,

```
class composite_part
 public:
   update_quality()
   begin
     var min_q : real;
     min_q := get_assem_quality()@self
     foreach p in self do
     begin
       var part_q := get_quality()@p;
       if (part_q < min_q) then
         min_q := part_q;
     end
     put_quality(min_q)@self;
   end
   . . .
end_class
```

FIGURE 18.2. Example ROCK method.

as is the case with composite_part, or private.

An example ROCK method is provided in Figure 18.2. This method ensures that the quality of a composite does not exceed that of the components or the composite assembly_quality attribute. The initial var declaration establishes a local variable min_q of type real. min_q is assigned using the value stored in the assem_quality attribute. The expression on the right-hand side of the assignment is a message-sending operation in which self references the composite_part that is handling the invocation of update_quality. The @ symbol is the message sending operator.

The foreach construct allows iteration over a class extent or the members of a collection type. Since self is a composite_part, it is constructed as an association. So, in this case, the foreach loop is executed repeatedly with the variable p bound to each each part that is a member of self. The quality of part p is retrieved and used to initialize another local variable, part_q. Since the type of p is known, the signature of the get_assem_quality method can be determined and the result type derived as real. This obviates the need to declare the type of part_q. As the loop executes, min_q retains the minimum quality for the composite and its components. Finally, once the loop is exited, this minimum value is used to assign the composite part's quality attribute.

18.2.3   ROLL

ROLL is a Horn clause logic language used to query the database. Like all logic languages, a ROLL program is organized as a set of clauses. Although ROLL is very similar to existing logic languages such as Datalog extended with negation and arithmetic operator, it differs from them in

```
class composite_part
 public:
  contains(part)
  begin
    contains(P)@CP :-
      is_in(P)@CP;
    contains(P)@CP :-
      contains(P)@Sub:composite_part, is_in(Sub)@CP;
  end
  . . .
end_class
```

FIGURE 18.3. Example ROLL method.

several important respects: ROLL is strictly typed, a type inference algorithm avoiding the need for most variable types to be declared; goals in the head and body of ROLL clauses are written using the same message-passing syntax as employed by ROCK, rather than the more usual predicate syntax; clauses are grouped into methods located in the type of the recipient argument in the clause head, which allows a subclass to override a method implemented by one of its superclasses, by providing an alternative set of clauses; and the reduction process implied by the clause structure bottoms out in built-in goals whose solution is determined with reference to the structure of and interrelation between objects in the database.

An example ROLL method is provided in Figure 18.3. The method has two clauses, each of which can be used to reduce a goal to subgoals identifying solutions to the goal as it does so. The head of the clause (the message term preceding the :- symbol) is a pattern representing a goal to be solved. The body of the clause is a list of ROLL method invocations. These constitute subgoals which, if they can be solved, will thereby provide a solution for the head goal. The two clauses of contains compute the transitive closure of the (stored) is_in relationship.

18.2.4 Queries

Queries over the databases are written using a syntax similar to a set or list comprehension. Queries contain a body that specifies a set of ROLL goals to be solved, and a projection, a list of goal arguments that should be collected from the various solutions derived for the goals and returned as the result of the query. An example query is provided in Figure 18.4. The query is written between square brackets on the right-hand side of the assignment to variable p. It retrieves all instances of class part whose name attribute has value "widget". The query body on the right-hand side of the | contains one goal that specifies that the result of running the get_name method on part P must be the string "widget", i.e., any solution for P must be a part whose name attribute is "widget". The projection on the

```
var ps : {part};

ps := [ ALL P | get_name()@P:part == "widget"];
foreach p in ps do
  write "Found part with id", get_id()@p, nl;
```

FIGURE 18.4. Example ALL query.

```
var cp : composite_part;
var ps : {part};

cp := [ ANY CP | get_id()@CP == 1000 ];
ps := [ ALL P | contains(P)@!cp ];

foreach p in ps do
  write "Composite part 100 contains component", get_id()@p, nl;
```

FIGURE 18.5. Example ANY query.

left-hand side of the | specifies that *all* bindings for variable P should be collected and returned as the result of the query. So, the type of the query expression is an association of part objects.

Note that the type of the query expression will be inferred from the fact that it is assigned to a variable ps of type {part}. Since this is an ALL query, this implies that the ROLL variable P must be of type part. So, there is no need to declare the type of P in the query goal. The type inference algorithm derives it from the context.

The fact that ROCK and ROLL both operate over the same data model makes it is very easy for data to be communicated between the two languages. Arguments to query goals may be variables, constant values, or ROCK variables bound to some value. Where a constant or a ROCK variable is supplied as a goal argument, this restricts the solution set for the goal to solutions that have the relevant constant or bound value for the argument. The example in Figure 18.5 uses an ANY query to retrieve a composite part with id 1000. If any such parts exist, one solution is chosen and the composite_part bound to variable CP is returned as the result of the query for assignment to the ROCK variable cp. The second query supplies the value bound to cp as the recipient argument to the contains goal. The ! character indicates that the argument is not a ROLL variable but a ROCK variable from the surrounding context that is bound to an input value. Solutions to the contains goal that have this value for the recipient argument are collected, and the relevant bindings for variable P are collected in an association returned as the result of the query expression.

It is also possible to collect a tuple of related objects or a set of such tuples from a query. Figure 18.6 contains a query that retrieves the name and id of each part in the database. The result of the query is an association

```
var pairs := [ ALL <Name, Id> | get_name()@P:part == Name,
                                 get_id()@P == Id ];

foreach pair in pairs do
  write "Part ", get_id@pair, " has name ", get_name()@pair, nl;
```

FIGURE 18.6. Example query with multiple projection arguments.

Event	Source	Structure Operation, Behavior Invocation, Transaction, Abstract
	Type	Primitive, Composite
	Granularity	Subset, Set
	Role	Mandatory
Condition	Role	Mandatory
	Context	$Bind_E$, DB_C
Action	Options	Structure Operation, Behavior Invocation, Abort, Inform, Do Instead
	Context	$Bind_E$, $Bind_C$, DB_A

TABLE 18.1. Dimensions for knowledge model.

whose members are aggregations containing two fields, a **name** and an **id**.

18.3   Knowledge Model

The knowledge model of RAP supports ECA rules for extending the behavior modeling facilities of ROCK & ROLL. ROLL and ROCK constitute powerful deductive and imperative programming languages in their own right, and so are natural candidates for the respective roles of condition and action language. As a result, the description of the RAP knowledge model mainly focuses on the event language. The dimensions for the RAP knowledge model are given in Table 18.1.

18.3.1   Event Language and Event Model

All RAP rules are required to contain an event part. The event language supports a variety of primitive events and an event algebra allowing the construction of complex events. Primitive events may specify any built-in operation on objects, new and delete operations, attribute fetches and updates, accesses to the construction of constructed types, etc. User method invocations, including new method invocations, may also be specified as events. All of these operations actually correspond to message send operations either invoking system-generated methods or user-defined methods.

Primitive message events are written using the same syntax as in ROCK or ROLL except that event arguments must be either constant values or variables. So, for example, the event `insert(P)@CP:composite_part` would match every insertion of a `part` into a `composite_part`. The keyword SENT may be appended to the event to specify that the event should be caught before the message is sent rather than after. So, the event `insert(P)@CP:composite_part SENT` would be matched before part P was added to composite CP. Return values may be specified for events with a functional syntax. For example, the event `get_name()@P == "widget"` would match every retrieval of a part name that returned the result `"widget"`.

Other primitive events include milestone events, such as program or transaction start and end, transaction commit and transaction abort.

An event algebra is provided for the construction of complex events. The following operators are provided:

```
[ALL | EARLIEST | LATEST] event AND event [WITHIN t]
[ALL | EARLIEST | LATEST] event THEN event [WITHIN t]
event OR event
event REPEATED n TIMES [WITHIN t]
event WITHOUT event [WITHIN t]
( event )
```

The first two operators support unordered and sequenced conjunctions of events, respectively. The WITHIN keyword may be employed to restrict triggering to cases where the events occur within a given number of seconds. The optional keyword preceding the events specifies a *Consumption Mode*, which describes how repeated occurrences of either component event are combined with occurrences of the other event. Given conjunction event A AND B, assume that two occurrences of A are followed by an occurrence of B. With consumption mode EARLIEST, the first occurrence of A is combined with the occurrence of B to trigger the event and, since it occurred before the B event that triggered the composite, the second occurrence is discarded. With LATEST mode, the second occurrence of A is combined with the occurrence of B and the first discarded. With mode ALL, both occurrences of A are combined with B, triggering the event twice.

The OR operator may be used to specify a set of alternative events that will trigger a rule.

The REPEATED operator allows an arbitrary number of repeats of a given component event to trigger a rule. The timeout defines the maximum allowable interval in seconds between the first and last such events.

The WITHOUT operator provides a controlled means of specifying that an event has not occurred. It is triggered if the first event occurs and the second event does not subsequently occur whether within the specified time interval or before the end of the current program run.

Event specifications are written using a similar notation to conditions, a list comprehension containing an event specification, and a projection. The projection is used both to specify the frequency with which events are triggered and to describe how event arguments are to be bound for use during condition or action evaluation. The following specification is the most simple case:

```
WHEN [ EACH | insert(P)@CP:composite_part]
IF . . .
```

Each time an insert operation is performed, the event is triggered and the rule either fired immediately or queued for (possibly repeated) deferred execution. With deferred processing, it is also possible to use the ALL or ANY keywords:

```
WHEN [ ANY | insert(P)@CP:composite_part]
IF . . .
```

However many times the insert event is performed, the rule is only triggered and queued once for deferred processing.

If event parameters are extracted from the operation for use in conditions, things get slightly more complicated. A binding must be established to an event variable that may be employed as a condition or action input. The following specification is triggered each time an insert operation is performed and the inserted part P is bound to variable p so that it may be accessed during condition and action evaluation:

```
WHEN p <== [ EACH P | insert(P)@CP:composite_part]
IF . . .
```

Each trigger may either be handled immediately or queued for deferred processing. If the rule employs deferred condition processing, then the ANY keyword may be used in place of EACH. If more than one occurrence of the insert operation occurs before deferred processing is initiated, one occurrence will be picked at random and the rule triggered once using the associated value for P to bind variable p. The ALL keyword may also be used with deferred condition mode:

```
WHEN ps <== [ ALL <P, CP> | insert(P)@CP:composite_part]
IF . . .
```

In this last example, the rule is still triggered once only. However, bindings for P and CP are collected from all insert operations and used to construct a binding for ps. Each pair of bindings is installed in an aggregation instance with two fields, part and composite_part. The aggregation instances are then collected in an association bound to ps.

18.3.2   Condition Model

The condition of a RAP rule is either a ROLL query or the keyword TRUE. If a ROLL condition is employed, it may refer to values bound in the event specification by mentioning the relevant event variable prefixed by a ! character.

If a ROLL condition is employed, it may be a boolean test with an empty projection or it may employ the ANY or ALL keywords. In the former case the action is run should the condition evaluate to true. Rules with non-empty projections are only useful when it is desired to collect bindings from the condition for use in the action. The following condition uses the pairs of parts P retrieved from the insert operations specified in the event and checks see if any of the inserted parts are linked in a cycle:

```
WHEN ps <== [ ALL <P, CP> | insert(P)@CP:composite_part]
IF bad_ps <== [ ALL <P, CP> |
                   Pair is_in !ps, get_composite_part@Pair == CP,
                   get_part@Pair == P, contains(CP)@P ]
DO . . .
```

The action of this rule will only be run if the query has solutions, or equivalently if the association bound to variable bad_ps is non-empty.

Although the use of bindings allows the condition to access data mentioned in the event specification, the state of any such objects at the time of binding is not preserved. So, the *Condition Context* is $\{Bind_E, DB_C\}$.

18.3.3   Action Model

RAP actions can be any ROCK statement. Normally, actions are additional to any operations triggering the rule. If the event specification matches a message before it is sent, then it is possible for the rule to DO INSTEAD an alternative action. If an event specifies a message event with a return value then the rule may RETURN an alternative value.

If the event or condition employ a binding, then the action code may reference either bound value by mentioning the relevant variable. As per the condition, such bindings only provide access to the current state of bound objects. So, the *Action Context* is $\{Bind_E, Bind_C, DB_A\}$.

An example set of RAP rules is shown in Figure 18.7. These rules ensure that the parts hierarchy is non-cyclic by rejecting attempts to create a circular link. They also ensure that every time the hierarchy is modified or a part has its cost or quality modified, the quality and cost of the composite parts of which it is a member are recalculated using the ROCK methods update_cost and update_quality. Since this involves modifying the cost and quality of the enclosing part, this invokes the same rule recursively for each enclosing part up to the root of the hierarchy. Note that the rule no_cycles is run immediately. It intercepts before any new link is added to

```
RULE no_cycles
    WHEN pair <== [ each <P, CP> | insert(P)@CP:composite_part SENT ]
    IF [ | get_part@!pair == P,
            get_composite_part@!pair == CP,
            contains(CP)@P ]
    DO INSTEAD NOTHING
END_RULE

COUPLING no_cycles CONDITION IMMEDIATE ACTION IMMEDIATE END_COUPLING
PRIORITY no_cycles 5.0 END_PRIORITY

RULE qual_rep1
    WHEN cpart <== [ each CP | insert(_)@CP:composite_part OR
                                remove(_)@CP OR
                                put_assembly_quality(_)@CP ]
    IF true
    DO update_quality@cpart;
END_RULE

COUPLING qual_rep1 CONDITION DEFERRED ACTION IMMEDIATE END_COUPLING
PRIORITY qual_rep1 4.0 END_PRIORITY

RULE qual_rep2
    WHEN apart <== [ each P | put_quality(_)@P:part ]
    IF cparts <== [ all C | !apart is_in C:composite_part ]
    DO foreach cp in cparts do
            update_quality@cp;
END_RULE

COUPLING qual_rep2 CONDITION DEFERRED ACTION IMMEDIATE END_COUPLING
PRIORITY qual_rep2 3.0 END_PRIORITY

RULE cost_rep1
    WHEN cpart <== [ each CP | insert(_)@CP:composite_part OR
                                remove(_)@CP OR
                                put_assembly_cost(_)@CP ]
    IF true
    DO update_cost@cpart;
END_RULE

COUPLING cost_rep1 CONDITION DEFERRED ACTION IMMEDIATE END_COUPLING
PRIORITY cost_rep1 4.0  END_PRIORITY

RULE cost_rep2
    WHEN apart <== [ each P | put_cost(_)@P:part ]
    IF cparts <== [ all C | !apart is_in C:composite_part ]
    DO foreach cp in cparts do
            update_cost@cp;
END_RULE

COUPLING cost_rep2 CONDITION DEFERRED ACTION IMMEDIATE END_COUPLING
PRIORITY cost_rep2 3.0 END_PRIORITY
```

FIGURE 18.7. Example RAP rule set.

the hierarchy and tests whether the new link will cause a cycle. If so, the insert operation is overridden with no alternative action taken. Note also that the repair rules are deferred. This means that triggers will be queued for each modified composite part, but repeated triggers for updates to the same composite will be elided.

18.4   Execution Model

RAP provides a general-purpose execution model, allowing alternative execution characteristics to be mixed in a variety of combinations where many rule systems only support one alternative. For example, *Condition* and *Action Modes* may be selected independently as either *Immediate* or *Deferred* (*Detached* execution is ruled out because of the limited transaction facilities of ROCK & ROLL). As the previous section has explained, the use of an EACH or ANY projection in an event specification corresponds to a *Transition Granularity* of *Tuple*, and an ALL projection corresponds to a *Transition Granularity* of *Set*.

Rules with immediate conditions and actions are executed using a recursive depth-first strategy, while deferred rules are executed using an iterative strategy, so the *Cycle Policy* is {*Iterative, Recursive*}. A numerical priority scheme allows users to prioritize rules during scheduling, and the *Scheduling Policy* is *All Sequential*. Errors during rule firing are ignored unless the rule condition or action detects the error, in which case it may choose to execute an ABORT.

RAP does not normally employ a net-effect policy. So once a rule has been triggered, the trigger is not normally removed in response to subsequent developments. However, in the case where an object is deleted, any outstanding triggers or any deferred actions that may reference the deleted object via a binding are updated to reflect the deletion. If a *Set* granularity rule has bound an association containing the deleted object, then the association is modified so that the deleted object is removed. If a *Tuple* granularity rule has bound the deleted object itself, then the associated trigger or pending action is canceled.

The dimensions for the RAP execution model are given in Table 18.2.

18.5   Implementation

The RAP extension to ROCK & ROLL is an integrated rule manager in that it is part of the kernel of the database. The ROCK & ROLL system is written in C++, and exploits persistent extensions of C++ for storage management. ROCK & ROLL is available over the WWW from http://www.cee.hw.ac.uk/Databases.

Condition-Mode	*Immediate, Deferred*
Action-Mode	*Immediate, Deferred*
Transition Granularity	*Tuple, Set*
Net-effect Policy	*No*
Cycle-Policy	*Iterative, Recursive*
Priorities	*Numerical*
Scheduling	*All Sequential*
Error Handling	*Abort, Ignore*

TABLE 18.2. Dimensions for execution model.

18.6 Conclusion

The RAP system is an example of a powerful active rule language for an object-oriented database that exploits the declarative features of the underlying passive database in the design of both event and condition languages. This has given rise to an event language that supports unification of event parameters, which, when combined with a range of consumption modes, allows unusually precise event description with corresponding reductions in space overheads compared with less precise composite event languages. The declarative language features have allowed the development of comprehensive rule analysis and optimization features for RAP [DPW96], although space precluded their description here.

The RAP system is probably most similar to Chimera (Chapter 17), which also adds active facilities to a DOOD system. The Chimera system allows more unrestrained access to intermediate states than in ROCK & ROLL, and thus has somewhat more expressive (and expensive) event detection and condition monitoring facilities; the execution model of ROCK & ROLL is more flexible than that of Chimera, which is more set-oriented. RAP differs from some earlier work on adding active functionality into deductive databases [Zan94, HD94] in not seeking to give a deductive semantics to the active rule functionality, as this is felt to complicate the semantics of the deductive language while at the same time restricting the execution model features that can be readily supported.

18.7 REFERENCES

[BFP+95] M.L. Barja, A.A.A. Fernandes, N.W. Paton, M.H. Williams, A. Dinn, and A.I. Abdelmoty. Design and Implementation of ROCK & ROLL: A Deductive Object-Oriented Database System. *Information Systems*, 20:185–211, 1995.

[BPF+94] M.L. Barja, N.W. Paton, A.A.A. Fernandes, M.H. Williams, and A. Dinn. An Effective Deductive Object-Oriented Database Through Language Integration. In J. Bocca, M. Jarke, and

C. Zaniolo, editors, *Proc. 20th Intl. Conf. on Very Large Databases (VLDB)*, pages 463–474. Morgan-Kaufmann, 1994.

[CGT90]   S. Ceri, G. Gottlob, and L. Tanca. *Logic Programming and Databases*. Springer-Verlag, Berlin, 1990.

[DPW96]   A. Dinn, N.W. Paton, and M.H. Williams. Active Rule Analysis and Optimisation in Object-Oriented Databases. 1996. submitted for publication.

[HD94]   J.V. Harrison and S.W. Dietrich. Integrating Active and Deductive Rules. In N.W. Paton and M.H. Williams, editors, *Proc. 1st Intl. Workshop on Rules In Database Systems*, pages 288–305. Springer-Verlag, 1994.

[Zan94]   C. Zaniolo. A Unified Semantics for Active and Deductive Databases. In N.W. Paton and M.H. Williams, editors, *Rules in Database Systems*. Springer-Verlag, 1994.

Part IV

Applications

19

Database Internal Applications

Suzanne M. Embury
Peter M.D. Gray

ABSTRACT
In this chapter, we consider the use of active rules to implement not user
applications but the database facilities that will later be used to support
application development. In particular, we focus on three important classes
of database functionality to which rules have been applied: integrity maintenance; support for database views and data integration; and the implementation of advanced transaction models. Finally, we consider the suitability
of ECA rules for the implementation of DBMS internals in general, and
draw some guidelines for the kind of behavior to which they can be most
successfully applied.

19.1   Introduction

While active rules were first suggested as a means of capturing the reactive behavior present in many real-world domains, database researchers
and programmers have been quick to spot the potentially rich vein of applications of ECA rules within database management systems themselves.
Database features such as integrity checking, view maintenance, security
checking, and audit trail generation all require the DBMS to respond to
some stimuli–an update to data, or an attempt to query a particular relation, for example. The ability of active rules to extend a DBMS with
new forms of behavior, without the need to modify the source code of
the system, means that an active database is an ideal platform both for
researchers, who wish to prototype and experiment with novel database
facilities [PDB93], and for application developers, who may require functionality not supported by the DBMS. Any active database can be extended
with, for example, a production rule style inference engine, novel logging
techniques, or a version management capability, simply by changing the
contents of its rule base, even though such an extension had not been envisaged by the original implementor of the system.

A wide range of proposals for the use of active rules in the implementation of database internals has appeared in the literature. A characteristic
of such research is that initial proposals demonstrate that ECA rules are a
suitable formalism for implementing the required behavior, but assume that

such rules will be generated manually by the database designer/application programmer. Subsequent work then focuses upon the design of high-level languages for specifying the new semantics declaratively, and shows how the required rules may be generated automatically from them. The clear structuring of active rules into event, condition, and action suggests a methodology with which to approach the design of compilers for such languages. For each construct in the high-level language, the compiler writer must consider how to identify the set of events for which rules must be generated, what conditions must be monitored when these events occur, and, finally, what action must be taken when situations of interest arise. Thus, the structure of the ECA rules helps to partition the code generation process into a series of smaller, more manageable stages.

In this chapter, we survey three areas that have received significant research attention–integrity maintenance (section 19.2), database views and data integration (section 19.3) and advanced transaction management (section 19.4)–and show how this methodology of compiler design applies in these different contexts. Other examples of using active rules for implementing database internals are:

- The use of ECA rules for error handling [WYW94]. Rules of this kind are triggered when exceptional situations arise, and their action is to execute some contingency plan that will allow processing to continue.

- The use of ECA rules for dynamic displays in database interfaces [PDDJ96]. Here, active rules are used to update user-interface displays when the database itself is updated, and conversely to react appropriately when the user updates the display (by copying the change to another part of the display, for example).

- The use of ECA rules to model the operational semantics of relationships [DE92, Día96]. In this proposal, declarative descriptions of relationship semantics, in terms of the delegation, propagation and anticipation of messages sent to relationship objects, are compiled into active rules that implement the required behavior.

- The use of ECA rules to maintain consistency in cooperative problem solving [eL94]. Active rules are automatically generated that inform the various problem solving agents in a system when the data over which they are computing has been updated.

- The use of ECA rules to implement forward chaining production rules [Pat95]. This proposal describes how production rules (i.e. condition-action rules) can be compiled into a set of ECA rules that will perform the equivalent inference steps.

19.2   ECA Rules for Integrity Maintenance

The problem of efficient maintenance of database integrity has long been a focus of database researchers. Briefly stated, the problem is this: given a declarative specification of some condition (called an integrity constraint, or a consistency constraint) that must be satisfied by a valid database, how can the DBMS ensure that this condition is never violated, without a corresponding unacceptable decrease in the efficiency of ordinary database access? Such constraints can range from simple local checks on single attributes, to highly complex relationships over large parts of the database. For example, one of the simplest constraint forms is the range constraint, as illustrated by the following first-order logic (FOL) expression:

$$(\forall\, p,\, a)\, person(p)\, \wedge\, age(p,\, a)\, \Rightarrow\, 0 \leq a\, \wedge a \leq 130$$

This expresses the constraint that the **age** attribute of the **person** class (or tuple) may take only values in the range 0 to 130 inclusive. Other examples of local constraints are uniqueness and optionality constraints on attributes.

More complex constraints can express conditions over multiple attributes and relationships. For example, this FOL expression describes the constraint that all postgraduate students must have a supervisor, who is an investigator for at least one of the projects on which that students works:

$$(\forall pg)postgrad(pg)\, \Rightarrow\, ((\exists s,\, pr)\, supervisor(pg,\, s)\, \wedge$$

$$project(pg,\, pr)\, \wedge\, investigator(pr,\, s))$$

ECA rules have been proposed as a suitable underlying mechanism for implementing the two major aspects of integrity maintenance: the efficient detection of constraint violations, and the execution of further updates that will restore database integrity. These two aspects are discussed below, followed by a brief summary of the way in which ECA rules can be used to implement checking of temporal integrity constraints, and constraints expressed over distributed databases.

19.2.1   ECA Rules for Checking Constraints

In its simplest form, constraint checking can be seen as evaluation of a query. The query describes violations of the constraint, so integrity is preserved if the query returns an empty results set. In general, it is a straightforward process to convert a declarative specification of an integrity constraint into a query for violations. If the language in which constraints are expressed is closely related to the query language, then it may only be necessary to identify the result variables and to negate the constraint predicate.

However, this form of constraint checking can be highly inefficient. A much better approach, as proposed by Nicolas [Nic82], is to check constraints incrementally. This approach relies on the following features of integrity constraints:

- A consistent database (i.e., one that satisfies all the integrity constraints) can only become inconsistent as a result of data update. Therefore, constraints need only be checked after an update has occurred.

- In general, the set of updates that may cause a constraint to be violated is a subset of the full set of updates expressible against a schema. For example, an update to the undergraduate records in a university database cannot violate the above constraint about postgraduates and their supervisors. Less obviously, it is also not possible to violate this constraint by deleting postgraduate students from the database. For updates of this kind, we say that the constraint is trivially satisfied.

  After each update, then, it is only necessary to check those constraints that are not trivially satisfied by that update.

- if the database is known to have been consistent before an update occurs, then it is only necessary to check the consistency of data that is affected by that update, and not the entire database. For example, if a new postgraduate student record is created, it is not necessary to recheck consistency for all the previously existing postgraduate records.

  In Nicolas's terminology, this process of specializing a constraint check according to the update that has occurred is called simplification.

These features mean that ECA rules are highly appropriate for the implementation of efficient integrity checking, and a large number of researchers have studied their use for this particular internal database application (e.g., [BG94, CW90, CFP94, Dia92, JQ92, UD92, YK92]). ECA rules can be generated that trigger only on the relevant set of update events, and in which the condition of the rule represents the check that the constraint is violated (preferably simplified relative to the triggering updates). Thus, rules for constraint checking have the general form:

```
on <update_event>
if not <constraint_predicate>
do abort or report_error
```

All the proposals follow this basic approach, but differ in the complexity of the constraint language, the number of rules generated for each constraint, the accuracy of the set of triggering events generated from each constraint, and the amount of simplification that is performed when generating the rule condition. To illustrate these differences, we will describe the process of rule generation in general, using example systems to show the effects of the different implementation choices.

The first stage of generating ECA rules from any high-level constraint specification is to identify the set of events that may cause that constraint to be violated. In fact, most proposals generate only an approximation to this set that may contain extra events for which the constraint is trivially satisfied. Providing that this approximation is always a superset of the required set, then integrity will be preserved.

All proposals for ECA-rule implementations of integrity checking use the same basic approach to the generation of the set of potentially violating updates. Each syntactic construct in the constraint language is characterized according to the update events that may violate it, given the sets of violating events for its syntactic constituents [EG95]. For example, a conjunction of predicates:

$$C \equiv A_1 \wedge \ldots \wedge A_n$$

may be violated (i.e., falsified) by any update event that may violate one of its constituent predicates:

$$FE(C) \equiv FE(A_1) \cup \ldots \cup FE(A_n)$$

where $FE(Pred)$ represents the set of update events that may falsify $Pred$ once it is satisfied. An implication $C \equiv P \Rightarrow Q$, on the other hand, may be violated by any event that falsifies Q, or that causes P to become satisfied:

$$FE(C) \equiv SE(P) \cup FE(Q)$$

Here, $SE(Pred)$ represents the set of events that may cause an initially false predicate $Pred$ to become true for some set of variable bindings. At the lowest syntactic level, a reference to some database value can be violated (made false) by a deletion event, and resatisfied (made true) by an insertion. For a full characterization of the set of events that may violate some constraint predicate, we must describe both the events that will violate a predicate form that is initially satisfied, and the events that will resatisfy that form when it is initially false. This dual characterization is required for any constraint language that supports negation, including the implicit negation present in the *implies* operator.

One significant factor in the generation of a close approximation of the set of potentially violating events is the expressiveness of the initial constraint language. In the work of Díaz [Dia92], for example, a limited form of constraint, known as a constraint equation (CE), is considered. Constraint equations allow equality or inequality constraints to be placed on values obtained by navigating from a single object [Mor84]. For example, the following CE represents the constraint on postgraduates and their supervisors given earlier:[1]

```
supervisor of postgrad :: leader of project of postgrad
```

In this case, since the language is so simple, a full characterization of the set of potentially violating events is possible. In the proposal for Starburst [CW90], on the other hand, the constraint language is much richer, and their update characterization, while giving good results in general, produces an approximation for more complex constraint forms involving aggregates. However, both these proposals fare better than that for the ODE system [JQ92]. ODE is grounded heavily in object-oriented programming, and allows the definition of methods on object classes that can modify the state of those objects arbitrarily. Since the constraint compiler cannot know which methods cause which updates, constraint checking rules must be triggered whenever any method is invoked on an object (even if it performs no updates). Thus, for ODE, the lack of semantics present in the data model means that only a very coarse approximation of the set of potentially violating events can ever be identified.

Once generated, the set of update events for which the constraint must be checked is used to form the event of the rule (or rules) that implement that constraint check. In the Starburst proposal, a single rule is generated for each constraint, which is triggered by the occurrence of any one of the identified updates. In this case, the rule so generated has the form:

```
on <potentially_violating_updates>
if exists <query_for_constraint_violations>
do <action>
```

Here, <query_for_constraint_violation> is derived directly from the initial constraint specification.

In Díaz's CE proposal, the more common approach is taken of generating a set of rules from each constraint, each one triggered by a single potentially violating event. This has the advantage of allowing more efficient constraint checking, as in each case the condition of the rule can be tailored (i.e., simplified) to the update by which it is triggered. As an illustration of this, compare the conditions of the following two rules, which might be generated

---

[1]In fact, the semantics here are slightly different, as all variables are assumed to be universally quantified in CEs. This constraint demands that the set of supervisors of each postgraduate be equal to the set of leaders of all projects associated with the student. There is no way to express our original constraint in the CE language.

as part of the implementation of the example constraint on postgraduate students:

```
on create supervisor(Pg, S)
if project(Pg, Pr) and leader(Pr, L) and not(L = S)
do <action>

on create leader(Pr, L)
if project(Pg, Pr) and supervisor(Pr, S) and not (L = S)
do <action>
```

Notice the importance, here, of being able to pass the parameters of the update event through to the condition. In Starburst, a similar effect can be achieved by making use of the virtual relations **inserted**, **deleted**, **old-updated** and **new-updated**, which describe the update that has taken place, in the rule condition. This allows a degree of incrementality in constraint checking, even if full simplification is not possible. Achieving a high-degree of simplification for arbitrarily complex predicates is as yet an unsolved problem. Díaz generates highly efficient conditions from the limited CE language, while other proposals, such as that for ODE, achieve a lesser degree of efficiency for more expressive constraint languages.

19.2.2   ECA Rules for Constraint Repair

We have considered the generation of the events and conditions for constraint checking rules. What of the rule actions? If the rule's function is simply to avoid the creation of an illegal database state, then the action must either prevent the violating update from occurring (if the rule is triggered before the update takes place), or undo its effects (if the rule is triggered after the update has completed). In the former case, rule actions will have the general form:

```
do instead <display_error_message>
```

In the latter case, actions will issue a **rollback** or **abort** command. For set-valued rule systems, such as Starburst, this last case is the only feasible alternative (since the details of the set-valued update, which may be required for the evaluation of the condition, will not be known until it has taken place).

In their original proposal for integrity constraints in Starburst, Ceri and Widom suggested a third option, which was to allow database designers to specify the action themselves. The action's function would then be to perform some further updates that would restore consistency. For example, if we had a constraint that no employee could earn more than 45K, the action in response to a violation of this constraint could be to update the illegal salary to the maximum legal value of 45K. This technique is called integrity repair (or transaction repair), and it is clearly preferable to a simple-minded rollback where possible.

An even better solution, however, would be for the constraint compiler itself to generate the repair action automatically from the declarative constraint specification [CFPT94, DE92, Ger94, IK93, ST94]. One of the earliest attempts at automatic integrity repair is by Urban et al. [UKN92]. In this work, each high-level constraint is converted into a number of skolemised horn clauses, from which all elements of the constraint rules (i.e. event, condition *and* repairing action) are generated [UD92]. However, the process is not completely automatic, since there will generally be more than one possible repair update for each constraint. After rules are generated, then, the database designer must use his or her deeper knowledge of the application domain to choose between the possible repairs. In addition to this compile-time assistance, user intervention is often required at runtime, to select from a set of possible values during execution of the repair itself. For example, the following rule (based on the example given in [UKN92]) maintains the constraint that the commander of every ship must be a citizen of the country in which that ship is registered:

```
on modify country_of_registry(s, c)
if not exists o such that commander(s, o) and
                          citizen_of(o, c))
  do select o1 from officer where citizen_of(o1, c)
     create new assignment o2
     modify commander(s, o2)
     modify officer_assigned(o2, o1)
```

Here, the select construct in the repair action requests the user to choose a new officer for the ship from the set of officers who are citizens of the country in which the ship is now registered.

One problem with this approach to constraint repair, identified by Urban et al., is that of anomalous rule behavior. Since constraint rules may now themselves perform updates, it is possible that the process of repairing one constraint violation may itself cause further violations of other constraints. In general, this presents no problem, as it will simply trigger further constraint rules to repair the new violations. Where difficulties may occur, however, is if the repair for one of these violations causes the first violation to reappear. This situation causes an infinite cycle of rule firing in which violations are continually repaired and recreated. Urban et al. suggest a hierarchical approach to this problem, in which rules are associated with a particular level of processing and cannot be triggered from outside that level.

In fact, much of the later work on automatic integrity repair using ECA rules has concentrated on this problem of overcoming anomalous rule behavior. Ceri et al. give a particularly thorough analysis of this problem (and indeed of all other aspects of automatic repair) [CFPT94]. However, other problems with the ECA-rule approach to repair have since been identified [Ger96, Emb96]. These are summarized by Gertz as:

> "The drawback of [active rule approaches to repair is] that they in general realize an autonomous repair of constraint violations. Though the user can choose between automatically derived repairing triggers at compile-time, these triggers are kept fixed at runtime. Once a repair is triggered in an inconsistent database, there is no way to interact with the repair process. Furthermore, often a repair of violations may introduce new violations which are then automatically repaired, and so on. Hence it is difficult for the user to identify why what happened. Interesting questions are also what happens if the result state does not reflect the user's intention or the application requirements? How can she/he choose between possible alternative repairs?" [Ger96], p. 42.

An additional problem is seen when multiple constraint violations have occurred, and a single repair strategy must be constructed that repairs them all. This is essentially a nondeterministic search problem: the repair for each individual violation must be chosen so that it does not prevent repairs being found for the violations that are still to be considered. Unfortunately, however suitable it might be for dealing with single violations, the forward-chaining search provided by ECA rules is too inefficient, both in terms of time and space, to yield a practical solution to the more general repair problem in which an arbitrary number of violations may exist.

19.2.3 ECA Rules for Non Standard Constraint Checking

ECA rules have also been applied to the implementation of two variations on the standard form of constraint checking: namely, checking of temporal constraints [Coh89, GL93, TC94] and of static constraints over distributed databases [CW93, CGMW94, GSE+97].

Temporal constraints (also called transition or dynamic constraints) describe legal sequences of state changes, rather than the static conditions over individual states described by ordinary integrity constraints. Examples of temporal constraints are:

- the age of a person can only ever increase,

- a student who has failed a particular exam twice may not retake it,

- only staff who have reached their productivity targets for the last three years are eligible for promotion.

Constraints of this kind are usually expressed using a form of temporal logic, with operators to express the fact that some formula was true in a previous state, or has been true ever since some other formula became true, for example. Gertz and Lipeck [GL93] convert such constraints into transition graphs describing the allowable sequences of state changes. The edges of these graphs represent particular state changes (i.e., updates), and they are labeled with static (i.e., non-temporal) conditions, representing the preconditions necessary for that state change to take place. An ECA-rule is generated for each edge of the transition graph, whose event is the update represented by the edge, and whose condition succeeds when the edge's formula is not satisfied by the pre-updated state. The default rule action is to rollback the current transaction, or the database designer may specify some alternative action if required.

Toman and Chomicki [TC94] give a different theoretical underpinning for what amounts to a similar approach. They use ECA rules to maintain a record of the values that satisfy some temporal predicate required for checking a temporal constraint. For example, consider the constraint that students may not retake an exam if they have already failed it twice. Three ECA rules must be generated to check this constraint, and two stored sets of values must be maintained. One rule watches for students who fail an exam for the first time, and records the details in the first stored value. The second rule fires when students recorded in this way fail the same exam. These are the students who have failed for a second time, and their details are recorded in the second stored value. The third ECA-rule fires when one of these students attempts to retake the same exam. Its action is to rollback the current transaction.

In another variant on standard integrity checking, Ceri and Widom [CW93] have proposed the use of ECA rules for incremental maintenance of certain constraints in distributed database systems.[2] Two kinds of constraint are considered: existence dependencies, which require that data should exist in one database if related data is present in the other, and value dependencies, which require that the value of data in one database should be determined by the value of related data in the other. The ECA rules generated from these constraints take the same basic form as those generated for non-distributed constraints, except that the condition may include a remote query to retrieve data from another database, and the action may invoke a remote transaction in order to propagate the effects of some change to the other database.

Grufman et al. [GSE+97] present an approach to distributing a wider class of constraints.[3] They suggest the use of ECA rules to remotely mate-

---

[2]The proposal is actually limited to constraints expressed over just two databases, but the basic principles could be expanded to cover an arbitrary distribution.

[3]They focus on constraints involving only universally quantified variables, although the approach is more widely applicable.

rialize sets of values required for the constraint check, so that all the data required to test for consistency is local to one particular database.

19.3   ECA Rules for Views and Data Integration

The growth of interest in the field of data warehousing has triggered a corresponding resurgence of research activity in the area of database views, and techniques for implementing them efficiently [Sin95]. Views on database schemas were originally aimed at the provision of restricted versions of full database schemas that were tailored to the needs of particular users, i.e. to their particular world view. Views also improve data security, as users are prevented from accessing (or even being aware of) the parts of the schema that are not explicitly included within their own particular view.

In addition to the inclusion within a view of whole classes or relations from the underlying (concrete) schema, it is also possible to specify virtual classes that are derived from the underlying database in some way. For example, a view of a university database containing data about undergraduate and postgraduate students as separate classes might define a single, virtual class student which covered both these concepts. The set of instances of this virtual class would be the union of the sets of instances of the undergraduate and postgraduate classes, and its attributes would be those attributes of the two concrete classes that are meaningful to the more general concept of a student. A virtual class like this would typically be defined by some sort of high-level description, for example:

```
define view class student
     as undergraduate union postgraduate
with attributes name(student) = ...
                age(student) = ...
                year(student) = ...
```

Alternatively, a virtual class might be specified as the subset of the instances of a concrete class that satisfies some predicate. For example:

```
define view mature_student
     as undergraduate where age > 22
with attributes
```

This virtual class has exactly the same attributes as the undergraduate class but contains only those instances representing students who are older than 22.

Ideally, a DBMS will provide seamless support for views so that the user can access both concrete and view data in the same way (i.e., without having to know which classes or relations are concrete and which are virtual). In order to meet this criterion, the implementor of a view mechanism must consider two issues: how to provide efficient retrieval of view data, and how to deal with attempts to update the view classes or relations.

One way to solve the view retrieval problem is to materialize the view class or relation by physically storing the derived form of the data [GS95]. This removes the need to recalculate the view data every time it is accessed, and means that retrieval for views is just as efficient as access to concrete data. However, the materialized view must be kept consistent when the underlying data is updated, so the view retrieval problem is simply transformed into the view maintenance problem.

Updates to views are problematic because they must be mapped into updates to the concrete data that underlies them, and in general there may be more than one legitimate way to do this. Consider, for example, the attempt to create a new instance of the virtual **student** class defined earlier. This must be transformed into either the creation of a new **undergraduate** instance, or a new **postgraduate** instance, but the original update does not give enough information for the DBMS to be able to decide which update is required in any given case. This is called the view update problem.

More recently, views have been seen as a way of integrating data from multiple distributed, and possible heterogeneous, data sources, both for data warehousing and in the more general context of distributed information systems. In data warehousing, data from the various production databases used by an organization is copied to a separate database (the data warehouse) where it is filtered and transformed in order to integrate it with the existing data. The idea here is that more complex analysis, such as that required for long-term planning and decision support, can be run against the data warehouse without affecting the performance or availability of the production databases.

In the wider context of distributed information management, components known as integration mediators [Wie92] have been proposed as building blocks for the construction of large-scale distributed information systems. An integration mediator encapsulates the knowledge required to integrate a number of underlying information sources.[4] Other components that need to access this data can request it from the integration mediator, rather than having to reimplement the code to perform the integration themselves. In addition, the mediator can buffer these other components against changes to the underlying data sources. The result is a more modular system architecture that is easier to maintain and more resilient to change.

Active rules have been proposed as suitable implementation platforms for all these aspects of database views, from traditional views, both materialized and virtual, to views for data integration. In the remainder of this

---

[4]In fact, not all the underlying sources need be databases. Some may be knowledge bases, inference engines, statistical packages, or constraint solvers, for example [GPF+97].

section, we survey some of these proposals.

19.3.1   ECA Rules for Database Views

One of the earliest applications of ECA rules to the implementation of a view mechanism, by Stonebraker et al. [SJGP90], illustrated how rules could be used to trap accesses to view data, and divert the query to the concrete data on which the view is defined. For example, using this approach, a hypothetical implementation of the student view given above would include the rules:

```
on get_name(Student, Name)
if UnderGrad = cast(undergraduate, Student),
do instead get_name(UnderGrad, Name)

on get_name(Student, Name)
if PostGrad = cast(postgraduate, Student),
do instead get_name(PostGrad, Name)
```

Here, cast(Class, Instance) returns a value if Instance is also a member of Class. The result is the identifier of the corresponding instance in Class. Notice that we need the ability to replace the action which triggered the rule with the rule's own action (do instead) to be able to use this approach to view implementation.

Rules such as this can be generated automatically from the original high-level view definition. Stonebraker et al. also showed how active rules could be used to solve the view-update problem, by allowing a particular update policy to be associated with each view. Under this scheme, a rule is created for each possible update to each virtual class, relation, or attribute, whose action describes the update that must be made to the base data in order to create the effect of the required update to the view. This is not an ideal solution, however, as the database designer is forced to commit to one particular policy per update at the time when the view is defined. In reality, this may not be a decision that can be made outside the context of the actual update. We saw this earlier with the example update of creating a new instance of the virtual student class. We cannot decide a priori that all new students will be undergraduates, since some may actually be postgraduate students. A safer, if less flexible, alternative therefore is to use a set of active rules triggered on updates to view data, with the default update of fail or rollback, to prevent any attempted updates to virtual data.

Active rules can also be used to implement the alternative strategy of explicitly materializing the view data within the database [CW91, ODSD94, UO94]. The problem here is to find an efficient way of ensuring that the materialized view remains consistent when the underlying data is updated.

In other words, the view should be maintained *incrementally*, so that only those parts of the view that are directly affected by the update are rematerialized.[5] This can be achieved by generating an active rule of the form:

```
on <update to base data>
if <set of changes to view required> = C and C <> 0
do <update view with C>
```

for each type of update on the base data that might cause a change in the contents of some view class or relation. For example, to materialize the mature_student view defined above, we must create the following rule:

```
on create undergraduate U
if age(U) > 22
do create mature_student MS
    let name(MS) = name(U)
    let age(MS) = age(U)
    let year(MS) = age(U)
```

Similar rules are also required to maintain view consistency when undergraduate student records are deleted, or when some attribute of an undergraduate instance is updated.

As with virtual views, the active rules required to implement a materialized view can be generated automatically from the initial specification of the view. For example, Ceri and Widom [CW91] propose a simple approach to rule generation in the context of a relational system, in which exactly four active rules are generated for each concrete table appearing in the view definition–one triggered on /tt insert events on that table, one triggered on /tt delete events, and two triggered on **update** events. However, a more efficient approach can be taken in which the events for which rules are generated are only those base data updates that may cause a change in the contents of the view [BLT86]. This set of events can be identified using the same sort of analysis that is used to identify the events that may cause a violation of an integrity constraint. The difference here is that we are interested in update events that can alter the value of some expression, rather than the set of events that can cause a true predicate to become false.

The conditions of rules for the incremental maintenance of a materialized view must compute the changes that must be made to the view as a result of the update that has occurred. Incremental conditions for active rules can be generated using the same basic techniques proposed for incremental view maintenance in non-active contexts, as in both settings the aim is to generate some expression that will evaluate the updates required. The

---

[5]This notion of incremental maintenance of views has much in common with the incremental checking of integrity constraints described in section 19.2.

most common approach is to turn the view definition expression into a set of differential expressions in which changes (i.e., additions and deletions) to the results set are described in terms of changes (again, additions and deletions) to the subexpressions. This is the basic idea of the approach taken by Ceri and Widom [CW91], for example. For an update on base table T, they generate incremental versions of the view definition expression by replacing references to T with the special transition tables **inserted T**, **deleted T**, **old-updated T**, and **new-updated T**, giving a set expression that computes just those tuples that have been added to (or deleted from) the view relation as a result of the transaction. The rules generated in this way fall into two categories–those that deal with deletions of data, and those that deal with insertions of data. All rules are prioritized so that the deletion rules are triggered before the insertion rules.

While ECA rules can also be used to allow updates to materialized views that are propagated to the base data, as we described for virtual views, all of the drawbacks of that approach also apply in this context.[6] Chen et al. [CHM94] have proposed a partial solution by generalizing the actions of their ECA rules to allow disjunctions of alternative actions. Thus, update rules containing several different update policies can be generated from view definitions. When updates occur, all possible rule firings are investigated, and alternatives that lead to violations of integrity constraints or other view dependencies are discarded. If only one of the possible rule firings results in a consistent database, then this state is committed. Otherwise, the consistent alternatives are presented to the user for selection.

19.3.2   ECA Rules for Data Integration

While the concept of a database view was originally seen as a way of partitioning a single large schema into smaller, more manageable units, more recently views have also been applied to the problem of integrating data from several distributed schemas. And, naturally, active rules have also been used to implement view mechanisms in this new context. Their role, however, is slightly different from that discussed in section 19.3.1 above, in that in these distributed systems, rules become a tool for managing communication between autonomous components (or, at least, for detecting the need for communication and triggering the necessary message passing). Thus, rules may be important for view maintenance in such systems, even when the view component itself is not implemented as a rulebase.

This point is clearly illustrated by the use of rules in the WHIPS data warehousing architecture [HGMW+95]. In this project, a central reposi-

---

[6]In fact, the rules themselves take exactly the same form as those used to handle updates to virtual views, the only difference being that the rule action is executed *in addition to*, and not *instead of*, the update to the view.

tory (i.e., the warehouse) containing an integrated materialized view of a number of underlying data sources must be maintained. In the ideal situation, each of the data sources would have an active capability, so that rules could be planted in each one to inform the integrator component (i.e., the software module responsible for maintaining consistency of the warehouse's contents) when updates have occurred. However, many of the data sources to be integrated may be legacy sources, which are not active and which cannot be easily extended with any such facility. In these cases, the WHIPS architecture places a monitor component between the legacy source and the integrator. The monitor is responsible for detecting when changes in its source have occurred (for example, by polling the transaction log or by arranging for regular differential snapshots of the source's contents to be created). Since the monitor is a custom component, it can be relied upon to have an active rule facility, and so communication of these updates to the integrator can be handled by rules.

In the WHIPS project, the incremental integration of these changes into the warehouse/view is also managed by rules, although at present these are generated manually. Research into the implementation of mediators for data integration, however, is already tackling the problems of automatically generating rule sets from high-level descriptions of the required integration [Con95, PGMU96, ZHK96]. For example, the Squirrel mediator generator [ZHKF95, ZHK96] compiles high-level descriptions of matching conditions into a set of ECA rules. A matching condition is a test that may be applied to pairs of entities from distinct data sources to determine whether they both represent the same real-world entity or not. The generated mediator is able to answer queries about method objects efficiently by maintaining a copy of the data needed to perform the matching operation, and by storing a cache of previously matched objects. Both these sets of data are a form of materialized view, and so can be kept consistent and up-to-date by active rules generated under the principles described earlier.

19.4   ECA Rules for Advanced Transactions and Updates

In the previous section, we saw how active rules have been used to propagate change notifications between components in distributed systems. The potential value of ECA rules in coordinating complex multi-agent activities has also been investigated in another context–namely, that of advanced transaction models for supporting long-running activities [DHL90], such as those found in process modeling and design applications. Conventional transaction models with the well-known ACID properties (Atomicity, Consistency, Isolation, and Durability) are not suitable for modeling such activities. It is not practical, for example, to use standard locking techniques to guarantee isolation of transactions when they may run for days or weeks. The impact on data availability for other transactions is too severe. However, relaxing the isolation property also compromises atomicity [RS95], since rollback is now no longer guaranteed to correctly undo all the effects of the transaction.

Recognition of these problems has prompted investigation into different transaction models specially designed for supporting long-duration activities. Most of these models allow transactions to be nested inside other transactions, and dependencies to be specified between otherwise independent transactions, so that if one commits (or aborts), then the other must also commit (or abort). Sets of related transactions may be chained to describe complex activities, and special visibility or conflict resolution policies may be defined that are tailored to the needs of these activities. The standard notion of rollback is replaced with compensation, in which each transaction can be associated with another transaction (its compensating transaction) which is its semantic dual. In other words, execution of the compensating transaction is guaranteed to restore the database to a consistent state in which the effects of the first transaction have been annulled.

The use of rules to specify and manage the complex control flows implied by these extended transaction models was suggested by Dayal et al. [DHL90]. For example, chaining of transactions T_1 and T_2 can be achieved by a rule that is triggered on the commitment of T_1. The condition of the rule may be used to check that any preconditions on chaining are satisfied, and the action simply starts execution of T_2. Similarly, an abort-dependency between transactions T_1 and T_2 can be implemented by a very simple rule of the form:

```
on abort T1
if true
do abort T2
```

While active rules of this kind may provide a very general and flexible mechanism by which to glue transactions together to model long-running activities, they remain highly procedural. It is difficult to infer the exact form of the activity that has been modeled from the set of rules created for it. A far better solution is to provide some higher-level formalism in which the semantics of long-lived activities can be specified, and from which active rules can be generated to coordinate transaction execution. Geppert and Dittrich [GD94] have shown how this may be achieved for transaction models specified according to the ACTA framework [CR92]. ACTA is a generalized framework for specifying and comparing different transaction models, using a small set of fundamental concepts. In particular, ACTA allows the description of different types of dependencies between transactions by the expression of predicates over the history of transaction execution. So, for example, an abort-dependency between transactions T_1 and T_2, given a history H, would be specified as:

$$Abort_{T_1} \in H \Rightarrow Abort_{T_2}$$

Geppert and Dittrich show how to convert ACTA predicates of this kind onto ECA rules that will implement the given semantics [GD94]. Rules are triggered on the occurrence of transaction primitives, such as `begin`, `commit`, and `abort`. Their conditions check any necessary pre- or post-conditions, and their actions either reject the event (if it is invalid in the current context) or ensure that the required semantics are followed by raising further associated events.

One type of long-running activity that has proved particularly amenable to implementation by active rules is the *workflow*. A workflow is some complex process, usually involving several processing agents (possibly working in parallel) that must be performed by some organization. Example workflows are arranging a mortgage from a building society, and processing an expense claim within some business organization. The task of a workflow management system (WfMS) is to assist in the design of workflows by providing suitable editing and analysis facilities, and in the execution (enactment) of workflows, by scheduling the workload amongst the available agents and by monitoring its progress.[7] It is in the implementation of this second aspect, of workflow enactment, that ECA rules have been employed [BJ94, GKT95, KLRSR95].

The enactment of a workflow requires the coordination of the execution of the steps of the workflow, according to some pre-specified partial ordering of steps. This can be achieved by using rules in a similar manner to that described above for handling chained transactions. Kappel et al. [KLRSR95], for example, show how different rule sets can be generated to implement and-branching, exclusive-or-branching, and inclusive-or-branching of processes. A rule is generated for each branched process P which has the general form:

```
on <end_of_preceding_activity>
if <precondition_for_execution_of_P>
do <schedule_process_P>
```

For an and-branching, in which all processes must be executed when the preceding one is complete, all rules have the same condition part (so that all the branched processes will be invoked when this condition is true). For an exclusive-or-branching, all the rules have mutually-exclusive conditions (so that only one of the branched activities is scheduled for execution). For an inclusive-or-branching, rule conditions are different but need not be

---

[7]It may be argued whether these kind of workflow management facilities are truly internal database applications, or whether the DBMS is really an internal facility for the WfMS.

mutually-exclusive (so that a subset of the subsequent activities may be executed).

Before any step may be enacted, however, the WfMS must select the agent (or agents) that will be responsible for its processing. This selection must be made according to the rules laid down by the organization, called agent selection policies. Policies may range from the highly general, such as allocate tasks to the agent with the lowest workload, to the highly specific, such as "temporary staff may not carry out any task with requires access to the safe in office 21." Each agent has an agenda (or worklist) of tasks that it is responsible for carrying out. An agent selection rule, therefore, chooses a suitable agent and updates the worklist of that agent, whenever some new task needs to be performed. Rules can also be used within the agent itself, to initiate processing when a task is placed on the agent's worklist.

A further application for active rules in workflow management is in monitoring the progress of workflow enactment, so that remedial action may be taken when some error occurs. Error conditions in this context are often complex, and an efficient implementation requires the ability to trigger rules on composite events [GKT95]. Events of this kind include negation events (i.e., events that are triggered when some other event has *not* occurred within some specified time interval), and time events, both absolute and relative. They enable the WfMS to monitor progress with respect to deadlines and timeouts, and to enforce policy constraints such as "expense claims must be submitted within one month of incurring the expense."

ECA rules seem to be particularly well suited to workflow enactment, as they allow the WfMS to react quickly and intelligently when the organizational context changes, even if this occurs in the middle of process enactment [KLRSR95]. Since rules can easily be added to or deleted from running systems, it is easy to keep agent selection policies up to date. Even more critically, rules can be used to trigger dynamic rescheduling of tasks in response to, for example, machinery failure or staff illness.

19.5   Conclusion

An active rule facility has a number of advantages as a mechanism for implementing database internal applications. Perhaps the most significant of these is the ability to extend an active database system with new functionalities simply by creating the rules that describe the required behavior. No modification or recompilation of source code is necessary. A further advantage is the ease with which the rule bases of many active databases can be modified. The ability to selectively add and delete rules from an operational database system is important for the implementation of database features, since it means that those features can also be selectively added and deleted. This is an obvious advantage for modern business applications, for example, which must keep pace with the changing semantics of the environment in which they operate. Integrity constraints, agent selection policies in workflow systems, and view maintenance strategies may all need to be altered over the lifetime of an application. Conventional implementation strategies, such as the modification of method code, do not provide such flexibility.

Programming an application using ECA rules, however, is itself a difficult task. It is all too easy for a fallible human programmer to omit rules for some important situations, or to generate rules that will never be triggered, particularly when modeling complex data integration tasks or coordinating the processing of multiple processing agents. Moreover, ECA rules are too low-level an expression of database semantics to be understandable to nonexpert users. This can mean that it is difficult to generate meaningful diagnostic error messages from ECA rules.

The solution to both these problems, as we have seen, is to allow the new behavior to be described using some high-level (preferably declarative) language, from which the necessary active rules can be generated automatically. This approach has the advantage that users do not need to be trained rule programmers in order to gain the benefits of the active rule capability. A second advantage is that the process of extending the behavior of a database management system becomes simply a matter of creating a new compiler component for the high-level language, and the changes required are, by and large, localized away from the existing system code. As we have mentioned earlier, the structured nature of active rules provides a useful discipline for compiler writers, and can often act as a framework for formally proving that the rules generated do indeed meet the initial specification. In fact, the experiences reported above in the automatic generation of ECA rules suggest that such rules represent a half-way house between procedural and declarative code. They combine enough procedural aspects to allow the possibility of efficient implementation, while retaining enough structure to allow the DBMS to be able to manipulate and reason about them intelligently. However, the business of automatically generating an efficient rule set from a wide range of high-level specifications is still an open research problem.

One seeming advantage of ECA rules for implementing database internals is their apparent modularity. When generating rules for a new functionality, the programmer can concentrate simply on the set of rules needed for the description of that particular semantics. However, if active rules are really to be used to implement database internals, and not just for prototyping prior to some more conventional implementation, we must expect ECA-rule implementations for several database functionalities to be able to coexist in the same DBMS. Since researchers have so far focused on the implementation of individual features, the practicality of a DBMS in which multiple features are implemented as ECA rules has not yet been established. Database internals tend to generate several rules from each high-level construct, and it is as yet an open question whether current active databases are able to process the large rule sets that would be required efficiently enough to be practically usable.

Another problem that arises when large rule sets are generated is that of controlling the interactions between rules. In many cases, we can rely on the standard rule mechanism to handle such interactions. So, for example, the implementor of a materialized view mechanism need not worry about whether the updates triggered by the ECA rules will violate any integrity constraints. Since updates executed by rule actions are themselves events, any relevant constraint checking rules will also be triggered and will abort the entire transaction if any inconsistencies are detected. Unfortunately, in other cases, rule interactions can cause unexpected and undesirable effects. At one end of the spectrum, such effects are irritating but essentially harmless. For example, on commitment of some transaction, a number of time-consuming constraint repair rules may be fired, only to be followed by execution of a transaction management rule that causes an unconditional rollback of the entire transaction. In this case, some redundant processing is carried out, but the correct database state is eventually reached.

At the other end of the spectrum, execution of rule sets may terminate in an unexpected, incorrect database state, or may fail to terminate completely. As an example of the former kind of undesirable effect, consider the execution of a compensating transaction, that has been triggered after a number of constraint repair rules have been processed. The compensating transaction is designed to undo the effects of the initial, unrepaired transaction; it's creator could know nothing about the repair updates that have been found to be necessary in this particular case. Therefore, its execution may result in only a partial retraction of the original transaction, producing a database state that does not correspond to the true real-world situation. As an example of ECA-rule interactions that may cause non-termination, consider the situation when a view update rule causes a violation of a constraint. This, in turn, causes a repair rule to be fired, which executes the update that triggered the initial view update. In such a case, the two rules will fire repeatedly, resulting in non-termination of the computation.

A rule precedence mechanism offers a partial solution to these problems. It would allow us, for example, to state that all rules that cause unconditional rollback of a transaction should be executed before constraint-repair rules, and thus avoid the problem of redundant repair generation. It is extremely difficult, however, to generate the correct relative precedences even for rule sets generated from just a single high-level specification, let alone coordinate the necessary rule firings for multiple rule sets generated from multiple compilers. Nor could rule precedences solve the problem of non-termination illustrated by our constraint and view repair example.

It appears, then, that the practicality of the ECA-rule approach to the implementation of database internals depends in some measure on our ability to analyze arbitrary sets of rules for conflicts and dependencies. The current state of the art in this area is surveyed in Chapter 3. For collections of rules generated from the same compiler (i.e., the same specification sublanguage), it may be easier to reason about rule interactions in terms of the higher-level, declarative specifications rather than the low-level rules, but this is not practical when it comes to analyzing interactions between rules generated from different compilers. It would be necessary to generate an additional analysis component for each existing sublanguage every time a new functionality was added to the system. The only hope of a more general solution in the short term is to exploit the uniformity of the generated ECA rules, and to accept the reduced amount of analysis that can be performed on their low-level form. This approach has a conceptual simplicity that is attractive–no matter how many extensions we make to the system, only one rule analyzer is required.

Having considered the current proposals for ECA-rule implementations of database functionalities, what lessons can be drawn about the kind of internal applications that are most suitable for this implementation technique? ECA rules appear to work most successfully when applied to problems that do not require overly complex conditions or actions. In particular, the state change that must be effected by the rules should be locatable using deterministic (database) search, rather than nondeterministic (state-space) search. Thus, ECA rules are suitable for view maintenance, for example, in which the update is computed by an ordinary database query, but are less successful when applied to integrity repair, in which the required update must be generated by (at the very least) some form of backtracking search through a number of alternatives. This problem becomes particularly acute when several ECA rules must coordinate their efforts to produce a globally consistent solution, as we saw with integrity repair. A similar situation may occur in workflow systems, where an optimal assignment of agents to tasks must be achieved. This is the downside of the modularity of ECA rules, which makes it difficult, if not impossible, to impose any guiding search principles on their execution.

On the other hand, one area in which active rules do seem to have been particularly successful is in handling communication between distributed, autonomous components. In such systems, rules are used to cope with the unpredictability of incoming requests, and also to monitor situations of interest in remote data sources. In both cases, the rules themselves are relatively simple, although their execution may trigger the invocation of more complex, non-rule-based processing steps within components. In the future, rules may find their role in the implementation of database internal applications focused on the handling of simple search tasks required for the coordination of components with more complex processing abilities.

19.6 References

[BG94]   N. Bassiliades and P.M.D Gray. CoLan: A Functional Constraint Language and Its Implementation. *Data and Knowl-*

edge Engineering, 14:203–249, 1994.

[BJ94]   C. Bussler and S. Jablonski. Implementing Agent Coordination for Workflow Management Systems Using Active Database Systems. In J. Widom and S. Charavarthy, editors, *Proc. 4th Int. Workshop on Research in Data Engineering (RIDE -ADS)*, pages 53–59. IEEE, 1994.

[BLT86]   J.A. Blakeley, P.-A. Larson, and F.W. Tompa. Efficiently Updating Materialised Views. In C. Zaniolo, editor, *Proc. of SIGMOD '86*, pages 61–71, Washington D.C., USA, May 1986. ACM Press.

[CFP94]   S. Ceri, P. Fraternali, and S. Paraboschi. Constraint Management in Chimera. *Data Engineering Bulletin*, 17(2):4–8, June 1994.

[CFPT94]   S. Ceri, P. Fraternali, S. Paraboschi, and L. Tanca. Automatic Generation of Production Rules for Integrity Maintenance. *ACM TODS*, 19(3):367–422, September 1994.

[CGMW94]   S.S. Chawathe, H. Garcia-Molina, and J. Widom. Flexible Constraint Management for Autonomous Distributed Databases. *Data Engineering Bulletin*, 17(2):23–27, June 1994.

[CHM94]   I.-M.A. Chen, R. Hull, and D. McLeod. Local Ambiguity and Derived Data Update. In J. Widom and S. Chakravarthy, editors, *Proc. of the 4th Intl. Workshop on Research Issues in Data Engineering (RIDE'94): Active Database Systems*, pages 77–86, Houston, Texas, February 1994. IEEE Computer Society Press.

[Coh89]   D. Cohen. Compiling Complex Database Transition Triggers. In J. Clifford, B. Lindsay, and D. Maier, editors, *Proc. of SIGMOD 89*, pages 225–234, Portland, Oregon, 1989. ACM Press.

[Con95]   NIIIP Consortium. NIIIP Reference Architecture: Concepts and Guidelines. Cycle 0, Revision 6. NIIIP Publication NTR95-01, November 1995.

[CR92]   P.K. Chrysanthis and K. Ramamritham. ACTA: The Saga Continues. In A.K. Elmagarmid, editor, *Database Transaction Models for Advanced Applications*, Series in Data Management Systems, Chapter 10, pages 349–397. Morgan Kaufmann Publishers, San Mateo, CA, 1992.

[CW90]   S. Ceri and J. Widom. Deriving Production Rules for Con-
           straint Maintenance. In *16th Intl. Conf. on Very Large
           Databases, Brisbane*, pages 567–577. Morgan Kaufman, 1990.

[CW91]   S. Ceri and J. Widom. Deriving Production Rules for In-
           cremental View Maintenance. In R. Camps G.M. Lohman,
           A. Sernadas, editor, *17th Intl. Conf on Very Large Databases*,
           pages 577–589. Morgan Kaufmann, 1991.

[CW93]   S. Ceri and J. Widom. Managing Semantic Heterogene-
           ity with Production Rules and Persistent Queries. In
           R. Agrawal, S. Baker, and D. Bell, editors, *19th Intl. Conf.
           on Very Large Databases*, pages 108–119. Morgan Kaufmann,
           1993.

[DE92]   O. Diaz and S.M. Embury. Generating Active Rules from
           High-Level Specifications. In R. Lucas P.M.D. Gray, editor,
           *Advanced Database Systems - Proc. British National Confer-
           ence on Databases 10*, pages 227–243. Springer-Verlag LNCS
           series, 1992.

[DHL90]   U. Dayal, M. Hsu, and R. Ladin. Organising Long-Running
           Activities with Triggers and Transactions. In H. Garcia-
           Molina and H.V. Jagadish, editors, *Proc. of SIGMOD '90*,
           pages 204–214, Atlantic City, May 1990. ACM Press.

[Dia92]   O. Diaz. Deriving Rules for Constraint Maintenance in an
           Object-Oriented Database. In I. Ramos A.M. Tjoa, editor,
           Proc. Intl. Conf. on Databases and Expert Systems DEXA,
           pages 332–337. Springer-Verlag, 1992.

[Día96]   O. Díaz. The Operational Semantics of User-Defined Rela-
           tionships in Object-Oriented Database Systems. *Data and
           Knowledge Engineering*, 16(3):223–240, 1996.

[EG95]   S.M. Embury and P.M.D. Gray. Compiling a Declarative,
           High-Level Language for Semantic Integrity Constraints. In
           R. Meersman and L. Mark, editors, *Proc. of 6th IFIP TC-2
           Working Conf. on Data Semantics*, Atlanta, GA, May 1995.
           Chapman and Hall.

[cL94]   K. el Hindi and B. Lings. Using Truth Maintenance Systems
           to Solve the Data Consistency Problem. In M.L. Brodie,
           M. Jarke, and M.P. Papazoglou, editors, *Proc. of the 2nd
           Intl. Conference on Cooperative Information Systems*, pages
           192–201, Toronto, Canada, May 1994.

[Emb96]   S.M. Embury. Coping wih Constraint Violation: The Prac-
            tical Face of Database Integrity. In S. Conrad, H.-J. Klein,
            and K.-D. Schewe, editors, *Proc. of the 6th Intl. Workshop
            on Foundations of Models and Languages for Data and Ob-
            jects: Integrity in Databases*, pages 141–148, SchloßDastuhl,
            Germany, September 1996.

[GD94]   A. Geppert and K. Dittrich. Rule-Based Implementation
            of Transaction Model Specifications. In N.W. Paton and
            M.H. Williams, editors, *Proc. 1st Int. Workshop on Rules In
            Database Systems*, pages 127–142. Springer-Verlag, 1994.

[Ger94]   M. Gertz. Specifying Reactive Integrity Control for Active
            Databases. In J. Widom and S. Chakravarthy, editors, *Proc.
            of the 4th Intl. Workshop on Research Issues in Data Engi-
            neering (RIDE'94): Active Database Systems*, pages 62–70,
            Houston, Texas, USA, February 1994. IEEE Computer So-
            ciety Press.

[Ger96]   M. Gertz. An Extensible Framework for Repairing Con-
            straint Violations. In S. Conrad, H.-J. Klein, and K.-D.
            Schewe, editors, *Proc. of the 6th Intl. Workshop on Foun-
            dations of Models and Languages for Data and Objects: In-
            tegrity in Databases*, pages 41–56, SchloßDastuhl, Germany,
            September 1996.

[GKT95]   A. Geppert, M. Kradolfer, and D. Tombros. Realisation
            of Cooperative Agents Using an Active Object-Oriented
            Database Management System. In T. Sellis, editor, *Proc.
            of 2nd Intl. Workshop on Rules in Database Systems (RIDS
            '95)*, Lecture Notes in Computer Science 985, pages 327–341,
            Glyfada, Athens, Greece, September 1995. Springer-Verlag.

[GL93]   M. Gertz and U.W. Lipeck. Deriving Integrity Maintaining
            Triggers from Transition Graphs. In *Proc. of the 9th Intl.
            Conference on Data Engineering (ICDE)*, pages 22–29, Vi-
            enna, Austria, April 1993. IEEE Computer Society.

[GPF+97]   P.M.D. Gray, A. Preece, N.J. Fiddian, W.A. Gray,
            T.J.M. Bench-Capon, M.J.R. Shave, N. Azarmi, M. Wie-
            gand, M. Ashwell, M. Beer, Z. Cui, B. Diaz, S.M. Embury,
            K. Hui, A.C. Jones, D.M. Jones, G.J.L. Kemp, E.W. Law-
            son, K. Lunn, P. Marti, J. Shao, and P.R.S. Visser. KRAFT:
            Knowledge Fusion from Distributed Databases and Knowl-
            edge Bases. In R.R. Wagner, editor, *Proc. of 8th Intl.
            Workshop on Database and Expert System Applications*

(DEXA'97), pages 682–691, Toulouse, France, September 1997. IEEE Computer Society Press.

[GS95]   A. Gupta and I. Singh Mumick. Maintenance of Materialised Views: Problems, Techniques and Applications. *Data Engineering Bulletin*, 18(2):3–18, June 1995.

[GSE+97]   S. Grufman, F. Samson, S. M. Embury, P. M. D. Gray, and T. Risch. Distributing Semantic Constraints Between Heterogeneous Databases. In A. Gray and P. Larson, editors, *Proc. of 13th Intl. Conference on Data Engineering (ICDE'97)*, pages 33–42, Birmingham, U.K., August 1997. IEEE Computer Society Press.

[HGMW+95]   J. Hammer, H. Garcia-Molina, J. Widom, W. Labio, and Y. Zhuge. The Stanford Data Warehousing Project. *Data Engineering Bulletin*, 18(2):41–48, June 1995.

[IK93]   H. Ishikawa and K. Kabota. An Active Object-Oriented Database: A Multi-Paradigm Approach to Constraint Management. In R. Agrawal, S. Baker, and D. Bell, editors, *Proc. of the 19th VLDB Conference*, pages 467–478, Dublin, August 1993. Morgan Kaufmann Publishers, Inc.

[JQ92]   H.V. Jagadish and X. Qian. Integrity Maintenance in an Object-Oriented Database. In L.-Y. Yuan, editor, *Proceedings of the 18th VLDB Conference*, pages 469–480, Vancouver, August 1992. Morgan Kaufmann Publishers, Inc.

[KLRSR95]   G. Kappel, P. Lang, S. Rausch-Schott, and W. Retschtzegger. Workflow Management Based on Objects, Rules and Roles. *Data Engineering Bulletin*, 18(1):11–18, March 1995.

[Mor84]   M. Morgenstern. Constraint Equations: Declarative Expression of Constraints with Automatic Enforcement. In *Proc. Intl. Conf. on Very Large Data Bases*, pages 153–299. Morgan Kaufmann, 1984.

[Nic82]   J.-M. Nicolas. Logic for Improving Integrity Checking in Relational Databases. *Acta Informatica*, 18:227–253, 1982.

[ODSD94]   D. Ohsie, H.M. Dewan, S.J. Stolfo, and S. Da Silva. Performance of Incremental Update in Database Rule Processing. In J. Widom and S. Chakravarthy, editors, *Proc. of the 4th Intl. Workshop on Research Issues in Data Engineering (RIDE'94): Active Database Systems*, pages 10–18, Houston, Texas, February 1994. IEEE Computer Society Press.

[Pat95]   N.W. Paton.   Supporting Production Rules Using ECA-
             Rules in an Object-Oriented Context. *Information and Soft-
             ware Technology*, 37(12):691–699, 1995.

[PDB93]   N.W. Paton, O. Diaz, and M.L. Barja.   Combining Active
             Rules and Metaclasses for Enhanced Extensibility in Object-
             Oriented Systems. *Data and Knowledge Engineering*, 10:45–
             63, 1993.

[PDDJ96]   N.W. Paton, K. Doan, O. Díaz, and A. Jaime. Exploitation
             of Object-Oriented and Active Constructs in Database Inter-
             face Development. In J. Kennedy and P.J. Barclay, editors,
             *Proc. of 3rd Intl. Workshop on User-Interfaces to Database
             Systems (IDS'96)*, Edinburgh, Scotland, July 1996.

[PGMU96]   Y. Papkonstantinou, H. Garcia-Molina, and J. Ullman.
             MedMaker: a Mediation Specification Subsystem Based on
             Declarative Specifications. In S.Y.W. Su, editor, *Proc. 12th
             Intl. Conference on Data Engineering (ICDE'96)*, pages 132–
             141, New Orleans, February 1996. IEEE Computer Society
             Press.

[RS95]   A. Reuter and F. Schwenkreis.   ConTracts — a Low-Level
             Mechanism for Building General Purpose Workflow Systems.
             Data Engineering Bulletin, 18(1):4–10, March 1995.

[Sin95]   I. Singh Mumick. The Rejuvenation of Materialised Views.
             In S. Bhalla, editor, *Proc. of 6th Intl. Conference on Infor-
             mation Systems and Data Management (CISMOD'95)*, Bom-
             bay, India, November 1995. Springer.

[SJGP90]   M. Stonebraker, A. Jhingran, J. Goh, and S. Potamianos. On
             Rules, Procedures, Caching and Views in Database Systems.
             In H. Garcia-Molina and H.V. Jagadish, editors, *Proc. of
             SIGMOD '90*, pages 281–290, Atlantic City, May 1990. ACM
             Press.

[ST94]   K.-D. Schewe and B. Talheim.   Achieving Consistency in Ac-
             tive Databases. In J. Widom and S. Chakravarthy, editors,
             *Proc. of the 4th Intl. Workshop on Research Issues in Data
             Engineering (RIDE'94): Active Database Systems*, pages 71–
             76, Houston, Texas, February 1994. IEEE Computer Society
             Press.

[TC94]   D. Toman and J. Chomicki.   Implementing Temporal In-
             tegrity Constraints Using an Active Database. In J. Widom
             and S. Chakravarthy, editors, *Proc. of the 4th Intl. Workshop
             on Research Issues in Data Engineering (RIDE'94): Active*

Database Systems, pages 87–95, Houston, Texas, February 1994. IEEE Computer Society Press.

[UD92]   S. Urban and M. Desiderio. CONTEXT: A CONstraint EXplanation Tool. *Data and Knowledge Engineering*, 8:153–183, 1992.

[UKN92]   S.D. Urban, A.P. Karadimce, and R.B. Nannapaneni. The Implementation and Evaluation of Integrity Maintenance Rules in an Object-Oriented Database. In *8th Intl. Conference on Data Engineering*, pages 565–572, Phoenix, Arizona, 1992. IEEE Computer Society.

[UO94]   T. Urpí and A. Olivé. Semantic Change Computation Optimisation in Active Databases. In J. Widom and S. Chakravarthy, editors, *Proc. of the 4th Intl. Workshop on Research Issues in Data Engineering (RIDE'94): Active Database Systems*, pages 19–27, Houston, Texas, February 1994. IEEE Computer Society Press.

[Wie92]   G. Wiederhold. Mediators in the Architecture of Future Information Systems. *IEEE Computer*, 25(3):38–49, March 1992.

[WYW94]   H. Wang, J. Yen, and J. Wolter. A Framework for Handling Errors During the Execution of Trigger Rules for an Active Object-Oriented DBMS. In J. Widom and S. Chakravarthy, editors, *Proc. of the 4th Intl. Workshop on Research Issues in Data Engineering (RIDE'94): Active Database Systems*, pages 132–136, Houston, Texas, February 1994. IEEE Computer Society Press.

[YK92]   J.P. Yoon and L. Kerschberg. A Framework for Constraint Management in Object-Oriented Databases. In *Proceedings of the 1st Intl. Conference on Information and Knowledge Management (CIKM'92)*, pages 292–299, Baltimore, MD, USA, 1992.

[ZHK96]   G. Zhou, R. Hull, and R. King. Generating Data Integration Mediators that Use Materialisation. *Journal of Intelligent Information Systems*, 6(2/3):199–221, June 1996.

[ZHKF95]   G. Zhou, R. Hull, R. King, and J.-C. Franchitti. Supporting Data Integration and Warehousing using H2O. *Data Engineering Bulletin*, 18(2):29–40, June 1995.

20

Active Database Systems: Expectations, Commercial Experience, and Beyond

Angelika Kotz-Dittrich
Eric Simon

ABSTRACT

We confront the promises of active database systems with the result of their use by application developers. The main problems encountered are the limitations of existing trigger languages, insufficient methodological support in analysis and design, missing development and administration tools for triggers, and weak performance. After analyzing each of these problems, we concentrate on performance because we discovered it is one of the main reasons that users are reluctant to use active rules in the development of large applications. We show, using simple concrete examples, that optimizing large applications is rendered difficult by the separation of transactions and triggers and the misunderstanding of their subtle interactions. We argue that tools, which provide assistance to both programmers and database designers to optimize their applications and master their evolution, are strongly needed. Finally, we outline several perspectives for the improvement of active database systems.

20.1 Introduction

The field of active database systems that originated in the mid-70s [Esw76] has for the last ten years received increasing interest from both database vendors and database researchers. A large number of research projects are ongoing to design and implement relational or object-oriented active database systems, as illustrated by the other chapters of this book. Many relational products already incorporate some limited form of active rule processing, and promote the active rule functionality as a key value of their system. Rules are also a prominent feature of the SQL3 standard [ISO94], currently under development. Finally, users have started using active rules in the development of real-life applications.

Active database systems have been presented as a very promising technology. They are expected to facilitate the design and maintenance of business rules, enable the development of general system extensions on top of an existing DBMS, improve the reliability of applications regarding the enforcement of business rules, and enhance their performance. In this chapter, we analyze the gap that exists between the potential benefits of active database systems and the actual capabilities of existing systems in the light of their use in the development of real-life applications. Our goal is to derive challenging research topics that we think should contribute to better establish the technology and encourage its dissemination.

We view an active database system as a black box and consider users that are either database designers, database administrators, or application programmers. Therefore, we study the problems that arise when users want to design a database schema including triggers, program transactions that automatically invoke triggers, verify the correctness of applications, optimize the performance of applications, and maintain applications, e.g., when transactions or triggers are changed. From this, we derive requirements for trigger languages, analysis and design methodologies, and development and administration tools.

Throughout this chapter, we consider a relational active database framework and most of our observations take their roots in the study of application development projects in the banking environment. Consequently, our concrete examples are mainly inspired from banking applications. However, we believe that most of the problems listed in this paper have their counterparts in object-oriented active database systems, and in other application domains.

The chapter is organized as follows. Section 20.2 states the expected benefits of active database systems, and describes several potential application domains. Section 20.3 presents the difficulties encountered by application developers using existing active database systems. Section 20.4 focuses on the need for administration tools that enable optimization and maintenance of large active applications. Section 20.5 offers perspectives for the improvement of active database systems. Section 20.6 concludes.

20.2   Expectations of Active DBMS's

20.2.1   Passive Vs. Active Database Applications

In most modern database management systems with widespread usage in the commercial world, we find some sort of limited active functionality (triggers, active rules, or similar constructs). In spite of the opportunities inherent in these new mechanisms, most database applications are still passive. By a *passive database application*, we mean an application that does not make use of any active features even though the underlying DBMS may offer them. In contrast, an *active application* in our sense is not only based on a DBMS with active capabilities, but actually makes use of these capabilities.

Passive DB applications use the DBMS only to create, retrieve, modify, and delete data by issuing corresponding operations. In particular, a considerable part of the *business rules*[1] essential to guarantee data quality and correct behavior are embedded into the application programs. It can be observed that applications that ignore the availability of active features also tend not to make full use of other features like referential integrity.

To better explain the differences between passive and active applications, let us consider the problem of implementing business rules. There are two commonly used approaches followed in passive applications. The most frequent approach is to encode business rules using *database procedures* explicitly invoked from within a transaction. For instance, a procedure can be called before or after every modification to the database, or before committing the transaction. Appropriate actions (e.g., an abort of the transaction) will–again explicitly–be taken in response to the execution of a procedure that checks some condition.

A second approach is to periodically poll the database in order to check and enforce business rules. For instance, companies send monthly retirement payments for their employees to a life insurance company. Sometimes the data sent are incomplete or incorrect. The strategy followed by some companies is to register all data in the database, and then run a separate application process that mines the database in order to discover anomalies that are subsequently handled either by dedicated repairing software (e.g., expert systems) or by humans. The rationale for this approach is to afford a high transaction throughput for a very large online database, given that the percentage of anomalies found in the database is reported to be below 1 percent. In contrast, incorporating controls in transactions would make transactions longer, thereby degrading the performance of applications. The problem with the polling approach is the difficulty tuning it: inconsistencies are introduced in the database and one has to carefully control the consequences of that for all transactions.

It is worthwhile noticing that with passive database applications, programmers have the full control over and responsibility for the application semantics, including the quality of stored data. Programmers also master how the processing of business rules is optimized within the application program.

In contrast, active database applications externalize part of their semantics and control structure, delegating it to the database system. In the context of this chapter, unless otherwise specified, we shall focus on the kinds of triggers offered by today's relational DBMS products, or described in the SQL3 proposal [ISO94]. We shall refer to these triggers as *SQL triggers*. In these triggers, typical actions are database modifications, procedures, or a

---

[1]In this paper, the term *business rules* covers semantic integrity constraints as well as statements about how the business is performed.

rollback statement that aborts the transaction or the statement. Events are issued by transactions and generally consist of database statements such as data modifications, data retrievals, or transactional commands. At specific points in a transaction's execution, the database system takes a set of events issued by the transaction, automatically retrieves the triggered rules, and processes them. There are two kinds of rule processing points: rules can be triggered immediately after (or before) each occurrence of an event in the transaction (*immediate* execution mode), or at the end of the transaction (*deferred* execution mode). Triggers are defined as immediate or deferred and this subsequently determines their execution mode in a transaction. In most active database systems (and at least, in all commercial active database systems), the execution of triggers is done within the triggering transaction. We refer the interested reader to Chapter 10 of this book for a comprehensive view of SQL triggers.

20.2.2   Advantages of Active Database Systems

We start this section with an example of rather encouraging results from a financial application. We then discuss the major benefits provided by active database systems. Though later in the chapter, we will elaborate on a number of difficulties encountered with commercial active database systems as well as on complex optimization problems still to be solved, we argue that the advantages described below justify the research and development efforts necessary to solve the still open design and optimization problems.

In [BZB97], Bruechert presents results from a financial application, namely a system used by several large banks for scanning, processing, and archiving of documents representing securities. The application comprises scanning and OCR processing of the documents, as well as archiving of images and data extracted from those images. The archived data are organized along a tree structure of trades, transactions, denominations, and shares (each trade consisting of 1 to n transactions, each transaction of 1 to n denominations, and each denomination of 1 to n shares). The paper shows how triggers can be used to simplify the application and make it more flexible. Since the application had been using a relational DBMS without any triggers before, a direct comparison between the passive and the active solution could be made.

In the active implementation of the application, triggers are used for four different tasks:

- cascading deletes in the tree structure (e.g., when a trade is deleted, all corresponding transactions, denominations, and shares will be deleted, too),

- cascading updates of status attributes along the hierarchy (e.g., if all shares of a denomination have changed their state from "check" to "correct", the status attribute of the denomination will be set accordingly),

- logging of all transactions that affect primary tables (shares, denominations, etc.),

- implementation of a former daemon process by database triggers (in the original passive application, the daemon's task was to poll the database to find out new securities with unknown document formats, which require initial interactive processing).

Only twenty five triggers were used to implement the above tasks (respectively, four, four, fifteen, and two of each above category). The performance measurements given for the new application show improvements in the range of 5 to 15 percent over the original passive application. Cascading deletes provided the best improvement (15 percent) but in this case, implementing them with declarative constraints resulted in an even better improvement. The results slightly vary according to the DBMS product used (Informix and Oracle) and according to whether stored procedures are used in the action part or not (not surprisingly, stored procedures performed much better). Though the numbers do not show huge performance improvements, they prove that, at least for some releases of commercial products (Informix release 7, and Oracle release 7.1.3), and for appropriate applications, triggers can compete with traditional solutions while at the same time offering clear advantages in terms of reduced system complexity, better maintainability of the application, improved data integrity, and higher stability of the whole system. In the sequel, we elaborate in more detail on the issues that make active databases a valuable mechanism for application development.

As a first benefit, *triggers enable a uniform and centralized description of the business rules* relevant to the information system. In fact, several conceptual modeling and information systems methodologies are being extended to handle restricted (e.g., [TKL90, HKMS94]), or general (e.g., [CF97]), forms of triggers. Triggers generally rely on the use of query constructs for expressing condition and action parts of rules. Their regular format can be exploited to understand how rules relate to events, or how rules interact with each other, for instance by analyzing the relationships that a rule action has with the event or condition parts of other rules. This knowledge is useful for checking the correctness of rules and tuning performance. In contrast, when business rules are embedded into application programs, they can be specified and implemented in a different way in several applications. It is thus difficult to get the specification of rules validated by users, and to verify that they are consistently implemented.

As a second benefit, *the use of triggers facilitates the maintenance of business rules.* Since triggers are modular, adding a business rule amounts to defining new triggers that will automatically be invoked by application programs when necessary. On the contrary, adding (changing, or removing) a constraint in a passive application requires changing application programs. Early studies have reported that a substantial maintenance effort in passive transaction processing applications is spent in the maintenance of integrity controls.

For a further advantage, triggers are reliable since they are automatically invoked whenever an appropriate event is issued by a transaction. This provides a safe way to *ensure that every application obeys specific rules*, regardless of the method used to access the database. Declarative integrity constraints (also called assertions) also do this, but are limited in what they can control. On the contrary, with passive applications, the correct enforcement of business rules is guaranteed only if every single transaction implements it correctly. This makes data quality dependent on the reliability of programmers and programming methodologies and may be the reason for severe inconsistencies as to the enforced policies. For instance, in the application mentioned earlier for the processing and archiving of securities, the use of triggers provided better integrity in the case of cascading deletes (no forgotten tuples filling up the database). It also provided better logging of transactions: for instance, it was not possible to add any code to the Informix-tool DBACCESS in order to log the operations initiated by that tool.

Finally, triggers are expected to *improve the performance of applications*. There are two main reasons for that. The first reason is rooted in the *centralization of application semantics by means of triggers*. Due to centralization, more and better optimization techniques can be applied, redundancy of checking and repair operations can be avoided, and changes in the environment (like the fact that a checking operation is no longer necessary) can more easily be incorporated. Audits conducted on very large passive database applications have shown that transactions often perform more controls than necessary. In fact, the number of database procedures invoked from succeeding releases of these applications tends to increase monotonically. Calls to database procedures are rarely removed from transactions, though it turns out that changes in the data acquisition process have made some controls obsolete. Discovering such situations requires a lot of effort usually not considered as deserving in individual application programs.[2] For instance, in the application mentioned earlier, the use of triggers for cascading updates enabled a reduction in application complexity: status changes are not spread throughout the application as before, SQL statements are simplified in a number of places, and module size was reduced

---

[2]The hidden rule is often that it is preferable to pay extra processing cost for superfluous checks rather than endangering the correctness of data by missing any useful controls.

by 10 to 20 percent.

As a second argument, one *use of triggers is as an effective tuning instrument* to make the application run faster [Sha92]. A typical example is to replace a polling transaction that impedes the transactional traffic by triggers. Suppose there is an application that wants to display the latest data inserted into a table $SELLS$ (insert_time, ...). A polling transaction would select data from $SELLS$ since the last time it looked at the table. This transaction will conflict with inserters and create inter-transaction blockings. Furthermore, if polling is done too rarely, recently inserted records may be deleted by some transaction before they have been displayed. An alternative is to use a trigger that displays inserted data whenever an insert occurs to $SELLS$. The trigger avoids concurrency conflicts since it executes within the same transaction that inserts into $SELLS$. Similar observations have been made in the case of our earlier application where the original daemon process was no longer needed and resulted in a better accuracy of data.

Another example of effective tuning is to create materialized views and maintain them with triggers. Suppose we have two relations $ORDER$ (ordernum, itemnum, qty, vendor), and $ITEM$ (itemnum, price), and we frequently ask the total dollar amount on order from a particular vendor. This query can be very expensive on the above schema. An alternative is to create a materialized view $TOTAL - VENDOR$ (vendor, amount), where amount is the total value of goods on order to the vendor. Each update to $ORDER$ causes an update to relation $TOTAL - VENDOR$, which can easily be maintained with a trigger. However, there is a trade-off between the use of a materialized view to speed up the query, versus the cost associated with the maintenance (i.e., updating) of the materialized view. In the past, the overhead associated with the update triggers was sometimes intolerable. With improved trigger implementations available today, and appropriate programming tuning, the maintenance of materialized views by triggers becomes feasible with reasonable performance.

As an example of the improvements in efficiency, triggers have been used with a loan management database, based on an early release of Oracle, for applications like portfolio management and customer support. The main fields of usage of triggers in this application are data replication, denormalization, and materialized views with appropriate update propagation. First attempts to implement the applications with triggers was made about three to four years ago. At that time, the performance was clearly too low to be tolerable. As a consequence, a passive solution using directly called stored procedures had been chosen. A new attempt has recently been made with a more recent release (Oracle 7.1.6) and better tuned programming, yielding now very reasonable performance values. For example, a benchmark was taken on 160,000 insert operations into tables triggering the update of the associated materialized views. The results show that triggers and stored procedures perform equally well, with triggers providing many advantages in terms of flexibility.

20.2.3   Application Domains for Active DBMS's

We have seen a major difference between the use of active rules to *implement* general system-level tasks such as data caching, security, data replication, etc., and the use of active rules to *model* and *implement* business rules. The first category includes what are called Database System Extensions in Chapter 1 of this book, and what has been described in Chapter 19 as Database Internal Applications. However, these extensions are not restricted to extensions of the internal capabilities of a database system such as integrity constraint checking or the management of materialized views. They may also consist, for instance, of middleware functionalities such as the management of events in a distributed heterogeneous environment composed of database and file systems. The second category comprises what are called open and closed database applications in Chapter 1.

When looking at applications based on commercially available active DBMS, we have made the following observations:

- In contrast to what one might expect, there are a lot of applications that try to implement system extensions (at least in part).

- The applications implementing general system extensions may have more demanding requirements as to the execution model and performance of the active DBMS than pure business rules-oriented applications.

- Closed applications prevail with respect to open ones, presumably due to the fear that users have of producing uncontrollable effects.

- In a number of cases, however, there is no clear borderline between open and closed database applications. Part of the application may stick to internal reactions within the system, while another part may trigger external effects (like sending e-mail, printing documents, initiating deals at the electronic stock exchange, etc.).

In the following, we examine implemented applications as well as potential application domains. Each time, we point out the benefits that can be expected from the use of an active DBMS. Note that we decided to illustrate the applications by simple examples to give a flavor of the problems in principle. The complexity encountered in practice is of a much higher degree in both the number of triggers and the structure of individual triggers. We first present active applications implementing system extensions, and then active applications implementing business rules.

20.2.4 Applications Implementing System Extensions

When referring to system extensions, we consider applications that use an existing DBMS. We first observed that many application developers are aware of triggers as a very flexible means to implement system extensions. Essentially, triggers enable the DBMS to interrupt the execution of user transactions, take control, and execute the programs, specified in the action parts of triggers, that implement the desired system extensions. From the application side, the behavior is the same as if the system extensions were actually part of the DBMS.

A second observation is that although most system extensions would certainly be implemented more efficiently within the DBMS, implementing them on the top may be advantageous: system extensions can be tailored to application needs, and applications that do not need the system extensions do not have to pay the price for them (they merely do not trigger the active rules that implement the functionality). As a consequence, the separation of the active functionality from the concrete DBMS was recommended in several companies.

Chapter 19 of this book has already explained how internal database functionalities such as integrity maintenance, materialized views maintenance, and advanced transaction management could be specified by means of high-level languages, and how compilers that translate these specifications into trigger definitions could be designed. In this section, we report on the following experiences of design and implementation of system extensions with SQL triggers: schema versioning, audit trail construction, replication and caching, security, and situation monitoring. In section 20.3, we shall focus on the main difficulties encountered by the designers of such system extensions.

Our first example is a loan management database application. Triggers have already successfully been used for denormalization and materialized views. Triggers have also been considered for automating database administration (e.g., user administration) in a workflow-like manner, thereby replacing manual tasks by program-supported processes. Triggers can be used to model the processes. Finally, in the same application, triggers have also been considered for the support of schema versioning.

The schema versioning functionality consists of maintaining two consistent versions of a relation for a predefined time after a schema modification so that the applications may switch gradually. As an example, think of switching to a new format for date attributes to cope with the Year 2000 problem. For some time, there will be old applications still using the old format: *MM.DD.YY*, while other applications will already use the new one: *MM.DD.YYYY*. A way to allow for a gradual switch would be to keep two versions for each relation concerned, namely one with the old and one with the new date format.

Both versions could be kept consistent by using update triggers that propagate the changes occurring in one version towards the other version. Of course, since the triggers work in both directions, one must prevent them from looping infinitely. A possibility would to be to deactivate a rule after firing once. In our examples, rules have the form: on *event* if *condition* then *action*. We use a natural English language syntax for events, conditions, and actions in order to be independent from any system-specific trigger language. The triggers for a simple relation recording the payment date of a mortgage might look like:

```
trigger t1_mortgage
on update to mortgage_old.date_due
then
    deactivate t2_mortgage
    mortgage_new.date_due = mortgage_old.date_due + 1900
    activate t2_mortgage

trigger t2_mortgage
on update to mortgage_new.date_due
then
    deactivate t1_mortgage
    mortgage_old.date_due = mortgage_new.date_due - 1900
    activate t1_mortgage
```

A second example is the use of triggers for auditing in a very flexible way. The idea is to implement a logging mechanism where the set of database operations to be logged can be specified dynamically and can easily be extended for new relations as well. The application provides skeletons, called trigger templates, to create triggers for some relevant database operations on demand. To generate new triggers for logging, the names of relations and columns to be audited are placed into special tables. The generation process reads these tables, fills in the trigger templates, and produces the trigger code which is then fed into the DBMS for rule definition. For instance, here is an example of an Oracle trigger template used:

```
create or replace trigger <trigger-name>
before insert or update or delete on <table_name>
for each row declare <variable_declarations>
begin
    if inserting then do
        <insert specific stuff>
    elsif updating then do
        <update specific stuff>
    elsif deleting then do
        <delete specific stuff>
    end if;
```

```
<do any work that is generic, e.g., create a row in the
audit table to indicate that a change has occurred>

if inserting or updating then
   <record the before images of the fields we are
   interested in>
elsif deleting then
   <record the after images of the fields we are
   interested in>
end if;
end;
```

A third example is the use of triggers to implement caching. The ADMS Project [NNS93] implements an enhanced client/server database architecture with caching from multiple heterogeneous commercial DBMS (including Oracle, Sybase, Informix and Ingres) for a number of clients. Each client creates its own set of materialized views from multiple heterogeneous DBMS and local data. When the result of a query is cached to a local relation for the first time, this new local relation is bound to the server relations used in extracting the results. Bindings can either be stored at the server's catalog or maintained by the individual clients. Every server relation is associated with an update propagation log that consists of timestamped inserted tuples and timestamped qualifying conditions for deleted tuples. The server is required to look up log portions of the query-involved relations, and only relevant fractions or increments are propagated to the client's site. There is a choice between eager or deferred (periodic, on-demand, event-driven) update strategies. Triggers can be used conceptually to initiate periodic or event-driven updates of the cached views. In the on-demand case, triggers can also be used if a special kind of event is introduced. One of the advantages would be that triggers provide a uniform mechanism on which to map all kinds of update strategies.

Our next example is the implementation of a security mediator ([Smi95]) carried out at MITRE Corporation. The security mediator is meant to detect unauthorized access to the database and react according to various policies (preventing the access, logging it, or various different reactions). Triggers are a very convenient mechanism for this kind of functionality. Of course, this kind of application requires as a prerequisite the detection of database read events (i.e., on select triggers).

The security mediator application has also come up with a system decomposition issue. There is a need to implement complex active functionality across a system consisting of several heterogeneous DBMS and a Distributed Object Manager (DOM). This requires capturing various kinds of DBMS as well as DOM events and responding to them according to a uniform policy. As an example, think of an environment with a marketing database targeted at home banking customers who access banking services via a distributed object manager. Events relevant for triggering reactions may be generated by the DBMS as well as the DOM. For example, a certain marketing action should be triggered either by a given attribute value in the customer relation or by statistics gathered on service usage in the DOM. Triggers can help monitor the marketing action according to such events as shown below:

```
on update to customer.category
if customer.category = "frequent_homebanking_user"
then <initiate marketing action>

on "call homebanking_service"
if number of service calls in 10 days > 20
then <initiate marketing action>
```

Our last system extension is the active monitoring of information that resides in autonomous, distributed data sources ([KSMR96]). For example, suppose we have the following two single-relation data sources.

```
US_customer (Cust#, Name, Address, Rank, Yearly_turnover)
EU_customer (Cust#, Name, Address, Rank, Yearly_turnover)
```

We define the schema of a federated view of all customers as follows.

```
all_customers (Cust#, Name, Address, Yearly_turnover)
```

The problem is to provide automated support for what is called standing requests for information (SRI) in [KSMR96]. Standing requests are expressed over the federated view (also called the situation). For example, considering the query that selects the average yearly-turnover of all customers ranked important, an SRI could specify that an alert must be produced if the result of this query falls below a given threshold. The role of the situation monitor is thus to transform the update events received from the data sources into appropriate user notifications. Triggers can be used to monitor the standing requests for information and execute alerts when necessary. Given an SRI specification, rules are automatically generated by a monitor generator in order to insulate the user from the technical details.

20.2.5   Applications Implementing Business Rules

An interesting survey about the applicability of triggers to implement business rules is reported in [GHM94]. Though the study identifies a number of problems with current active DBMS's, their survey of DBMS users reveals that the general awareness of and interest in active database technology for business rules is high. The interviewed database users were categorized along the DBMS used (Sybase, Ingres, and Oracle users). The results are given in the table below. We also observed that the major usage of triggers as business rules in running applications is integrity constraint checking,[3] alerting (i.e., rules whose action part only consist of messages), as well as pre- and postprocessing of database updates.

Categories of users	Sybase	Ingres	Oracle
Using triggers	74%	50%	31%
Planning to use triggers	13%	33%	44%

Most of the experiences reported in this section stem from the financial environment. In this area, there are a considerable number of existing and potential applications for business rules. For more examples illustrating the application of active DBMS's in financial applications, see also [CS94]. Typical implementations use sets in the order of some hundred triggers (in three different banks, we came across applications using, e.g., 150, 200, and 220 triggers, respectively). Besides financial applications proper, such as account management or management of guarantees in international markets, implementations also include system extensions like the management of a bank's inhouse communication network.

An interesting application scenario (henceforth called market watcher) is the electronic stock exchange or any financial trading environment with prices provided by a ticker service. The decision to buy or sell must be based on the recent market trend data. The traditional solution relies on human supervision, i.e., traders constantly watch data on the screen or poll the database by regularly submitting queries. More recent solutions try to automate this by installing processes that automatically poll the database. Clearly, triggers can be helpful to supervise the market trends by either notifying the human trader, or (to a certain extent) automatically kicking off the deals. In this respect, the market watcher can be classified as an open database application.

We give a simple example of a trigger watching a *PRICES* relation. In a realistic environment, the number of triggers will depend on the number of financial instruments and the number of traders' strategies and can easily reach some tens of thousands.

```
on insert to PRICES
if the price for Microsoft stocks is larger than the
   price for IBM stocks for the last 10 ticks
then notify trader A
```

The advantage of using triggers is that the conditions for trading decisions can be made explicit and can easily be inspected. An active DBMS can guarantee that interesting data constellations are never missed by the trader (provided that appropriate performance is guaranteed under real-time utilization).

---

[3]In one application this amounts to 77 percent.

A second example is portfolio management. Following a specific investment strategy (degree of risk, customer preferences, etc.), each portfolio
is supervised and modified according to market opportunities. The investment strategy can be expressed (at least partly) as a constraint system
on the minimum/optimum/maximum volume of different financial instruments in the portfolio (for example, the volume of bonds has to be between
10 percent and 15 percent, the volume of options less than 5 percent, the
volume of gold preferably around 10 percent, etc.). In practice, such constraint systems tend to get rather large, involving an ever-growing number
of financial derivatives, foreign currencies, etc. Triggers can help to automatically supervise the constraint set, notify the portfolio manager when
constraints are about to be violated, suggest modifications of the portfolio
to approach the optimum, or prevent violating transactions. We give two
examples of rules below. Again note that the number of triggers will grow
rapidly with the number of investment strategies and the variety of new
financial instruments and derivatives.

```
on update to PORTFOLIO.bonds
if bonds < 10% or bonds > 15%
then rollback
```

```
on update to PRICE.gold
if gold < threshold and PORTFOLIO.gold < optimum - 5%
then notify
```

In many financial applications, the notion of time plays an important
role, either for timely reactions, or reactions based on historical data. We
give below an example of triggers that handle time-related events and conditions over the database. In large financial institutes, there are a large
number of deadlines and time limits to supervise, especially accumulating
around specific points like end-of-business hours or end-of-month processing.

```
on end_of_month + 2 workdays
if balance is not available from branch Z
then notify
```

```
on update to CUSTOMER.address + 1 day
then send new forms to customer
```

As to historical data, time series analysis provides another attractive application domain for triggers. Time series on stock prices or macroeconomic
data are analyzed to produce forecasts and to base decisions on interesting historical developments. Triggers can be used to automatically notify
the analyst on historical trends based, for instance, on moving averages, as
shown below.

```
on insert to TIMESERIES
if moving average over last 30 days equals moving average
    over last 120 days and moving average over last 30
    days is rising
then suggest to sell
```

For this area, good performance is again important, as the conditions are usually quite complex and extend over a possibly large time window in the historical database. The competitive advantage resulting from timely notification as provided by the triggers can be tremendous in today's highly volatile markets.

Though the potential benefits of specifying business rules using triggers seem obvious, developers keep asking us questions like "How should business rules be implemented?", "Should we use the trigger mechanisms offered by database systems?". We have come across strategic guidelines in companies that categorically recommend not to code business rules into triggers at all, though the reasons for that decision remain more or less fuzzy. Sometimes, in the same companies, designers are advised to describe business rules (e.g., on paper) using the concept of event-condition-action rules. At this stage, our answer is to code an application with triggers when the benefits mentioned earlier–i.e. uniform and centralized definition, maintenance, guaranteed invocation, effective tuning–are of high importance. The crucial point here is to know whether the practical reality of active database systems matches the expected benefits of triggers, which is the topic of the next section.

20.3   Realities of Active Database Systems

In this section, we examine the realities of active database systems in light of their use in the development of applications. Our analysis of applications first revealed that we need to distinguish between applications that can be adequately implemented using SQL triggers available in commercial systems, and applications that cannot. Note that the distinction that we made earlier between system extensions and business rules is blurred here. For instance, in their study [GHM94], the authors show that the mapping of business rules to triggers can be carried out to some extent with today's active DBMS. In one application developed at Swiss PTT for the administration of owned and rented buildings, the total number of business rules was compared to the number of these rules that can actually be implemented using Oracle triggers. It was found that 65 percent of the business rules (342 out of 523) can be implemented by triggers. Similarly, we observed that there are a number of simple system extensions for which SQL triggers work quite well, and others that could not be implemented with existing active DBMS.

There are three main factors that impede the development of applications with SQL triggers. First, existing active systems only accept the definition of triggers that are limited in their expressiveness and execution model. Second, there is a lack of administration tools and design methodologies, which generates problems of security, reliability, and predictability for active applications. Finally, applications implemented with SQL triggers may suffer from severe performance problems. Each of these factors is analyzed in the subsequent sections. We shall introduce several tenets that highlight the result of our analysis. There are other reasons that are not considered in this chapter such as the impossibility of adding triggers to legacy applications (this obstacle was encountered within the security mediator application of section 20.2.4).

20.3.1   Limitations of SQL Trigger Systems

A first problem of existing DBMS's is given below.

> **Tenet 1:** SQL trigger languages have a too limited expressiveness, in particular for specifying event clauses.

For instance, with business rules, triggers are often considered in the analysis and design phase, but there are a number of cases where triggers are ruled out at that stage because of a lack of expressiveness of the proposed implementation platform. We start with those cases where the limited expressiveness can be circumvented at the time triggers are defined at the expense of an increase in trigger's complexity.

First, condition-action rules are usually not directly expressible. This problem is emphasized by restrictions of the trigger language, e.g., the event part of a rule must be associated with a single relation, or a disjunction of elementary events (even for the same relation) is not allowed. Coding a simple business rule, such as "the volume of bonds must be between 10% and 15%" in a portfolio management application, may entail the definition of many triggers because one trigger is needed for every data modification event capable of violating the constraint. A negative consequence is the proliferation of rules that complicate the verification of their correctness. For this reason, most development guides recommend not to use triggers for coding integrity constraints that can be expressed by means of assertions in the data definition language.

As explained in Chapter 19 of this book, a way to circumvent this limitation is to develop a system extension that offers a high-level language in which declarative constraints can be specified and automates the generation of SQL triggers from these specifications.[4] However, [KSMR96] reports

---

[4]Note that some degree of automatic generation (e.g., for referential integrity) is already available in several commercial database design tools.

that this solution is not always applicable: it was investigated for the development of a situation monitoring application (as described in section 20.2.4), but rejected by the local database administrators of autonomous data sources because it required the definition of too large a number of triggers in their data sources. As a result, an ad-hoc replication mechanism was finally chosen to propagate changes from a data source to the federated materialized view. Similarly, other experiences with the direct implementation of high-level monitoring mechanism instead of using triggers are reported in [Ris89], and in the framework of Syntel [Dud87], an expert system tool for loan officers and insurance underwriters that relies on monitoring changes to combined materializations of database queries and user inputs.

As another limitation, the possible number of triggers associated with each relation is sometimes limited. The number of rules that can be triggered by any specific event is also limited (in many cases to one).[5] This is a severe restriction in applications managing history relations (e.g., a Withdraw relation) or central data (e.g, insurance claims), where a single change to a relation can trigger a very large number of actions.

Once again, this limitation can somehow be circumvented by the definition of a single trigger whose action part consists of a sequence of if-then-else statements. For instance, a single trigger in a market watcher application can be defined as shown below. In this trigger, rule1 always precedes rule2 and rule3, which are executed sequentially; rule2 and rule3 are exclusive and rule2 has priority over rule3.

```
on insert to PRICES
do
   if condition1 then notify trader A /* rule1 */
   if condition2 then <sell action> /* rule2 */
      else if condition3 then notify trader B /* rule3 */
end-do
```

This solution may be advantageous. First, a single rule is watching the *PRICES* relation. Second, the flow of control within that rule is essentially a sequence of conditionals, which can be easier to understand for SQL application programmers and designers than atomic rules with more opaque control. Nevertheless, modular rules are also extremely useful, specially when rules that turn out to have the same triggering event are actually performing very different tasks. Furthermore, with existing SQL application programming languages, monitoring the conditions in rules 1 to 3 requires the use of auxiliary variables. This complication is avoided if the watching

---

[5]In the current SQL3 proposal, there are eighteen distinct types of triggers available for each relation, plus additional update triggers for the different columns of a relation. However, multiple triggers for the same event are possible, and their order of execution can be specified using priorities.

rules are specified as individual triggers.

Unfortunately, there are limitations of the trigger language that cannot be easily bypassed. The detection of specific events is one example. As an illustration, the security mediator application presented earlier required to support triggers with external events other than database events, while time series analysis required temporal events. Some other applications require to trigger business rules at the end of transactions (that is, the commit statement should trigger the rule). Imagine, for instance, an entry-order transaction that requires to check global information at the end of the transaction, such as the total amount on order to take decisions about preferential prices. Existing SQL trigger languages do not support these types of events.

In order to support the detection of such events and the monitoring of triggers accordingly, application developers can be led to implement special modules that interface at runtime between the application programs and the DBMS. To illustrate this point, consider again the problem of triggering a rule, such as the one below, at the end of an entry-order transaction that merely consists of a sequence of SQL insert statements in a relation ORDER.

```
on insert to ORDER
if the total amount on order for supplier A
   is greater than 1,000 and customer's status = ''gold''
then apply a 10% discount on the ordered items to A
```

To implement this rule with SQL triggers that only support immediate triggering, before or after the occurrence of a data modification event, we can first define an SQL trigger as shown below, which appends all the tuples inserted by every individual insert statement into a specific HISTORY relation.

```
on insert to ORDER
then log the inserted tuples into relation HISTORY
```

Then, the entry-order transaction would be modified to include a statement:

```
call Event_manager()
```

just before the commit statement of the transaction. Event_manager() is a procedure that performs the following:

```
if the total amount on order for supplier A
   is greater than 1,000 in the HISTORY relation
   and customer's status = ''gold''
then apply a 10% discount on the ordered items to A
```

If the transaction also includes delete and update statements, then special SQL triggers should be defined to maintain the HISTORY relation appropriately. For temporal events, it would be necessary to implement a specific temporal event manager, and to invoke it from the action part of triggers that react on elementary events. Thus, although a solution can be envisaged in each case, it may be quite difficult to engineer.

Other problems concern the SQL trigger's execution models:

> **Tenet 2:** SQL trigger's execution models are too limited for some applications.

For instance, in the situation monitoring application presented in section 20.2.4, because of source autonomy, a source database update in one process must trigger a database update to the federated materialized view into a different process. If such a possibility of openness is not provided, it is almost impossible to rely on the active system for this task. Other examples concern the possibility of activating and deactivating triggers dynamically (as in the schema versioning application of section 20.2.4), or executing the action part of a trigger in a separate transaction whose commitment depends on the commitment of the parent transaction that generated it (as in the situation-monitoring example). All these possibilities are usually not offered by SQL trigger execution models, and supporting them at the application level may require the development of a complete active rule monitor on top of the target active DBMS. However, because developers lack some familiarity with the active database systems technology, they usually abandon the idea of using triggers at this stage and prefer to adopt instead a specific ad-hoc solution for their problem.

20.3.2 Administration Tools and Design Methodologies

Many developers we talked to, e.g., concerning the applications in section 20.2.5, like the market watcher or the portfolio management system, are asking for design guidelines and reference applications to find out how to use triggers.

Below, we mention the most frequently asked questions:

- What kind and amount of semantics has to be externalized into triggers as compared with semantics that has to stay in the application? For example, should all the stock prices be polled within the application, or should each check be encoded into a separate trigger?

- What are the criteria for deciding when to choose stored procedures and when to choose triggers? For example, even if the basic decision is to store the code for price checking in the database, this code could either be invoked explicitly or triggered automatically.

- What conditions have to be observed for the design of correct and terminating trigger sets? For example, in the portfolio example, contradicting conditions like bonds < 10% and bonds ≥ 10% should not both trigger a rollback action.

- Is there a classification of constraints that require different treatment? For example, should simple integrity constraints like deriving an account balance be treated differently from complex business rules like reacting to specific customer patterns?

- Which criteria are there for the complexity of triggers? Should expressions in constraints and/or actions be limited, should a trigger refer to no more than one relation, should the action touch no other data than the triggering transaction, etc.? For example, with the market watcher example, should the action be limited to notification (no automatic buying and selling), and should each trigger be limited to touch only one financial instrument?

- Is it more advantageous to design transactions and triggers in close connection or to develop them in isolation from each other? For example, can the transactions modifying a portfolio be coded and/or modified independently of the investment constraints?

- Are there quantitative design rules like optimal size of a trigger set (absolute size, number of triggers per relation, etc.)? For example, is a set of triggers corresponding to 1,000 financial instruments multiplied by 100 traders with individual strategies feasible?

In our view, a design and maintenance environment for active databases must support a methodology that allows for the initial design and subsequent modification of triggers in close connection with the database schema and the transactions. One difficulty is that trigger languages lack a simple, clear, and standardized semantics. They vary considerably in their syntax and semantics, which means that applications developed with triggers are not portable from one system to another. However, developers can expect the upcoming SQL3 standard to alleviate these problems. An important difference is the level of granularity (tuple-level or statement-level) of triggering. For languages that have both, conflicts may occur yielding an incorrect or nondeterministic behavior, as shown in [Hor94]. Languages also differ in the restrictions (usually not clearly justified) placed on triggers. Although these differences strongly determine the behavior and the possible usage of triggers, there is no clear indication as to which style of design is appropriate for some given rule semantics. Finally, in systems that support both triggers and integrity assertions, the exact execution behavior of both is not well defined in existing products, although a recent proposal [CPM96] has been adopted to clarify this issue. It is worth noticing that the successful experiences we have reported earlier (such as [BZB97]) concern applications with a small number of triggers that do not have complex interdependencies between them.

Real life experiences show that both project managers and senior developers are often reluctant to use active DBMS facilities because they consider triggers as insecure, unreliable, and unpredictable. In this respect, their reaction is the same as with deductive rules in expert systems or knowledge-base systems because they wonder how a set of individual, isolated rules will interact with each other and with application programs in concrete situations. With active rules, this suspicion is even greater because these rules act on their own and may directly affect the real world.

For mission-critical financial applications like the ones mentioned in section 20.2.5 where triggers may automatically execute stock deals, influence the structure of large portfolios, or rate customers as non credit-worthy, this attitude is well founded. The same is true for applications in plant control, patient care, or aviation systems. Without guarantee (or at least very high probability) of correctness and predictable, unambiguous behavior, triggers will not be used in these fields.

There are less critical ways of using triggers, e.g., triggers that react just by notifying a human user. Nevertheless, the impression that less security is needed may be misleading. To argue about it, we consider a trade support system similar to the market watcher from section 20.2.5 that has recently been introduced at a bank for the New York Stock Exchange. In the beginning, for about the first three months, traders resented the new system. After that, they got accustomed to it to such an extent that they now consider it a major problem if the software goes down for a single day. Traders are now reported to completely rely on the information delivered by the system and to no longer cross-check the automatically generated buy and sell suggestions. As a result, generating incorrect notifications will have the same disastrous effect as erroneous automatically triggered deals. It is therefore crucial for an active DBMS to offer all kinds of support to make triggers reliable and predictable.

A first impediment to this requirement is given by our next tenet:

Tenet 3: It is difficult to validate a large number of rules.

As an example, think of the portfolio management application with the modification that the triggered actions do not only notify or rollback, but automatically adjust the portfolio to the various constraints. In this case, contradicting constraints will cause the triggers to bounce, e.g., one trigger's action will violate the condition of another trigger and vice versa, causing the restructuring to continue indefinitely.

We will now mention a number of concrete problems that have to be solved in order to support the design of more reliable and predictable active applications. First, most active database languages provide few or no facilities for imposing a structure on the rules in the database schema. Rules can be structured according to their triggering operations (e.g., all rules triggered by an insert to a particular relation are grouped together).

But this will be undesirable when a set of rules with different events correspond to the same integrity constraint. For example, when an investment strategy is changed, all triggers defined to impose this strategy must be identified and updated, or when a financial instrument is no longer traded, all corresponding triggers have to be removed.

Second, existing active DBMS's do not provide rule analysis tools that enable to predict how rules will behave in realistic scenarios. For instance, the authors in [BCMP94] report that in most of their examples, the first set of rules produced by the design was indeed looping.[6] Recently, several papers have proposed techniques to predict if a set of rules is guaranteed to terminate or to behave deterministically (see Chapter 3 of this book). However, these techniques have not been validated on large-scale applications, and their effectiveness has still to be proven.

The definition of isolated triggers tends to rely on implicit assumptions about constraints that are observed in the application environment at the time of trigger design. For example, the termination of triggers related to two financial instruments may rely on the fact that the two instruments are never traded at the same stock exchange. However, a change of such real-world assumptions may easily occur at some later point in time, invalidating the original trigger design. Therefore, design and monitoring tools must support the explicit extraction of constraints from a trigger set, the addition of user-supplied constraints, as well as the supervision of constraint modifications and violations during the whole lifetime of the triggers.

A further point revealed by our study of real applications is the following:

> **Tenet 4:** It is difficult to understand the behavior of database transaction programs in the presence of triggers.

Adding a rule may alter the correctness of an existing transaction if the rule is triggered by the transaction and modifies the database in a way that is not expected by the rest of the transaction. Thus, analysis tools are also needed to understand how rules interact with transactions. Similarly, suppose you defined an instance-oriented rule (e.g., a for-each-row trigger) as below in a context where all entry-order transactions are assumed to insert a single tuple into *ORDER*. If a newly defined transaction performs a set-oriented insert into *ORDER*, the rule will not react as expected (it will not consider the total amount on order for A).

```
on insert to ORDER
if the amount on order for supplier A is greater
    than 1,000 and customer's status = ''gold''
then apply a 10% discount on the ordered item to A
```

---

[6]In current systems, the maximum number of cascading triggers is bound; thus, infinite triggering does not actually occur even if there is a loop.

Intuitively, although in theory rules should be defined independently from transactions, in practice they are often associated in a designer's mind with a set of transactions that implement a certain business activity. Thus, a rule triggered by an insert into *ORDER* may not be expected always to behave the same regardless of the business activity in which it has been triggered by a transaction.

It cannot be expected that formal verification tools will guarantee correct behavior of triggers in all cases. Therefore, further components will be needed in an active DBMS to support simulation and testing of triggers together with their triggering transactions. The tracing of triggered executions at runtime can help to discover dysfunctions. For instance, in a trading system, the conditions under which deals have been executed must be logged to be investigated and cross-checked regularly. Accumulation of incorrect reactions can easily be imagined (compare this to recent cases where the ruin of a bank was brought about by the decision of one trader–though definitely not with the help of an active DBMS).

Two further methods to make active rules more secure and reliable in critical cases are generated triggers and explicit limitations. The idea to generate lower-level trigger definitions from higher-level specifications has been mentioned before. At this higher level, more comprehensive verifications are possible. The portfolio scenario is a typical example for this approach.

Limitations to what a trigger may execute or access should not be imposed by the DBMS, but be individually definable for each trigger or subset of triggers, depending on the application. Limitations may relate to the maximum depth of cascaded rule triggering, the database elements that may be accessed by the trigger, operations that may be included in the action part, etc. For example, one might demand that all triggers on modifications of sensitive relations are neither allowed to write these relations in their action part nor to perform operations that are capable of triggering other rules. Or a trigger on modifications of a customer account may in its action part modify data of the same customer and specific global balance data. In certain applications, one even wants to impose the restriction that all actions are either rollback or notify (think of triggers that check for inconsistencies in an accounting system where all irregular transactions must either be prevented or checked by a human supervisor).

Last, regarding security, we found the following problem:

Tenet 5: Triggers need to be (better) protected from unauthorized accesses.

In fact, most systems having triggers offer the possibility to associate privileges with users to define, modify, or consult triggers (e.g., using a grant command). This can be problematic. First, programmers may need to see which rules can be triggered by the transaction they write, in particular with immediate rules whose action consists of changing the database. Now, the programmer may have the privileges for executing a trigger but not for reading it. Second, if a transaction (or a statement) is rolled back by a trigger, the associated error message must take into account the level of confidentiality associated with that trigger. As an example of the latter, think of an employee in a bank executing a transaction on a collegue's account. In this case, the bank's strategy is not to reveal the total assets of the fellow employee (as would be the case with usual customers). However, a trigger that checks the available total assets and rolls back the transaction in case a limit is violated may implicitly reveal this information. Much remains to be done in that area.

20.3.3   Performance

One of the main reasons that users are reluctant to use triggers in the development of large applications is their anxiety about performance. This feeling is consolidated by recent experiences conducted with the development of applications that involve several hundred triggers on various DBMS platforms (e.g., account management applications for large commercial customers). When developers compare the performance of the same application coded with and without triggers (i.e., all the checks and reactions to updates are programmed linearly in the application programs), they observe that the trigger-based version sometimes runs significantly slower. As a consequence, many consultants recommend not to use triggers intensively, although they are convinced by the functionality.

This disquiet deserves some analysis. A natural question is to wonder if the immaturity of the implementations of triggers suffices to explain such a gap of performance. In fact, the overhead taken by the binding mentioned earlier, and the retrieval of rules remains quite small.[7] We mentioned earlier examples where triggers improved the performance of the application. There may, however, be a scalability problem. For instance, the performance of one active DBMS was seriously damaged when triggers were used on set updates with some hundred tuples. It is a fact that a trigger system is a general-purpose mechanism that carries some overhead. Using this system can be valuable if one wants to implement various applications relying all on event detection (the benefit comes from the cross-section of several applications that share a common mechanism). However, if there is only a single reason to use triggers, a specific optimized solution can be better, especially if developers can take advantage of low-level system functionalities. This observation is backed up by several attempts to use triggers for caching and replication (e.g., in the ADMS project mentioned before or

---

[7] Note, however, that the only measurements available to us actually concern a small number of rules.

the Smallbase project at HP Labs). In those cases, developers implemented specifically tailored solutions using log files and incremental algorithms.

Another possible track of investigation is the lack of experience of developers in the programming of triggers. With respect to performance, we have to distinguish between two kinds of trigger-based applications. The first category is generally obtained when only a few triggers are selectively added to an existing passive application. With available active database technology, such applications may not encounter any performance problems and run satisfactorily without sophisticated optimization techniques.

However, the relevant active applications now coming into existence are one or more orders of magnitude larger in terms of defined triggers, ranging from hundreds to thousands of triggers. Some examples and reasons for this fact have been given in sections 20.2.4 and 20.2.5. In these applications, triggers are used for all kinds of tasks like coding integrity constraints, alerters, business rules, time constraints, etc. With applications of this kind that actually intend to exploit active databases to a significant degree, we have observed that performance problems represent a severe obstacle. In the following, we will try to reason about what is behind this performance deficiency and what needs to be done about it. In fact, we suggest the following tenet:

> **Tenet 6:** the separation between transactions and triggers renders difficult the *global optimization* of the application.

In practice, designers define triggers from application semantics specifications, and programmers code transactions knowing that some properties of the data are guaranteed. Thus, design phases are separate, and the levels of abstraction provided by the language used for transactions and triggers are different. This leads to what we call the *Iceberg Problem* in active database programming. From the database designer's perspective, the visible part of the application is the database schema including triggers, and the immersed part is transactions. From the programmer's perspective, the situation is reversed. This complicates the tuning of active applications, i.e., the activity of reconsidering the design of data structures, triggers, and transactions to make the application run more quickly. In particular, it is hard, and sometimes impossible, to reproduce optimizations that programmers used to do in passive applications. Finally, there is no design methodology that guides application developers in the design of efficient active applications.

20.4 Optimizing Active Applications

Tuning is a well-known difficult activity that requires a comprehensive understanding of the components of a DBMS [Sha92]. We argue that triggers further complicate the picture. In this section, we show that most difficulties for optimizing applications come from the misunderstanding of the interactions that exist between triggers and transactions. We review effective tuning techniques, show how to apply them in active applications, and explain the precautions that must be taken. From that, we derive various requirements, e.g., for administration tools.

20.4.1 Relaxing of Constraints

Suppose we have a purchase transaction that withdraws an amount X from a given bank account, and a business rule saying that "The balance of a bank account must never become negative." Suppose the rule is implemented by a trigger that checks the balance whenever an insert occurs in relation $WITHDRAW$. Every time the transaction inserts a tuple into $WITHDRAW$, relation $ACCOUNT$ is read by the trigger. Therefore, the purchase transaction conflicts with transactions that update relation $ACCOUNT$ periodically, which entails transaction blockings. A good optimization is to relax the constraint in a controlled way, e.g., for small withdrawals. This approach requires the computation of a function that gives the proportion of transactions run in relation to the amount withdrawn (X, in our example). Then, depending on the degree of consistency desired for the application, designers may decide to add an extra condition on the withdrawal amount to the condition of the trigger. In our example, the balance might be checked only for withdrawals above $30. If the remainder represents 45 percent of the withdrawals, the optimization will certainly improve the transaction throughput of the application.

However, two precautions must be taken with this approach. First, changing the definition of the trigger may impact the correctness of existing transactions that rely on the strict satisfaction of the integrity constraint. Thus, the change to the trigger must be notified to programmers who can then check that no incorrect behavior is introduced in the application. This is also true with passive applications, but there programmers have full control over the implementation of the constraint relaxation. Second, imagine that withdrawals originate from different transactions. For instance, a withdrawal is issued either by a purchase transaction (using a credit card), or by an automatic teller machine. Both transactions perform inserts to $WITHDRAW$, but their policies can be different regarding the above integrity constraint: violations can be accepted for purchases but not for ATM transactions. If the condition of the trigger defined for inserts to $WITHDRAW$ is changed, then the effect will apply to *all* transactions that perform inserts to $WITHDRAW$. In our example, this will prevent the constraint from being relaxed. Dirty solutions may circumvent the problem by duplicating the $WITHDRAW$ table, but such a decision may have important secondary effects on the design of the transactions. Thus,

> **Tenet 7:** It would be useful to enable the specification of the context of invocation within the event part of triggers.

Note that this problem does not occur with passive applications because programmers directly control when and how checks are performed within transactions.

20.4.2 Optimizing a Relational Schema

Another tuning technique is to create redundant data in order to speed up the evaluation of queries that involve costly operations.

Creating redundant data can also improve the evaluation of trigger conditions. Suppose we have a relation SEC_PRICES (securityNo, stockExchange, date, price), and a trigger that implements a London_better_than_NY_rule:

```
on insert to SEC_PRICES
if a new price from London is inserted and it is higher than
    the average price for the same security in NY for the past
    10 days
then notify
```

The evaluation of the trigger's condition involves several costly operations: a join on securityNo between the set of inserted tuples and SEC_PRICES, a selection on stockExchange, and an aggregate. Creating a new relation, say $NY\_AVERAGES$ (derived from SEC_PRICES), which contains the average prices from the NY Stock Exchange over the last ten days, facilitates the evaluation of the trigger when new prices for London are inserted. One must check that the new price is higher than the value in $NY\_AVERAGES$. This involves only a join between two relations one of which is rather small. Thus, a different trigger can be defined when London prices are inserted into SEC_PRICES.

Additional triggers are needed, however, to keep $NY\_AVERAGES$ up-to-date when SEC_PRICES is updated. A primary effect of this maintenance is that transactions that do not need to check the London_better_than_NY_rule (e.g., those inserting prices from NY) now have to maintain the redundant relation. Thus, the value of the decision depends on the proportion of transactions that benefit from the optimization with respect to transactions that have to maintain the redundant relation. Sometimes a global optimization may not be possible because of local autonomy and ownership. In a cost-center situation, a region may not be prepared to pay in terms of performance for the benefits of another region.

However, understanding the implications of this decision is delicate in an active application. In fact, insertions to SEC_PRICES can be caused directly by transactions that update this relation but also by transactions that update another relation that triggers the execution of a rule that inserts tuples into SEC_PRICES. Thus:

Tenet 8: It is useful to know which transactions may directly or indirectly cause some changes to any relation.

20.4.3 Select Lower Isolation Modes

Previous tuning techniques concern the rewriting of triggers or the redesign of the relational schema. We now look at techniques concerning the writing of transactions.

When transactions follow the strict two-phase locking protocol, they run in total isolation (SQL isolation degree 3) [BN97]. This protocol implies that before reading or writing a database item, the transaction must acquire a lock on the item and hold it until a particular *lock point*, after which no new lock will be acquired. The performance effect of this protocol is to create inter-transaction blockings and deadlocks. Most database systems offer the possibility to run transactions with a lower degree of isolation. For instance, if a transaction runs in degree 2, then its read locks are released just after the read operation. This diminishes the waiting time for transactions that want to write the same database item. So, when consistency is not sacrificed,[8] selecting a lower degree of isolation is an effective tuning technique [Sha92], [BN97].

We analyze the implications of this technique on active database transactions. Suppose we have two relations *WITHDRAW* and *ACCOUNT*. A purchase transaction inserts a tuple into *WITHDRAW* and then updates the balance of the corresponding bank account. This transaction can be run in isolation degree 2 since it does not issue any read operation.

Now, suppose we add an immediate trigger:

```
on insert to WITHDRAW
if ACCOUNT.balance is less than the amount of the
    withdrawal
then rollback
```

Suppose the balance for an account X is 1,000 when two occurrences of the purchase transactions, called T1 and T2, start to run concurrently with the following history:

```
T1 - insert 500 into WITHDRAW for account X
T1 - execute immediate trigger
T2 - insert 700 into WITHDRAW for account X
T1 - execute immediate trigger
T1 - update balance in ACCOUNT
T2 - update balance in ACCOUNT
```

At the end of the execution, the balance for account X is negative. The reason is that when T1 executes its trigger immediately after the insert, it

---

[8]Or, more generally, the inconsistencies possibly introduced are acceptable.

reads account X (value is 1,000) and then releases its lock on X because the transaction runs in degree 2. When T2 executes its trigger, X is not locked and can be read (its value is 1,000); thus, T2 continues its execution. When T1 updates the balance, the value becomes 300, and when T2 does its update, the value of balance is -200.

First, observe that if the trigger were declared as deferred, i.e., it executes at the end of the transaction, the problem would not exist. Second, suppose that the transaction only does an insert to $WITHDRAW$, and we define two immediate triggers:

```
trigger1: on insert to WITHDRAW
   then update to ACCOUNT.balance
```

```
trigger2: on update to ACCOUNT.balance,
   if ACCOUNT.balance is less than the amount of
      the update
   then rollback
```

This implementation is correct even if the transaction runs in degree 2. The lesson learned from this example is this:

> **Tenet 9:** Selecting lower isolation modes for active database transactions requires understanding of the invocation relationships that exist between the transaction and the triggers.

In particular, note that optimizations that turn out to be correct at some point may become incorrect if the set of triggers is changed.

This problem is already acknowledged by many development guides as a source of unreliability when referential integrity is enforced by means of triggers. It is necessary for the programmer writing the trigger procedure to explicitly lock (degree 3 isolation) the appropriate data for the duration of the transaction, and this must be done in triggers for all related tables.

Note that this problem does not occur with passive applications, since adding a trigger requires redefinition of the transaction.

20.4.4 Chopping Transactions

Transaction length has some effect on performance: the more locks a transaction requires, the more it will have to wait, and the longer it executes, the more it will cause other transactions to wait. Making transactions shorter may improve the performance of concurrent transactions when blocking situations occur and is thus an effective tuning technique. However, chopping a transaction into separate transactions must be done cautiously and requires a clear understanding of the possible concurrent transactions. Otherwise, inconsistencies can be introduced in the database. When all transaction programs are known in advance, it is possible to automatically chop transactions into smaller transactions without sacrificing isolation guarantees [SLSV95].

In an active application, chopping is more complicated. Suppose a purchase transaction T first updates the balance of some bank account and then inserts a tuple into $WITHDRAW$. If the only possible concurrent executions are instances of T, then it is safe to chop the transaction into an update transaction, T_1, and an insert transaction, T_2, since the relations involved in each statement are distinct. Suppose the following deferred trigger is added later:

```
on update to ACCOUNT.balance
if the balance becomes negative or if the total amount of
    the withdrawals this week exceeds 1000$
then rollback
```

This trigger will be executed within T_1. However, the chopping of T into T_1 and T_2 is no longer correct. Suppose the total amount of withdrawals for account X is $800, and the balance is $400 when two instances of the (chopped) purchase transactions (noted T_1, T_2, T_1', and T_2') execute concurrently with the following history:

```
T1  - decrement balance of $200
T1  - execute trigger
T'1 - decrement balance of $100
T'1 - execute trigger
T2  - insert $200 into WITHDRAW
T'2 - insert $100 into WITHDRAW
```

At the end of the execution, the balance for account X is positive but the total amount of withdrawals is $1100, which exceeds the authorized threshold value. Thus, *chopping needs to take into account the rules that are capable of being triggered by the transaction.*

Suppose now that every instance of a chopped purchase transaction for an account X can either execute concurrently with other instances of purchase that concern accounts different from X, or with debit transactions that simply increment the balance of some bank account. The above inconsistency problem cannot occur any longer, and isolation is guaranteed. However, the problem is that if we execute the trigger in T_1, then its condition is evaluated on a state of $WITHDRAW$ which does not take into account the new withdrawal (only visible after T_2 executes). Thus, chopping T violates the internal consistency of the transaction with regard to the condition of the trigger. Thus,

> **Tenet 10:** Assuring the correctness of a chopping requires understanding the data dependencies between the conditions of triggers and the statements of the transaction.

20.4.5   Choosing the Instants for Rule Processing

Defining a trigger as immediate may be a good optimization technique if the trigger rolls back the transaction when a particular condition is violated. Immediate processing enables the trigger to execute as soon as possible in the transaction, which avoids waiting until the end of the transaction if the transaction must be rolled back. However, defining triggers as immediate may introduce inconsistencies.

Suppose we have a transaction that does the following operations:

```
x = select balance from ACCOUNT where ...;
insert into WITHDRAW ...;
if x < 1000 then ...  else ....
```

Suppose trigger1 in section 20.4.3 was defined as deferred and one changes its definition into an immediate trigger. This change clearly alters the correctness of the transaction because variable x may not be up-to-date after executing the trigger that reacts on insert to $WITHDRAW$. Thus, *immediate triggers may introduce side-effects into transactions that are difficult to control manually.*

Another problem with immediate rules is that the programmer must be aware of which rules can be triggered and what their effect is. In some sense, this subverts the original idea that the programmer should concentrate on the logic of the transaction without worrying about business rules that have been externalized in the database schema. This yields security problems because some business rules need to be protected against unauthorized accesses. For instance, the writer of a transaction that inserts employees may not be allowed to see which (immediate) rules are triggered by updates to employee's salaries (e.g., bonus rules). Thus:

> **Tenet 11:** It is necessary to provide programmers with enough information about existing triggers in order to program correct transactions, without at the same time sacrificing confidentiality.

Some systems (e.g., Oracle version 7) provide a restriction to what a trigger can change. For example, a before-row-trigger cannot change any values provided by the triggering statement, and an after-row trigger cannot change a new column value. A row trigger cannot change a *constraining table* of the triggering statement, i.e., a table that a triggering statement may need to read. For instance, if a statement issued by the transaction conflicts with the processing of triggers, then the statement is not allowed. Under these restrictions, the above subvertion problems cannot occur.

As a last point, it is interesting to compare the implementation of integrity constraints in passive and active applications. Generally, passive applications perform integrity checks as soon as possible, e.g., at the beginning of update transactions, if possible. The rationale is to minimize the time during which write locks associated with the update operations are held. Furthermore, if rollbacks occur due to integrity violation, no write lock is acquired. If the read operations entailed by the integrity checks are not involved in any read-write lock conflict, then this strategy is profitable as the simulation study in [LST97] shows. With SQL triggers, the best way to do early checks is to use immediate before-trigger. Simulating the checks at the beginning of the transaction would require rules that can be triggered by an event such as: `on begin-transaction(T)`.

20.4.6   Detached Processing of Triggers

Detaching the processing of triggers from their triggering transaction is sometimes a valuable optimization technique. For example, suppose we have two relations *ACCOUNT* and *BRANCH* (branch_id, balance, ...). Take a rule that computes the total balance of the branch (attribute balance in *BRANCH*) as the sum of a branch's individual account balances, and suppose we want to implement it using triggers. A possible solution is to define triggers that react to every update on *ACCOUNT*.balance, and every insertion or deletion on *ACCOUNT*. However, this would make heavier all transactions that update *ACCOUNT*. A typical optimization is to run the rule when the transactional traffic is low (e.g., at night), provided that it is acceptable to have less actual data in *BRANCH*.[9] To implement such an optimization, we need to *detach* the processing of the trigger from its triggering transaction and defer its execution until a given time. This is tricky to do with most systems.

20.5   Perspectives

In this section, we outline several perspectives for the improvement of active database systems with respect to the three following problems: limitations of SQL trigger systems, lack of administration tools and design methodologies, and performance.

20.5.1   Extensions of SQL Trigger Systems

First, triggers should be open, that is, it should be possible to execute the action of a rule in a different process from the process in which it has been triggered. The situation monitoring application of section 20.2.4 is an illustration of this need. Note that some systems such as Informix already offer this possibility.

---

[9]This turns out to be the case for many applications that use materialized views or replicated data.

Second, the class of primitive events accepted in the event clause of a trigger should be enlarged. Ideally, for any SQL command, there should be an associated primitive event. We illustrated this need with transactional commands such as begin-transaction, commit, or rollback. If such primitive events are provided, rich languages for composite events and a variety of trigger's execution models can be implemented at the application level.

Third, it would be useful to parametrize a trigger with an execution context such as a transaction program name, or a set of transactions (e.g., a procedure or a package). Tenet 7 in section 20.4.1 illustrates this need for optimization purposes. Another potential benefit is a more accurate analysis of the behavior (e.g., termination) of triggers that takes into account their execution contexts.

Fourth, it should be possible to use transactional commands in the action part of a trigger, for instance to abandon a transaction or to initiate an independent transaction. System extensions, such as situation monitoring or caching, call for this extension.

Last, an important extension is the possibility to manipulate light-weight tables in the DBMS, that is, tables that do not persist after a transaction (like temporaries). These tables should reside in main memory, and their changes do not have to be recorded in the database log (they are not recoverable). Finally, key indexing should be possible. In section 20.3.1, we showed how to use a table *HISTORY* to accumulate the insertions made by an entire transaction into a table *ORDER*. This *HISTORY* table should be a light-weight table. More generally, these tables are essential to implement application-defined events or specific execution models efficiently.

In summary, we propose to extend SQL trigger systems in a way that they provide the necessary primitives to support the implementation of a wide variety of trigger rule languages and trigger's execution models. Our proposed extensions address limitations that are quite difficult, or even impossible, to circumvent at the application level. On the contrary, almost all the other limitations we encountered can be reasonably simulated at the application level.

Therefore, our approach radically differs from the SQL3 standard committee's approach, which aims at defining and progressively enriching a specific execution model for SQL triggers systems.

20.5.2 Administration Tools and Design Methodologies

Regarding administration tools and design methodologies, we wish to distinguish between predefined system extensions and business rules, and ad-hoc ones. For well-understood system extensions (e.g., integrity checking, maintenance of materialized views, or replication) and common business rules, there is a need for optimized modules that implement them on a variety of database platforms. Essentially, a module provides some functionality via a dedicated interface, and the user specifications are automatically translated into trigger definitions within the target active DBMS. A product like USoft Developer [Mal97] is an example of a third-party module for business rules.

For ad-hoc system extensions and business rules, there is first a need for tools that considerably ease the development of a dedicated rule monitor on top of an existing system. As explained in section 20.3.1, due to the limitation of SQL trigger's execution models, developers are sometimes led to implement the detection of events or the runtime monitoring of rules at the application level. We do not quite believe in the pure compiler approach, whereby a developer would specify in a powerful high-level language a desired execution model, and a compiler would automatically generate the necessary programs to interface between the application programs and the DBMS. We instead think that a toolbox approach can be more practical. With this approach, reusable softare components, which implement the generic part of an active rule system, are provided. Then, a toolbox helps the application developer to implement the parts of the active rule system that are specific to his/her application requirements. Current work in that direction is presented in [BFL+97].

20.5.3   Optimization of Triggers

The last problem is performance, which we believe is a major factor in explaining why the usage of triggers remains limited to niche areas. Therefore, solving this problem is a major challenge for the database community. This problem can be addressed at two different levels: improving the implementation techniques for SQL triggers in DBMS kernels, and devising optimization, or tuning, techniques for the development of active applications.

The work presented in [LST97] illustrates a way to improve the DBMS kernel. There, the authors present a simple multiversion protocol that improves the performance of update transactions that execute read-only integrity checking rules at the end of the transaction.

Finally, in [LFS97], the authors present a powerful and complete solution to eliminate redundant computations of SQL triggers when they are costly. In particular, they provide a model to describe programs, rules, and their subtle interaction, which addresses the points raised by Tenets 8, 9, and 10. This work illustrates the development of optimization techniques at the application level.

20.6   Conclusion

In this chapter, we assessed the maturity of active database technology as it is available in existing commercial systems. We observed that many projects have attempted to use triggers to implement database or general system extensions, and business rules. Usually, triggers are regarded as an attractive concept and technology by application programmers and designers. The most promising results of using triggers were found for simple system extensions, such as integrity checking, maintenance of materialized views, daemon processes, or logging, and for equally simple business rules such as alerters or event-action rules. There, triggers can effectively improve the reliability, maintenance, and performance of applications. However, we observed that there is a scalability problem: successful experiences concern applications with a reasonably small number of triggers. When the number of triggers grows, the administration of triggers and the tuning of the active applications become much harder. We were unable to give a quantitative evaluation of the difficulties related to the maintenance of applications with many triggers because there are not such applications in production use (we did not find such a thing as a legacy active application).

We also analyzed the problems that impede the successful development of applications with triggers. These problems are of three kinds: limitations of SQL trigger systems, lack of administration tools and design methodologies, and performance. We have indicated several possible perspectives for improving the available technology with respect to the three previous problems. First, we proposed that SQL trigger systems should be extended in such a way that they provide the necessary *primitives* to support the implementation of a wide variety of ECA rule languages and execution models. In this sense, our approach is conservative and differs from the SQL3 standard committee's approach, which aims at defining and progressively enriching a specific execution model for SQL triggers systems. Second, we suggested a toolbox approach based on reusable components to facilitate engineering arbitrary active applications on top of an SQL trigger system. Last, we pointed out the need for new optimization techniques that take into account both the transactions and the triggers.

20.7   Acknowledgments

We wish to thank Mokrane Bouzeghoub, Eric Dujardin, Francoise Fabret, Irene Kunz, Francois Llirbat, Dennis Shasha, and Dimitri Tombroff for the many constructive discussions we had on the topic of this chapter. We also want to thank Phil Bernstein for his help obtaining introductions within the French banking application domain.

20.8   References

[BCMP94] E. Baralis, S. Ceri, G. Monteleone, and S. Paraboschi.   An Intelligent Database System Application: the Design of EMS. In T. Risch and W. Litwin, editors, *Applications of Databases.* LNCS, Springer-Verlag, 1994.

[BFL+97] M. Bouzeghoub, F. Fabret, F. Llirbat, M. Matulovic, and E. Simon. ACTIVE-DESIGN: A Generic Toolbox for Deriving Specific Rule Execution Models. In *Proc. of the 3rd Intl. Workshop on Rules in Database Systems*, Skovde, Sweden, June 1997. Springer Verlag.

[BN97] P. Bernstein and E. Newcomer. *Principles of Transaction Processing.* Morgan Kaufmann, 1997.

[BZB97] L. Bruechert, J. Zimmermann, and A. Buchmann. Possibilities for Using Trigger Mechanisms and Their Performance in a Security Archiving System. In *Proc. of BTW'97*, Ulm, Germany, March 1997.

[CF97] S. Ceri and P. Fraternali. *The IDEA Methodology.* Addison-Wesley Publisher Ltd., 1997.

[CPM96] R. Cochrane, H. Pirahesh, and N. Mattos. Integrating Triggers and Declarative Constraints in SQL. In *Proc. of the 22nd Intl. Conference on Very Large Databases*, September, 1996.

[CS94] R. Chandra and A. Segev. Active Databases for Financial Applications. In J. Widom and S. Charavarthy, editors, *Proc. 4th Intl. Workshop on Research In Data Engineering (RIDE-ADS)*, pages 46–52. IEEE, 1994.

[Dud87] R.O. Duda. SYNTEL: Using a Functional Language for Financial Risk Assessment. *IEEE Expert*, 2(3):18–31, 1987.

[Esw76] K.P. Eswaran. Specifications, Implementations and Interactions of a Trigger Subsystem in an Integrated Database System. IBM Research Report RJ 1820, IBM San Jose Research Laboratory, San Jose, California, August 1976.

[GHM94] G. Knolmayer, H. Herbst, and M. Schlesinger. Enforcing Business Rules by the Application of Trigger Concepts. In *Proc. of the Priority Programme Informatics Research, Information Conference.* Swiss National Science Foundation, November 1994.

[HKMS94] H. Herbst, G. Knolmayer, T. Myrach, and M. Schlesinger. The Specification of Business Rules: A Comparison of Selected

Methodologies. In A. Verrijn Stuart and T. Olle, editors, *Methods and Associated Tools for the Information System Life Cycle.* Elsevier, Amsterdam, 1994.

[Hor94] B. Horowitz.   Intermediate States as a Source of Non-Deterministic Behavior in Triggers. In J. Widom and S. Charavarthy, editors, *Proc. 4th Int. Workshop on Research In Data Engineering (RIDE-ADS).* IEEE, 1994.

[ISO94] ISO-ANSI working draft: Database Language SQL3, 1994. X3H2/94/080; SOU/003.

[KSMR96] K. Smith, L. Seligman, D. Mattox, and A. Rosenthal. Distributed Situation Monitoring, Issues and Architecture. In I. Mumick and A. Gupta, editors, *Proc. of the Intl. Workshop on Materialized Views: Techniques and Applications*, Montreal, June 1996.

[LFS97] F. Llirbat, F. Fabret, and E. Simon. Eliminating Costly Redundant Computations from SQL Trigger Executions. In *Proc. of the ACM SIGMOD Intl. Conference on Management of Data,* Tucson, Arizona, May 1997.

[LST97] F. Llirbat, E. Simon, and D. Tombroff. Using Versions in Update Transactions: Application to Integrity Checking. In *Proc. of the 23rd Intl. Conference on Very Large Databases*, Athens, Greece, august 1997.

[Mal97] P. Mallens. The Approach for Business Rule Automation. Usoft approach, USoft, http://www.usoft.com/products, 1997.

[NNS93] N. Roussopoulos, N. Economou, and A. Stamenas. ADMS: A Testbed for Incremental Access Methods. *IEEE Transactions on Knowledge and Data Engineering*, 5(5):762–774, 1993.

[Ris89] T. Risch. Monitoring Database Objects. In *Proc. of the 15th Intl. Conference on Very Large Databases*, Amsterdam, The Netherlands, August 1989.

[Sha92] D. Shasha. *Database Tuning: A Principled Approach.* Prentice-Hall, 1992.

[SLSV95] D. Shasha, F. Llirbat, E. Simon, and P. Valduriez. Transaction Chopping: Algorithms and Performance Studies. *ACM Transactions on Database Systems*, 20(3), September, 1995.

[Smi95] K. Smith. Autonomy and Confidentiality: Secure Federated Data Management. In *Proc. of NGITS*, 1995.

[TKL90]   A. Tsalgatidou, V. Karakostas, and P. Loucopoulos. Rule-Based Requirements Specification and Validation. In *Proc. of the 2nd Nordic Conf. on Advanced Information Systems Engineering*, Springer-Verlag, LNCS N. 436, May, 1990.

21

Active Real-Time Database Systems

Jörgen Hansson
Mikael Berndtsson

ABSTRACT

Real-time systems are systems where correctness not only depends on the logical result of a computation, but also when the result was produced. In complex real-time applications, real-time systems have to handle a significant amount of information efficiently, motivating the need for real-time database management facilities. Characteristically, real-time systems are normally highly interactive with their environment, reacting to stimuli in the environment. However, no uniform method for specifying thir reactive behavior has yet been developed. This chapter addresses issues and problems associated with incorporating active functionality and real-time constraints into a single database system. As of now, there are no database systems available that provide support for both active and real-time capabilities. This is in contrast to the envisioned rather large number of applications that can benefit from the use of such a system. In this chapter, we provide a general introduction to real-time systems. Then, we elaborate on identified problems, potential solutions, and current research projects within active real-time database systems.

21.1 Introduction

Active databases and real-time databases have gained increased interest in recent years. Both active and real-time databases are considered as important technologies for supporting non traditional applications such as computer integrated manufacturing (CIM), process control, and network management. These applications are often event-driven and need to react to events in a timely and efficient manner.

In general, applications that require automatic situation monitoring of their environments and need to react to events in an efficient way require an active database system. Most active database systems adopt ECA rules, which are triggered and executed within the context of database transactions. Applications that require execution of transactions with respect to time constraints require a real-time database system.

In real-time systems, the correctness is not only dependent on the functional and logical result produced by a computation, but also the time at which the result was produced. By timeliness, we mean the ability of the system to fulfill the timing requirements, e.g., meeting time constraints, where a time constraint may be a deadline. When designing real-time systems, mainly two approaches have been used: event-triggered and time-triggered real-time systems. Event-triggered systems react to external events directly and immediately, as opposed to time-triggered systems which react to external events at prespecified instants [KV93]. Event-triggered systems are prone to overloads and event showers. Moreover, static scheduling is not applicable due to no a priori knowledge on when events will occur. Dynamic scheduling is a must, and often preemption is allowed [KV93]. In time-triggered systems, schedules are computed at pre-runtime and are not changed during execution. Characteristically, time-triggered systems are not subject to overloads and event showers. It is not hard to see commonalities between the methodologies used when designing and building active database systems, and how active database systems can fit into the system model of event-triggered, real-time systems.

Applications that need to react to events with respect to time constraints require a database system that combines both active database capabilities and real-time database capabilities, i.e., an active real-time database system (ARTDB). The need for active real-time database applications will require several modifications to an active database system with respect to system issues such as scheduling, concurrency control, rule execution, and event detection, since neither a traditional active database system nor a traditional real-time database system can support the requirements of an active real-time database application. Thus, a new database system needs to be developed that synthesizes research carried out both within active databases and real-time databases. Although extensive research has been carried out in both active databases and real-time databases, few proposals have been made to combine active and real-time capabilities into one system.

Initial research on active databases and time-constrained data management was carried out in the HiPAC project [CBB+89]. The combination of active rules and time-constrained data management was mainly left out as future work, due to its complexity. Furthermore, both the fields of active databases and real-time databases were in their early stages. Thus, most of the research after the HiPAC project focused on either the active aspect or the time-constrained aspect. However, currently there are several projects developing active real-time database systems, e.g., DeeDS [ABE+95, AHE+96], REACH [BBKZ92], and STRIP [AGMW97]. The recent interest in having another attempt at combining active database technology and time-constrained data management mainly relies on three premises:

- In recent years, the active database field has matured and become mainstream [Day95]; thus, the field is now becoming well-defined with respect to concepts, semantics, and working prototypes.

- The ECA formalism has in recent years gained interest from other research communities. One of these communities is the real-time database community [Gra92, Ram93, BH95a].

- Applications that require both active and real-time requirements have been identified, e.g., air traffic control systems [LPN], cooperative distributed navigation systems, and network services database systems [PSS93, SPSR93].

Section 21.2 introduces real-time systems and real-time database systems. In section 21.3, we will elaborate on characteristics of active time-constrained applications. In section 21.4, we discuss system aspects and give an overview of related research projects. Finally, we present a summary together with potential future research directions on active real-time database systems.

21.2   Real-Time Database Systems

21.2.1   What Is a Real-Time System?

When comparing real-time systems with other computer systems, they differ significantly in design goals, requirements, and implementation. The fundamental difference is the importance of time in different aspects. With respect to time, computer systems have traditionally been designed and optimized to guarantee high throughput and minimize the response time. New applications requiring prompt response at certain time-points, implies that the strict notion of time and timeliness are addressed and handled in the underlying computer system. This system we call a real-time system.

Several good definitions of real-time systems exist. Lawson defines a real-time system to be

> "... a system that assures that controlled activities "progress" and that stability is maintained and further, that the values of outputs **and** the time at which the outputs are produced are important to the proper functioning of a system." [Law92]

A more general definition is presented by Young, who defines a real-time system to be:

> "... any information processing activity or system which has to respond to externally-generated input stimuli with a finite and specified period." [You82]

Hence, a real-time system is a system that, in order to maintain system external/internal correctness, has to respond to input stimuli and produce logical results of computation within a finite and sufficiently small time bound. It is often stated in the literature that real-time system must feature *predictability*. Three questions are obvious: 1) what is predictability, 2) how do we measure predictability, and 3) how do we build predictable systems? The last two questions are beyond the scope of this chapter. However, let us look at some attempts made on describing predictability.

Stankovic and Ramamritham [SR90] describe predictability to be the ability to, in some way, show that the system meets the specified requirements under the various conditions, e.g., failures and workloads, the system is expected to work under. A similar view is given by Le Lann [LL91], where predictability means that the system behaves according to the specifications. Le Lann argues that predictability is the likelihood that assumptions made at specification and design time are not violated at runtime, and that the system behaves as anticipated whenever runtime conditions match specification and design assumptions. If the system behavior deviates from the specification, the system acts under conditions that have not been foreseen, jeopardizing predictability, which may have severe consequences.

In some safety-critical applications, the timeliness is an imperative requirement, leaving no room for lateness, but instead may have weaker requirements on the quality of the result. Hence, the logical correctness can be traded for timeliness, implying that the correctness of a real-time system is a function of (1) the logical correctness of the computation, and (2) the timeliness of result delivery. The most important property of a real-time system is predictability, i.e., the functional and temporal behavior is deterministic to such an extent that the system specification is satisfied [Sta88]. Given this, it is not hard to see that real-time computing is not an issue of high-performance computing.

Real-time systems are typically embedded systems, where the system can, on a high-level, be decomposed into one *controlled* system, representing the environment in which the real-time system acts, and one *controlling* system, interfaced with (intelligent) sensors and actuators. Moreover, a human operator is connected to the controlling system for monitoring purposes. The main characteristics of a real-time system are that they (1) interact with their environment, (2) react to stimuli in the environment, and that (3) the correctness of the result not only depends on the functional result, but also *when* the result is delivered.

21.2.2   Categorization of Real-Time Systems

Real-time systems in their various subtleties can be categorized considering different aspects, such as the granularity of the deadline and the laxity of tasks; the strictness of a deadline; reliability; the size of a system and degree of coordination; and the environment in which the system operates [SR90].

By studying the severity of the consequences when the real-time system's behavior is temporally incorrect, i.e., time constraints are not satisfied, the importance of timeliness can be quantified, and hence, used for categorizing real-time systems. By analyzing the strictness of deadlines, two fundamentally different types of systems exist: in *hard real-time systems*, it is an imperative requirement that deadlines are met, due to the catastrophic and costly consequences caused by delays; in *soft real-time systems*, tasks should execute to completion and their deadlines should be met, but can be missed occasionally without violating system correctness.[1] The former can be classified further into (1) *hard critical real-time systems*, where it is absolutely imperative that deadlines are met, and failing to meet these is equal to system failure, and (2) *hard essential real-time systems*, where a missed deadline will have severe consequences but system services, although at a degraded level, can still be provided.

21.2.3   The Role of ARTDBS in Real-Time Systems

When studying different, and especially complex applications, several common characteristics and requirements appear. First, massive amounts of data are often retrieved by the controller system from the environment, which must be computed and stored. Second, in some applications the amount of data needed to produce an output, given a specific input, is significant, i.e., the size of the database used for making a decision is significant. For example, geographic information systems (maps) in airplanes. Third, systems are responding to physical events, i.e., the systems incorporate reactive behavior. Fourth, the systems act in environments with dynamic elements, implying that dynamicity and adaptability are desirable, and sometimes necessary properties of real-time systems. Fifth, the real-time system must be able to handle complex workloads, since tasks differ in strictness, tightness, arrival patterns, etc. A complex real-time system needs database functionality (efficient storage and manipulation of data), and support for specifying reactive behavior. Moreover, it must be able to adapt to its environment in order to cope with dynamic situations.

Conventional database systems are not suitable as repositories for real-time systems, due to the inherently different design goals and criteria. Conventional databases are designed to maximize throughput and minimize the average response time while maintaining database consistency. Hence, real-time guarantees cannot be given, and therefore, time-cognizant techniques for transaction processing must be developed, where transactions have time constraints. A system that supports this is referred to as a *real-time database system*. Conventional and real-time database systems differ

---

[1] A special case of soft real-time systems is the *firm real-time system*, in which no tasks are executed after the deadline.

in several aspects. As mentioned, the performance metrics are different, and in a real-time database system the metric is usually to maximize the *guarantee ratio,* or to minimize the number of missed deadlines. Hence, the scheduling algorithm must be time-cognizant. Moreover, concurrency control protocols are used to increase the concurrency of transaction execution, and still maintain database consistency. Where the concurrency control algorithm and the scheduler are seen as autonomous entities, decisions made of the former algorithm can override scheduling decisions made by the scheduler [YKLLS94], and therefore both the concurrency control algorithm and the scheduler in a real-time database system must be time-cognizant, ensuring timeliness. Although database consistency is desirable, in hard real-time database systems it can be that timeliness must be traded for consistency, i.e., the timely delivery of a result with less quality or accuracy is preferred to having an exact result delivered too late. Data-access conflicts are also handled differently. In conventional databases data access conflicts are resolved based on fairness or resource consumption, while in real-time database systems, the preference tends to be criticality of the transaction [YKLLS94].

As mentioned earlier, real-time systems respond to external events in the physical environment. The events are signaled to the real-time system which, based on the event type, determines what the next step should be. Even though real-time systems have possessed reactive behavior, to the best of our knowledge, no general methods or techniques for uniform specification of reactive behavior have been developed in the real-time research community. While active databases use the ECA concept as a building block for specifying reactive behavior, active database systems do not explicitly consider the time constraints of transactions; hence, even though the ECA rules can be used for specifying timeouts, active database systems do not guarantee the timeliness of the triggered action(s).

In HiPAC [CBB+89], it was proposed that a time constraint could be attached to the action part of a rule. This implies a change in semantics as pointed out by [Ram93], were it is identified that traditional ECA rules cannot express the following semantics:

ON event E
IF condition C
DO <COMPLETE> action A <WITHIN t seconds>

The semantics of the above rule action are to *complete* action A within t seconds. In general, the time constraint can refer to (1) the time of event occurrence, or (2) the time of event detection. The former refers to the actual time when the event was generated, T, whereas the latter refers to the time when the event was detected by the system, which can be a time-point $T+n$. For example, an event manager is most likely to spend a nontrivial amount of time when detecting a composite event [GBLR96].

Depending on whether the deadline is relative to the time of event occurrence or event detection, the importance of the triggered transactions has a dramatic impact on the requirements of the real-time system. If the deadline is relative to the event occurrence, time-cognizant mechanisms for event handling transaction triggering must be catered for explicitly in the system, as opposed to when deadlines are relative to event detection, where no upper bound can be obtained for the time between event occurrence and detection. However, real-time systems are inherently reactive and have to respond to external events within an upper bound, implying that transaction deadlines are relative to the time of occurrence (for the event that triggered the transactions). Hence, to guarantee that triggered transaction deadlines are met, the transactions should be triggered before the latest start time of the transaction, with enough time to perform scheduling operations and meet the deadlines of the triggered transactions.

21.2.4   Real-Time Transaction Characteristics

The indivisible executable entity in a real-time database system is the transaction, where the real-time transaction adds the issue of time constraint to the management of the conventional transaction. Conventional databases have been designed for ensuring that data integrity is maintained for permanent data and that concurrent transaction execution is correct, i.e., the database is not left in an inconsistent state due to the interleaved transaction execution. This can be ensured by transactions having the ACID-properties, namely, atomicity, consistency, isolation and durability. However, real-time database systems require additional support because not all data may be temporal, i.e., data becomes invalid after some time, as opposed to archival data [Ram93]. Moreover, in many applications, timeliness is more important than correctness. Hence, correctness can be traded for timeliness by relaxing the ACID properties.

21.2.5   Temporal Scope

The execution time of a transaction is often very hard to predict accurately due to its dynamic behavior and the different execution paths that can be taken depending on the contents of the database. To guarantee timeliness of critical transactions, an upper bound of the execution time must be determined, referred to as the worst-case-execution time. This bound is used for scheduling and schedulability test purposes. Moreover, transactions have (1) deadlines determining when the result must be delivered, and (2) ready times denoting the earliest times for starting transaction execution.

Schedulers determining the transaction execution order at runtime are said to be dynamic. At the other end of the scale, static schedulers are found that perform scheduling before runtime, implying that transaction arrival patterns must be known a priori.

For more material regarding real-time database management, see the work of Graham [Gra92], Kao and Garcia-Molina [KGM92], Ramamritham [Ram93] and Yu et al. [YKLLS94], Eriksson [Eri97], O'Neil et al. [nei96], and Özsoyoğlu and Snodgrass [OgS95].

21.3   Applications

Different categories of applications such as air-traffic control, network management, workflow management systems, coordination infrastructure for distributed object systems, stream-oriented systems, and multimedia systems have been mentioned in the literature as applications that would benefit from ARTDB technology [BH96].

Despite the envisaged benefits, little research has been carried out to identify the applications suitable for an ARTDB. Most of the above enumerated potential ARTDB applications do not have a documented case were the active and real-time functionalities required by applications are identified. As a general guideline for ARTDBs, it has been pointed out that ARTDBs should target real-time capabilities of non mission-critical applications, as they seem to need the functionality of database management systems [BH96].

We next briefly describe two applications for where the requirements of ARTDB functionalities have been identified and documented: cooperative distributed navigation systems [PSS93], and network management [BB95].

21.3.1   Cooperative Distributed Navigation Systems

Cooperative distributed navigation systems typically consist of multiple semi-autonomous sensor-based agents, which are coordinated by a high level controller [PSS93], see Figure 21.1.

Each agent is equipped with sensors/cameras that sense the surrounding environment. The data from the sensors serves as input to the front-end system, which is responsible for filtering of sensor data, reflexive actions in response to sensor data, and prefetching of maps.

The high-level controller can be seen as the central coordinator for the sensor-based agents. It maintains a map database, and it provides support for sophisticated control knowledge. The high-level controller may be implemented by an ARTDB.

When the front-end system detects events that it cannot handle, e.g., potential threats/obstacles, the events (sensor data) are forwarded to the high-level controller. The high-level controller can then perform more sophisticated analysis of the current situation and then relay the appropriate commands (actions) back to the agent.

The above control loop has to be executed with very high priority until

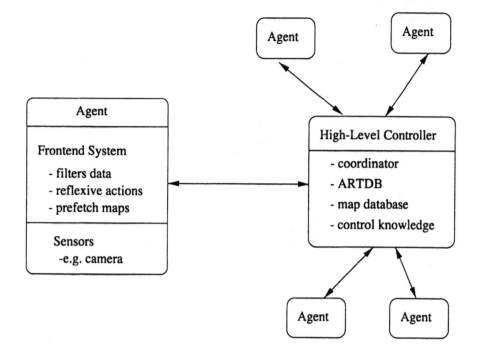

FIGURE 21.1. Cooperative distributed navigation system.

it has been identified if any threat is present or not. If threats are present, then a hard real-time task is triggered. The triggered task is a preventive command to the agent to, for example, avoid the threat.

In this application, the ECA rule paradigm is used to model the control knowledge in the system. Furthermore, the application showed that time-triggered actions and aperiodic actions could be conveniently specified using the ECA rule paradigm.

From an active database perspective, the investigated application does not shed any light on what the requirements are in terms of coupling modes or event consumption modes.

21.3.2   Network Management

A network management system typically consists of a network manager and several network agents [BB95]. The network manager monitors and controls an operational environment which includes entities such as terminals, gateways, and routers. A network agent can be seen as the interface between hardware and a management transaction.

In a traditional network management system, interaction between the network manager and the network agents is performed by polling and/or event notifications. It is discussed in [BB95] how a network management application can benefit from the use of a database system that provides active capabilities and enforces timeliness:

- *time-critical jobs*: computation of network indicators is time-critical, since they describe the state of the network and are used for network management decisions and corrective actions,

- *overload situations*: contingency actions and rule execution under hard time constraints are applicable in overload situations for performance and fault management.

21.4   System Aspects

In real-time database systems, timeliness and predictability are of paramount importance, which is achieved by eliminating the sources of unpredictability. Ramamrithmam [Ram93] identified several sources of unpredictability: dependence of the transaction's execution sequence on data values; data and resource conflicts; dynamic paging and I/O; and transaction aborts resulting in rollbacks and restarts. Distributed systems has the additional complexity of communication delays and site failures. Due to space constraints, we will not go into detail about inherent differences between conventional and real-time database systems. Instead, we will focus our discussion on sources of unpredictability when combining active and real-time database systems.

When incorporating reactive behavior in a real-time database system by using techniques and methods developed within the active database community, or vice versa, several incompatibilities and sources of unpredictability can be identified. We will in this section identify incompatibilities and discuss how these can be addressed in real-time applications.

21.4.1   Execution Model: Coupling Modes

Actions are carried out during the execution phase. As transactions are executed, new events may be generated that may cause cascaded rule firing, which will impose additional workload on the system. Unrestricted cascading of rule firings causes system overload. Hence, cascading must either be bounded with respect to execution time, restricted, or prevented. The core issue is how rule execution should be executed with respect to the triggering transactions. Some of the coupling modes are not appropriate for real-time purposes.

When studying the set of coupling modes for event-condition, and condition-action, the following combinations of modes are possible in active database systems[2]: (1) immediate-immediate, (2) immediate-deferred, (3)

---

[2]Detached coupling may be either dependent or independent, but will not affect the

immediate-detached, (4) deferred-deferred, (5) deferred-detached, (6) detached-immediate, and (7) detached-detached. Predictability can be enforced by restricting the set of coupling modes to those not affecting the execution of the triggering transactions.

Event-Condition Coupling

The coupling modes used for event-condition coupling may be a source of unpredictability. The real-time scheduler has, based on the worst-case execution time of the triggering transaction, guaranteed that the deadline of the triggering transaction will be met. Given that the triggering transaction generates new events, and that immediate or deferred coupling is used, this implies that the event detection and condition evaluation cost will be charged to the triggering transaction due to the necessary blocking of the currently executing transaction. Hence, in order not to override the allocated worst-case-execution time, the time consumed on event detection and condition evaluation must be controlled. If this is not done, the coupling combinations 1-5 cannot be adopted in real-time environments. Moreover, this also implies that the rules are reduced to detached event-condition coupling.

For detached event-condition coupling, condition evaluation is performed in a separate transaction, which is scheduled in the same way as any other transaction. The detached coupling mode does not jeopardize the timeliness of the guaranteed transactions nor predictability of the system. However, an additional workload is imposed on the system that must be resolved by the real-time scheduler.

Condition-Action Coupling

Given that condition evaluation in the former phase passes the test, i.e., an action should be executed, immediate and deferred actions are then executed as subtransactions on behalf of the triggering transaction. Actually, similar reasoning as for the immediate and deferred event-condition coupling can be applied. As we can see, immediate and deferred condition-action coupling may to a greater extent jeopardize the timeliness of the already-guaranteed triggering transaction. If the number of cascaded triggered subtransactions cannot be bounded, and thereby also the worst-case-execution time, immediate and deferred condition-action coupling have limited applicability in real-time systems. As pointed out by Branding et al. [BB95], the execution time of the transaction is prolonged in proportion to the number of rules triggered in immediate and deferred mode, which may cause blocking delays of other transactions that arrived before that the rules were triggered.

---

list for analysis.

As detached condition-action coupling is performed in separate transactions, and provided that the event detection and condition evaluation is predictable, the temporal behavior of the triggering transaction is not affected, i.e., neither predictability nor timeliness is jeopardized. Going back to the list of coupling modes, this means that the coupling combinations 3, 5, and 6 can be adopted in a real-time environment.

Three types of dependent detached actions have been suggested by Branding et al [BBKZ94]: parallel, sequential detached, and exclusive with causal dependency.

Parallel detached coupling with causal dependency implies that the triggered transaction must not commit until the triggering transaction has performed a commit. The triggered transaction may start execution before this, though.

The execution of actions having sequential detached coupling with causal dependency implies that the triggered transaction should only start executing after the triggering transaction commits. Temporal behavior of the triggering transactions is not affected.

Exclusive detached coupled actions with causal dependencies are mainly used for defining contingency actions, that is, actions that should only commit if and only if the triggering transaction aborts. The execution of the contingency may very well be executed in parallel.

21.4.2   Execution Model: Action Scheduling and Execution

A considerable amount of research has been carried out within the area of real-time scheduling. Surveying the area of all the work carried out in real-time scheduling requires a book itself. We will here only provide a brief and general introduction to the area, covering some different scheduling dimensions, and then focus on some research carried out in transaction real-time scheduling in active real-time database systems specifically. The interested reader can look at the survey articles by Stankovic et al. [SSDNB95], Xu and Parnas [XP93], and Burns [Bur91].

Real-time scheduling deals with searching for an action execution order such that timeliness is enforced, or optimizing action execution according to a defined metric, e.g., minimize the number of missed deadlines or guarantee ratio. The vast number of scheduling problems is underpinned by the number of different dimensions and constraints that must be fulfilled. The following list explores some of the options:

- Static vs. dynamic scheduling. Static schedules are computed pre-runtime, which implies that complete information about the workload must be known a priori, as opposed to dynamic schedules which are computed at runtime.

- Single-processor vs. multi-processor. Scheduling algorithms developed for uni-processor systems can, in general, not be used on multi-processor systems to guarantee timeliness.

- Non-preemptive vs. preemptive scheduling. Non-preemptive scheduling indicates that action execution cannot be interrupted after it has started, even though more important actions may be released during the execution. If preemptive scheduling is adopted, action execution will be interrupted in case a higher prioritized action arrives to the system.

- Mutually exclusive vs. dependent actions.

- Non-precedence-constrained vs. precedence-constrained actions. In the former, the execution order between action is arbitrary, as opposed to the latter in which precedence constraints exist expressing acceptable execution order between two (or more) actions.

- Periodic, sporadic, vs. aperiodic arrival of actions. Periodic actions means that the arrival time of the actions are periodic. Sporadicity implies that the minimum inter arrival time is known. Aperiodic means that the arrival time is unknown.

- Hard, firm, vs. soft deadline of action.

- Non-overload vs. overload scheduler. This merely indicates whether a scheduler should be able to handle an overload or not.

In real-time database systems, the scheduling entity of the system normally was the action. In active real-time databases, additional issues and activities have to be considered: How should event detection, rule evaluation, and condition evaluation be performed? Should actions encompass these activities, or should each one of the activities be considered as schedulable entities and thereby handled by the scheduler?

In active real-time database systems, new transactions are triggered imposing additional workload. Sivasankaran et al. [SST$^+$96] studied the problem of priority assignment policies for active real-time, main-memory resident database systems, where the workload consists of two types of transactions, both having firm time constraints: triggering transactions and non-triggering transactions, denoted T and NT respectively. Upon an event occurrence, T-transactions can trigger simple subtransactions, which are executed in immediate or deferred coupling mode. The transaction model has three types of events, namely transaction events (begin, commit, and abort), object events (occurring upon method invocation), and temporal events (occurring at a given timepoint). Three different scheduling algorithms were developed and then evaluated by simulation, each one performing well under different conditions. They show that, for workload consisting of T and NT, the guarantee ratio for triggering transactions is increased

significantly when priority assignment policies take into account the dynamically generated workload. The cost is a small decrease in the guarantee ratio. Moreover, dynamically evaluating and changing the priorities of
the transactions also results in a significantly increased guarantee ratio.

21.4.3   Event Detection

In real-time applications, the system must respond to a stimulus within an
upper bound, where the response is performing a computation and reporting the result. Mapping this to the ECA model, actions are triggered by
event occurrences.

Given this, it is interesting to investigate the origin of the time constraints. Time constraints are often assigned to actions, where the time
constraints are relative to the event occurrences, i.e., the time association
between event occurrences and actions implies that the time constraints of
the actions are inherited by the events. By studying the temporal scope
of the events, three types can be seen [Ram95]: maximum delay of events,
minimum delay between events (also known as minimum interarrival time),
and duration of an event. Moreover, events can be input or stimulus events;
output or response events; and internal or invisible events (external events
outside the (sub)system) [Ram95]. In other words, events can be classified
according to whether they are in- or outgoing events with respect to the
system, and whether the system has awareness of the events or not.

ECA rules provide a good model for specifying the reactive behavior and
enforcing constraints, and for triggering actions upon event occurrences.
The ECA model, at least in its basic form, neither provides mechanisms for
specifying time constraints, nor for guaranteeing that time constraints are
enforced. Timeliness in this case is no longer only a matter of transaction
scheduling, since the time constraints of the actions are determined by
the time constraints of the events. Depending on the characteristics of
the event, the deadline may be relative to the event occurrence, which is
typical for external events occurring in the physical environment, or it may
be relative to the time when the system detected the event, in which it is
more likely that the event is internal. Hence, in order to obtain a notion of
guarantee or schedulability, not only must the set of triggered transactions
be considered, but methods and algorithms that are performed between
event detection and transaction triggering must be predictable or time-
cognizant. Hence, methods for event detection, rule selection and triggering,
and condition evaluation should be predictable.

If traditional rule detection is adopted, i.e., events are detected in the
same order as they occurred, then uncontrolled behavior can result with
the timeliness being jeopardized as an effect due to event showers and
transient overloads. Berndtsson and Hansson [BH95b] suggested a scheme
for prioritized event detection and rule handling, where events are detected
and rules evaluated with respect to the time of event occurrence and the

criticality of the actions that may be triggered upon that event. The event detection scheme is appropriate for multi level real-time systems, where deadline criticality varies, but can also be applied on real-time systems where the tightness between time of event occurrence and the latest start time of the action determines the priority.

The scheme suggests that events are handled in a strictly prioritized manner, where the priority is determined by the degree of criticality of the most critical action that may be triggered upon that event. Moreover, the tightness of the time constraint of the triggered deadline may also be reflected in the priority assigned. It is suggested that the rule set is analyzed statically in order to determine the criticality of events, which are then parameterized with this information. It is suggested that event showers can be handled by using filtering mechanisms that are sensitive to critical events and thereby can filter out these and present them to the system.

One implication with this approach is that in systems where it is likely that an event will be involved in rules where the actions vary in criticality and where the event is likely to be part of at least one rule with a critical action, there is risk that the system will be loaded with critical events.

Until now we have described the applicability of the method when it comes to prioritizing primitive events. The method can be applied to composite events but with the constraint that the criticality of the composite event cannot be higher than lowest criticality among the constituents of the rule, with the effect that composite events are likely to be handled as less critical ones.

21.4.4   Rule Triggering

Upon event detection, the appropriate rules should be selected, that is, those rules that should be triggered as a response to the event occurrence. Within active object-oriented database systems, techniques can be broadly categorized into the centralized approach; rules indexed by classes, and rules associated with specific events. With the centralized approach, all the rules have to be notified to determine which rules are subjects for evaluation. By indexing the rules by classes, efficiency is increased [BH95b]. Neither methods can guarantee that no unnecessary rule triggering is performed. It has been suggested that rules should be associated with specific events, and then notified when the event takes place [BH95b].

In HiPAC, it was suggested that the cost of evaluating rules should be embedded in the execution cost of the transaction, which results in problems when cascaded firing of rules occurs. Two ways of solving this problem were suggested: (1) restrict rule behavior, or (2) limit the coupling modes. The first approach implies that rule behavior can be restricted to only allow non-cascaded firing of rules. Thus, rules cannot trigger other rules as part of their action part. The second approach implies that coupling modes can be limited to only detached, thereby disallowing immediate and deferred.

21.4.5   Condition Evaluation

Rule conditions in active databases are implemented as either boolean expressions, methods, or database queries. Sophisticated implementations of active databases can apply techniques proposed for query optimization in order to speed up the condition evaluation [GBLR96].

21.4.6   ARTDBS Prototypes and Platforms

We will elaborate here on active real-time database systems that have been built or that are currently under development. We will highlight the specific research problems that have been/are under investigation in each one of the following projects: HiPAC, REACH, DeeDS, STRIP and RT-Genesis.

Initial work on active databases and time-constrained data management was carried out in the HiPAC project [CBB+89]. Although, the combination of active rules and time-constrained data management was mainly left out as future work, some novel ideas were presented concerning a strawman architecture and the cost of evaluating rules.

In the strawman architecture presented in [CBB+89], the scheduler is considered as the controlling component, which tightly couples the operating system and the database management system. Further, the architecture assumes that all events are routed through the scheduler, since the response to the event needs to be scheduled like any other task in the system.

The REACH project [BBKZ92, BZBW95] is an active object-oriented database being built at the Technical University of Darmstadt, Germany. One of the issues addressed in REACH is time-constrained rule processing in an active database system.

A special type of relative temporal event, *milestones*, was introduced in REACH [BBKZ94]. Milestones are used for time-constraint processing. The semantics of milestones are: if a transaction does not reach its milestone in time, then the probability of meeting the deadline of the transaction is low. It is also possible to invoke a contingency plan in the case of a missed milestone.

Temporal constraints on rules can be specified, where the constraints specify the point in time when the rule action must have been completed.

The work in [BB95] elaborates on providing soft and hard real-time capabilities for a network management application. One of the conclusions is that contingency rules can be used to handle emergency situations in the application or overload situations in the active real-time database system.

DeeDS [ABE+95, AHE+96] is a [D]isributed Activ[e] Real-Tim[e] [D]atabase [S]ystem prototype, currently under development at the University of Skövde. The project focuses on the following:

- integration of reactive mechanisms for uniform and time-cognizant handling of internal and external events in complex real-time systems, where the complexity is in terms of the amount of information that is handled, the varying degrees of criticality of the transactions, and the need for distribution;

- issues concerning time-cognizant and uniform reactive behavior by using modified ECA rules;

- dynamic real-time transaction scheduling where transaction criticality goes from hard to soft; and

- replication mechanisms and algorithms guaranteeing an upper bound for replicating data to all nodes in the distributed system.

The database system is incorporated at the system level. Nodes have to maintain their own main-memory resident database. Guaranteed local data availability is provided by full replication of data, where transaction updates are made locally, without a distributed commit, and then propagated to other nodes. Data is replicated on a BASAP (Bounded ASAP) basis, i.e., updates are propagated as soon as possible but within some bounded time. Hence, timeliness is achieved at the cost of temporary inconsistencies. All over, unpredictable disk delays are avoided and the need for real-time communication is avoided.

STRIP, the [ST]anford [R]eal-time [I]nformation [P]rocessor, is a soft, real-time, main-memory resident database system, designed for heterogeneous environments with special support for importing and exporting data from conventional databases. The design goals were to provide (1) support for soft time constraints for both transactions and data, (2) high performance, (3) high availability, and (4) good interoperability, i.e., sharing data with other components in open systems [AKGM96]. Transaction timeliness is enforced by earliest deadline first, highest value first, highest value density, or custom scheduling algorithms. Temporal constraints on data is supported by defining a maximum age, reflecting how often data must be refreshed to not become stale. High performance is obtained by placing the data in main memory.

Reactive behavior is modeled in a special-purpose rule language, based on SQL3-type triggers. Only internally generated events are considered, namely, insertion, deletion, and update. Event checking and condition evaluation of the triggered rules are performed at the end of each transaction prior to commit [AGMW97]. Triggered transactions are released after committing the triggering transaction (sequentially casually dependent coupling). Hence, transactions trigger new transactions, and are currently limited to internally generated events.

The development of RT-Genesis, by modifying an existing commercial database system, Genesis, shows the feasibility of converting non real-time

DBMS to real-time DBMS for firm deadline transactions [AGN+96]. The approach necessitated a priority-based transaction execution where the priorities are assigned with respect to the deadlines where priorities are under the control of the DBMS, time-cognizant conflict resolution methods for data and resource contention. In addition, the SQL language was extended to handle transaction deadline specification.

21.5   Conclusion

There are several applications that require both active and real-time capabilities. For now the designers of such applications are faced with several problems when considering the underlying implementation platform.

Currently, there are no commercial, off-the-shelf, active real-time database platforms available; hence, the designer has to either use an active database platform, use a real-time database platform, or build an active real-time database platform. The two first alternatives make trade offs between either active capabilities or real-time capabilities. Even if an active database is chosen, the current support for active capabilities in commercial systems is limited. The last alternative is most likely to satisfy the application's requirements. However, it will also imply that a nontrivial amount of time will be spent on building a new type of database system. Typically, this is something that cannot be accomplished within the time frame of a short-term project.

When building an active real-time database system, some incompatibilities can be identified by studying existing methods within each discipline. These incompatibilities are also sources of unpredictability, and often these jeopardize the timeliness and predictability directly. When combining active and real-time database technology, methods and algorithms executed during signaling, triggering, scheduling,[3] evaluation, and execution phases must be time-cognizant and enforce predictability. We have in this chapter elaborated on some of the issues that need to be resolved in order to make the marriage between active database systems and real-time database systems a successful one. Timeliness and predictability can be enforced by restricting the set of coupling modes to those not affecting the execution of the triggering transactions. Unrestricted cascaded rule firing may cause overloads, implying that cascaded rule firing must be bounded. In addition, more work must be done in the area of predictable event detection and monitoring methods, rule triggering methods, and dynamic action priority assignment algorithms, to turn active real-time database systems into practical systems.

---

[3]By the scheduling phase, it is meant how rule conflict sets are processed and the time of condition evaluation and action execution.

We conclude this chapter by quoting Buchmann [Buc95]:

> "...the interest of real users is not triggered by yet another research paper but by working prototypes on which at least limited applications can be implemented."

21.6   Acknowledgments

The authors would like to thank Joakim Eriksson, Krithi Ramamritham and the editor Norman Paton for comments and suggestions on earlier versions of this chapter.

21.7   REFERENCES

[ABE+95]   S. Andler, M. Berndtsson, J. Eftring, B. Eriksson, J. Hansson, and J. Mellin. DeeDS–Distributed Active Real-Time Database System. Technical Report HS-IDA-TR-95-008, Department of Computer Science, University of Skövde, 1995.

[AGMW97] B. Adelberg, H. Garcia-Molina, and J. Widom. The STRIP Rule System for Efficiently Maintaining Derived Data. *SIGMOD*, 1997.

[AGN+96]   R.F.M. Aranha, V. Ganti, S. Narayanan, C.R. Muthukrishnan, S.T.S. Prasad, and K. Ramamritham. Implementation of a Real-Time Database System. *Information Systems: Special issue of Real Time Data Base Systems*, 21(1):55–74, 1996.

[AHE+96]   S.F. Andler, J. Hansson, J. Eriksson, J. Mellin, M. Berndtsson, and B. Eftring. DeeDS Towards a Distributed and Active Real-Time Database System. *SIGMOD Record*, 25(1):38–40, March 1996.

[AKGM96] B. Adelberg, B. Kao, and H. Garcia-Molina. Overview of the STanford Real-Time Information Processor STRIP. *SIGMOD RECORD*, 25(1), 1996.

[BB95]   H. Branding and A.P. Buchmann. On Providing Soft and Hard Real-Time Capabilities in an Active DBMS. In Berndtsson and Hansson [BH95a], pages 158 – 169.

[BBKZ92]   A.P. Buchmann, H. Branding, T. Kudrass, and J. Zimmermann. Reach: A Real-Time, Active and Heterogeneous Mediator System. *IEEE Quarterly Bulletin on Data Engineering, Special Issue on Active Databases*, 15(1-4):44–47, December 1992.

[BBKZ94] H. Branding, A. Buchmann, T. Kudrass, and J. Zimmermann. Rules in an Open System: The REACH Rule System. In N.W. Paton and M.H. Williams, editors, *Rules in Database Systems*, pages 111–126. Springer-Verlag, 1994.

[BH95a]   M. Berndtsson and J. Hansson, editors. *Active and Real-Time Database Systems (ARTDB-95), Proc. of the 1st Intl. Workshop on Active and Real-Time Database Systems*, Workshops in Computing. Springer-Verlag (London) Ltd, June 1995.

[BH95b]   Mikael Berndtsson and Jörgen Hansson. Issues in Active Real-Time Databases. In Berndtsson and Hansson [BH95a], pages 142–157.

[BH96]   M. Berndtsson and J. Hansson. Workshop report: The 1st Intl. Workshop on Active and Real-Time Database Systems (artdb-95). *ACM SIGMOD Record*, 25(1):64–66, 1996.

[Buc95]   A.P. Buchmann. Wrap-Up Statement. In Berndtsson and Hansson [BH95a], pages 264–266.

[Bur91]   Alan Burns. Scheduling Hard Real-Time Systems: A Review. *Software Engineering Journal*, X(X):116–128, May 1991.

[BZBW95] A.P. Buchmann, J. Zimmermann, J. Blakely, and D. Wells. Building an Integrated Active OODBMS: Requirements, Architecture, and Design Decisions. In *Proc. IEEE Data Engineering*, 1995.

[CBB⁺89] Sharma Chakravarthy, Barbara Blaustein, Alejandro P. Buchmann, Michael Carey, Umeshwar Dayal, David Goldhirsch, Meichun Hsu, Rajiv Jauhari, Miron Livny, Dennis McCarthy, Richard McKee, and Arnon Rosenthal. HiPAC: A Research Project in Active Time-Constrained Database Management – final technical report. Technical Report XAIT-89-02, Reference Number 187, Xerox Advanced Information Technology, July 1989.

[Day95]   U. Dayal. Ten Years of Activity in Active Database Systems: What Have We Accomplished? In *Proc. of the 1st Intl. Workshop on Active and Real-Time Database Systems (ARTDB-95)*, Workshops in Computing. Springer-Verlag, 1995.

[Eri97]   Joakim Eriksson. Real-Time and Active Databases: A Survey. In *Proc. of the 2nd Intl. Workshop on Active, Real-Time, and Temporal Database Systems (ARTDB-97)*. Springer-Verlag, 1997.

[GBLR96]   A. Geppert, M. Berndtsson, D. Lieuwen, and C. Roncancio. Performance Evaluation of Object-Oriented Active Database Management Systems Using the Beast Benchmark. Technical Report 96.07, University of Zurich, 1996.

[Gra92]   Marc H. Graham. Issues in Real-Time Data Management. *The Journal of Real-Time Systems*, (4):185–202, 1992.

[KGM92]   Ben Kao and Hector Garcia-Molina. An Overview of Real-Time Database Systems. In *Proc. of NATO Advanced Study Institute on Real-Time Computing*. Springer-Verlag, October 1992.

[KV93]   Hermann Kopetz and Paulo Verissimo. *Design of Distributed Real-Time Systems*, chapter 16. Addison-Wesley Publishing Company, 1993.

[Law92]   Harold W. Lawson. *Parallel Processing in Industrial Real-Time Applications*. Prentice-Hall, Inc., 1992.

[LL91]   Gerard Le Lann. Designing Real-Time Dependable Distributed Systems, April 1991.

[LPN]   Kwi-Jay Lin, Ching-Shan Peng, and Tony Ng. An Active Real-Time Database Model for Air Traffic Control Systems. In *Proc. of the 2nd Intl. Workshop on Active, Real-Time, and Temporal Database Systems (ARTDB-97)*.

[nei96]   P. O'Neil and O. Ulusoy, editors. *Information Systems Journal: Special Issue on Real-Time Database Systems*, 1996.

[OgS95]   Gultekin Özsoyoğlu and Richard T. Snodgrass. Temporal and Real-Time Databases: A Survey. *IEEE Transactions on Knowledge and Data Engineering*, 1995.

[PSS93]   B. Purimetla, R. M. Sivasankaran, and J. A. Stankovic. A Study of Distributed Real-Time Active Database Applications. In *Proc. of the IEEE Workshop on Parallel and Distributed Real-Time Systems*, 1993.

[Ram93]   Krithi Ramamritham. Real-time Databases. *Intl. Journal of Distributed and Parallel Databases*, 1(2), 1993.

[Ram95]   Krithi Ramamritham. The Origin of TCs. In Berndtsson and Hansson [BH95a], pages 50–81.

[SPSR93]   R. M. Sivasankaran, B. Purimetla, J. A. Stankovic, and K. Ramamritham. Network Services Databases–A Distributed Active Real-Time Database (dartdb) Application. In *Proc. of the IEEE Workshop on Real-Time Applications*, 1993.

[SR90]   John A. Stankovic and Krithi Ramamritham.   What is
            Predictability for Real-Time Systems? *Real-Time Systems*,
            4(2):247–254, Novemeber 1990.

[SSDNB95]   John A. Stankovic, Marco Spuri, Marco Di Natale, and
            Girogi C. Buttazzo. Implications of Classical Scheduling for
            Real-Time Systems. *Computer*, 28(6):16–25, June 1995.

[SST+96]   R. Sivasankaran, J. Stankovic, D. Towsley, B. Purimetla, and
            K. Ramamritham. Priority Assignment in Real-Time Active
            Databases. *VLDB Journal*, 1996.

[Sta88]   John A. Stankovic. Misconceptions About Real-Time Com-
            puting: A Serious Problem for Next-Generation Systems.
            IEEE Computer 21(10), 21(10), October 1988.

[XP93]   Jia Xu and David Lorge Parnas. On Satisfying Timing Con-
            straints in Hard-Real-Time Systems. *IEEE Transactions on
            Software Engineering*, 19(1):70–84, January 1993.

[YKLLS94]   Philip S. Yu, We. Kun-Lung, Kwei-Jay Lin, and Sang H. Son.
            On Real-Time Databases: Concurrency Control and Schedul-
            ing. In *Proc. of the IEEE*, volume 82, pages 140–157, January
            1994.

[You82]   S. J. Young. *Real Time Languages: Design and Development*.
            Chichester: Ellis Horwood, 1982.

Part V

Summary

22

Summary

Norman W. Paton

ABSTRACT

Many of the lessons that can be learned from earlier chapters relate to details and are embedded in contexts from which they should be extracted only with care. Thus, this chapter does not attempt to present general conclusions, but rather to summarize the principal achievements in the area of active databases, and to identify areas in which further effort is required.

22.1   Introduction

Active database systems have received significant attention in the database research community for at least ten years. Many of the fruits of this activity are presented in earlier chapters, and it is clear that a range of issues relating to languages and systems have become well understood. This implies that the area is now quite mature. However, the lack of practical experience with many of the more powerful constructs means that understanding of how best to exploit active facilities is less comprehensive than is required to reassure many of the practitioners who might benefit from active facilities. The lack of experience with more powerful active rule systems stems from the relatively recent completion of comprehensive implementations of certain constructs and from the limited capabilities of current commercial systems.

The following section summarizes the contributions and needs in a range of topic areas.

22.2   Topic-Based Summaries

22.2.1   Architectures

Contributions. Researchers have developed a wide range of prototype active database systems over a range of data models, adopting both layered and integrated approaches. This means that issues such as primitive and composite event detection and the relationship between rule languages and the transaction manager have been comprehensively studied, although it took many years for systems to be developed that supported all the facilities proposed in the HiPAC project [DBM88].

Needs. Active database systems have tended to be monolithic software systems, even where relatively distinct components can be identified [FGD97], and few active systems take account of distributed delivery environments (for a discussion see section 8).

22.2.2   Event Detection

Contributions. The development of powerful languages for describing composite events based on a range of underlying formalisms, along with the notion of consumption modes [CKAK94], provides a firm foundation for the development of future composite event detectors.

Needs. The question as to how powerful an event detection language should be is still not widely agreed (e.g., what operations should be provided for testing event parameters in the event language?), and there is relatively little application experience reported in the use of composite event detectors in practice. The use of composite event detectors in distributed systems is a topic for ongoing research.

22.2.3   Specification of Active Systems

Contributions. Most active database systems are specified in an informal and imprecise manner. Formal description techniques have been used to give a semantics to specific systems [Wid92] and to allow comparison of a range of systems [FT95, CPW97], but there is no generally accepted approach. Some of the later active database systems (e.g., NAOS (see Chapter 15) and ROCK & ROLL (see Chapter 18)) were formally specified before they were implemented, but it is not yet clear that this is standard practice or that the specifications are ever consulted by users.

Needs. Developers of active database systems will be encouraged to exploit formal techniques where the specification can be used not only to describe the system precisely and concisely, but when the specification can also be used to underpin analysis and optimization. To date, with real systems, the exploitation of specifications for understanding the semantics of rule bases has been limited.

22.2.4   Rule Analysis

Contributions. The development of algorithms for detecting termination, confluence, and observable determinism in Starburst [AWH92], along with complementary techniques for indicating how conditions and actions interact in rule analysis [BW94], means that a solid starting point exists for the development of analyzers for active systems.

Needs. Most analyzers have been developed with relatively straightforward rule systems, and few have been implemented that support confluence analysis. Thus, there is little experience in communicating the results of analyses to users or in using analysis in the development of real rule bases.

22.2.5   Rule Optimization

Contributions. The optimization of individual rules in isolation generally involves straightforward extensions to existing query optimizers. Some work has been carried out on multiple query optimization (see Chapter 4) and on parallel evaluation of rules [CM95].

Needs. There has been little or no work on the analysis of how rule optimization can be used to improve the performance of real or benchmark applications.

22.2.6   Condition Monitoring/Production Rule Algorithms

Contributions. Considerable amounts of work have been done on the development and comparison of techniques for incremental condition evaluation, especially in condition-action rules (for example, see Chapter 11). Many speed-space trade-offs are thus quite well understood.

Needs. Few of the incremental condition evaluation techniques have been applied to ECA rules, so the situations and applications in which ECA rules might benefit from these techniques are less than fully explored (one approach is described in section 5). In addition, few recent systems support both ECA rules and condition-action rules, although Ariel (see Chapter 11) and AMOS [SR95] are exceptions. More work is needed on the development of incremental rule optimizers that optimize rule condition checking based on knowledge about, e.g., access costs and update frequencies.

22.2.7   Performance Assessment/Improvement

Contributions. The 007 benchmark has been extended in BEAST (see Chapter 6) to support comparison of different aspects of the performance of active object-oriented databases, and in particular event detection.

Needs. There is currently no benchmark for active relational systems, and understanding of the performance implications of active solutions as opposed to alternative techniques remains limited (see Chapter 21.3 for a discussion).

22.2.8 Design Methods

Contributions. The development or extension of design methods that account for active behavior has lagged significantly behind the development of active database systems. The IDEA method [CF97] is probably the most comprehensive to date, in that it supports mappings of designs onto a number of active systems and is associated with comprehensive tool support. An approach more linked to support for business policies, but also exploiting active capabilities, is described in [DP97].

Needs. Most work to date has involved the development of new methodologies that make active functionality a major focus. The extension of existing methods is probably more likely to encourage the use of active facilities in practice [TPC94].

22.2.9 Tool Support

Contributions. Tools have been developed that support design, simulation, and debugging of active applications (see Chapter 7). These give an indication of the sorts of support facilities that users of active systems will require.

Needs. There is currently a lack of integration of tools for different parts of the development life cycle, and little evidence of the evaluation of tools in use.

22.2.10 Distribution

Contributions. Work on active databases can be seen to overlap with some activities relating to event-based distributed computing. This has given rise to the use of ECA rules in distributed systems and to the development of event models that account for the idiosyncrasies of distributed environments (see Chapter 8).

Needs. Although active database constructs are beginning to be exploited in a distributed setting, active database systems are generally monolithic and centralized.

22.2.11   Applications

Contributions. A significant number of applications have been developed using active facilities, as outlined in Part 4 of the book. Application areas vary in the extent of their ambition and in the range of active facilities exploited. As might be expected, given the limited power of early commercial active rule facilities, the greatest number of practical applications involves the exploitation of relatively straightforward active facilities. As such, active databases have not so much served to extend the range of applications supported by database systems, but rather have provided new ways in which certain aspects of application functionality can be supported.

Needs. There are relatively few large and well documented applications in which active databases have been used, and experience to date with more advanced features (e.g., composite events, complex execution models) is limited.

22.2.12   Standards

Contributions. Relational database vendors have been quick to incorporate active facilities, which should become more consistent and comprehensive in the context of the SQL3 standard (see Chapter 10).

Needs. Object-oriented database vendors have been slow to incorporate active facilities into their products. The inclusion of active rules in object-oriented products would certainly benefit from appropriate extensions to the ODMG standard.

22.3   REFERENCES

[AWH92]   A. Aiken, J. Widom, and J.M. Hellerstein. Behaviour of Database Production Rules: Termination, Confluence, and Observable Determinism. In *ACM SIGMOD*, volume 21, pages 59–68, 1992.

[BW94]   E. Baralis and J. Widom. An Algebraic Approach to Rule Analysis in Expert Database Systems. In J. Bocca, M. Jarke, and C. Zaniolo, editors, *Proc. 20th VLDB*, pages 475–486. Morgan-Kaufmann, 1994.

[CF97]   S. Ceri and P. Fraternali. The Story of the IDEA Methodology. In A. Olive and J. Pastor, editors, *Proc. CAiSE*, pages 1–17. Springer-Verlag, 1997.

[CKAK94]   S. Chakravarthy, V. Krishnaprasad, E. Anwar, and S.-K. Kim. Composite Events for Active Databases: Semantics, Contexts and Detection. In J. Bocca, M. Jarke, and C. Zaniolo, editors, *Proc. 20th Intl. Conf. on Very Large Databases*, pages 606–617. Morgan-Kaufmann, 1994.

[CM95]   C. Collet and J. Manchado. Optimization of Active Rules with Parallelism. In M. Berndtsson and J. Hansson, editors, *Proc. Active and Real Time Database Systems (ARTDB)*, pages 82–103. Springer-Verlag, 1995.

[CPW97]   J. Campin, N.W. Paton, and M.H. Williams. Specifying Active Database Systems in an Object-Oriented Framework. *Intl. J. Software Engineering and Knowledge Engineering*, 7:101–123, 1997.

[DBM88]   U. Dayal, A.P. Buchmann, and D.R. McCarthy. Rules Are Objects Too: A Knowledge Model for an Active Object Oriented Database System. In K.R. Dittrich, editor, *Proc. 2nd Intl. Workshop on OODBS*, volume 334, pages 129–143. Springer-Verlag, 1988. Lecture Notes in Computer Science.

[DP97]   O. Diaz and N.W. Paton. Stimuli and Business Policies as Modelling Constructs: Their Definition and Validation Through the Event Calculus. In A. Olive and J. Pastor, editors, *Proc. CAiSE*, pages 33–46. Springer-Verlag, 1997.

[FGD97]   H. Fritschi, S. Gatziu, and K.R. Dittrich. Framboise–An Approach to Constructing Active Database Mechanisms. Technical Report 97.04, University of Zurich, 1997.

[FT95]   P. Fraternali and L. Tanca. A Structured Approach for the Definition of the Semantics of Active Databases. *ACM TODS*, 20(4):414–471, 1995.

[SR95]   M. Skold and T. Risch. Using Partial Differencing for Efficient Monitoring of Deferred Complex Rule Conditions. In S. Su, editor, *Proc. IEEE Data Engineering*, pages 392–401, 1995.

[TPC94]   M. Teisseire, P. Poncelet, and R. Cichetti. Towards Event-Driven Modelling for Database Design. In J. Bocca, M. Jarke, and C. Zaniolo, editors, *Proc. 20th Intl. Conf on VLDB*, pages 1–12. Morgan-Kaufmann, 1994.

[Wid92]   J. Widom. A Denotational Semantics for the Starburst Production Rule Language. *ACM SIGMOD Record*, 21(3):4–9, 1992.

Index

CPSIA information can be obtained at www.ICGtesting.com
Printed in the USA
LVOW09s0746120616

492225LV00002B/15/P